161 681886 0

D0353238

Towards *Pax Sinica*?

China's Rise and Transformation: Impacts and Implications

Two week loan

Benthyciad pythefnos

urn on or before the due date

With compliments from

Institute Of China Studies
University of Malaya
50603 Kuala Lumpur
MALAYSIA

Towards *Pax Sinica*?

China's Rise and Transformation: Impacts and Implications

Editor

Emile Kok-Kheng Yeoh

UNIVERSITY OF MALAYA

Institute of China Studies

327.51 TOW

28 JAN 2011

Institute of China Studies
University of Malaya
50603 Kuala Lumpur
Malaysia
Tel: 603-79565663   Fax: 603-79565114
http://ics.um.edu.my

© Institute of China Studies
First published in 2009

COPYRIGHT

All rights reserved. No part of this publication may be reproduced, copied or transmitted, in any form, or by any means, electronic, mechanical, photocopying, recording or otherwise, without written permission from the publisher. Under the Copyright Act 1987, any person who does any unauthorized act in relation to this publication shall be liable to prosecution and claims for damages.

Perpustakaan Negara Malaysia   Cataloguing-in-Publication Data

Towards pax sinica? : China rise and transformation : impacts and
    implications / editor Emile Kok-Kheng Yeoh.
    Bibliography: p. 304
    ISBN 978-967-5148-50-7
    1. China—Foreign relations. 2. China—Economic conditions. I. Yeoh,
    Emile Kok-Kheng.
    327.51

Printed by Vinlin Press Sdn. Bhd.
No. 2, Jalan Meranti Permai 1
Meranti Permai Industrial Park
Batu 15, Jalan Puchong
47100 Puchong, Selangor Darul Ehsan

Contents

China's Future: International Milieu, Ethnoterritoriality and *Realpolitik*

List of Tables

List of Figures

Contributors

Dr **Đỗ Tiến Sâm** 杜进森, Director and Associate Professor, Institute of Chinese Studies and Centre for ASEAN and China Studies, Vietnam Academy of Social Sciences. *Email: dtiensam@yahoo.com*

Dr John A. **Donaldson**, Assistant Professor of Political Science, School of Social Sciences, Singapore Management University, Singapore. *Email: jdonaldson@smu.edu.sg*

Hà Thị Hồng Vân 何氏红云, Department of Chinese Socio-economic Studies, Institute of Chinese Studies and Centre for ASEAN and China Studies, Vietnam Academy of Social Sciences. *Email: vanhongha@yahoo. com*

Dr Sukhee **Han** 한석희 / 韓碩熙, Director, China Division, Institute of East-West Studies; Assistant Professor, Graduate School of International Studies, Yonsei University, Republic of Korea. *Email: shan65@yonsei.ac.kr*

Dr Kate **Hannan**, Associate Professor and Principal Research Fellow, School of History and Politics, Faculty of Arts, University of Wollongong, Australia. *Email: kateh@uow.edu.au*

Takashi **Hoshiyama** 星山隆, Minister and Deputy Chief of Mission, Embassy of Japan in Malaysia. *Email: takashi.hoshiyama@mofa.go.jp*

Dr Samuel C.Y. **Ku** 顧長永, Professor, Institute of China and Asia-Pacific Studies, National Sun Yat-sen University, Taiwan. *Email: cyku@mail.nsysu. edu.tw*

Dr **Mutahir** Ahmed, Professor, Department of International Relations, University of Karachi, Pakistan. *Email: mutahir62@yahoo.com*

Dr Emile Kok-Kheng **Yeoh** 楊國慶, Director and Associate Professor, Institute of China Studies, University of Malaya, Malaysia. *Email: emileyeo@correo. nu, emileyeo@gmail.com*

Dr Im-Soo **Yoo** 유임수 / 劉壬洙, Senior Research Fellow, Institute of China Studies, University of Malaya, Malaysia; Emeritus Professor of Economics, Ewha Womans University, Seoul, Republic of Korea; President, Asia-Europe Perspective Forum; former President, Korean Association for Contemporary European Studies, Korean-German Association of Social Science and Korean-German Association of Economics and Management. *Email: isyoo@ewha. ac.kr, isyoo42@gmail.com*

Dr Forrest **Zhang** 张谦, Assistant Professor of Sociology, School of Social Sciences, Singapore Management University, Singapore. Email: *forrestzhang@smu.edu.sg*

Introduction

Chapter 1

China's Rise and Transformation

Emile Kok-Kheng **Yeoh**[*]

In recent years, probably no other events than the successful hosting of the 2008 Olympics and the first spacewalk better heralded the return of China to the centre of the world. Yet other incidents during the same year – whether in the form of natural calamities, man-made food scares, or socio-political disturbances – have not failed to dampen the optimism that would have otherwise marked unequivocally the country's year of success. Among the series of natural calamities that struck the People's Republic of China (PRC) in 2008, which included snowstorms, sandstorms, floods and droughts, was that devastating earthquake that hit the Sichuan province's Wenchuan 汶川 County, Ngawa 阿坝 *Zizhizhou* 自治州 ("autonomous prefecture") of the Tibetan/Zang 藏 and Qiang 羌 nationalities, and surrounding areas on 12th May 2008 which killed at least 68,000 people and left long-lingering socioeconomic and even political fallout, especially those involving the "tofu-dregs schoolhouses"[1] scandal, on the country. Yet, fading from collective memory is another even more devastating earthquake that came to pass three decades earlier. Slightly over thirty years ago in 1976, two events shook China – one literally. One of the modern world's largest earthquakes, in terms of the loss of life, devastated the industrial city of Tangshan in the northeast province of Hebei on 28th July 1976. Six weeks later, on 9th September, Mao Zedong (Mao Tse-tung) died, and with him, so did the decade-long Cultural Revolution and his languid socialist collectivist autarky[2]. When Deng Xiaoping launched his "Reform and Open" (*gaige kaifang* 改革开放) policy in the late 1970s by bringing the reformists Hu Yaobang and Zhao Ziyang into the politburo, around 250 million people in China were living below the international poverty line, with incidence of poverty as high as 31 per cent. The *gaige kaifang* policy truly, and amazingly, transformed China. Napoleon once suggested that China be allowed to sleep, "for when she awakes, she will shake the world." China has indeed shaken the world – not with her armies, but with her factories.[3] Today the world's most populous nation of 1.3 billion people is also the third largest economy in terms of GDP, and a global investor with operations established in more than 160 countries (Schmidt, 2006: 3), while absolute poverty has dropped to below 22 million, with incidence of poverty just around 2 per cent[4]. The phenomenal rise of China as an economic power, as well as her heightened political and military clout that has been growing in tandem with this, inevitably brought forth, both regionally and globally, increasing concern over whether she is posing a threat to regional stability and prosperity, and if so, in what way. Despite also being viewed as a threat, China is more often regarded as an opportunity for her trade partners. Unlike the earlier economic "miracles" of East Asia, China has been following a liberal foreign investment regime in recent decades (McGregor, 2005), opening its domestic markets and "not building an export powerhouse behind a wall of protective tariffs"[5]. The country's rapid economic growth has generated great opportunities for large volumes of imports of both primary and manufactured goods from her regional trade partners. This has served to compensate the latter for their losses of market share in the US and Japan (Weiss, 2005: 72).

Being a newly emerging economic entity and the world's third largest economy, as well as the United States' largest creditor holding US bonds totaling US$727 billion as at end of 2008 which reached US$801.5 billion by May 2009, and the only major country that is possibly still able to maintain a growth rate of 7 or 8 per cent this year amidst the current global financial crisis, China's importance as the possible saviour of the global economy cannot be overstated.[6] Out of the four countries of the BRIC[7] (the four major newly emerging economic entities of Brazil, Russia, India and China) that encompass over 25 per cent of the world's land coverage, constitute 40 per cent of the world's population and hold a combined Gross Domestic Product of US$15.5 trillion (purchasing power parity), China, with the largest GDP (PPP) of US$7.9 trillion (compared to India's US$3.3 trillion, Russia's US$2.3 trillion and Brazil's US$2 trillion)[8], is without doubt the BRIC's bright spark second to none, especially in view of the unenviable economic performance of Russia and Brazil during the current global economic crisis – though the recent rise in oil prices has benefited Russia much and Brazil's 1.9 per cent GDP growth in the second quarter of 2009 has exceeded market forecast of 1.7 per cent[9] – and India's continued sociopolitical instability stemming particularly from her troubled relationship with her equally nuclearized foe Pakistan and the problem of Kashmir. With the support of the rest of the BRIC, China, which is holding a foreign exchange reserve exceeding US$2 trillion[10], has recently proposed to challenge the status of the US dollar as the international reserve currency, though this was subsequently played down in the first BRIC Summit held in Yekaterinburg[11], Russia, on 16th June 2009 and the final BRIC communiqué did not mention the issue.[12] On the regional front, with the establishment of the world's largest free trade area[13] – the China-ASEAN Free Trade Area (CAFTA/ACFTA)[14] encompassing a total population of 1.9 billion – on the horizon, and the Association of Southeast Asian Nations (ASEAN) being the fourth largest trade partner of China with bilateral trade still reaching US$230 billion[15] in 2008 – a growth of 14 per cent over the preceding year even during the current global financial crisis[16], China is set to become an even more formidable pivotal power in the vibrant Southeast Asian region in the years to come[17], and the economic well-being of countries big and small in this region is now very much tied to China's rise as an economic power and the engine of growth in the region.

Nevertheless, notably, one of the major factors in many of China's PTA/FTA negotiations has been her urgent need for greater access to raw materials, particularly of energy, to fuel her sustained rapid economic growth.[18] Increasingly attracting global attention is China's fervent resource diplomacy in Africa, Latin America, and West and Central Asia, often with geopolitical implications. Early in March 2004, US Assistant Secretary of State for Western Hemisphere Affairs Roger F. Noriega warned the US government that China had been translating its economic success and its search for resources to fuel its economic growth into greater influence in Latin America and the Caribbean, and of the political and strategic threat to the US from China's enhanced influence in Central America, reflected not least by China's successful lobby to keep democratic Taiwan (Republic of China)[19] out of the observer position in the Organization of American States (OAS) despite OAS's stated goal of advancing democracy, according to John Tkacik, Jr., senior research fellow in China policy at the Asian Studies Center of the Heritage Foundation, US, who noted the threat of another CAFTA (Central American Free Trade Agreement) to China's interest in world textile production (Tkacik, 2005). Similarly, on the part of China, geopolitical, probably more than economic rationale, is dictating her continued emphasis on Sino-ASEAN relations, including the formation of CAFTA/ACFTA as part of her *mulin youhao* 睦邻友好 (good neighbourliness and friendship) foreign policy.

Hence, to a world that is watching her rise with a mix of curiosity, hope and trepidation, the rapidly transforming China remains an enigma. Almost a decade ago, an observer noted, "Is China a threat to the region, a potential hegemon busy establishing an economic power base on which to build an invincible military force? Or is she a large yet insecure country with painful memories of various colonial predators, fearfully aware of the immense technological superiority of the United States military, but intent on international and regional cooperation? Then there is the question of China's economy, and whether the Middle Kingdom will ever be anything more than a middle power." (Arnott, 2001: 70-71) A decade later today, it is indubitable that the world has witnessed China's rise maturing from a work in progress into a *fait accompli*, and there is increasing prognosis among the pundits that, with the waning of *Pax Americana* that has held sway since the end of World War II, the dawn of a new era of *Pax Sinica* might be in the making. One thing for sure is, amidst mixed signals, where China is headed, how she will get there and in what ways she will impact upon other countries and herself along the way have become questions urgently needing to be answered. While China's material rise and miraculous accomplishments are beyond doubt, her direction at this stage could be less than certain and the next phase of the country's ascendancy under the rule of the Chinese Communist Party (CCP)[20] and her trajectory of transformation could be an even more complex phenomenon, and understanding them is hence even more strategically critical for both her ASEAN neighbours and the world at large.

Against this backdrop, this book presents a collection of research papers that examine and discuss the breadth and depth of China's strategic development in the coming years and its potential impact on the East and Southeast Asian regions as well as the world at large. Reflecting on China's accomplishments during the past thirty years of reform, this book also sets out to contemplate the country's future, and how this would affect her immediate neighbours and the world, in terms of the impact upon the international *status quo*, whether socio-politico-economic or military, and whether and how this could also ultimately be subordinate to the country's domestic challenges. Earlier versions of some of the chapters in this book were presented at the international conference "China's Future: Pitfalls, Prospects, and the Implications for ASEAN and the World" organized by the Institute of China Studies (ICS), University of Malaya, in May 2009. Chapters 2, 3, 5, 6 and 8 of this volume are revised versions of papers presented in the said conference. The editor and the Institute of China Studies would like to thank these conference presenters who have since taken the effort to revise their papers for inclusion in this volume as well as the other authors who have contributed some great new papers to this book.

China's Rise: Regional Challenges

After this introductory chapter, the book begins with the section *China's Rise: Regional Challenges*, with a chapter by Samuel C.Y. Ku, "China's Changing Relations with Southeast Asia: A Political Analysis" (Chapter 2), that analyzes

China's changing politico-economic relations with Southeast Asia, from the confrontational relationship of the 1950s-70s to the implementation of three key policy initiatives, viz. the open-door policy that began in 1979, the "good neighbour" policy of 1990 and the "go global" strategy of 2002 that have laid a foundation for the rapidly improving relations – political, economic as well as social – with ASEAN. Acknowledging the existence of major problems, in particular territorial disputes and economic disparities between the two sides, Ku contends that China's political manoeuvre with respect to Southeast Asia is the contributing factor of both her changing relations with the latter as well as the emerging problems between them, and hence he asserts, China needs to take another political initiative to handle the disputes between them. In a sense, in China the origin of the problem lies and paradoxically, in China, also the solution is to be found.

China has been relentlessly emphasizing that her growing influence in Asia and the world arena – her "peaceful rise" (*heping jueqi* 和平崛起) – is a threat to no one but a benefit for all, and with the formalization in the 1990s of the framework of her foreign relations with the surrounding countries (*zhoubian guanxi* 周边关系)[21] as "*zhoubian shi shouyao, daguo shi guanjian, fazhanzhong guojia shi jichu, duobian shi wutai* 周边是首要, 大国是关键, 发展中国家是基础, 多边是舞台" ("relations with the surrounding countries are primary; those with the great powers are the key; those with the developing countries are the foundation; multilateral relations are arenas")[22], her overall foreign policy is guided by the principle of *mulin fuli* 睦邻富邻 (in harmony with neighbours and prosper together) and her diplomatic relations with her neighbouring countries are guided by the principles of *mulin, fulin, anlin* 睦邻、富邻、安邻 (in harmony with neighbours, prosper together with neighbours, and assuring the neighbours) and *yi lin wei ban, yu lin wei shan* 以邻为伴，与邻为善 (to be partner of neighbours and do good to neighbours). Nevertheless, on the part of her immediate neighbours in East and Southeast Asia, diplomatic manoeuvres of this overshadowing giant could not probably be seen but through the smoky prism of *Realpolitik*, wherein the primary alignment response of states is often a bid to balance against a potential or actual power or constellation of power due to the fear of being dominated or destroyed by the latter, or alternatively, to bandwagon with this rising, stronger power to gain from the benefits the latter makes possible (Yeoh and Hannan, 2008: 8).

This section continues with Sukhee Han's chapter, "The Rise of China, Power Transition and South Korea's Soft Hedging" (Chapter 3), which analyzes "dual bandwagoning" as fundamental to South Korea's "soft hedging" in which South Korea maintains economic interdependency and cooperative relations with the rising China while at the same time expanding diplomatic and security cooperation with the US, or in other words, soft hedges against China with the blessings of the US, given her economic dependence on China and the latter's diplomatic influence over North Korea, as well as her traditional alliance upon the US, her long-time ally. Such strategy, he contends, has gain particular cogency in the light of recent developments concerning nuclear weapons in North Korea. While deviating from other types of hedging carried out by the other regional states – such as reciprocal hedging, twin hedging and dual hedging – South Korea's policy of soft hedging under the new Lee Myong-bak 이명박 / 李明博 administration since 2008 is particularly tailored to maintain her faithfulness to the trusted strategic alliance with the US strained during the anti-American, pro-Chinese and North Korea-friendly presidency of the late Roh Moo-hyun 노무현 / 盧武鉉, and through increasing economic interdependence and societal interactions with China, coincides with the latter's interest of maintaining her one-party regime legitimacy through economic performance. On the part of the US, according to Han, the effort to curtail China's potentially revisionist inclinations by weaving her into the international community and integrating her with the global economy indeed concurs with South Korea's policy of soft hedging.

Also within the context of East Asia, Takashi Hoshiyama, in the third chapter on *China's Rise*, "Japan's Perspective on the Threat and Opportunity of China" (Chapter 4), examines Japan's perspective on China as one of her major neighbouring countries, focusing on China as not only a possible "opportunity" but also a potential "threat" not only in economic terms but also, more often perceived in the context of a potential security risk to Japan. Six decades after the end of World War II, Hoshiyama notes, shadow of the past still lingers to haunt the bilateral relations between the two East Asian powers. Prominent recent examples he gives include issues from the complex entwinement of historical legacy and national honour and dignity like former prime minister Junichiro Koizumi 小泉純一郎's visits, widely considered as official, to the Yasukuni Shrine (*Yasukuni Jinja* 靖国神社) to territorial disputes such as that related to the Senkaku Islands[23] to military concerns such as the June 2009 incident around the atoll of Okinotori-shima 沖ノ鳥島. Problems as such notwithstanding, Hoshiyama foresees the potential of Japan-China cooperation and joint leadership in the region in building and developing multi-faceted and multi-layered regional mechanisms for the maintenance of regional peace and stability, within a larger framework that includes the US in Japan-China relations and further multilateral frameworks that include ASEAN, India, South Korea, Australia, etc. based on collective security and related concerns, on a path that would increase the opportunities and at the same time, decrease the potential risks of China's ascendance not only as a global and regional economic power and engine of growth, but also as a political force and potential military juggernaut that her neighbours have learnt to fully reckoned with.

Complex legacies from modern history such as that which is still haunting Sino-Japanese relations are not unknown either in the case of Sino-Vietnamese relations. Despite their close alliance during the Vietnam War, relations between the two countries have been plagued by regional rivalries and territorial disputes such as the delineation of territorial waters in the Tonkin/Beibu Gulf[24] and sovereignty over the Paracel Islands[25] and Spratly Islands[26] in the South China Sea[27]. The potential of offshore oil deposits in the Gulf of Tonkin also raised tensions over territorial waters. Such disputes and post-Vietnam War political realignment finally resulted in the brief but deadly Sino-Vietnamese border war in early 1979 after Vietnam invaded Democratic Kampuchea[28] in 1978 and overthrew China's genocidal ally, Pol Pot's Khmer Rouge regime. The ending of open enmity and the resumption of Vietnam War-era friendship between China and Vietnam did not arrive until the official normalization of ties in late 1991 after the collapse of the Soviet Union and Vietnam's military withdrawal from Cambodia in 1990. The normalization of ties also saw in subsequent years genuine efforts by the two sides in resolving territorial disputes – both regarding land border and maritime rights – between them both on a bilateral basis and as part of the Sino-ASEAN endeavour for peaceful resolution to territorial disputes and guarantees against armed conflict. Meanwhile, since resuming trade links in 1991, Sino-Vietnamese commercial ties blossomed and China has risen to become a leading trade partner of Vietnam. Such impressive development in economic relations between Vietnam and China since normalization of relations is detailed in Do Tien Sam and Ha Thi Hong Van's chapter on *China's Rise*, "Vietnam-China Relations and Building the 'Two Corridors, One Economic Belt'" (Chapter 5). The strengthening of relations is evident on various fronts, ranging from regular meetings between the two country's leaders to meteoric rise in bilateral trade and China's direct investments (FDI) and official development assistance (ODA) projects in Vietnam to equally remarkable advancement in the spheres of tourism and cultural and educational cooperation. Besides that, Do Tien Sam and Ha Thi Hong Van observe, the two countries have also made truly remarkable progress, given the bitter conflict in the past, in their genuine efforts to resolve the various thorny land and maritime territorial disputes. Although development in political relations has not adequately kept pace with that in economic relations, the authors note, the recent plan to construct the "two economic corridors and one economic belt", first proposed in 2004 and followed by the signing of a Memorandum of Understanding in 2006, could prove to be the catalyst for further breakthroughs in the improvement of bilateral relations of the two countries not only from the economic perspective, but also from the political and social, which augurs well for enhancing the wellbeing of the people of the two countries in an atmosphere of peace, cooperation and development.

China's Dilemma: Rural and Urban

After looking at the regional implications of the contemporary rise of China from the perspectives of various major neighbouring countries in East and Southeast Asia, the book proceeds to examine the mainly domestic challenges that China is confronted with in the course of her breakneck economic advancement in the section *China's Dilemma: Rural and Urban* with two chapters analyzing respectively the country's fast-transforming rural sector and urban landscape.

John A. Donaldson and Forrest Zhang, in the first chapter on *China's Dilemma*, "Whither China's Agriculture and Rural Sector? Some Thoughts on Changes in Rural China and Possible Effects on ASEAN" (Chapter 6), introduce a fivefold typology of agribusiness-farmer relations to analyze the growth of agribusiness and the role it has played in the rise of agrarian capitalism in China and the resultant changes to the rural society. Looking at the various forms in which agribusiness companies are transacting with individual agricultural producers, Donaldson and Zhang contend that China's unique system of land rights has played an important role in shaping agribusiness-farmer interactions and served to provide the individual agricultural producers a source of income and political bargaining power and protected them from being dispossessed of their land by corporate actors. Finally, noting the strong economic ties between China and ASEAN, the authors also examine the effects of the increase in scale and involvement of agribusiness in China on the member countries of ASEAN.

From agriculture and rural sector of China this section shifts its focus onto urban China in Kate Hannan's chapter "Finding a Home in China's 'Restless Urban Landscape'" (Chapter 7). The cities of China are undergoing a significant change in the use of urban space, Hannan notes, wherein the use of "convenient" urban sites for manufacturing industries, particularly for state-owned enterprises and their attendant worker housing, has given way to the use of these areas for shopping malls as both market outlets and public spaces, high-rise office blocks and privately owned apartments. In this changing landscape, she observes, permanent urban residents with market clout and good connections occupy the new urban housing, while less favoured residents find that they are relocated to more distant parts of the city. The *nongmingong* 农民工 (rural-to-urban migrant workers), on the other hand, have been obliged to find housing where they can, which may mean living in hostels provided by their employers or finding a home in the satellite towns that have now been established around China's largest cities, or they may be obliged to resort to renting accommodation in overcrowded, unheated and often unsanitary conditions on the outskirts of town. In the light of such disturbing development, Hannan analyzes the problems associated with finding a home in China's "restless urban landscape" and possibility of a solution through urban re-development.

China's Future: International Milieu, Ethnoterritoriality and *Realpolitik*

The year 2009 marks the anniversaries of several significant critical junctures for China, some triumphant, some tragic: 4th May 1919, 1st October 1949, 4th June 1989. Having focused on the regional challenges raised by a China in the ascendant and the domestic problems and dilemmas, rural and urban, caused by the country's breakneck economic transformation, the book moves on to its last section, *China's Future: International Milieu, Ethnoterritoriality and Realpolitik*, to contemplate the way forward in the context of the global environment, consequential policy responses at momentous critical junctures and subsequent State policy development, and the exigencies engendered by the questions of ethnic diversity, ethnoterritoriality and interplay of central State and peripheral nationalisms.

In the first chapter on *China's Future*, "China after Thirty Years of Reform and Open Policy: *Quo Vadis?*" (Chapter 8), Im-Soo Yoo reflects upon China's past three decades of economic reform and ruminates on the next thirty years down the road in the country's continued growth and transformation. China's economic miracle has prompted Joshua Cooper Ramo to introduce into the mainstream political lexicon in 2004 the concept of "Beijing Consensus" (Ramo, 2004) as an alternative economic development model in view of the perceived failure of the well-known "Washington Consensus" codified in Williamson (1990), a failure particularly attributed to over-adherence to "market fundamentalism"[29]. From the perspective of China's ruling CCP, "Beijing Consensus" clearly not only vindicated the three decades of economic reform policy, but also the caution against parallel reform in political system as well as the final decision taken in June 1989 in the face of the pro-democracy demonstrations in Tiananmen Square, as typified, for instance, by a Chinese scholar's opinion of the four cornerstones of the

"Beijing Consensus": 1) Contrary to "neo-liberalism" and the "Washington Consensus", in China there exist a powerful political party and a powerful government led by the said party constituting a crucial political prerequisite for the success of the country's "reform and open" policy; 2) Inductive, not coercive, institutional change and "gradualist", not "radical", reform; 3) "Rationally advancing (radical)" in economic reform and "rationally holding back (conservative)" in political reform; and 4) Unswervingly persisting in the market economic reform direction, yet maintaining sharp vigilance against market fundamentalism by means of firmly upholding the reform target of "socialist market economic system" (Zou, 2006: 411-412). This year, 2009, marks the 60th anniversary of the founding of the People's Republic of China which in 1949 marked the birth of the first major Marxist-Leninist country in Asia, preceded only by the establishment of the Mongolian People's Republic in 1924. It is a time to reflect, Yoo observes, upon the apparent contradictions inherent in this unique Chinese model – Zou's cornerstones of the "Beijing Consensus" – of combining pragmatic open-market economy with one-party political centralism, and as he proceeds to caution, to seriously appraise the sustainability of this model and the possible pitfalls along the way, which cast aspersions upon the present "China miracle" – whether it would be a lasting leading light in the world arena, or just a transient bright spark of the moment. Such pitfalls do not only stem from the unusual combination of open-market economy and political authoritarianism, but also from the instabilities engendered by the State's nationality policy and the growth of peripheral ethnonationalism, as exemplified again by the recent troubles in China's western frontier regions of Xinjiang and Tibet.

This section continues with Mutahir Ahmed's chapter, "Emerging Threats in South, Central and West Asian Regions: China's Strategy and Responses" (Chapter 9), which analyzes China's ethnoregional instabilities in the context of the nationalism of the Chinese central State linked to regime legitimization and peripheral nationalism in Xinjiang connected to the post-Afghan War regional rise of religious fundamentalism and radicalism and ethnic economic disparity which have led to ethnic riots in Xinjiang in recent years including the latest, most deadly, disturbance on 5th July 2009. Recognizing the source of tension in the South, Central and West Asian regions as one of the factors for the country's ethnoregional instabilities, Mutahir highlights China's attempt to address this issue by initiating the idea of Shanghai Five in 1996 which later on transformed into the Shanghai Cooperation Organization. To sustain economic growth within, he notes further, China depends heavily upon a stable security and peaceful environment in her neighbourhood which is constantly under threat from the Indo-Pakistan tension in South Asia, the presence of the US in Central Asia and violent religious extremism in the Southwest Asian region which directly affects the stability of Xinjiang. Noting the threat of a "New Great Game" stemming from the permanent pressure of the US in Afghanistan and reactions from the South, Central and West Asian regions in the forms of ethnonationalism and violent religious extremism, the author analyzes role of these regional and extra-regional powers[30] in affecting China's economic, political and security interests, and China's responses to these threats.

At the beginning of this introductory chapter we have brought up the 1976 Tangshan earthquake that has very much faded from collective memory. Not so much as fading from collective memory but more a subject of collective selective dementia is the 1989 Beijing-Tiananmen[31] massacre. This year 2009 is the 20th anniversary of that tragedy and various recent events related to civil rights development in China – be they State response to the "tofu-dregs schoolhouses" scandal[32] and the Xinjiang crisis or the latest incident involving exiled Tiananmen activist Zhou Yongjun[33] – have brought back limited attention to that harrowing event of 1989. The recent prime-time six-episode thematic programme of the China Central Television (CCTV) *Liu ge Wei Shenme* 六个为什么 [six "why"][34], in a way an antithesis of *He Shang*[35] of 1988 considered proemial to the 1989 Tiananmen demonstrations, reaffirmed CCP's position against multi-party democracy and tripartite separation of power in its argument that these would bring disaster to the country and the people who are currently enjoying China's unprecedented period of peace and prosperity – in other words, a domestic *Pax Sinica* (*Zhonghua taiping shengshi* 中华太平盛世), but *sans trias politica*. Emile Kok-Kheng Yeoh, in the closing chapter of this book, "China and Spain: Critical Junctures, Ethnoterritoriality and Paths of Reform and Devolution", examines the significance of the tragic monumental event of 1989 as a critical juncture, *à la* Katznelson (1971), central to State policy development in a comparative analysis of the evolution of the Spanish *Comunidades Autónomas* project and the state of Chinese decentralization against the backdrop of momentous critical structural junctures of the two countries since the 1970s. Placing such State policy development within a complex nexus of the trichotomy of society, economy and polity, Yeoh proceeds to provide a detailed analysis of the impacts of such critical junctures and the subsequent public policy development on the exigencies engendered in multiethnic societies characterized by ethnoterritoriality, with special reference to the El Ejido riots in 2000 and the Ürümqi riots in 2009. While the paths of decentralization and devolution may differ in many aspects between the two countries, as this closing chapter of the book shows, the experience of the Iberian nation in successfully negotiating her way through the treacherous undercurrents of centrifugal forces so far from the monolithic Franquist "no-party" State to the present "State of the Autonomies" could shed much light on the Asian giant's continued odyssey of development, modernization and reform, wherein at stake, as evidence increasingly shows, is not only the wellbeing of the country's population of one fifth of humanity but also that of the international community in this era of globalized commercial linkages and politico-socioeconomic nexus of an increasingly borderless world. *Pax Americana* on the wane might or might not be succeeded by a *Pax Sinica* in the making, but that may no longer be the heart of the matter, for out there in the uncharted waters, *Pax Humanica* could ultimately be the dark silhouette that is standing out boldly against the fading light of power politics, parochialism, schism and conflict.

Notes

* Dr Emile Kok-Kheng Yeoh 楊國慶 is Director and Associate Professor of the Institute of China Studies, University of Malaya, Malaysia. Emile graduated with a PhD from the University of Bradford, West Yorkshire, England (1998), and his research interests include institutional economics, China studies, decentralization and fiscal federalism, and socioracial diversity and the role of the State in economic development. His works have been published in journals and occasional paper series such as *The Copenhagen Journal of Asian Studies*, *GeoJournal: An International Journal on Human Geography and Environmental Sciences*, *Malaysian Journal of Economic Studies* and the Copenhagen Discussion Paper Series, and his recent books, as both editor and contributor, include *Ethnic Interaction and Segregation on Campus and at the Workplace* (2004), *Economic Kaleidoscope: Current Issues and Perspectives* (2005), *China and Malaysia in a Globalizing World: Bilateral Relations, Regional Imperatives and Domestic Challenges* (2006), *Emerging Trading Nation in an Integrating World: Global Impacts and Domestic Challenges of China's Economic Reform* (2007), *Facets of a Transforming China: Resource, Trade and Equity* (2008), *China in the World: Contemporary Issues and Perspectives* (2008), *CJAS Special Issue (26(2)): Transforming China* (2008), *Regional Political Economy of China Ascendant: Pivotal Issues and Critical Perspectives* (2009), *China-ASEAN Relations: Economic Engagement and Policy Reform* (2009).

1. *Doufuzha xiaoshe* 豆腐渣校舍.
2. A cognate of the ideal, *juche* 주체 / 主體, survives in Kim Il Sung's, and now Kim Jong Il's, Orwellian state of North Korea, China's close ally in East Asia.
3. "An Awakening Dragon Shakes up the World" (Editorial), in *China Goes Global*, Financial Times' Asia Insight series, 2005, p. 14.
4. See Chapter 10 of this book, Table 10.2.

5. "An Awakening Dragon Shakes up the World" (Editorial), in *China Goes Global*, Financial Times' Asia Insight series, 2005, p. 14.

6. *Dongfang Jeubao* 东方日报 (*Oriental Daily News*, Malaysian daily), 1st April 2009, 20th July 2009. For note on transliteration, see Appendix to Chapter 10 of this book.

7. Coined by economist Jim O'Neill of the Goldman Sachs investment bank in 2003, the BRIC thesis argues that given the economic potential of Brazil, Russia, India, and China, these four countries may become the four most dominant economies by the year 2050.

8. *Ibid.* Following the US (rather than British) convention, billion = 1000,000,000 and trillion = 1000,000,000,000.

9. *Dongfang Jeubao*, 17th September 2009.

10. *Dongfang Jeubao*, 20th July 2009.

11. Yekaterinburg/Ekaterinburg (Екатеринбург) is a major city in central Russia. It was named Sverdlovsk (Свердловск) between 1924 and 1991, after the Bolshevik party leader Yakov Mikhaylovich Sverdlov (Яков Михайлович Свердлов).

12. *Dongfang Jeubao*, 18th June 2009.

13. Ravenhill and Jiang (2007: 33, note 2) preferred the term "preferential trading agreements" (PTAs) to "regional agreements" (RAs) or "free trade agreements" (FTAs) for the fact that their membership is often not "regional" in any conventional geographic sense of the word and "relatively few of the large number of preferential arrangements negotiated in the last decade come close to conventional criteria for 'free' trade".

14. China calls this China-ASEAN Free Trade Area (CAFTA); ASEAN calls this ASEAN China Free Trade Area (ACFTA). Incidentally, CAFTA is also the English acronym of the Central American FTA. As China is anticipated to sustain relatively high growth rates in the foreseeable future, ASEAN countries including Malaysia are positioning themselves to take advantage of the growth opportunities, and seeing ACFTA/CAFTA as not only able to promote intra-regional trade but also to enhance market integration, leading to potential substantial gains through competition and scale effects, which could be used strategically to serve the growth objective, though such positive outcomes may not really be possible without long-term careful policy design (Yeoh, 2008a: 141-142).

15. Roughly equivalent to 828 billion Malaysian ringgit. For Malaysia, a member of ASEAN, her bilateral trade with China reached US$53.5 billion (192.6 ringgit) in 2008, realizing before schedule the target of US$50 billion by 2010 fixed earlier by the two countries (*Dongfang Jeubao*, 26th March 2009.).

16. *Dongfang Jeubao*, 11th April 2009.

17. Proportion-wise, China-ASEAN bilateral trade actually constitutes only 9 per cent of China's total foreign trade, which throws doubt in some way on the extent of advantage in terms of market access when CAFTA/ACFTA is fully implemented, and gives rise to the view that China's proposal of CAFTA/ACFTA is in fact predominantly politically motivated with an over-emphasis on its geo-

strategic implications for herself at the expense of the objective assessment of the economic realities (see, e.g. Yeoh, 2007: 7-8).

18. See Yeoh (2008b: 14). China's continued shielding of Burma's ruthless ruling military junta from international opprobrium over its dismal human rights record is usually attributed to China's wish to gain a foothold in the untapped energy resources of this Southeast Asian nation amidst the former's increasing reliance on imported oil and gas and on the latter's military bases, though Lee, Chan and Chan (2009) contended that the scramble for energy was not the principal reason for China to adopt an accommodating approach towards this Southeast Asian pariah ally of hers. Further on Burma and the ruling junta, see note 57 in Chapter 10 of the book.

19. On Taiwan, Republic of China (ROC), see note 133 in Chapter 10 of this book.

20. Or more officially, the "Communist Party of China" (CPC).

21. See Yeoh (2008b: 8).

22. "Jiedu Zhongguo Xin Waijiao Zhanlüetu: Quanfangwei Heping Waijiao Chuxian Jinzhan 解读中国新外交战略图: 全方位和平外交出现进展" [Interpretation of China's new diplomatic strategy chart: progress in all-direction peaceful diplomacy], by *Liaowang Dongfang Zhoukan* 瞭望东方周刊 (weekly) reporter Huang Lin 黄琳, 9th November 2005. <*http://news3.xinhuanet.com/world/2005-11/09/content_3756767.htm/*>

23. The Pinnacle Islands – a group of uninhabited islands currently controlled by Japan who calls them the Senkaku Islands 尖閣諸島, a part of Okinawa prefecture 沖繩県, but claimed by both the ROC and the PRC as the Diaoyutai Islands 釣魚台列嶼 / 钓鱼台群岛, part of the Taiwan province. The largest island of the group is the Uotsuri Jima 魚釣島 / Diaoyu Dao 釣魚島.

24. Chinese: *Dongjing Wan* 东京湾 / *Beibu Wan* 北部湾; Vietnamese: Vịnh Bắc Bộ / Vịnh Bắc Phần / Vịnh Bắc Việt (泳北部 / 泳北分 / 泳北越). Tonkin (東京) – Vietnamese "Đông Kinh" [eastern capital] – is today's Hà Nội, the capital of Việt Nam.

25. Chinese: *Xisha Qundao* 西沙群岛; Vietnamese: Quần Đảo Hoàng Sa (群岛黄沙). The Paracels are a group of islets, sandbanks and reefs in the South China Sea (East Vietnam Sea/East Sea).

26. Chinese: *Nansha Qundao* 南沙群岛; Vietnamese: Quần Đảo Trường Sa (群岛長沙). The Spratlys are a group of islets, atolls, reefs, cays and islands in the South China Sea. Besides China (both PRC and ROC) and Vietnam, Malaysia and the Philippines also claim sovereignty over some of the islands of the Spratlys (Malay: Kepulauan Spratly; Tagalog: Kapuluan ng Kalayaan).

27. Chinese: *Nan Zhongguo Hai* 南中國海 / *Nan Hai* 南海 [south sea]; Vietnamese: Biển Đông [east sea].

28. The official name of Cambodia under the murderous Khmer Rouge regime.

29. Critique from, among others, Nobel Laureate Joseph E. Stiglitz (see Williamson, 1999).

30. Regarding the role of the regional and extra-regional powers, an example is the formation of the Six plus Two (China, Iran, Pakistan, Tajikistan, Turkmenistan and Uzbekistan, along with Russia and the US) in 1998 to contain the Taliban regime, though the group was soon locked in internal power politics linked to the member states' different priorities and interests (Mutahir, 2007: 193; Mutahir, 2001: 69).

31. See note 31 in Chapter 10 of this book for an elaboration of this appellation.

32. Subsequent to the earthquake, grieving parents, social activists and civil right lawyers who have questioned the authorities regarding the shoddy "tofu-dregs" buildings (*doufuzha gongcheng* 豆腐渣工程) that caused heavy casualties among schoolchildren during the 3-minute 8.5-Richter-magnitude quake have been continuously harassed, rounded up, detained, and threatened.

33. Zhou Yongjun 周勇军, a student leader during Tiananmen days and one of the three student representatives down on their knees on 22nd April 1989 on the stairs of the People's Great Hall in their futile attempt to submit a petition letter to Premier Li Peng 李鹏 in the prelude to the full-scale pro-democracy demonstrations that shook China and the world, was arrested in Hong Kong and handed over to China in his failed attempt to enter China in 2009 (*Dongfang Jeubao*, 21st September 2009).

34. *Dongfang Jeubao*, 19th September 2009.

35. On the consequential six-part CCTV documentary *He Shang* 河殇 [river elegy] of 1988 as an overture to the 1989 Tiananmen demonstrations, see note 32 in Chapter 10 of this book.

References

Arnott, David (2001), "Challenges to Democratization in Burma: Perspectives on Multilateral and Bilateral Responses", International IDEA. <*http.//www.idea.int/ asia_pacific/burma/upload/chap3.pdf#search='david arnott burma china'*>

Katznelson, Ira (1971), "Power in the Reformulation of Race Research", in Peter Orleans and William Russell Ellis, Jr (eds), *Race, Change, and Urban Society* (*Urban Affairs Annual Reviews*, Vol. 5), Beverly Hills, California: Sage.

Lee, Pak K., Gerald Chan and Lai-Ha Chan (2009), "China Engages Myanmar as a Chinese Client State?", in Emile Kok-Kheng Yeoh (ed.), *Regional Political Economy of China Ascendant: Pivotal Issues and Critical Perspectives*, Kuala Lumpur: Institute of China Studies, University of Malaya, pp. 70-95.

McGregor, Richard (2005), "The World Should Brace for China's Expansion", in *China Goes Global*, Financial Times' Asia Insight series, p. 11.

Mutahir Ahmed (2001), "Fundamentalism in Afghanistan and Its Impact on Central Asia", in *ЕВРАЗИЙСКОЕ ПРОСТРАНСТВО В ПОСТСОВЕТСКИЙ ПЕРИОД: ЭТНОКУЛЬТУРНАЯ СПЕЦИФИКА СОЦИАЛЬНЫХ И ПОЛИТИЧЕСКИХ ПРОЦЕССОВ*, Vol. 1, Volgograd: Ethno-cultural Centre, Volgograd State University Centre for Regional and Trans-border Studies.

Mutahir Ahmed (2007), "Challenges of Religious Fundamentalism to China: Policies and Responses", in *Emile Kok-Kheng Yeoh and Evelyn Devadason (eds), Emerging Trading Nation in an Integrating World: Global Impacts and Domestic Challenges of China's Economic Reform*, Kuala Lumpur: Institute of China Studies, University of Malaya, pp. 186-196.

Ramo, Joshua Cooper (2004), *The Beijing Consensus*, London: The Foreign Policy Centre.

Ravenhill, John and Yang Jiang (2007), "China's Move to Preferential Trading: An Extension of Chinese Network Power?", Copenhagen Discussion Paper Series, No. 18, Copenhagen: Asia Research Centre, Copenhagen Business School, May.

Schmidt, Johannes Dragsbæk (2006), "China's 'Soft Power' Re-emergence in Southeast Asia", Copenhagen Discussion Paper Series, No. 13, Copenhagen: Asia Research Centre, Copenhagen Business School, June.

Tkacik, John J., Jr. (2005), "CAFTA's Covert Opponent: China", WebMemo #778, 28th June 2005. <*http://www.heritage.org/Research/TradeandForeignAid/wm778. cfm*>

Weiss, John (2005), "China and Its Neighbours: Partners or Competitors for Trade and Investment?", in UNCTAD, *China in a Globalizing World*, New York and Geneva: United Nations, pp. 47-74.

Williamson, John (1990), "What Washington Means by Policy Reform", in John Williamson (ed.), *Latin American Adjustment: How Much Has Happened?*, Washington, DC: Peter G. Peterson Institute for International Economics.

Williamson, John (1999), "What Should the World Bank Think about the Washington Consensus?", paper prepared as a background to the World Bank's *World Development Report 2000*, Washington, DC: Peter G. Peterson Institute for International Economics.

Yeoh, Emile Kok-Kheng (2007), "Domestic Reform and Global Impact: Political Economy of China's Changing Trade Policy", in Emile Kok-Kheng Yeoh and Evelyn Devadason (eds), *Emerging Trading Nation in an Integrating World: Global Impacts and Domestic Challenges of China's Economic Reform*, Kuala Lumpur: Institute of China Studies, University of Malaya, pp. 3-45.

Yeoh, Emile Kok-Kheng (2008a), "Sino-Malaysian Trade Relations: Economic Prospects and Challenges", in Đỗ Tiến Sâm, Hoàng Thế Anh, Phạm Ngọc Thạch and Hà Thị Hồng Vân (eds), *ASEAN-China Trade Relations: 15 Years of Development and Prospects*, Hanoi: Thế Giới Publishers (for the Centre for ASEAN and China Studies, Vietnamese Academy of Social Sciences), pp. 141-175.

Yeoh, Emile Kok-Kheng (2008b), "Perspectivas y retos económicos del crecimiento de China: desde una perspectiva del Sudeste asiático" [Economic prospects and challenges of the rise of China: A Southeast Asian perspective], paper presented at VIII Reunión de la Red de Estudios de América Latina y el Caribe sobre Asia Pacífico [the Latin American and the Caribbean Studies Network on Asia Pacific (REDEALAP) 8th Annual Meeting], Universidad Externado de Colombia,

Bogotá, Colombia, 27th-28th August 2008, organized by Universidad Externado de Colombia and Instituto para la Integración de América Latina y el Caribe del Banco Interamericano de Desarrollo [Institute for the Integration of Latin America and the Caribbean of the Inter-American Development Bank (IDB-INTAL)]. *<http://www.iadb.org/intal/detalle_evento.asp?Origen=CA&cid=386&tipo=&id ioma=esp&id=360>, < http://www.iadb.org/intal/articulo_carta.asp?tid=5&idio ma=esp&aid=583&cid=234&carta_id=810>*

Yeoh, Emile Kok-Kheng and Kate Hannan (2008), "Introduction: Transforming China", in Emile Kok-Kheng Yeoh and Kate Hannan (guest editors), *The Copenhagen Journal of Asian Studies*, Vol. 26, No. 2 (*Special Issue: Transforming China*), pp. 5-10.

Zou Dongtao 邹东涛 (2006), "'Huashengdun Gongshi', 'Beijing Gongshi' yu Zhongguo Dute de Fazhan Daolu '华盛顿共识'、'北京共识' 与中国独特的发展道路" [Washington Consensus, Beijing Consensus and China's unique development path], in China Institute for Reform and Development (CIRD) 中国(海南)改革发展研究院 (ed.), *Zhengfu Zhuanxing yu Shehui Zaifenpei: Jingji Shehui Xietiao Fazhan yu Hexie Shehui Goujian* 政府转型与社会再分配 —— 经济社会协调发展与和谐社会构建 [Government transformation and social income redistribution: balanced economic and social development and building-up of a harmonious society], Beijing: Zhongguo Jingji Chubanshe 中国经济出版社 (China Economic Publishing House), pp. 408-415.

China's Rise:
Regional Challenges

Chapter 2

China's Changing Relations with Southeast Asia: A Political Analysis

Samuel C. Y. Ku*

Introduction

China (People's Republic of China, PRC) and Southeast Asia have been suspicious and, to some extent, hostile towards each other during the first three decades after the Chinese Communist Party (CCP) took over the Chinese mainland in October 1949. The weak Asian giant was then associated with the former Soviet Union in fighting against the United States, its then enemy. When China broke off relations with the Soviets in the late 1960s, the still weak Asian giant changed its policy from relying upon the Soviets to seeking an alliance with the United States. This was a turning point for China in entering the global community, particularly after its accession to the United Nations in October 1971.

China began to change its relations with Southeast Asia since the mid-1970s, when the PRC exchanged diplomatic recognition with three Southeast Asian countries, i.e. Malaysia, Thailand, and the Philippines. China made another significant change in December 1979 with implementation of an open-door policy, which opened the Asian giant's door to the world and changed China's relations with the world. Since then, China has been perceived as a rapidly changing society, with changes exceeding those of any period in Chinese history.

China has continued changing its relations with Southeast Asia since the early 1990s, and has changed speedily since the beginning of the 21st century. Three questions are then raised. What is driving the changing relations between China and Southeast Asia? While China's relations with Southeast Asia are moving forward, are there any problems between the two? Are these problems clouding the existing shining relations between China and Southeast Asia and how are they dealing with these emerging clouds?

This chapter argues that the development of China's recent genial relations with Southeast Asia is directed and pushed forward, among other factors (Robinson and Shambough, 1995), by three important political initiatives that started in the early 1980s, which are later developed as three important policies, i.e. (1) the open-door policy, (2) the Good Neighbour policy, and (3) the Go Global strategy. These three policies have laid a foundation for the rapidly improving relations between the two sides, at least in the following four areas, i.e. (1) political engagements, (2) economic relations, (3) social interactions, and (4) linkages with ASEAN.

While China develops a comprehensive relationship with Southeast Asia, two major problems (i.e. territorial disputes and economic gap) are also emerging between the two sides, although other problems exist. This chapter contends that the territorial disputes involve political manoeuvre, while the economic gap of the two also results from the above three policies, which has become a gulf between China and its neighbours in Southeast Asia. In other words, the change of China's relations with Southeast Asia is because of the mainland's political initiatives towards Southeast Asia; the emerging problems between the two sides have also to do with political manoeuvre; therefore, China should take another political initiative to handle the disputes between the two parties.

This chapter is divided into three sections. The first section introduces the bases and programmes of China's thriving relations with Southeast Asia, while the second section explores the two problems between the two sides. The last section discusses another political initiative for both China and Southeast Asia, which tends to propose a mechanism to avoid possible future conflicts on both sides on the one hand, and continue current cordial relations on the other.

China's Changing Relations with Southeast Asia

This section is divided into two parts. One introduces China's three key political initiatives that have enlightened improving relations between the Asian giant and its neighbours to the South, and the other demonstrates programmes that contribute to thriving relations between China and Southeast Asia, showing speedily changing relations between the two previously hostile parties.

Three Political Initiatives

Since the early 1980s, China has started three political initiatives which have dominated the Asian giant's policymaking process in its relations not only with countries in Southeast Asia (Haacke, 2005), but also with countries in other parts of the world.

The first political initiative, introduced in late 1978, is the so-called open-door policy, which has not only changed the modern development of China's political economy, but also the directions of international political and economic orders. Although the open-door policy does not specifically concentrate on China's relations with Southeast Asia, it is a political initiative that has changed China's foreign relations with major countries in the region. To countries in Southeast Asia, for example, China, in 1981, for the first time, established a Commercial Representative Office in Singapore, as did Singapore in Beijing. China and Indonesia restored direct trade with each other in 1985, and also began to conduct indirect trade with Brunei in 1985. Although the PRC had not yet exchanged diplomatic recognition with these three countries, the open-door policy made possible China's improving relations with Southeast Asia.

The second political initiative started with the implementation of the Good Neighbour Policy in 1990.[1] While the 1980s witnessed the beginning of China's open door to the world and Southeast Asia, the 1990s was an era in which China rapidly strengthened its relations with Southeast Asia. This political move was particularly significant after the brutal Tiananmen Square massacre on 4th June 1989, because long-isolated China desired a new image and a new genial relationship with its neighbours in Southeast Asia. The Good Neighbour policy, according to S.D. Muni, contains seven elements, four of which have to do with Southeast Asia, i.e. (1) energy tapping potential in the South China Sea, (2) seeking access to the Indian Ocean through Myanmar, (3) securing, enlarging and integrating markets, and mobilizing capital, technology and managerial skills from ASEAN, and (4) filling the power vacuum in Indochina created by the collapse of the Soviet Union (Muni, 2002.)

China's relations with Southeast Asia entered a new page since 1990. Indonesia restored full diplomatic relations with China in August 1990, and, two months later in October 1990, the Asian giant exchanged diplomatic recognition with Singapore. The year 1990 also started a series of visits of Chinese leaders to Southeast Asian countries, including Premier Li Peng's trip to five major countries in Southeast Asia, i.e. Indonesia, Singapore, Thailand, Malaysia and the Philippines. Similarly, three heads of governments in Southeast Asia were also invited to visit China in 1990, including President Suharto of Indonesia, Prime Minister Lee Kuan Yew of Singapore, and Prime Minister Chatichai Choonhavan of Thailand. In addition, China normalized its relations with Laos in 1989,[2] and also with Vietnam in October 1991.[3]

Finally, China started the third political initiative by proposing the "Going Global" strategy in 2002. China was admitted to the World Trade Organization (WTO) in 2002, and 2002 also witnessed China's closer linkages with ASEAN. The "Going Global" strategy aimed at taking Chinese enterprises overseas. Several measures, according to China's Ministry of Commerce, were taken in 2002 to promote the "Go Global" policy, such as (1) enacting laws for enterprises' overseas investment, (2) improving employment administration for foreign contract workers, (3) helping enterprises undertake large-scale projects in key countries,[4] (4) fulfilling the achievements of leaders' visits to foreign countries, and (5) assisting enterprises to develop foreign investment in various ways.[5]

When China initiates the "Go Global" strategy, the mainland also notably continues its "Good Neighbour" policy. Hu Jintao visited three Southeast Asian countries (i.e. Indonesia, Brunei, and the Philippines) in April 2005, and publicly reiterated three key elements for China's policy towards Southeast Asia, i.e. in harmony with neighbours (*mulin*), enriching neighbours (*fulin*), and stabilizing neighbours (*anlin*). Continual practice of the "Good Neighbour" policy in the new century has actually empowered the "Go Global" strategy.

Programmes for China's Relations with Southeast Asia

Due to the above three political initiatives, China has conducted a series of programmes on its interactions with Southeast Asia, which can be demonstrated in the following four areas, i.e. political engagements, economic relations, social interactions, and linkages with regional organization (i.e. ASEAN).

a) Political Engagements

The most important indicator showing China's political engagements with Southeast Asia is on the exchanges of the visits of high-level officials between the two sides. In the 1960s and 1970s, China rarely dispatched delegations to Southeast Asia, with only a few exceptions, but things have changed since the late 1980s. China and Malaysia, for example, began to exchange visiting high-level officials only since the late 1980s, in spite of their mutual diplomatic recognition exchange in 1974. In 1988, China and Malaysia exchanged visits of cabinet ministers responsible for trade affairs, and two years later in 1991, China and Malaysia started the first Joint Committee on Trade and Economic Cooperation. This story similarly applies to China's relations with Thailand and the Philippines, the other two countries that also exchanged diplomatic recognition with China in the mid-1970s, but both countries did not increase visit exchanges of high-level officials until the late 1980s.

China's relations with Indonesia have also greatly improved with the restoration of full diplomatic relations in August 1990.[6] President Suharto led a large delegation to visit China three months later in November 1990, the first time that the leader of the Muslim state paid a state visit to Mainland China since the 1965 abortive Communist coup in Jakarta. One year later in 1991, China and Indonesia began the first Joint Committee on Trade and Economic Cooperation in 1991.[7] President Susilo Bambang Yudhoyono was also invited to visit China in July 2005, after becoming the head of state in October 2004.[8] In return, most Chinese leaders have visited Indonesia during the last decade, including President Hu Jintao's recent visit for the 50th anniversary celebration of the Asia-Africa Summit in April 2005.

China's relations with Singapore were also strengthened when both countries exchanged diplomatic recognition in October 1990, and since then the visits of high-level officials from both sides have been frequent, despite Mr Lee Kuan Yew's first visit to China in the mid-1970s. Regarding China's relations with Vietnam, its former enemy in the 1970s, most Chinese leaders have visited Vietnam since the late 1990s, including Hu Jintao's first state visit to Vietnam on 1st November 2005, after assuming China's top leadership post in March 2003.[9] As for Vietnam, almost all of its leaders have paid a visit to China since 1998, including Phan Van Khai, Le Kha Phiew, Tran Duc Luong, and Mr Nong Duc Manh, the current Secretary General of the Communist Party of Vietnam.[10] As for China's relations with Cambodia, Laos, Burma, and Brunei, the exchange of visits among top leaders has also been frequent in the last decade, showing a closer relationship between China and these neighbouring countries.

b) Economic Relations

China's economic relations with Southeast Asia mainly include trade and investment. China did not experience a favourable trade relationship with Southeast Asia before implementation of the open-door policy, but things have gradually changed since that time. According to official ASEAN statistics, China, since 1994, began to enjoy trade surplus with Southeast Asia however, while the latter, in the mean time, suffered from trade deficits. The volume of ASEAN's trade with China, based on official ASEAN statistics, has shown great progress since the early 1990s, as demonstrated in Table 2.1.[11] Southeast

Table 2.1 ASEAN's Trade with China (US$ billion)

	1993	1995	1997	1999	2000	2002	2003	2004	2005	2006	2008
Imports from China	4.33	7.12	13.4	12.3	18.13	23.21	30.57	47.71	61.13	74.95	109.6
Exports to China	4.52	6.20	9.1	9.59	14.17	19.54	29.05	41.35	52.25	65.01	85.5
Total	8.86	13.33	22.65	21.92	32.31	42.75	59.63	89.06	113.38	139.96	192.5
Share of ASEAN's total trade	–	–	–	–	–	–	–	9.2%	9.3%	10.0%	11.3%

Sources: (1) *ASEAN Statistical Yearbook 2006* (Jakarta: the ASEAN Secretariat, 2007), Table V.9 (pp.78-79), Table V.10 (pp. 80-81), and Table 11 (pp. 82-83). (*http://www.aseansec.org/13100.htm*, accessed 24th February 2009)

(2) The figure of 2008 is from *http://www.aseansec.org/stat/Table19.xls*, accessed 1st September 2009.

Asian countries, however, continue to experience widening trade deficits since the turn of the century.

ASEAN trade with China has changed significantly since 2000, including continually expanding bilateral trade volume and China's increasing surplus in its trade with Southeast Asia. The bilateral trade volume has exceeded US$32.3 billion in 2000, and continued to expand to US$42.7 billion in 2002, US$59.6 billion in 2003, US$89.1 billion in 2004, US$139.96 billion in 2006, and US$192.5 million in 2008, as shown in Table 2.1. As China's economy has continued to thrive since the turn of the century, the share of ASEAN-China trade to total ASEAN trade volume has also continued to increase, from roughly 6.0 per cent in the early 1990s to 9.2 per cent in 2004, 10.0 per cent in 2006, and 11.3 per cent in 2008 (Table 2.1).

It is also significant that China's trade with Southeast Asia has continued to be in China's favour since the turn of the century. China's trade surplus with Southeast Asia has kept expanding from US$3.9 billion in 2000 to US$6.3 billion in 2004, US$9.9 billion in 2006, and US$21.4 billion in 2008, implying Southeast Asia's increasing import dependence on the mainland. This trend will continue in the near future.

Regarding China's investment relationship with Southeast Asia, both sides are major destinations for foreign direct investments (FDI), rather than sources of FDI for each other. According to ASEAN's statistics, China's investment in Southeast Asia was only US$156.7 million in 1995, which has declined a little since then to US$62.5 million in 1999, US$147.5 million in 2001, and even to negative US$74.3 million in 2002 (see Table 2.2). The share of China's FDI inflows into Southeast Asia in the region's entire FDI has also declined during the same period of time, from 0.5 per cent in 1995 to 0.2 per cent in 1999, 0.8 per cent in 2001, and to negative −0.5 per cent in 2002 (see Table 2.2). The years of 2000 and 2002 even showed negative growth in both China's FDI inflows into Southeast Asia and the share of China's investments in the region's entire FDI inflows.

Things have changed recently, however. According to the ASEAN Secretariat, China's FDI inflows into Southeast Asia increased to US$195.2 million in 2003, US$731.5 million in 2004, US$936.9 million in 2006, and US$1,437 million in 2008, so did the share of China's FDI to ASEAN's total net inflow from 1.0 per cent in 2003 to 2.6 per cent in 2004, 1.8 per cent in 2006, and 2.4 per cent in 2008 (Table 2.2). According to China's statistics, the figures of Chinese investments in Southeast Asia are even larger than ASEAN's statistics. By the end of 2002, for example, the Chinese enterprise invested US$1,201 million in Southeast Asia, US$716 million of which was

Table 2.2 China's FDI Flow into ASEAN and Its Share
(Value in US$ million; Share in per cent)

	China's FDI Inflow into ASEAN	Share of China's FDI Inflow into ASEAN
1995	156.7	0.5%
1996	117.9	0.4%
1997	62.1	0.2%
1998	295.3	1.3%
1999	62.5	0.2%
2000	−533.4	−0.6%
2001	147.5	0.8%
2002	−74.3	−0.5%
2003	195.2	1.0%
2004	731.5	2.1%
2005	502.1	1.2%
2006	1,016.2	1.8%
2007	1,226.9	1.8%
2008	1,437.8	2.4%

Sources: (1) Figures for 1995 to 2003 are from *ASEAN Statistical Yearbook 2006*, Table VI.2 (p. 163), and Table VI.5 (p. 168). (*http://www.aseansec.org/13100.htm*, accessed 25th February 2009)
(2) Figures for 2004 and 2005 are from *http://www.aseansec.org/Stat/Table26.pdf*, accessed 25th February 2009.
(3) Figures for 2006, 2007, and 2008 are from *http://www.aseansec.org/Stat/Table27.pdf*, accessed 1st September 2009.

from China.[12] The Asian giant's entire investment in Southeast Asia further reached US$775 million by the end of 2004.[13]

Singapore has obtained the largest amount of Chinese investments during the last two decades, and has become a platform for Chinese enterprises doing business in the region. The five largest banks in China have already established branch offices in the city-state; it is thus predictable that the Asian giant's investment in Southeast Asia will continue to expand in the years ahead as China's economy continues to grow.

c) Social Interactions

China's social interactions with Southeast Asia are best presented by tourism, which is not seen as a basic economic activity in nature; rather it is regarded as part of the entertainment industry. International tourists from a sending country to a receiving country, however, bring about progress in a series of industries (e.g. hotel, restaurant, transportation, and entertainment-related manufacturing) to the receiving country, which then contributes to creating new job opportunities for the receiving country. Tourism, thus, demonstrates the closeness of social interactions between sending and receiving countries; hostile countries will not promote tourism with one another.

China's tourism course with Southeast Asia in the last decade has explained the close social interactions of the Asian giant to its neighbours in the South. International arrivals from China to ASEAN countries in the 1980s were insignificant; the ASEAN Secretariat even did not record the number of Chinese visitors to ASEAN by 1994. It is only since 1995 that the ASEAN Secretariat began to reveal the number of arrivals from China to ASEAN countries, and since then China has rapidly played a significant role in the tourist industry in Southeast Asia. In 1995, international arrivals from China to ASEAN was 794,876, but, four years later in 1999, the number of Chinese visitors to ASEAN has almost reached 2 million. China has also become the fourth largest tourist sending country to Southeast Asia since 1999, next to Singapore, Malaysia, and Japan. The year 1999 also shows for the first time that the number of China's visitors to Southeast Asia exceeded that of Taiwan's and South Korea's.[14]

More importantly, excluding Singapore and Malaysia, the number of China's visitors to Southeast Asia was next only to Japan during the period between 2000 and 2007. China, however, has significantly shown a much faster growth rate than that of Japan, not only during the period from 1995 to 1998 (22.74 per cent for China versus –2.33 per cent for Japan), but also during recent years from 1998 to 2004 (13.09 per cent for China versus 2.12 per cent for Japan).[15] Comparing China's and Japan's share of visitor arrivals to Southeast Asian countries, Japan's share has gradually declined since 1997 (i.e. from 11.7 per cent in 1997 to 8.4 per cent in 2001, 6.9 per cent in 2004, 5.9 per cent in 2005, 5.9 per cent in 2007, and 5.5 per cent in 2008) whereas China's share shows an increase from 4.1 per cent in 1997 to 5.8 per cent in 2001, 6.3 per cent in 2004, to 5.2 per cent in 2005, 6.3 per cent in 2007, and 6.9 per cent in 2008 (see Table 2.3).

Apparently, the year 2007 has demonstrated that China has over passed Japan as the largest source of international arrivals to ASEAN countries.

Table 2.3 Visitors from China and Japan to ASEAN
           (unit: thousands)

	1997	2001	2004	2005	2006	2007	2008
China	–	–	–	3,007	3,315	3,926	4,487
(Share of total)	(4.1%)	(6.3%)	(6.3%)	(5.2%)	(5.8%)	(6.3%)	(6.9%)
Japan	–	–	–	3,650	3,364	3,701	3,631
(Share of total)	(11.7%)	(8.4%)	(6.9%)	(7.1%)	(5.9%)	(5.9%)	(5.5%)

Sources: (1) Figures for 1997, 2001, and 2004 are from *ASEAN Statistical Yearbook 2005* (Jakarta: ASEAN Secretariat, 2006), pp. 234-235.
         (2) Figures for 2005 and 2006 are from *http://www.aseansec.org/Stat/Table30.pdf*, accessed 25th February 2009.
         (3) Figures for 2007 and 2008 are from *http://www.aseansec.org/Stat/Table30.pdf*, accessed 1st September 2009.

As economic regionalization sustains to develop in the coming decade, it is anticipated that China will play an even more significant role on Southeast Asia's tourist industry in specific and economic development in general.

d) Linkages with ASEAN

Since the early 1990s, China has been very active in establishing ties with the Association of Southeast Asian Nations (ASEAN), the most important organization in the region. The PRC was, for the first time, invited to participate in ASEAN in July 1991 for the Twenty-fourth ASEAN Post-Ministerial Meeting as a consultative partner. In July 1994, while the PRC joined and became one of the founding members of the ASEAN Regional Forum (ARF),[16] the Asian giant was accepted as a full dialogue partner of ASEAN in July 1996. The outbreak of the 1997 Asian financial crisis gave China another opportunity to upgrade its relations with ASEAN due to the convention of the First ASEAN-China Summit (i.e. the "10+1" Summit) in November 1997, which has continued to the present.[17]

China's linkages with ASEAN continue to expand since the new century. In November 2000 at the Fourth ASEAN-China Summit,[18] Chinese Premier Zhu Rongji initiated a proposal to strengthen China's economic relations with ASEAN by establishing a free trade area (FTA) between the two sides. This proposal was officially announced in the November 2001 ASEAN-China Summit, and was enacted on 4th November 2002 at the Sixth ASEAN-China Summit,[19] when Zhu Rongji and ASEAN leaders signed the "Framework

Agreement on Comprehensive Economic Co-operation between the ASEAN and the PRC".[20] In addition, as China initiated the "Go Global" strategy in 2002, China and ASEAN started the First Economic and Trade Meeting for Economic Ministers and the First Meeting for Ministers of Transportation in September 2002.

At the Sixth ASEAN-China Summit on 4th November 2002, leaders of China and ASEAN also publicized the Joint Declaration of ASEAN and China on Cooperation in the Field of Non-Traditional Security Issues, including bilateral cooperation on combating illegal drug trafficking, people-smuggling, piracy on the high seas, terrorism, arms-smuggling, money-smuggling, money-laundering, international economic crime and cyber crime.[21] In October 2003 at the Seventh ASEAN-China Summit, China endorsed the Instrument of Accession to the Treaty of Amity and Cooperation (TAC) in Southeast Asia. During the Eighth China-ASEAN Summit on 29th November 2004, leaders from both sides signed three more important documents, i.e. (1) Agreement on Trade in Goods, (2) Agreement on Dispute Settlement Mechanism of the Framework, and (3) Agreement on Comprehensive Economic Cooperation between ASEAN and PRC for China-ASEAN Free Trade Area.

Chinese Premier Wen Jiabao recently promised again at the 15th anniversary of ASEAN-China dialogue in October 2006 that China is strengthening its ASEAN linkages on a wide range of issues [22] The ASEAN Plus Three (known as "10+3") also expanded to the East Asian Summit (EAS) when the EAS was firstly held in Kula Lumpur on 14th December 2005, providing the Asian giant another opportunity to play a larger role in its overall relations with Southeast Asia.

Two Major Problems between China and Southeast Asia

While China and Southeast Asia enjoy their thriving interactions, both sides are also facing two major problems, i.e. territorial disputes and economic development gap.[23] These two problems have to do with policy-making process. While the dispute over the sovereignty of the Spratly Islands in the South China Sea has long existed but without practical and concrete solutions, the issue of economic development gap has recently emerged but with little attention being paid.

Territorial Disputes

The most significant problem between China and Southeast Asia is territorial disputes over the Spratly Islands in the South China Sea, involving six countries, i.e. China, Vietnam, the Philippines, Malaysia, Brunei, and Taiwan (Snyder, 1996; Tonnesson, 2000). China and Vietnam have the most severe disputes over sovereignty of the Paracel Islands in the East Vietnam Sea. Both sides even initiated the first armed conflict in January 1974 when PRC forces overran the South Vietnamese position, and have occupied the islands since then. China and the Philippines also have disputes over sovereignty of the Scarborough Reef and Mischief Reef. In January 1995, Chinese troops detained a Filipino fishing vessel around the Mischief Reef area; tensions between both sides erupted again in 1997 and 1998 when Chinese warships upgraded the construction structures on Mischief Reef and nearby islands.

In order to settle these territorial conflicts, China and ASEAN states signed a Declaration on the Conduct of Parties in the South China Sea in November 2002, promoting a peaceful, friendly, and harmonious environment in the South China Sea (Buszynski, 2003). Since then, China and Southeast Asian countries have generally abided by the provisions of the Declaration; both parties have also reiterated their willingness in obeying the spirit of the Declaration. In May 2007, for example, when Vietnamese President Nguyen Minh Triet visited China, Mr Nguyen and Chinese President Hu Jintao stated before a joint news conference that both sides desire to seek peaceful means for settling territorial disputes in the Paracel Islands.

Given these efforts by China and ASEAN countries, China, Vietnam, and the Philippines, however, have continued to take a series of actions in protecting their sovereignty in the South China Sea in recent years. In January 2007, for example, China constructed several targeting objects in the Paracel Islands, causing Vietnam protest against China for invading Vietnam's territory. In April 2007, Vietnam proclaimed that elections for members of the National Assembly were held in the Paracel Islands occupied by the Vietnamese. Similarly, the Philippine government announced, on 14th May 2007, that 247 registered citizens on Kalayaan in the Spratly Islands had finished voting in the May 2007 nationwide elections. The Philippine government further announced on 11th March 2009 that the 2009 baseline bill was signed, which has officially legalized some islands and reefs in the South China Sea as the Philippine territory. The Chinese Embassy in Manila immediately, on the same day, issued a strong and solemn protest against the Philippine government, contending that Huangyan Island and Nansha Islands, claimed by the Philippines, "have always been part of Chinese territory and the People's Republic of China has indisputable sovereignty over these islands and their adjacent waters."[24]

Regarding China, instead of using military means, the PRC has recently intensified its "fishery patrol ships" (retired naval ships) in the South China

Sea. In mid-March 2009, for instance, China sent its largest fishery patrol ship, Yuzheng 311, to the waters around the Spratly Islands, following a confrontation between Chinese boats and a US naval ship in early March 2009.[25] A few days later, the *China Daily* interviewed Wu Zhuang, director of the Administration of Fishery and Fishing Harbor Supervision of the South China Sea, who said that China, while facing a growing amount of illegal fishing and other countries' unfounded territorial claims of islands in Chinas' exclusive economic zone, is necessary to step up to fishery patrols to protect China's rights and interests in the South China Sea.[26]

Accordingly, territorial disputes on the islands in the South China Sea clearly remain unresolved. Before the final resolution is legally reached, China, Vietnam and the Philippines are likely to confront each other again over this issue in the foreseeable future.

The Gap of Economic Development Level

Prior to the open-door policy, China's economic development was falling behind that of most countries in Southeast Asia, with only a few exceptions. China's economy has speedily changed, however, since the new century. While China continues to play the role of the biggest market magnet in absorbing foreign capital, Chinese enterprises have also become strong enough to invest overseas.

With this huge amount of foreign capital and domestic investment, China has, in the meantime, greatly improved its domestic infrastructures, making the Asian giant more efficient in absorbing capital and investment from overseas and more capable in reshaping its economic development. While China continues to maintain its shining macro-economic growth records, the Chinese people have also, since the turn of the century, upgraded their living standards, including higher income, better housing, overseas vacations, engaging in international businesses and activities, etc. In the year 2000, China's GDP per capita (US$967) has already exceeded that of Indonesia's (US$807) and almost reached the same level of the Philippines (US$973), as demonstrated in Table 2.4.

While China is improving its economy, Southeast Asian countries have only made minor progress. According to statistics of the Asian Development Bank, China's GDP growth rates, since the beginning of the new century, are higher than almost all countries in Southeast Asia. During the five years from 2003 to 2007, China has even experienced double digit economic growth rates, which were higher than all Southeast Asian countries (see Table 2.4). This has made China's GDP per capita continue growing in the meantime,

Table 2.4 China's and ASEAN's GDP Per Capita and Economic Growth Rates
(Unit: US$ for GDP per capita; per cent for economic growth rates)

	2000	2001	2002	2003	2004	2005	2006	2007
China (Economic growth rates)	967 (8.4%)	1,060 (8.3%)	1,034 (9.1%)	1,308 (10.0%)	1,535 (10.1%)	1,776 (10.4%)	2,027 (11.1%)	2,380 (11.9%)
Indonesia (Economic growth rates)	807 (4.9%)	793 (3.8%)	970 (4.3%)	1,113 (4.8%)	1,163 (5.1%)	1,279 (5.6%)	1,640 (5.5%)	1,919 (6.3%)
Philippines (Economic growth rates)	973 (4.4%)	917 (4.5%)	956 (4.4%)	973 (3.7%)	1,038 (6.2%)	1,155 (5.0%)	1,355 (5.3%)	1,652 (7.4%)
Thailand (Economic growth rates)	1,910 (4.8%)	1,855 (2.2%)	2,020 (5.3%)	2,265 (7.1%)	2,525 (6.3%)	2,721 (4.5%)	3,293 (5.1%)	3,740 (4.8%)
Malaysia (Economic growth rates)	3,811 (8.9%)	3,690 (0.3%)	3,899 (4.4%)	4,155 (5.5%)	4,831 (7.2%)	5,006 (5.2%)	5,890 (5.9%)	6,880 (6.3%)
Singapore (Economic growth rates)	23,066 (10.0%)	20,735 (-2.3%)	21,218 (4.0%)	22,161 (2.9%)	25,366 (8.7%)	26,564 (6.9%)	29,499 (7.9%)	35,206 (9.3%)
Vietnams (Economic growth rates)	403 (6.8%)	415 (6.9%)	440 (7.0%)	489 (7.4%)	565 (7.8%)	635 (8.4%)	724 (8.2%)	836 (8.5%)
Laos (Economic growth rates)	312 (5.0%)	324 (5.7%)	327 (5.0%)	376 (6.8%)	431 (6.9%)	480 (7.3%)	645 (8.3%)	736 (6.0%)
Cambodia (Economic growth rates)	285 (8.4%)	295 (5.5%)	310 (5.2%)	325 (7.1%)	362 (7.7%)	404 (9.8%)	512 (10.8%)	598 (10.1%)
Burma (Economic growth rates)	112 (13.7%)	135 (10.5%)	136 (5.5%)	220 (5.1%)	193 (5.0%)	199 (4.5%)	210 (6.9%)	215 (6.0%)

Sources: (1) Figures for China are from website of the Asian Development Bank, *http://www. adb.org/Documents/Books/Key_Indicators/2008/pdf/PRC.pdf*, accessed 26th February 2009. The ADB recorded China's GDP per capita in the unit of Rmb (i.e. Rmb7,732 in 2000, Rmb8,467 in 2001, Rmb9,271 in 2002, Rmb10,460 in 2003, Rmb12,277 in 2004, Rmb14,128 in 2005, Rmb16,214 in 2006, and Rmb19,033 in 2007), but the author calculated and transferred to American dollar with exchange rate of one American dollar to eight Rmb.

(2) Figures for ASEAN are from *ASEAN Statistical Yearbook 2006* (Jakarta: the ASEAN Secretariat, 2007), Table IV.2 (pp. 38-39) and Table IV.39 (pp. 40-41) (*http://www.aseansec.org/13100.htm*, accessed 26th February 2009). Figures for 2006 and 2007 are from *http://www.aseansec.org/stat/Table7.pdf*, accessed 26th February 2009.

reaching Rmb19,033 (roughly US$2,380) in 2007, higher than that of Indonesia's (US$1,919) and the Philippines' (US$1,652), and closer to that of Thailand's (US$3,740), as shown in Table 2.4. As a result, the economic development level gap between China and Southeast Asia, already surfaced in the mid-1990s, has become wider since the turn of the century.

Global economic recession occurred in mid-2008, which badly hit China and most Southeast Asian countries. Given this economic tsunami, it is believed, however, that China, with greater resources and markets, will have better opportunities to develop its economy than its neighbours in the South. Chinese Prime Minister Wen Jiabo said, in January 2009, that China will achieve the target of 8 per cent economic growth in 2009, although China's exports dropped 17.5 per cent and imports plunged 43 per cent in January 2009 from the same month a year earlier.[27] While China's economy keeps growing, this would, on the one hand, continue to enlarge China's economic development level gap with countries already falling behind the Asian giant (i.e. Burma, Laos, Cambodia, Vietnam, Indonesia, and the Philippines) and, on the other hand, narrow the gap with countries ahead of China (i.e. Thailand, Malaysia, Singapore, and Brunei).

Given China's role of a political and military hegemony in the region, China's economic growth has also upgraded the Asian giant's status from region to the world. As economic regionalization (i.e. 10+1) becomes a reality starting from 2010, Southeast Asian countries will receive an even more direct and strong economic impact from China. This problem has already surfaced and will be even more apparent in the coming decade. Is the economically stronger Asian giant a threat to the neighbouring countries in the South or a stabilizing force to the region? This is the question that both China and ASEAN countries have to respond in the near future.

Another Political Initiative to Sustain a Cordial Relationship

This chapter has pointed out, on the one hand, the on-going comprehensive relationship between China and Southeast Asia, and the two problems that shade the cordial China-Southeast Asia relationship on the other. This chapter then continues to argue that China and Southeast, particularly China, are obligated to take another political initiative to establish a practical and constructive problem-solving mechanism, in order to sustain a harmonious bilateral relationship in the years ahead.

The key reason for this is that China is still under the leadership of a power-centralized regime, which directs policy initiation and conducts policy implementation. Without the political initiative from the above, it is not possible to face these problems seriously and efficiently. The other reason is that the two major problems have to be addressed through political arrangements that are decided by the leaders who are in charge, rather than by ordinary decision-making process. Both China and Southeast Asian countries already have government agencies handling bilateral affairs, but, as this chapter has demonstrated, they are not successful to manage the two worsening problems between the two sides. Thus, both China and Southeast Asian countries are obligated to take further actions towards these two issues before their bilateral relations are stumbled.

Taking the ASEAN as an example, this is the most important multi-national organization in Southeast Asia, but the ASEAN, according to the ASEAN Declaration, is established for two aims, i.e. (1) "to accelerate economic growth, social progress and cultural development in the region," and (2) "to promote regional peace and stability through abiding respect for justices and the rule of law in the relationship among countries in the region." Apparently, the ASEAN is designed as an advisory institution that is obligated to present policy suggestions and policy initiatives to the ruling leaders of Southeast Asia. ASEAN is not authorized to execute policies; ASEAN is not fully in charge of China-ASEAN affairs either, though the ASEAN Secretariat is responsible to provide suggestions on the development of China's relations with Southeast Asia. Each ASEAN member country has its own foreign ministry in handling its relations with China; the ASEAN Secretariat is not responsible to manage the region's affairs with the Asian giant.

Similarly, China does not have a specific high-level agency in managing affairs with ASEAN; rather, the Asian giant has several different government institutions in dealing with its affairs with each ASEAN member country. Without a specialized high-level government institution in charging with bilateral affairs, problems between China and Southeast Asia are then emerged, and will become worsened with the passage of time. This is why this chapter contends that ruling leaders of China and Southeast Asian countries are obligated to take another political initiative to constructive a more effective mechanism to manage the worsening problems between the two.

This chapter then argues that China and Southeast Asian countries must, based on an already established foundation (e.g. the Agreement of Dispute Settlement Mechanism of the Framework signed at the 2004 China-ASEAN Summit), do something further to construct a comprehensive problem-solving mechanism, which should contain at least the following five characteristics: (1) assigning a specialized agency in charge of China-ASEAN affairs, (2) involving ministerial officers, (3) holding regular meetings, (4) having a regular budget, and (5) equipping with enforcement authority. As regionalization continues to prevail in this part of the world, China-ASEAN affairs will become even more complicated, and, to some extent, more difficult to handle. This is the political mandate for the establishment of a specialized agency to manage the on-going bilateral relations.

In addition, this chapter also argues that China, as a rising political and economic hegemony in the region, should engage in more of what Joseph Nye calls "soft power" to Southeast Asia, changing China's image from a big hegemonic power to a big responsive partner and a big constructive helper in the region. Although China has been extending its soft power to Southeast Asia for some years and has been confirmed somewhat successful by Joshua Kurlantzick,[28] this chapter argues that China's soft power to Southeast Asia is not yet successful, and, thus, China should extend more soft power to the region. Mr Kurlantzick points out that China's soft power to Southeast Asia includes culture, investment, academia, foreign aid, and public diplomacy (Kurlantzick, 2006 and 2007), but this chapter argues that China should do more in the following two "soft power" areas, laying a foundation for the establishment of a comprehensive mechanism and a cordial relationship with Southeast Asia in the coming decade.

Expanding Economic Assistance

China was a receiver of international assistance during the last two decades of the 20th century, but the Asian giant has changed its role since the beginning of the new century from a country receiving assistance to a country that offers assistance to third parties. China has also widened its economic development level with its neighbours to the South since the new century, as indicated earlier, and this gap will likely become wider in the coming decade. In order to respond this issue in an appropriate way, this chapter thus argues that China should play a more active role in issuing economic assistance to a wider scope of less developed countries in Southeast Asia, such as Laos, Cambodia, Myanmar, Indonesia, and the Philippines.

China has actually provided assistance to many less developed countries (mostly in Africa) for years, but much of this assistance has been for political reasons. Since 1988, however, China has designed three new technical assistance methods to desired countries, including (1) integrating bilateral assistance and multilateral assistance (there were twenty-six items in 1988), (2) incorporating governmental assistance and foreign contracted projects, and (3) putting together China's assistance with other countries.[29] In 2000, for example, China undertook thirty-seven complete plant assistance projects in twenty-eight countries, including an agricultural machinery factory in Burma.[30] In 2002, China undertook thirty-nine new complete plant projects, including constructing the Kunming-Bangkok Road through Laos, and No. 7 Road in Cambodia from Kratie to the border of Cambodia and Laos.[31]

China's economic assistance to Southeast Asia also includes foreign aid and financial assistance. China began expanding foreign aid to its neighbours in the South in the late 1980s,[32] and, later in the late 1990s, has become one of the major foreign aid contributors to Southeast Asian countries. During the Asian financial crisis in 1997, for example, China offered a loan of US$1 billion to Thailand, which was eligible to apply to other affected countries under the International Monetary Fund. In 1997, China also presented preferential loans to Burma, Vietnam, Laos and delivered free economic aid to Burma, Vietnam, Laos, Cambodia, and Indonesia.[33] China has continued to do so in recent years.

China has recently begun to remit debts for heavily indebted poor countries (HIPCs) and least-developed countries (LDCs) due to the "Going Global" strategy. The Chinese government announced, in the ASEAN SEOM consultations with Japan, Korea and China in November 2002, relieving partial debts owed by seven friendly Asian HIPCs and LDCs in 2003, including Vietnam, Laos, and Burma.[34]

Finally, China has started opening up training classes for recipient country personnel since the new century, which has largely expanded since then. The Asian giant, for example, received twenty-one members from ten ASEAN countries to attend Training Courses for Entrepreneurs of Small- and Medium-sized Enterprises, and another twenty trainees to attend the Trade and Investment Training Course for five Mekong River countries in 2002.[35] In October 2003, China invited seventeen officials from Southeast Asia to attend the "First ASEAN Seminar on Economic and Technological Development Zones", which has not only upgraded China's overall relations with participating countries, but has also laid a sound basis for bilateral economic cooperation in the years ahead.

Given China's assistance to Southeast Asian countries, this chapter argues that China, a rising economic giant (with a foreign reserve of US$1.95 trillion at the end of 2008), should continue to extend its economic assistance to Southeast Asian countries, but also should expand the scope of its assistance to its neighbours in the South. For example, China is experienced in basic infrastructure construction, the weakness of several Southeast Asian countries. China should continue in the years ahead to execute projects helping its southern neighbours in constructing more roads, dams, houses, schools, factories, etc. Improving basic infrastructures of Southeast Asian countries would upgrade the development level of local people and narrow the economic gap between China and its southern neighbours.[36]

China's economic assistance to Southeast Asia would also notably reduce political involvement and environmental worries, often criticized by international media.[37] Environment protection has become a key concern behind economic development, and China, a big power in the region, should take the lead to play a role model in this regard.

Playing the Peace-Making Role

Given China's status as a rising power in the foreseeable future, the Asian giant should therefore play a bigger role in peace making in the area. This is particularly directed to the territorial disputes over the Spratly Islands in the South China Sea that involves China and several other countries in Southeast Asia, not to mention other cross-border problems in the region, including terrorist movement, transnational crimes, sea piracy and sea lane security in the South China Sea.

Given these problems in Southeast Asia, this area currently lacks reliable major power involvement or a stabilizing force when crisis or conflicts arise, in spite of the existing mechanisms between China and ASEAN. Southeast Asian countries had relied on United States intervention over the area's conflicts during the Cold War period, but the role of the US on regional affairs has been declining since the turn of the century. China, on the contrary, has been using its soft power to replace the US as a moderator on regional affairs since the new century, as Joshua Kurlantzick argues. Yet, as China has intensified its influence over Southeast Asia, worries about China in the mean time arise. A recent Pentagon study, released on 25th March 2009, indicates that China has continued its defense modernization since the new century and secrecy surrounding China's military has created the potential for miscalculation on both China and the United States.[38] The Pentagon annual report implies America's worry over China's growing military power and strategic intentions, although China slammed the US report as "a gross distortion of facts and interference into China's internal affairs".[39]

China, therefore, should do more to play the role of peacemaker in regional affairs in Southeast Asia, in order to reduce the worry of threat by countries in the region. As a rising major power, China owns resources that Southeast Asian countries lack, including technology, market, investment, finance, construction, huge foreign reserve, and, most importantly, a permanent member of the United Nations Security Council. Given the soft power that

China has extended to Southeast Asia since the early 1990s, this chapter argues that China is not yet successful in shaping the role of peace-maker in the region. China, thus, is obligated to take more responsibility over regional affairs management, even if the Asian giant is not directly involved.

The mass anti-government demonstration in Yangon in late September 2007, for example, is a Burmese domestic affair, although it attracted grave concerns from major countries, including the US, European countries, and the United Nations. As a regional major power and a long ally of the Burmese military government, China, unfortunately, kept silent on this matter. One scholar even accused China of manipulating the policy of "blood for oil", mainly because of the Asian giant's hunger for Burma's natural-gas reserves.[40] This chapter argues that China, as a rising dominant power in the region, should play the role of peace-maker over the Burmese crisis more actively, advocating universal common values of human rights.

During the Cold War period, the then weak China suffered its relations with most countries in Southeast Asia, which generated negative perceptions from both sides towards each other. It is now the time for a change. China is not only a major power in the region, but is also likely to become stronger in the near future. China was afraid of its southern neighbours' alliance with the United States, but China now is confident in building up close relations with all countries in the region. Given these changing scenarios between China and Southeast Asia, this chapter argues that China, as the leading major power in the region, is obligated to play the role of peace-making in this part of the world, which in turn will benefit China's relations with Southeast Asia and other parts of the world.

Conclusion

This chapter demonstrates China's changing relations with Southeast Asia, starting in the early 1980s with three key political initiatives. The open-door policy, introduced in 1979, was a comprehensive mechanism that changed China's overall relations with the world, including Southeast Asia. The Good Neighbour policy of 1990 was directed at China's neighbours, and Southeast Asia is regarded as one of China's most important neighbours. The Go Global strategy of 2002 aimed at bringing China's investments and enterprises abroad, in contrast to the open-door policy that brought foreign capital into the Chinese market. China's strengthening relations with Southeast Asia can be seen from frequent political engagements, increasing economic relations, expanding social interactions, and closer links with ASEAN, as demonstrated in the chapter.

As China begins a comprehensive relationship with Southeast Asia, both sides are also clouded by two major problems, i.e. territorial disputes in the South China Sea and the gap of economic development level. While the sovereignty disputes have existed for years, the gap of economic development level is emerging and will become wider in the coming decade. These problems, this chapter argues, will shade the ongoing development of a close relationship between China and Southeast Asia.

This chapter therefore contends that China should take another political initiative in constructing a comprehensive mechanism between China and Southeast Asia, in order to avoid possible escalated conflicts between the two on the one hand and to sustain the ongoing bilateral cordial relationship on the other. A specialized government agency should be established to be in charge of all affairs between China and Southeast Asia, and this official institution should be led by ministerial officials, holding regular meetings on all issues involved, with regular budget, and empowered with law-enforcement authority.

Finally, this chapter also argues that China, as a rising dominant power in the region, is obligated to do something more in two areas, i.e. economic assistance and the role of peace-making. With these efforts, China and Southeast Asia may hopefully strengthen mutual trust and sustain the cordial relationship in coming decades. Worries and troubles may fall upon China's relations with Southeast Asia in the near future should both sides are not making enough efforts.

Notes

＊   Dr Samuel C.Y. Ku 顧長永 is Professor at the Institute of China and Asia-Pacific Studies of the National Sun Yat-sen University (NSYSU) in Kaohsiung, Taiwan. He was Director of Institute of Interdisciplinary Studies for Social Sciences (2001-2006) and Center of Southeast Asian Studies (1999-2006) at NSYSU. Professor Ku's research interests include Taiwan's and China's relations with Southeast Asia, political development in Southeast Asia, comparative political reforms between Taiwan and Southeast Asia, etc. In addition to Chinese publications, Professor Ku's articles have also appeared in such international journals as *Contemporary Southeast Asia*, *Asian Profile*, *Asian Perspectives*, *Contemporary China*, *World Affairs*, *Issues and Studies*, etc.

1. In the *Yearbook of China's Diplomacy 1991*, China for the first time pointed out the focus of its diplomacy in 1990 was on the development of its relations with neighbouring countries, which initiated the so-called Good Neighbour Policy (Editorial Office of Diplomatic History, *Yearbook of China's Diplomacy 1991*, Beijing: World Knowledge Publisher, May 1991, p. 11).

2. The PRC established diplomatic relations with Laos in April 1961, but both sides

experienced a strained relationship during the period from the late 1970s to the mid-1980s.

3. China dispatched an official delegation to visit Vietnam in October 1991, the first of its kind since the birth of the PRC in October 1949.

4. For instance, railway building in the south of Malaysia and a cement mill in Burma were two of the major projects undertaken in 2002 (*Yearbook of China's Foreign Economic Relations and Trade 2003*, English edition, p. 53).

5. *Yearbook of China's Foreign Economic Relations and Trade 2003*, English edition, pp. 52-53.

6. Afterwards, China established full diplomatic relations with Singapore in October 1990 and with Negara Brunei Darussalam in October 1991.

7. Indonesia also removed the restrictions on its citizens to visit China in 1991.

8. After a two-round presidential election, Yudhoyono finally won the campaign and was sworn in as the sixth President of Indonesia on 20th October 2004.

9. Hu Jintao actually succeeded Jiang Zemin as Secretary General of the Chinese Communist Party at the 16th National Party Congress in November 2002.

10. Nong Duc Manh became the new leader of the Communist Party of Vietnam at the Ninth National Party Congress in April 2001.

11. Southeast Asia could generally be represented by ASEAN (Association of Southeast Asian Nations), which has since 1999 included all countries in Southeast Asia, with the exception of East Timor that declared independence on 20 May 2002.

12. *Yearbook of China's Foreign Economic Relations and Trade 2003*, English edition, pp. 257-258.

13. *China Commerce Yearbook 2005*, English edition, p. 123.

14. In 1999, China's visitors to Southeast Asia were 1.9 million, whereas those of Taiwan were 1.7 million and South Korea's were 1.1 million in the same year.

15. *ASEAN Statistical Yearbook 2005*, Jakarta: ASEAN Secretariat, 2006, pp. 234-235.

16. Founded in July 1994, the objectives of the ARF include: (1) to foster constructive dialogue and consultation on political and security issues of common interest and concern; and (2) to make significant contributions to efforts towards confidence-building and preventive diplomacy in the Asia-Pacific region. (*http://www.aseansec.org/3530.htm*)

17. The ASEAN Plus Three Summit (the "three" refers to China, Japan and South Korea) was also, for the first time, convened in November 1997, and China has been participating in the "10+3" Summit since then.

18. The Sixth ASEAN Summit was held at the same time.

19. The Eighth ASEAN Summit was held at the same time.

20. There is a great deal of studies on the ASEAN-China FTA, see, for example, Kevin G. Cai, "The ASEAN-China Free Trade Agreement and East Asian Regional Grouping", *Contemporary Southeast Asia*, Vol. 25, No. 3, December 2003, pp. 387-402; S. Chirathivat, "ASEAN-China FTA: Background, Implications and Future Development", *Journal of Asian Economics*, No. 13, 2002, pp. 671-686.

21. For details, visit *http://www.aseansec.org/13185.htm*.

22. Recently on October 30, 2006, Chinese Premier Wen Jiabao said, at a summit marking the 15th anniversary of ASEAN-China dialogue, that China and ASEAN should expand already blossoming economic links and "step up cooperation on cross-border issues concerning counter-terrorism, transnational crimes, maritime security, rescue operations and disaster relief." (*http://today.reuters. com/news/articlenews.aspx?type=politicsNews&storyid=2006-10-30T100539Z_ 01_SP196546_RTRUKOC_0_US-CHINA-ASEAN.xml*, accessed 2nd November 2006)

23. Many scholars share a similar point of view. Chia Oai Peng, a Chinese scholar, for example, has pointed out four hurdles in China-ASEAN relations, i.e. (1) their disparity in status, (2) unbalanced economic capacity, (3) disputes in border demarcation and sovereignty over islands, and (4) difference in resources exploration in disputed waters. Please see Chia Oai Peng, "China-ASEAN Relations: Towards Global Stability, Peace and Sustainable Growth", in Emile Kok-Kheng Yeoh and Hou Kok Chung (eds), *China and Malaysia in a Globalizing World*, Kuala Lumpur: Institute of China Studies, University of Malaya, 2006, pp. 114-115.

24. *http://www.gov.cn/english/2009-03/11/content_1257094.htm*, accessed 24th March 2009.

25. China accused the US ship of conducting surveillance within its exclusive economic zone, whereas US admiral Timothy Keating blamed China's manner as "aggressive and troublesome" and "not willing to abide by acceptable standards of behavior." (Website of *The Washington Post*, 19th March 2009 <*http://www. washingtonpost.com/wp-dyn/content/article/2009/03/19/AR2009031901726. html*>)

26. This news is from the website of *The Washington Post*, 19th March 2009 (*http:// www.washingtonpost.com/wp-dyn/content/article/2009/03/18/AR2009031804285. html*).

27. Website of *The Washington Post*, 12th February 2009.

28. Joshua Kurlantzick, under the invitation of the Carnegie Endowment for International Peace, delivered his point of view in a speech, entitled "China's Soft Power in Southeast Asia: What Does It Mean for the Region, and for the U.S.?" on 13th June 2006.

29. The Editorial Board of China's Foreign Economic Relations and Trade, *Yearbook of China's Foreign Economic Relations and Trade 1989/90* (Beijing: China's Foreign Economic Relations and Trade Publishing House, the Chinese edition, 1989), pp. 56-57.

30. *Almanac of China's Foreign Economic Relations and Trade 2001*, the English Edition, p. 110.

31. *Almanac of China's Foreign Economic Relations and Trade 2003*, the English Edition, p. 54.

32. China actually started its foreign aid quite early with a focus on Africa, but China began to focus on Southeast Asia since the late 1980s.

33. *Almanac of China's Foreign Economic Relations and Trade 1998-1999*, the English edition, p. 420.
34. The Editorial Board of the China Commerce Yearbook, *China's Commerce Yearbook* (Beijing: China Commerce and Trade Press, 2004, the Chinese edition), p. 99.
35. *Almanac of China's Foreign Economic Relations and Trade 2003*, the English Edition, p. 55.
36. Chinese Premier Wen Jiabao announced, on 18th April 2009 at Boao Forum for Asia, that China will collect a fund of US$10 billion for China-ASEAN investment to support infrastructure projects in the region (*http://www.chinapost. com.tw/china/national-news/2009/04/19/204809/China-to.htm*, accessed 20th April 2009).
37. China's recent assistance to Indonesia and the Philippines has caused environmental criticism (*http://www.foreignpolicy.com/story/cms.php?story_id=3732*, accessed 1st October 2007).
38. *http://www.nytimes.com/2009/03/26/washington/26military.html?_ r=1&ref=world*, accessed 30th March 2009.
39. *http://www.washingtonpost.com/wp-dyn/content/article/2009/03/26/ AR2009032600365.html*, accessed 30th March 2009.
40. Peter Navarro, "Beijing's Lust for Oil and Gas Perpetuates Atrocities in Southeast Asia and Africa". *<www.PeterNavarro.com>*

References

ASEAN Statistical Pocketbook, Jakarta: ASEAN Secretariat, 2006.

Buszynski, Leszek (2003), "ASEAN, the Declaration on Conduct, and the South China Sea", *Contemporary Southeast Asia*, Vol. 25, No. 3, December, pp. 343-361.

Cai, Kevin G. (2003), "The ASEAN-China Free Trade Agreement and East Asian Regional Grouping", *Contemporary Southeast Asia*, Vol. 25, No. 3, December, pp. 387-402.

Cai, Peng Hong (2005), "Non-traditional Security and China-ASEAN Relations: Co-operation, Commitments and Challenges", in Ho Khai Leong and Samuel C. Y. Ku (eds), *China and Southeast Asia: Global Changes and Regional Challenges*, Singapore: Institute of Southeast Asian Studies.

Chirathivat, S. (2002), "ASEAN-China FTA: Background, Implications and Future Development", *Journal of Asian Economics*, Vol. 13, pp. 671-686.

Curley, Melissa G. and Hong Liu (eds) (2002), *China and Southeast Asia: Changing Socio-Cultural Interactions*, Hong Kong: Centre of Asian Studies, The University of Hong Kong.

Haacke, Jurgen (2005), "The Significance of Beijing's Bilateral Relations: Looking 'Below' the Regional Level in China-ASEAN Ties", in Ho Khai Leong and Samuel C. Y. Ku (eds), *China and Southeast Asia: Global Changes and Regional Challenges*, Singapore: Institute of Southeast Asian Studies.

Ho, Khai Leong and Samuel C.Y. Ku (eds) (2005), *China and Southeast Asia: Global Changes and Regional Challenges*, Singapore: Institute of Southeast Asian Studies.

Jeperson, Ronald L., Alexander Wendt and Peter J. Katzenstein (1996), "Norms, Identity, and Culture National Security", in Peter J. Katzenstein (ed.), *The Culture of National Security: Norms and Identity in World Politics*, New York: Columbia University Press.

Kurlandtzick, Joshua (2006), *China's Charm: Implications of Chinese Soft Power*, Los Angeles: Carnegie Endowment.

Kurlandtzick, Joshua (2007), *Charm Offensive: How China's Soft Power Is Transforming the World*, New Haven: Yale University Press.

Linz, Juan J. and Alfred C. Stepan (1996), *Problems of Democratic Transition and Consolidation: Southern Europe, South America, and Post-Communist Europe*, New York: Johns Hopkins University Press.

Liu, Hong (2002), "The Contact Zones and Socio-Cultural Interactions between China and Southeast Asia during the Twentieth Century", in Melissa G. Kurley and Liu Hong (eds), *China and Southeast Asia: Changing Socio-Cultural Interactions*, Hong Kong: Centre of Asian Studies, The University of Hong Kong.

Muni, S.D. (2002), *China's Strategic Engagement with the New ASEAN*, Singapore: Institute of Defense and Strategic Studies, IDSS Monograph No. 2.

Navarro, Peter (2007), "Beijing's Lust for Oil and Gas Perpetuates Atrocities in Southeast Asia and Africa". <*www.PeterNavarro.com*>

Robison, Thomas W. and David Shambaugh (eds) (1995), *Chinese Foreign Policy: Theory and Practice*, Oxford: Oxford University Press.

Shambough, David (1996a), "China's Military: Real or Chapter Tiger?" *Washington Quarterly*, Vol. 19, No. 1, Spring, pp. 180-209.

Shambough, David (1996b), "Containment or Engagement of China? Calculating Beijing's Response", *International Security*, Vol. 21, No. 2, Autumn, pp. 180-209.

Snyder, Scott (1996), *The South China Sea Dispute. Prospects for Preventive Diplomacy*, Washington, D.C.: The United States Institute of Peace.

Tonnesson, Stein (2000), "Vietnam's Objective in the South China Sea: National or Regional Security?", *Contemporary Southeast Asia*, Vol. 22, No. 1, April, pp. 199-220.

Wong, John, Zou Keyuan and Zeng Huaqun (eds) (2006), *China and Southeast Asia: Economic and Legal Dimensions*, London: World Scientific.

Yang, Xiaohui (2002), "Transnational Drug Trafficking in the Golden Triangle", in Melissa G. Kurley and Liu Hong (eds), *China and Southeast Asia: Changing Socio-Cultural Interactions*, Hong Kong: Centre of Asian Studies, The University of Hong Kong.

Zhu, Zhenming (2002), "Drugs in Southeast Asia and China's Efforts to Curb Drug Smuggling in the Golden Triangle", in Melissa G. Kurley and Liu Hong (eds), *China and Southeast Asia: Changing Socio-Cultural Interactions*, Hong Kong: Centre of Asian Studies, The University of Hong Kong.

Chapter 3

The Rise of China, Power Transition and South Korea's Soft Hedging[+]

*Sukhee **Han***

Introduction

For almost two decades, the rise of China has been one of the major themes in the discussions of international politics and the global economy. China's rapid economic growth and its expanding influence over the global economic developments have put China at the very centre of these debates. Commensurate with its growing economic clout and its upgraded international status, China has consistently pursued its great power aspirations, and has subsequently been identified as a member of the world's great power community.[1] In general, the issue of China's ascent to possible superpower status has been evaluated in two diametrically opposing ways. On the one hand, some scholars and policy makers have tended to identify the rising China as a source of a strategic threat in the Northeast Asian region and/or in the global context; while others have rather emphasized the rising China's contributing factors to the world security and prosperity.[2] Regardless of the evaluations the international community has made, however, one of the most important issues relating to the rise of China at this moment is whether China with its consistent development would take over the lone superpower status of the United States (US): the issue of power transition.

Since the start of the new millennium, the issue of the potential power transition from the US to China has been a key question in the international relations community.[3] Given the challengers' capabilities and intentions as the core indicators for the evaluation of the power transition, however, common conclusions have thus far been that China cannot initiate the power transition for the time being. Reviewing the capabilities of both powers, the US still maintains its supremacy in terms of military capabilities, usage of IT technologies and physical quality of life, and therefore China would take another decade to develop its capabilities to reach parity with the US.[4]

China is also claimed to be facing fundamental difficulties in eliciting power transition from the US, because the US is a different type of hegemonic power than that have faced previous rising states. Representing the Western civilization, the current international order led by the US is easy to integrate in to, but difficult to deconstruct. In this perspective, China's power transition from the US seems to be hardly possible for the time being.[5]

However, although the power transition from the US to China seems to be unconvincing in the global context, China's neighbouring states have faced significant geostrategic changes caused by the rise of China. Over the past decade, China's unhindered economic growth and subsequent expansion of contribution to the prosperity of the Northeast Asian region has made these states reconsider their relations with the growing China and simultaneously with the other major powers in the region. Eschewing the simple dichotomy of balancing versus bandwagoning, in particular, China's neighbouring states do not want to choose either one of the two major powers, the US and China. As one of the closest neighbour of China, South Korea is not an exception. With the inauguration of the new administration under the leadership of Lee Myong-bak in 2008, South Korea has implemented what can be called a policy of soft hedging against China, through which South Korea hopes to maintain amicable and favourable relationships with both powers.[6] This is possible because the policy of soft hedging, for the moment, is fulfilling the needs of both the US and China. Soft hedging, in short, adheres to the US strategic policy of enmeshing China in to the established security and economic order, while the policy suits China with its unimpeachable aim of economic growth.

Assuming the continuing growth of China in the future, this chapter analyzes South Korea's policy of soft hedging as a response to the rising China. Given its dependency on China's economy and China's diplomatic influence over North Korea, South Korea prefers to maintain cooperative relations with China. But as a long time ally, South Korea also has to strengthen its traditional alliance relationship with the US, particularly in light of recent developments concerning nuclear weapons in North Korea. Reflective of the contextual situation that South Korea has to maintain friendly relationship with both powers, this chapter addresses the detailed conditions under which South Korea has to soft hedge against China with the blessings of the US.

The Rise of China and the Persistence of US Interests in the Region

The most significant feature of the Northeast Asian balance of power, brought to the fore by the end of the East-West confrontation of the Cold War, is the steady rise of Chinese economic and military strength,[7] as well as the spread of its soft power[8] in the region. China has been re-emerging as the present-day great power of the region (Yahuda, 1996: 257), expanding its military capabilities as well as her economic and political influence in the region. As China constantly increases and upgrades both her conventional and nuclear arms with her newfound wealth, the countries around her have looked on nervously. A feeling of apprehension towards the future policies of a powerful China has become commonplace among the governments of the region since the end of the Cold War. Many have argued that China's emphasis on economic development and the consequent interdependence with the other states of the region will broaden the foundation for peace and prosperity in Northeast Asia (Medeiros and Fravel, 2003). Furthermore, it is argued that, because China's military hardware is outmoded and because of the ever-widening gap between the military technology of the US and China, China is in no way a real competitor of the US (Eland, 2003).

It is true that both economic and military data show that China is nowhere close to threatening the global position of the US yet, she has, nevertheless, been encroaching upon American influence in Northeast Asia.[9] Whether this encroachment signals a more profound change in the overall global balance of power is a question that merits further study. However, it seems certain that it adds uncertainty to the already very fluid situation in the region thereby contributing to the tendency of short-term power balancing. Chinese perception of US interests, and vice versa, in the region is certainly the most important and relevant issue to any discussion concerning the formulation of policies with all the states that have a stake in the future of Northeast Asia.

Three overarching goals are evident when one looks to analyze America's interests in Northeast Asia. First, the US has remained concerned with maintaining a balance of power in the region that is favourable to American interests. This implies that US policy opposes efforts at domination of the region by a power or a group of powers. Second, the US has endeavoured to advance its economic interests in the region through involvement in economic development and the expansion of US trade and investment. A third major goal, centred on American culture and values, has involved efforts to foster democracy, human rights, and other trends deemed progressive by American (Sutter, 2003: 21). Of the three goals, the first is the most important in that it sets the foundation for the other two goals. And it is this goal which has been labeled a "vital interest" by many American officials.

In order to achieve and maintain these goals, the order that the US most prefer in Northeast Asia is the completion of a hegemonic order centred on it. The most important unfinished task would be to convince China that, despite its size, economic power or political ambition, it is best served as a partner in a US-centred order. Beyond that, great transformations in the foreign policies of other major states or the development of new regional institutions would not be required. Robust multilateral security institutions, in fact, would run counter to this image of order – unless they were crafted and dominated by the US.[10] US officials are unlikely to abandon a set of security arrangements that have worked well – and, that have afforded the US a considerable measure of hegemonic control – in favour of a security experiment that is appealing ideologically but unlikely to bear fruit in the near term politically (*ibid.*: 436).

The historically unusual preeminence of the US in world affairs at the dawn of the twenty-first century has obliged other countries to define themselves in relation to this declaration (Dittmer, 2004: 359). The recent strategy of the US, in Northeast Asia as well as generally, has been to pursue hegemony as cheaply, and as, quietly as possible. They have sought to satisfy geopolitical objectives in Northeast Asia and Europe while avoiding direct military intervention.[11] When they have judged intervention necessary, they have tried to circumscribe missions so that casualties are minimized and exit strategies are emphasized. To manage the economic costs of hegemony, they have pursued burden sharing aggressively, prodding allies to bear the costs of US led initiatives. For the US, its geopolitical interest of preventing a rise of a hegemon in any of the significant regions of the world, and the economic returns and the promise of future returns in Northeast Asia, proves to be a powerful incentive to maintain peace and stability, through its presence and role as a balancer, in the region.

On the other hand, considering that China traditionally has been a great regional power, China's attempt to throw her weight around in Northeast Asia is deemed normal and expected. It has been precisely this prospect upon which much of the policies of the major players of Northeast Asia are contingent; not least, the US. Because accommodation is tricky, and because China is emerging on to the scene in a fluid regional environment lacking most of the elements that can mitigate conflict, the future of Northeast Asian international politics seems especially problematic. (Rose, 1998: 171) This outlook is based on two assumptions: (1) growing Chinese power could produce a dangerous security dilemma leading to a region wide arms race, and (2) the expansion of Chinese security interests could conflict with the established network of regional security arrangements[12] as well as preventing a multilateral security mechanism from appearing (Murphy, 1994: 64). It is not what China is doing now that is confounding policy makers in Washington, Tokyo and Seoul, but what it might do in ten, twenty, or fifty years later on. It is precisely this potential that has South Korea, as well as the other countries in Northeast Asia, feeling uneasy about the possible establishment of a new security mechanism in Northeast Asia.

The US has been seen by many Chinese as an aggressive and powerful force in international affairs. Some Chinese claim that the US, has, all along, wanted to establish a security regime that would be dominated by itself, and to make the issue of security an excuse for interfering in the other countries' internal affairs (Song, 97: 45). The fundamental geopolitical interests of the major powers in the region in general, and with the Sino-American relations in particular, simply does not match-up to provide a fertile foundation for stability to prosper. The US geopolitical objective in Northeast Asia is as simple as it is difficult to achieve and maintain: prevent the rise of a potentially hegemonic[13] power. The same goal applies for the European theatre. The US has fought World War I and II, as well as the Korean War, among others to achieve this goal. Disengagement of the US from the Northeast Asian region has both been advocated and predicted by many. But from a geopolitical point of view, it is simply not in the American interest to do so. The American geopolitical objective of preventing a hegemonic power to arise in the Pacific Asia has remained constant since the acquisition of the Philippine Islands (Cohen, 2000: 26-54). The complexity of the situation arises from both the speculations concerning China's aspirations as well as its actual and latent power. Moreover, the containment of China became a significant issue, as Chinese economic and military development could have unpredictable consequences for the overall balance of forces, not only in Northeast Asia, but in the world.[14] Thus, in a current regional setting, concerns arise from the changing distribution of power among the major players, along with the perceived negative implications of American hegemony, the perception of a China threat,[15] and the fear of a remilitarized Japan. Much will depend on how the US manages to exercise its geopolitical interest in this setting.

As mentioned above, the American strategy for Northeast Asia is to prevent any single power from dominating the region. Thus, coping with a rising China is an important diplomatic challenge for Washington. It is safe to say that the rise of China, and how that is being perceived by other powers in the region, brought to the fore a competition for regional influence among the great powers in a region formerly dominated by the US. If history is any indicator, great powers have never tended to entrust their interests in an international institution nor saw eye to eye with multilateral approaches in conducting their security policies. The mere presence of the four largest powers in the world makes Northeast Asia a prime target of balance of power politics. It is by no mistake that a recent Pentagon report has labeled China as an "emerging rival," stating that the peaceful rhetoric of China cannot be taken at face value.[16] The US and China are realizing that they have no overarching motive for strategic co-operation despite their growing economic ties. China seems poised to expand its strategic reach and regain its traditional prominence in Northeast Asia.[17] As for the US, the continued ability to intervene in the Northeast Asian region rests heavily on its forward-based military presence in Japan and South Korea and its guarantees of protection to South Korea, Japan, and to some extent, Taiwan. Adding to the complexity, relations between China and Taiwan remain strained because of China's long-held aim to restore Taiwan to Chinese rule. All this is not to imply that the spectre of war looms over the horizon, nor that potentially significant tensions cannot be diffused, only that the search for stability faces a number of significant challenges.

There is no question that open security competition among the great powers in Northeast Asia has been subdued since the end of the Cold War. And with the possible exception of the 1996 dispute between China and the US over Taiwan, there has been no hint of war between any of the great powers. Periods of relative peacefulness like this one, however, are not unprecedented in history. For example, there was little open conflict among the great powers in Europe from 1816 to 1852, or from 1871 to 1913. But this did not mean then, and it does not mean now, that the great powers stopped thinking and behaving according to geopolitical logic. Indeed, there is substantial evidence that the major states in Northeast Asia still fear each other and continue to worry about how much relative power they control. Moreover, sitting below the surface the region is significant potential for intense security competition (Mearsheimer, 2001: 373).

Thus, the future of Northeast Asia greatly depends on the future of China, the most populous country in the world, and the US, the preeminent global power house. Therefore, the direction of US-China relations has had, and will continue to have, a crucial impact on the future of the region. It seems, fortunately, however transitional it may be, that a fairly stable form of balance is forming in Northeast Asia between the continental force that is China and the traditional maritime force that is the US for the time being. However, the substance, and the rules of maintenance, of this balance of influence[18] between the two powers remain vague, and it is altogether possible that it will work as a negative force in maintaining peace and stability in Northeast Asia because the vital interests of the two powers can become conflictual. One thing is for certain: the ramifications of this relationship will continue to be felt all over the world, especially by the countries of Northeast Asia.

South Korea and the Need for the Policy of Soft Hedging

South Korea has maintained a strong security alliance with the US for more than half a century. It has been one of the most formidable and enduring military alliances in the world, not only preserving peace and stability in the Korean peninsula but also ensuring nuclear restraint among Asian powers. Most American and South Korean strategists agree that the value of the alliance has gone far beyond security in the Korean peninsula and it has extended to the comprehensive fields of economy, culture and diplomacy. For South Korea, the US has provided multifaceted roles for its political development, economic prosperity and military security. The US has not only opened its domestic market for South Korea's exporting products, but also served as the major source of advanced and cutting-edge technologies for Korea's industrial development and expansion. Intimate bilateral relations on the basis of the strategic alliance has also established valuable conduits for improving cultural exchanges, increasing mutual visits and expanding value sharing. The US's economic, cultural, diplomatic and strategic influence over South Korea has been so dominant that South Korea's development thus far would not have been guaranteed without the consideration of the US-ROK alliance, and the alliance will continue to be regarded as the most essential partnership for South Korea's future security and prosperity.[19]

Despite the US's undisputed importance to South Korea's security and development, however, the rise of China has also been well addressed in South Korea. In light of its geographical proximity, its growing diplomatic clout, and its expanding economic influence, China has been considered as one of the most powerful neighbours with which South Korea should develop a constructive relationship with. In particular, China's growing economic influence over South Korea's development has been the initial impetus for South Korea to cooperate with China. Since 1992 when South Korea and China have established formal diplomatic relations, in particular, China has been South Korea's major trading partner and the bilateral trade between South Korea and China has been rapidly increasing ever since. As seen in Table 3.1, by the year of 2003 China has already surpassed the US in terms of trade volume with South Korea, and has consolidated its status as South Korea's largest trading partner as well as its largest source of trading surplus. As far as China's economic supremacy continues for South Korea, the South Korean government has had to consider the Sino-South Korean relationship as another fundamentally essential partnership along with the US-ROK alliance.[20]

Table 3.1 Korean Export/Import/Trade Balance against the US and China
(Unit: US$ billion)

Year	Country	In hundred million dollars		
		Export	Import	Trade Balance
2008	US	46.4	38.4	8.0
	China	91.4	76.9	14.5
2007	US	33.6	27.5	61.0
	China	59.0	45.3	13.7
2006	US	43.2	33.7	9.5
	China	69.5	48.6	20.9
2005	US	41.3	30.6	10.7
	China	61.9	48.6	20.9
2004	US	42.8	28.8	14.0
	China	49.8	29.6	20.2
2003	US	34.2	24.8	9.4
	China	35.1	21.9	13.2
2002	US	32.8	23.0	9.8
	China	23.8	17.4	6.4
2001	US	31.2	20.6	10.6
	China	18.2	13.3	4.9
2000	US	37.6	29.2	8.4
	China	18.5	12.8	5.7
1999	US	29.5	24.9	4.6
	China	13.7	8.9	4.8
1998	US	22.8	20.4	2.4
	China	11.9	6.5	5.4
1997	US	21.6	30.1	-8.5
	China	13.6	10.1	3.5
1996	US	21.7	33.3	-11.6
	China	11.4	8.5	2.8
1995	US	24.1	30.4	-6.3
	China	9.1	7.4	1.7
1994	US	20.6	21.6	-1.0
	China	6.2	5.4	0.7
1993	US	18.1	17.9	0.2
	China	5.2	3.9	1.2
1992	US	18.1	18.3	-0.2
	China	2.7	3.7	-1.1

Source: *http://www.mofat.go.kr/economic/economicdata/statistics/index.jsp*

China's importance to South Korea has also been recognized in the issues regarding North Korea. As a divided state, South Korea has always considered the issues related to North Korea, including the unification and the nuclear development, as the top priority in its conduct of international affairs. Also, China has been considered as the most important partner for cooperation whenever South Korea deals with North Korean issues. As a diplomatic patron, economic benefactor, and military sponsor, China has taken an indispensable role in the survival of Kim Jong-il's moribund regime. Given its economic aid and material assistance to Pyongyang, China has been a unique power to exert strategic influence over North Korea's decision-making process as witnessed in the Six-Party Dialogues. Also, given its diplomatic protection as a permanent member of the UN Security Council, China has been a *sui generis* mediator managing the relationship between North Korea and the world. As North Korea's diplomatic isolationism has strengthened, its public starvation has worsened, and its nuclear brinkmanship has continued, South Korea has felt the growing need for its cooperation with China.[21]

As the rise of China has become more conspicuous in South Korea's economy, security and diplomacy, one of the most sensitive issues that South Korea has had to face is how to manage simultaneously the US-ROK alliance and the Sino-South Korean partnership in a harmonious way. As a long-term ally of the US and also China's strategic cooperative partner, South Korea needs to maintain friendly relations with both great powers. China's economic viability and its diplomatic leverage over Pyongyang are two key factors that the current South Korean government desperately hopes to use from China, while the US involvement in South Korea's security and economy through the US-ROK alliance and the potential conclusion of the bilateral Free Trade Agreement (FTA) serves as major determinants for the future development of the peninsula. Given this situation, therefore, it is not conducive to its national interests if South Korea promotes relations with either one power at the cost of the other. For its future stability and prosperity South Korea should maintain constructive relationships with both China and the US by the implementation of what the author of this chapter call the soft hedging policy.[22]

States have tended to implement the policy of hedging for reducing the risks against future uncertainties. Hedging generally implies a national strategy to combine the engagement and balancing, and implement them toward the target states simultaneously. The major reason that the states hedge against the rising power is that they are not certain about the future consequences of the rising power towards them. Unsure of the rising power being a threat or a partner to them, the concerned states try to establish a friendly relationship with the rising power as well as preparing for the unexpected risks from the rising power. On the one hand, the concerned states tend to engage with the rising powers (mostly economically) and promote the relationship by increasing mutual economic interdependence and promoting bilateral diplomatic co-relationship. They also tend to balance against the rising state by either extending itself with another alliance or partner, or enmeshing the rising power into multilateralism or the established order, on the other.[23]

There are several types of hedging in international relations. First, there is reciprocal hedging. It is indicative of recent Sino-American relations, in which both the US and China mutually pose economic cooperation and security (and diplomatic) competition to each other at a same time. Sino-American reciprocal hedging reflects that both powers recognize the necessity of mutual cooperation for co-prosperity but at the same time they are very cautious of each state's potential threat to the other.[24] Second, there is "twin hedging," which the ASEAN states have recently emphasized to adopt in dealing with the rising China. Twin hedging implies a pragmatic mixture between soft balancing and engagement. On the one hand, it means adopting a strategy of deep engagement with China. On the other, it also involves a soft (or indirect) balancing against potential Chinese aggression or disruption of the *status quo*. In the case of the ASEAN states, soft balancing mainly involves persuading other major powers, particularly the US, to act as counterweights against Chinese regional influence, or potentially aggressive Chinese dominance.[25] Finally, there is a dual (double) hedging. As was the case with Japan during the US war in Afghanistan, the state mobilizes the dual-pronged approach, through which it has relied on its alliance with the US as a hedge against uncertain but possible military threats, while it has cultivated different partners to hedge against potential economic danger.[26]

South Korea's Soft Hedging against China while Strengthening the US-ROK Alliance

The growing importance of China along with the strong US-ROK alliance has made South Korea adopt the policy of soft hedging. The major goal of South Korea's soft hedging strategy is to manage both the US-ROK alliance and the Sino-South Korean economic cooperative partnership in a smooth manner.[27] Given its geopolitical environment with both the US and China, it is a very sensitive issue where South Korea has shaped its strategic position in between the US and China, and therefore South Korea seems to feel very uncomfortable when it considers how to implement the policy of soft hedging. In order to succeed with South Korea's soft hedging policy, South Korea has to manage a type of hedging among a variety of alternatives which will be more conducive to its diplomatic environment: reciprocal hedging, dual hedging, twin hedging, and what we have termed soft hedging. The reciprocal hedging seems to be unsuitable to South Korea, because it implies that South Korea be cooperative and competitive with the two powers simultaneously. The twin hedging is not pertinent to the Sino-South Korean relations either, because it is composed of deep engagement and soft balancing. It is true that South Korea's China policy has mostly been composed of accommodation, largely lacking the factors of balancing. Regardless of soft or hard balancing, South Korea has no interest in balancing against China.[28]

Given its strategic situation that requires inevitable promotion of the US-ROK alliance, and that requires further economic interdependence under the Sino-South Korean strategic cooperative partnership, South Korea has to deploy soft hedging against China in full cooperation with the US. Soft hedging is a kind of dual hedging but the range of application is much wider than dual hedging. Given that dual hedging is an efficient structure to combine the alliance and partnership simultaneously, South Korea's soft hedging has to adopt the format of hedging against a rising power, but it also has to be differentiated from dual hedging in two perspectives. First, the major objective of South Korea's soft hedging in contrast to dual hedging is not aimed at balancing the two powers, but aimed at accommodating or to some degree bandwagoning with the counterparts. Since the major goal of South Korea's soft hedging is to maintain favourable relationships with both the US and China, South Korea tends to emphasize the bilateral cooperation in the fields with comparative advantages for the mutual development, respectively. As a token of it, South Korea tends to underscore the security and diplomatic cooperation with the US, while it features economic collaboration with China.[29] Since both the US and China have been cautious and sensitive to South Korea's tight relationship with the other power, South Korea's dual bandwagoning *per se* would pose a balance of power structure in the region.

Another difference comes from the distribution of diplomatic weights between the US and China. As witnessed in the diplomacy of the Lee Myong-bak administration, South Korea has deployed soft hedging against the Sino-South Korean strategic cooperative partnership with the full backing of the US-ROK alliance; it has tended to put more diplomatic weight on the US, reflective of its strategic calculation. Despite China's undisputed economic importance for Seoul and its incomparable diplomatic clout over Pyongyang, however, more than five decades of US-ROK alliance has been seen as much more valuable for the South Korean citizens. Reviewing the recent US-South Korea relationship, the US also seems to recognize desperately the necessity and the importance of the US-South Korea bilateral cooperation, especially after the anti-American, pro-Chinese, and North Korea-friendly Roh Moo-hyun's five-year tenure.[30] In addition to the mutual commitment of alliance reinforcement, the US has demonstrated its strong sense of cooperation including its effort to ratify the US-South Korea FTA agreement; its permission of South Korea into the VWP (Visa Wavered Program); and its information sharing on North Korea.[31]

The major rationale for South Korea to put more emphasis on its relationship with the US than that of China is closely related to the US role and status in the global community. As a unique superpower, the US has managed a variety of international affairs, and has distributed public goods and resources for the benefits of the world. Without the US contribution, international security and prosperity cannot be maintained under the current international system.[32] As a member of the international community, South Korea has a responsibility to contribute to preserving and developing the system, and the US-ROK alliance should be readjusted to the global needs. Despite its growing economic viability and expanding financial affluence, on the other hand, China has provided limited contribution to defending the international system. In fact, at least for the China threat proponents, China constitutes a possible threat to the established international order of things. It is true that China is rising to become a possible superpower, but its capabilities *vis-à-vis* the US are far behind and much limited. Reflective of the situation, the Sino-South Korean partnership has largely remained as a regional level cooperation and therefore has been limited to bilateral economic cooperation for mutual development and bilateral diplomatic cooperation in dealing with the North Korean issues. Given the gap between the two powers, South Korea at least for now has to put more diplomatic emphasis on the US-ROK alliance.

However, South Korea's soft hedging is not static. At least theoretically, South Korea's diplomatic weight can be shifted depending on the wider international power transition. As we have witnessed in South Korea's previous government under Roh Moo-hyun, the US-ROK alliance does not always guarantee cooperative relationship between the US and South Korea. Overestimating China's economic supremacy and its diplomatic clout over Pyongyang as well as his innate anti-American sentiment, Roh during his tenure had put strategic distance from the US and simultaneously had tilted toward China.[33] With his policy of tilting toward China, which was far off from a correct reflection of the contemporary international power structure, Roh's diplomatic stance could not last long. However, South Korea's experience during the Roh administration had shown that US-South Korea cooperation is not a constant variable, but always subject to shifts.

Consequently, if and when a power transition occurs from the US to China, it will result in South Korea's shift of diplomatic weight. The key point is whether China can instigate the power transition from the US, and if possible, when? Although the signs of US decline and the rise of China are visible, as we've witnessed in the recent financial crisis, nobody has seriously considered the event to be the beginning of the power transition. Power transition critics tend to point to China's capabilities, being far behind that of the US, as the major point to vindicate their argument. It is widely believed that that it is still too premature to recognize China as a superpower and it will take decades for China to replace the US as the world's superpower if indeed it happens at all. As far as China's economic viability continues, as Chinese leaders declare, South Korea will keep its policy of soft hedging against China with the full support of the US. After all, the US strategic goal of containing China, and with enmeshing China in to the international order as it is as an integral part of that strategy, South Korea's soft hedging policy fits in to the American scheme of things very nicely indeed. Since the US-ROK alliance and the Sino-South Korean strategic cooperative partnership are the two most important features to influence South Korea's national interests, South Korea has to manage both relationships with its policy of soft hedging. And for the time being, the disposition of diplomatic weight in the strategic hedging has to be on the US's side.

Conclusion

The issue of the rise of China has long been a source of various discussions in the international relations community. Recently the issue has been developed into a new ramification: the power transition. Created in 1950s by A. F. K. Organsk, the power transition theory assumes the possibility of war between the challenger and the dominant power. The power transition theory has thus far added a number of valuable contributions to the development of international relations theories, and also provided persuasive translations and explanations of a variety of international relations phenomena. In a more recent manifestation of a possible power transition from the US to China, power transition theory has not attracted comprehensive attention yet, mostly because of China's lack of relevant capabilities. Given China's consistent growth not only in the field of economy, but also in the fields of diplomacy, security and even culture, power transition theory has the potential to denominate a much wider range of explanation.

Another ramification of the rise of China is the advent of more sophis-ticated security strategies among China's neighbouring states, including

South Korea. Northeast Asian states around China, having enjoyed security stability with the preservation of friendly relations with the US, have to reconsider their security strategies with the rise of China. Most states share the similar position – undecided between the eagle and the dragon, and generally adopting the policy of hedging. South Korea has been one of the participants in the strategic dilemma. However, in contrast to the other states' implementation of types of hedging, including reciprocal hedging, twin hedging, and dual hedging, South Korea pursues the policy of soft hedging. Given the diplomatic goal of South Korea as maintaining friendly relations with both the US and China, the fundamental substance of soft hedging is "dual bandwagoning," under which South Korea, on the one hand, should precipitate economic interdependency with China while it expands diplomatic and security cooperation with the US, on the other. At the current stage, South Korea has put more emphasis on the US-ROK alliance rather than the Sino-South Korean strategic cooperative partnership. But China's potential power transition from the US would trigger South Korea's substantial shift of diplomatic weight from the US to China.

As of now, it seems certain that South Korea is remaining faithful to its trusted strategic alliance with the US. The US's strategic goal of containing China and refraining China from possible revisionist tendencies shows through its positioning of its global partnerships as well as its armed forces forward deployment positions. The US's effort to enmesh China in to the international community and the global economy, thereby curtailing potentially revisionist inclinations, goes hand in hand with South Korea's policy of soft hedging. By increasing economic interdependence as well as increasing societal interactions with China, South Korea's policy of soft hedging is contributing to not only the interest of the US, but, for the time being, coincides with China's interest of maintaining regime legitimacy through its economic performance. The policy of soft hedging is unique in every sense; the target state is unique in its rise, the collaborating state is unique in its lone superpower status and, in between them, the practitioner of the soft hedging is unique in its geopolitical setting.

Notes

+ A version of this work is under review for publication in the *Pacific Review*, Warwick University, Great Britain.

* Dr Sukhee Han 한석희 / 韓碩熙 is Assistant Professor at the Graduate School of International Studies, Yonsei University, South Korea. Before joining Yonsei University, he had served as a research professor at the Institute of Korean

Unification Studies and as an acting professor for China CEO Advanced Management Program – both at Yonsei University. In China, he had taught at the School of Government, Peking University, for two years and had worked as a visiting scholar at the Institute for Asia-Pacific Studies, Chinese Academy of Social Sciences (CASS). Currently, he widely writes at the SSCI-listed *The Korean Journal of Defense Analysis*, *The Korean Journal of International Relations* (Korean), and the *Journal of Korean Political Science Association* (Korean). He completed both undergraduate and MA programmes at the Department of Political Science and Diplomacy, Yonsei University. He continued his M.A.L.D. and PhD degree programmes at the Fletcher School of Law and Diplomacy. Dr Han's main research interests are Sino-American relations, Sino-Korean relations, Sino-North Korean relations, and China's interactions with international institutions.

1. There have been a number of literatures, analyzing the political, security, economic, and diplomatic implications of the rise of China. See Deng and Wang (eds) (2005); Ross and Zhu (eds) (2008); Sutter (2005); Goldstein (2005); Kang (2007).
2. For the China threat argument, see Timperlake and Triplett (eds) (2002); Roy (1994); Roy (2003). For positive evaluation of China's international behaviour, see Medeiros and Fravel (2003); Shambaugh (2004/2005).
3. It has been more than a decade since the international relations scholars have evaluated the rise of China with the application of the "power transition theory". For comprehensive discussions of it, see Tammen *et al.* (eds) (2000); and also refer to the special issue of *International Interactions* (Vol. 29, No. 4, October-December 2003) to address the issues related to power transition theory and the rise of China – Lemke and Tammen (2003), Lemke (2003), Efird, Kugler and Genna (2003), and Rapkin and Thompson (2003) respectively. Also, see Chan (2005) and Chan (2004).
4. Chan (2005) argued against the potential power transition from the US to China. Reviewing China's capabilities in terms of traditional power measures and soft power indicators, he concluded that there is scant evidence pointing to a power transition between these two countries in the foreseeable future.
5. For a detailed argument, see Ikenberry (2008).
6. For South Korea's new China policy after the inauguration of President Lee Myong-bak of Korea, see Han (2008).
7. See Brown *et al.* (eds) (2000); Roy (1996); Eland (2003); and Yee and Storey (eds) (2002).
8. See Nye (2004).
9. *New York Times*, 3rd December 2003.
10. Ikenberry and Mastanduno (eds), 2003: 424.
11. Ikenberry and Mastanduno (eds), 2003: 431.
12. Particularly concerning the security arrangements that the US deems necessary to maintain a balance of power that is favourable to American interests.

13. For theories of hegemony or hegemonic transition, see Rapkin (1990); Wight, Bull and Holbraad (eds) (1978); and Keohane and Nye (1989).
14. Tkachenko (1997: 25).
15. For articulations of the "China Threat" theory, see Bernstein and Munro (1998); Overholt (1993); Segal (1996); Gertz (2000); Fishman (2005); Brown *et al.* (eds) (2000); Roy (1996); Eland (2003); and Yee and Storey (eds) (2002).
16. *Choongang Ilbo*, 26th May 2005.
17. See Friedberg (1993); Betts (1993); Kupchan (1998: 62-66); and Stuart and Tow (1995).
18. See Moon and Kim (2003).
19. Recently Scott Snyder has published a research report, arguing for the importance of the US-South Korean alliance and the strengthening it for the future. See Snyder (2009).
20. For a detailed explanation of the intimate economic interdependence between China and Korea, see Chung (2008).
21. For a detailed study of the Sino-North Korean relations, see Scobell (2004); International Crisis Group (2006). Also, for a recent study about China's perceptional change of North Korea, see Glaser, Snyder and Park (2008).
22. See Han (2008).
23. For a conceptualization of the hedging strategies, see Art (2004).
24. Both the US and China still lack trust. The US has retained its strategic suspicion on China's military build-up and its expansion of influence over the East Asian region. China has long identified US policy goals toward China as containment or at least constraintment of China's reemergence. Chinese policymakers and analysts are also convinced that the US poses the most significant long-term external threat to China's national rejuvenation and regional aspirations. For a detailed analysis of the Sino-American strategic hedging, see Tkacik (2006); and Medeiros (2005/06).
25. For a detailed explanation of twin hedging, see Goh (2005). For the ASEAN version of soft balancing, see Khong (2004).
26. For a comprehensive analysis of "dual hedging", see Heginbotham and Samuels (2002).
27. After his inauguration as the president of Korea, Lee Myong-bak upgraded the Korea-China bilateral relations to the "Korea-China Strategic Cooperative Partnership" in August 2008 when he had a summit meeting with the Chinese president, Hu Jintao.
28. For a detailed analysis of the Sino-American reciprocal hedging, see Medeiros (2005/06). For the Sino-ASEAN twin hedging, see Goh (2005); Chung (2004); and Limaye (ed.) (2009).
29. For an argument which insists that Korea's response to China is accommodation instead of balancing, see Kang (2009).
30. Since the inauguration of President Roh Moo-hyun the US and Korea have been struggling to manage the perceptional differences about the alliance and security.

For a comprehensive analysis of the issue, see Lee (2007). For Korea's anti-Americanism, see Kim (2002).

31. For the recent events between the US and Korea, and for more detailed study of strengthening the relationship, see Forrester (2007).
32. For the US's role and responsibility in a unipolar world, see Wohlforth (1999).
33. For a succinct but analytical review of Korea's perception of China and its policy of tilting toward China, see Sheen (2009).

References

Art, Robert J. (2004), "Europe Hedges Its Security Bets", in T.V. Paul and James Wirtz (eds), *Balance of Power Revisited: Theory and Practice in the 21st Century*, Palo Alto, C.A.: Stanford University Press, pp. 179-213.

Bernstein, Richard and Ross H. Munro (1998), *The Coming Conflict with China*, New York: Random House Inc.

Betts, Richard K. (1993), "Wealth, Power, and Instability: East Asia and the US after the Cold War", *International Security*, Vol. 18, No. 3, pp. 34-77.

Brown, Michael E., Owen R. Cote, Jr, Sean M. Lynn-Jones and Steven E. Miller (eds) (2000), *The Rise of China*, Cambridge: The MIT Press.

Chan, Steve (2004), "Exploring Puzzles in Power-Transition Theory: Implications for Sino-American Relations", *Security Studies*, Vol. 13, No. 3, Spring, pp. 103-141.

Chan, Steve (2005), "Is There a Power Transition between the US and China?: The Different Faces of National Power", *Asian Survey*, Vol. 45, No. 5, September/October, pp. 687-701.

Choongang Ilbo 중앙일보 / 中央日報, 26th May 2005.

Chung, Chien-peng (C.P.) (2004), "Southeast Asia-China Relations: Dialectics of "Hedging" and "Counter Hedging", in Chin Kin Wah and Daljit Singh (eds), *Southeast Asian Affairs*, Singapore: Institute of Southeast Asian Studies Publications Unit, pp. 35-53.

Chung, Jae Ho (2008), *Between Ally and Partner: Korea-China Relations and the US*, New York: Columbia University Press.

Cohen, Warren I. (2000), *America's Response to China: A History of Sino-American Relations*, New York: Columbia University Press.

Deng, Yong and Fei-Ling Wang (eds) (2005), *China Rising: Power and Motivation in Chinese Foreign Policy*, New York: Rowman & Littlefield Publishers, Inc.

Dittmer, Lowell (2004), "The Emerging Northeast Asian Regional Order", in Samuel S. Kim (ed.), *The International Politics of Northeast Asia*, Oxford: Rowman & Littlefield Publishers, Inc., pp. 331-360.

Efird, Brian, Jacek Kugler and Gaspare M. Genna (2003), "From War to Integration: Generalizing Power Transition Theory", *International Interactions*, Vol. 29, No. 4, October-December, pp. 293-313.

Eland, Ivan (2003), "Is Chinese Military Modernization a Threat to the US?", *Policy Analysis*, No. 465, 23rd January.

Fishman, Ted C. (2005), *China Inc.: How the Rise of the Next Superpower Challenges America and the World*, New York: Scribner.

Forrester, Jason W. (2007), "Congressional Attitudes on the Future of the US-South Korea Relationship", A Report of the International Security Program, CSIS, May. *<http://www.csis.org/media/csis/ pubs/ 070504_congressionalattitudes_final.pdf>*

Friedberg, Aaron L. (1993), "Ripe for Rivalry: Prospects for Peace in a Multipolar Asia", *International Security*, Vol. 18, No. 3, pp. 5-33.

Gertz, Bill (2000), *The China Threat: How the People's Republic Targets America*, Washington D.C.: Regnery Publishing, Inc.

Glaser, Bonnie, Scott Snyder and John S. Park (2008), "Keeping an Eye on an Unruly Neighbor: Chinese Views of Economic Reform and Stability in North Korea", USIP (US Institute of Peace) Working Paper, 3rd January. *<http://www.csis.org/ media/csis/pubs/071227_ wp_china_northkorea.pdf>*

Goh, Evelyn (2005), "Meeting the China Challenge: The US in Southeast Asian Regional Security Strategies", *Policy Studies*, 16, Washington, D.C.: The East-West Center. *<http://www.eastwestcenter.org/fileadmin/stored/pdfs/PS016.pdf>*

Goldstein, Avery (2005), *Rising to the Challenge: China's Grand Strategy and International Security*, Stanford, C.A.: Stanford University Press.

Han, Sukhee (2008), "From Engagement to Hedging: South Korea's New China Policy", *The Korean Journal of Defense Analysis*, Vol. 20, No. 4, December, pp. 335-351.

Heginbotham, Eric and Richard J. Samuels (2002), "Japan's Dual Hedge", *Foreign Affairs*, Vol. 81, No. 5, September/October, pp. 110-121.

Ikenberry, G. John (2008), "The Rise of China and the Future of the West", *Foreign Affairs*, Vol. 87, No. 1, January/February, pp. 23-37.

Ikenberry, G. John and Michael Mastanduno (eds) (2003), *International Relations Theory and the Asia Pacific*, New York: Columbia University Press.

International Crisis Group (2006), "China and North Korea: Comrades Forever?", *Asia Report*, No. 112, 1st February. *<http://www.nautilus.org/fora/security/0610.pdf>*

Kang, David C. (2007), *China Rising: Peace, Power, and Order in East Asia*, New York: Columbia University Press.

Kang, David C. (2009), "Between Balancing and Bandwagoning: South Korea's Response to China", *Journal of East Asian Studies*, No. 9, pp. 1-28.

Khong, Yuen Foong (2004), "Coping with Strategic Uncertainty: The Role of Institutions and Soft Balancing in Southeast Asia's Post-Cold War Strategy", in J.J. Suh, Peter J. Katzenstein and Allen Carlson (eds), *Rethinking Security in East Asia: Identity, Power, and Efficiency*, Stanford, C.A.: Stanford University Press, pp. 172-208.

Kim, Seung-Hwan (2002), "Anti-Americanism in Korea", *The Washington Quarterly*, Vol. 26, No. 1, Winter, pp. 109-122.

Koehane, Robert O. and Joseph S. Nye (1989), *Power and Interdependence*, Boston: Center for International Affairs, Harvard University, 1989.

Kupchan, Charles A. (1998), "After Pax Americana: Benign Power, Regional

Integration, and the Sources of Stable Multipolarity", *International Security*, Vol. 23, No. 2, Fall, pp. 40-79.

Lee, Sanghee (2007), *Changes in Perceptions of the ROK-US Alliance and the Way Ahead to Achieve Common Interests*, Washington, D.C.: The Brookings Institution. *<http://www3.brookings.edu/fp/cnaps/events/20070711.pdf>*

Lemke, Douglas (2003), "Investigating the Preventive Motive for War", *International Interactions*, Vol. 29, No. 4, October-December, pp. 273-292.

Lemke, Douglas and Ronald L. Tammen (2003), "Power Transition Theory and the Rise of China", *International Interactions*, Vol. 29, No. 4, October-December, pp. 269-271.

Limaye, Satu P. (ed.) (2009), *Asia's China Debate. <http://www.apcss.org/Publications/ SAS/AsiaBilateralRelations/Asias%20Bilateral% 20Relations%20Complete.pdf>*

Mearsheimer, John J. (2001), *The Tragedy of Great Power Politics*, New York: W.W. Norton & Company, Inc.

Medeiros, Evan S. (2005/06), "Strategic Hedging and the Future of Asia-Pacific Stability", *The Washington Quarterly*, Vol. 29, No. 1, Winter, pp. 145-167.

Medeiros, Evan S. and M. Taylor Fravel (2003), "China's New Diplomacy", *Foreign Affairs*, Vol. 82, No. 6, November/December, pp. 22-35.

Moon, Chung-in and Yongho Kim (2003), "Balance of Influence vs. Balance of Power: An Eclectic Approach for East Asian Security", in Woosang Kim (ed.), *Northeast Asian Regional Security Order and Strategic Calculus on the Taiwan Straits*, Seoul: Yonsei University Press, pp. 205-230.

Murphy, William J. (1994), "Power Transition in Northeast Asia: US-China Security Perceptions and the Challenges of Systemic Adjustment and Stability", *Journal of Northeast Asian Studies*, Vol. 13, No. 4, Winter, pp. 61-84.

New York Times, 3rd December 2003.

Nye, Joseph S., Jr (2004), *Soft Power: The Means to Success in World Politics*, New York: Public Affairs, 2004.

Overholt, William H. (1993), *The Rise of China: How Economic Reform is Creating a New Superpower*, New York: W.W. Norton & Company, Inc.

Rapkin, David P. (1990), "The Contested Concept of Hegemonic Leadership", in David P. Rapkin (ed.), *World Leadership and Hegemony*, London: Lynne Rienner Publishers, Inc.

Rapkin, David and William R. Thompson (2003), "Power Transition, Challenge and the (Re)emergence of China", *International Interactions*, Vol. 29, No. 4, October-December, pp. 315-342.

Rose, Gideon (1998), "Neoclassical Realism and Theories of Foreign Policy", *World Politics*, Vol. 51, No. 1, pp. 144-172.

Ross, Robert S. and Zhu Feng (eds) (2008), *China's Ascent: Power, Security, and the Future of International Politics*, Ithaca, N.Y.: Cornell University Press.

Roy, Denny (1994), "Hegemon on the Horizon?: China's Threat to East Asian Security", *International Security*, Vol. 19, No. 1, Summer, pp. 149-168.

Roy, Denny (1996), "The 'China Threat' Issue: Major Arguments", *Asian Survey*, Vol. 36, No. 8, August, pp. 758-771.

Roy, Denny (2003), "China's Reaction to American Predominance", *Survival*, Vol. 34, No. 3, Autumn, pp. 57-78.

Scobell, Andrew (2004), "China and North Korea: From Comrades-in-Arms to Allies at Arm's Length", SSI (Strategic Studies Institute) Monograph, March. <*http://www.carlisle.army.mil/ssi/pdffiles/PUB373.pdf*>

Segal, Gerald (1996), "East Asia and the Constrainment of China", *International Security*, Vol. 20, No. 4, Spring, pp. 107-135.

Shambaugh, David (2004/2005), "China Engages Asia: Reshaping the Regional Order", *International Security*, Vol. 29, No. 3, Winter, pp. 64-99.

Sheen, Seongho (2009), "Tilting toward the Dragon: South Korea's China Debate", in Satu P. Limaye (ed.), *Asia's China Debate*. <*http://www.apcss.org/Publications/SAS/ChinaDebate/ChinaDebateSheen.pdf*>

Snyder, Scott (2009), "Pursuing a Comprehensive Vision for the US-South Korea Alliance", CSIS, April. <*http://www.csis.org/ media/csis/pubs/090409_snyder_pursuingcompvision_web.pdf*>

Song, Yimin (1997), "China and North-East Asia's Regional Security", in Takashi Inoguchi and Grant B. Stillman (eds), *North-East Asian Regional Security*, Tokyo: United Nations University Press.

Stuart, Douglas T. and William Tow (1995), "A US Strategy for the Asia-Pacific: Building a Multipolar Balance-of-Power System in Asia", *Adelphi Papers*, No. 229, London: International Institute for Strategic Studies (IISS).

Sutter, Robert G. (2003), *The US and East Asia: Dynamics and Implications*, Oxford: Rowman & Littlefield Publishers, Inc.

Sutter, Robert G. (2005), *China's Rise in Asia: Promises and Perils*, New York: Rowman & Littlefield Publishers, Inc.

Tammen, Ronald, Jacek Kugler, Douglas Lemke, Allan Stam, Carole Alsharabati, Mark Abdollahian, Brian Efird, and A.F.K. Organski (eds) (2000), *Power Transition*, New York: Chatham House.

Timperlake, Edward and William C. Triplett II (eds) (2002), *Red Dragon Rising: Communist China's Military Threat to America*, Washington, D.C.: Regnery Publishing, Inc.

Tkachenko, Vadim (1997), "The Consequences of Korea's Unification for Russia and Security in Northeast Asia", *Far Eastern Affairs*, Vol. 4, pp. 23-40.

Tkacik, John J., Jr (2006), "Hedging against China", *Backgrounder* (Heritage Foundation), No. 1925, 17th April.

Wight, Martin, Hedley Bull and Carsten Holbraad (eds) (1978), *Power Politics*, Leicester: Leicester University Press.

Wohlforth, William C. (1999), "The Stability of Unipolar World", *International Security*, Vol. 24, No. 1, Summer, pp. 5-41.

Yahuda, Michael (1996), *The International Politics of the Asia-Pacific 1945-1995*, London: Rutledge.

Yee, Herbert and Ian Storey (eds) (2002), *The China Threat: Perceptions, Myths and Reality*, London: RoutledgeCurzon.

Chapter 4

Japan's Perspective on the
Threat and Opportunity of China

Takashi **Hoshiyama***

Introduction

Most intellectuals in Malaysia usually regard contemporary China only as
an "opportunity". On the other hand, those in Japan, in general, rather view
China as both an "opportunity" and a "threat." This chapter focuses on Japan's
view towards China's threat so that we can clarify the present situation
and the prospects of the bilateral relations between Japan and China. The
relationship among the major regional powers of Asia inevitably affects peace
and prosperity in this region. Thus the deterioration of the relationship and
inter-confrontation would overshadow the prospect of creating a new regional
order which is essential for the region to further develop economically and
politically. Under this recognition, this chapter concludes that the entire region
should pay more attention as well as exert more emphasis on the Japan-China
relations than ever before.

In using the word "threat", it is necessary to clarify its meaning first.
Roughly defined, some threats are real and imminent, but on the other hand,
some are deemed potential (not conspicuous at present) and not so immediate.
The application of the term "threat" in this chapter relates to the meaning of
the latter[1]. For most Malaysians, the term "China's threat" seems to largely
suggest an economic one where the Malaysian economy might be damaged
with China's mounting economic competitiveness which could attract foreign
investments; otherwise they would come to Malaysia. In Japan as well, the
threat in economic terms is quite often referred and related to the kind of
effect that China's economic downturn could create, especially when it could
catastrophically damage Japan's economy. But more often, "China's threat"
is recently perceived in the context of security as a potential risk to Japan.
Issues like China's rapid military build-up and China's approach to North
Korean nuclearization could seriously change the security environment

around Japan. Also of concern is the negative diplomatic influence caused by China's increased military presence, a pressure that might force Japan to diplomatically compromise various bilateral issues. If China's upcoming doldrums lead to its domestic political and social instability, Japan could be faced with serious uncertainties given the enormity of China. In fact, this is also a part of China's threat to Japan.

Probably what is more important and fundamental is the viewpoint that with China's enhanced presence in the regional and international arena, the present power balance that Japan enjoyed so far in the international society would change drastically, a situation that might pose a risk to regional security and prosperity, including Japan, in a sense that the future outlook is unforeseeable. In other words, China's rise might unfavourably change the status quo of the international community, a move that will threaten Japan's critical national interests. Future state of affairs in China is fluid and unpredictable. Therefore, China's intention as to what kind of new world it wants to build has inevitably come under the spotlight among the regional and international communities.

This chapter tries to outline Japan's perspective towards China as one of its neighbouring countries. To this end, 8 pillars of the policy recommendations "A New Chapter in Japan-China Relations", issued by the Institute for International Policy Studies (IIPS)[2] in April 2008, are quoted in order to clarify Japan's perception on China's threat and opportunity. This set of policy recommendations[3], to which the author contributed as a researcher, was compiled by summing up various views expressed by a number of Japanese scholars and several incumbent and former government officials. Thus the recommendations can be regarded as a standard perception of Japanese intellectuals. Each of these 8 pillars includes Japan's rationale of threats towards China and the remedies to the issues. Highlighted below are brief summaries of them.

1. Building a Broadly Perceived and Amicable Major Power Relationship Fitting for a New Era

After several years of stalled relations between Japan and China, leaders of both countries agreed to develop a "strategic mutually beneficial relationship" in 2006. The reasons for the Hu Jintao administration's final consent can be summed up as follows:

(1) Amid frequent outbursts of terrorism and ethnic conflict worldwide and the gradual unraveling of nuclear non-proliferation system internationally

and regionally, international expectation that Japan and China should coexist and cooperate to build a desirable international order has intensified, reflecting a global longing for sustainable economic growth in a peaceful environment. The expectations of East Asian nations, including the nations of ASEAN, are especially high. In this situation, China came to recognize the necessity to position Japan as a partner for creating a new regional order.

(2) In concert with Japan, China recognized that it must carefully manage its potentially antagonistic bilateral relationship by emphasizing its "increasing common interests", given the new relations where both countries have become equal partner, at least economically, for the first time in history.

(3) For Chinese leaders, stability within China is extremely important. Fears are rising that loss of control over diversifying domestic public opinions driven by the advance of globalization and the IT revolution would result in internal political disorder. To avoid this to happen, China judged that intrinsically fragile relations with Japan must not be a flashpoint and Japan's economic strength should be made better use of. If anti-Japan sentiment among the Chinese public explodes, the chaos could ignite domestic instability within China.

Since China's recognition of the necessity to change the relations qualitatively, Japan-China relationship has been recovering well. In 2008, there were five mutual visits of leaders between the two countries, which is a record high. In 2009, three summit meetings were successfully concluded as of August. But the prospect to advance the newly-born relations cannot be so optimistic, due to mounting nationalism among the Chinese and still-existing historical issues, to name a few. In overcoming the history-dominated relations to become real joint partners in creating a new regional order, the IIPS Recommendations pointed out, "it will above all be vital to build 'a relationship in which the two sides can frankly say with courtesy to one another what needs to be said', and to maintain a continuous dialog based on a relationship of trust between leaders of the two countries. What should be reminded of the lesson is that misunderstandings and conflicts have arisen instead because Japan has attempted to this day to guard against a backlash over the history issue by refraining from saying much about its opinion." It can be concluded that a healthy diplomatic relationship is required where the two nations can assert views frankly and thereby find common ground. Japan is now expected to speak frankly to China not only about bilateral issues but also about regional issues and global issues as an opinion leader in the region.

2. Advancing Measures Sufficient to Overcome the Problems of History

There have been many instances where Japan-China relations have soured due to various problems originating from history. Even now, more than 60 years after the war, the past still haunts bilateral relations. Very recently, Prime Minister Junichiro Koizumi's visit to the Yasukuni Shrine has caused bilateral relations to stall for almost five years, forcing leaders of both sides to suspend mutual visits. The deteriorated relation was not only due to his visits to the Yasukuni Shrine, but history issues such as the Yasukuni shrine, school history textbooks, the Nanking incident, comfort women, and abandoned chemical weapons – these issues which are related to national honour and dignity had stirred up the emotions of people of both countries. History also relates to the frictions over Taiwan and the Senkaku Islands. These problems have been made more complex by internal political situations in both countries, in addition to the differences in historical perspective and interpretation of these historical events.

With regard to history, Premier Wen Jiabao addressed the Japanese Diet in April 2007, saying, "Since the normalization of diplomatic ties between China and Japan, the Japanese government and leaders have on many occasions stated their position on the history issue, admitted that Japan had committed aggression and expressed deep remorse and apology to the victimized people. The Chinese government and people appreciate the position they have taken." In the joint press communiqué issued then, China also stated that China applauds Japan's post-war progress as a peaceful state and its economic cooperation with China. President Hu also echoed Premier Wen's statement in May 2008 when he visited Japan. The expressions of China's leaders appealed to the deeply rooted sentiments of amity that Japanese harbour towards China.

The drastic change of China's stance towards history, which has long been a thorny issue between both countries, should be greatly welcomed and appreciated. Nevertheless, historical issues will inevitably rise up between the two countries even hereinafter[4]. In Japan, where freedom of speech is guaranteed to the maximum, any untoward statements occasionally released from Japan are unavoidable. Notwithstanding that, the Japanese side should exercise maximum self-control in discussions on historical views, particularly by leaders of the Japanese government in order not to unnecessarily offend the sensitivities of the Chinese people.

In requesting both sides to react appropriately, the IIPS recommendations to the Chinese side advise, "In this search for a new start for Japan-China relations, the Chinese government is also urged to take appropriate actions against those found for fomenting anti-Japanese sentiments in the past. For instance, the patriotic education campaign introduced in 1994 to influence the Chinese people has had the side effect of fomenting anti-Japanese sentiments. If the situation accelerates, it will have undesirable effects on the rule in China itself, in addition to the negative effects on Japan-China relations. Thus, Japan should sincerely ask China to make the correction. The negative explanation in history textbooks heavily influences the views of the Chinese younger generation. Thus, it should reflect the results of the joint historical research initiated by both governments, and statements that cultivate anti-Japanese sentiments should be re-examined. Institutions (such as museums) related to Japan should also have future-oriented exhibitions befitting the new Japan-China relationship."

Both sides should be reminded of the lesson that as long as negative sentiments towards "history" exist among Chinese people, the risky condition that history continues to be a potential flashpoint between Japan and China cannot be changed.

3. Japanese Cooperation to the Various Problems that China Faces such as Environment, Energy, Water

As China undergoes rapid economic growth, environmental problems such as atmospheric pollution (given China's reliance on coal for approximately 70 per cent of its energy consumption), water contamination and shortages, and soil contamination have become major social issues. If the environmental problems get any worse, this will hinder the continual growth of the Chinese economy – and naturally be harmful to the health of the Chinese. These problems might also cause political and social turmoil. Since China's mounting environmental problems have direct consequences to Japan, in the form of airborne yellow sand, acid rain damage, and rubbish washed ashore from the sea, cooperation between Japan and China is now a matter of urgency.

China's rapidly growing consumption of energy and natural resources has caused instability in international markets in terms of supply and prices. Therefore, China's domestic and foreign policies on energy and natural resources will greatly affect the Japanese economy. Japan is compelled to pay attention to China's moves and to continue to enhance cooperation with China in fields such as energy conservation technology and safety in nuclear power generation. The problem of food shortage will also be on the international agenda in the near future.

As for global warming, though it is not an issue in the context of Japan-China relations, it is one of the most serious problems faced by the international community. China is the top CO_2 emitter in the world exhausting 20 per cent of total CO_2, a level on par with the USA. China's participation in global efforts to combat global warming is essential. Otherwise, the future of human society *per se* will be at risk. In this area too, Japan's cooperation with China should be enhanced in the future.

China's evolution in such fields is attracting international attention. Although China's progresses *per se* may not be criticized, they are easily recognized as threats, because its sheer size itself inevitably makes a huge impact on the international community.

4. Cooperation between Japan and China on the Building of a New Regional Order

The worldwide trend towards political and economical regionalism is intensifying. East Asia too, should in the long term, aim to build strong mechanisms for political, economical, security and cultural cooperation in the region. In the course of this process, Japan and China should cooperate closely and jointly display leadership, with a view to building and developing multi-faceted and multi-layered regional mechanisms. To put it the other way round, if Japan-China relationship is neither close nor cooperative, it will be difficult to create such desirable regional mechanisms, which will in turn pose challenge to the maintenance of regional peace and stability. Considering the characteristics of this region, it is no easy task to create one single integrated regional organization that provides comprehensive coverage for all important fields as the example of Europe. Instead, an alternative approach worthy of consideration (with the view of acting in a way that would be materially conducive to the peace and prosperity of the region) would be to adjust the member nations according to the scope of cooperation, and to build up cooperative relationships that are multi-faceted and multi-layered. For example, it has been difficult for ARF (ASEAN Regional Forum) – the only all-inclusive security mechanism for East Asia – to reach consensus on meaningful conflict prevention measures although it has been useful in providing a platform for dialog to enhance mutual trust. Instead, there should be more attempts to set up various specific cooperation groupings to pursue concrete results. Such examples are the PSI (Proliferation Security Initiative) on nuclear non-proliferation and the Regional Cooperation Agreement on Combating Piracy and Armed Robbery against Ships in Asia.

The debate is still on-going as to which countries should be included as member states of the community in this region, i.e. whether ASEAN+3,

ASEAN+3+3, APEC or some other configuration. With the future shape of the international order yet unknown, it would be unwise to attempt to determine what it may look like. The status of the USA will be a crucial factor. Although the USA is not geographically part of East Asia, it does play an essential role in the region's politics, economy, and in particular security. Since security in East Asia is maintained by means of a network of alliances based around the USA, it will be necessary to design a regional mechanism that includes the USA as a constituent member, and which is distinct from the "East Asian Community" and can act as a support to it. It is neither realistic nor responsible to categorically exclude the USA from the region by neglecting its effective role in this region.

As for the Japan-China cooperation in creating a new regional order, the North Korean issue is at the core. Entering 2009, North Korea has intensified its provocative behaviour by carrying out nuclear tests and ballistic missile launches repeatedly. In response, the UN Security Council Resolution 1718 adopted new additional sanctions. In order to give rise to the denuclearization of North Korea and to make the sanctions effective, the key lies in China, on whom North Korea is greatly dependent. It is said that around 50 per cent of North Korea's external trade is with China. Thus, China's determination on its action will ultimately steer the direction of North Korea's denuclearization and impact the possible proliferation of weapons of mass destruction and thus, the security environment of East Asia as a whole.

5. Strengthening Mutual Understanding between Japan and China

Mutual understanding is much easier said than achieved between any two countries. This can be clearly seen by looking at the relations between Malaysia and its neighbours, i.e. Indonesia and Singapore, let alone the relations between Japan and China who engaged in war only three generations earlier. Certainly, the relations are improving in the past few years. But in terms of the sentiments of people at the grassroots level, the situation is rather deteriorating, particularly in the Japanese people who have been consistently favourable to China, partly due to their strong atonement for the war. In the 1980s (when statistics became available[5]), roughly around 70 per cent Japanese had a favourable feeling towards China. However, in recent years, the figure has continuously dropped until 32 per cent in 2008. The problem lies in the fact, unfortunately, that the figure is decreasing even during the Hu Jintao administration whose policy towards Japan has played a major role in enabling the positive turnaround in Japan-China relations. On top of the case of poisoned frozen dumplings imported from China which directly affect the Japanese consumers' health, China's military build-up, China's response to energy development in the East China Sea, China's manner in treating historical issues, mass demonstration against Japan (in 2005), Tibetan turmoil and other accounts seem to have infiltrated a sense of fear and discontent into the grassroots level Japanese. In contrast, there is an improvement in the Chinese views towards the relations since last year. More than half of the Chinese populace surveyed (54.3 per cent) responded that the present Sino-Japan relations were good in 2008 though the percentage stood at a mere 24.9 in 2007[6]. At any rate, the serious problem is that if the foundation of public support for the bilateral relations is fragile, it is difficult to control the situation once issues stimulating national sentiments arise.

Therefore, it is significant to enhance various grassroots activities like those being undertaken by the Japanese government now, to promote mutual understanding and exchange programmes, for example, annual exchange of 4000 youth and exchange of 1500 teachers for a 3 year-period. Of course, as stated in point number 2 earlier; the Japanese leaders must exercise maximum restraint on their actions and expressions, given the deep remorse of Japanese people for the past. On the other side, it would be difficult to alter the sentiments of the Chinese youths towards Japan entirely and to impact the foundation of bilateral relations on a national level, unless the Chinese government embarks to modify its educational approach related to its history with Japan. The dilemma for the Communist Party (and the Chinese government) would be that its legitimacy to rule China lies in its sheer victory over Japan and it is only through education can the Party thrusts its views into people's mind from generation to generation.

6. Continuous Support for China's Policy of Reform and Openness

World-wide financial crisis swooped down from the USA in 2008 seriously affecting even the Chinese economy which is now the engine of the world economy. But the stimulus package of as much as 4 trillion Chinese yuan announced last November appears successful so far. GDP in the 2nd quarter of 2009 rose 7.9 per cent from the same period last year according to the China National Statistics Bureau. On the other hand, China's export fell by 21.8 per cent in the first half of 2009 compared with 2008 due to the slowdown of the US and European economy. Even though China is able to weather through the present crisis, it will have to face difficulties one after another in terms of achieving continued high growth.

China's economic expansion has been supported by vigorous investments, and now there is a real danger that excessive investment and bad debt could become more overt dangers to the economy. Japan has experienced just this type of problem. Between 10 and 20 years from now, China will also experience its aging society, and domestic personal savings that supported investment will dry up as well. Crucial is to what degree China will be able to absorb the price increase of resources and energy. In addition to that, if environmental problems become more serious, it will become increasingly difficult to continue to invest in China. It will be critical for China to take the necessary and appropriate environmental measures to continue to introduce foreign capital. Furthermore, it will also have to work to correct the income gap as part of the efforts to build a more stable society. For China to continue to be stable politically and socially, it has to secure high growth rate and, through which, create huge employment opportunity. But there are a lot of unfavourable phenomena arising in recent years. For example, there are huge unemployed migrant workers, insufficient job opportunities for new university graduates, frequent mass protest (which is numbered 70,000-80,000 annually) against governmental acts such as inappropriate way of condemnation of personal fortunes. Such social dissatisfaction could seriously rock social stability and damage its economic progress.

If China fails to devote its full attention to dealing with these structural issues and continues to attach greater importance to its policy of economic expansion, the country is sure to face a severe economic downturn, sooner or later. If that happens, it will give a serious adverse effect on the Japanese economy and in the light of the size of the Chinese economy from an international perspective, it will also have a serious negative impact on the world economy.

The IIPS recommendations conclude in this aspect, "The economies of Japan and China have a strong mutual dependence, and strengthening this economic relationship is an important element of the strategic mutually beneficial relationship between the two countries. Japan has supported reform and openness in China through official development assistance (ODA[7]) and private investments. Japan should continue in this vein by assisting China's development through transfers of technology, know-how and private investments."

7. Resolving Bilateral Conflict through Consultation Based on International Law and Justice

Japan and China are neighbouring countries with a high degree of mutual dependency, which at the same time provides a constant source of potential conflicts. There are the problems related to history, the East China Sea, and broad-based economic relations. The problems involving Taiwan, which often create discord between China and the United States as a serious regional issue, have at times become a source of friction between Japan and China.

The IIPS recommendations summarize, "Dealing with individual problems requires restraint from both sides so as not to exacerbate the situation, and each must hold tight to a position of peaceful resolution based on international law and justice. This requires the establishment of high-level strategic talks at the right moment, followed by a final decision at the leadership level as a customary practice."

For instance, regarding the energy development issue revolving around the median line in the East China Sea faced by both countries, the problem should be resolved through talks. The trouble began when China decided to develop natural gas in a potentially conflicting area with Japan. Although both countries achieved a basic agreement on joint development on both sides of the median line, further negotiation has not been in progress. Under such circumstances, some media reported in July 2009 that China is unilaterally building more facilities for gas-digging and the Japanese government is protesting against it[8]. This issue concerns the demarcation line between exclusive economic zones in the East China Sea in which Japan asserts legitimacy of the intermediate line, while on the other hand, China argues the theory of the natural extension of the continental shelf. The argument relates to the control of the area which may cause a military clash. In order to avoid such military confrontation, IIPS recommendations suggest, "If these talks fail to produce a resolution, seeking a resolution in an international court should be considered" and "to establish conflict prevention mechanisms such as the installation of a hotline" is advised.

The Senkaku Islands, which is Japanese territory (China and Taiwan call them "Diaoyu") are also situated in the East China Sea. The 2009 White Paper on Defense announced by the Japanese government stated, in this Japanese territorial area, "China's ocean survey ships took actions such as offences like prowling in December 2008, which are against international laws. The IIPS also recommends that in the case of this kind of issue which is related to international laws, the possibility of remitting the case to international court should be examined in order to avoid any possible military clash. Apart from these issues, there are also other potential causes for confrontation around this area, and these may, through unforeseeable circumstances, embroil Japan into conflict. Some examples of situations which may embroil Japan into conflict include military provocation by North Korea or a clash between China and Taiwan in the Taiwan Strait.

8. Response to China's Military Rise

The above-quoted 2009 White Paper on Defense also discussed the Chinese military power: "The Chinese Navy is improving its capabilities to perform operations in distant waters", "In recent years it has begun to work on acquiring capabilities for missions other than the Taiwan issue" and so on. This shows the concern on the rise of China's military.

IIPS recommendations summarize the rise of China as follows, "The rapid expansion of both the scope and capabilities of China's military, centring on air and sea power as well as missile capability, together with the fact that its military strategy and capabilities are unclear, has become a source of concern not only for Japan but also for the entire East Asian region, from the point of view of the balance of military power. Incidents such as violations of Japan's territorial waters by Chinese naval vessels, the recently confirmed satellite destruction test, and the actions of the People's Liberation Army in maritime areas close to the South China Sea, have given rise to international suspicion of China's decision-making processes and methods of implementation with regard to political processes and military strategy formulation. Although it champions "peaceful development" as a foreign policy, China is also pursuing a strategy of military expansion. Its military preparedness and strategy, thus, warrant a close examination into the effect they exert on the overall security environment in East Asia, and these must be assessed comprehensively and strategically. Even if the strategic aims of the Chinese government should prove to be non-invasive and non-aggressive, we need to be aware that the expansion of Chinese military power projection beyond its territorial waters and airspace and onto the regional or global stage increases the likelihood of unexpected conflict. Given China's current state, Japan must assess the military balance in East Asia and employ national security policies aimed at maintaining the status quo and guaranteeing the stability of the region."

As a very recent example, at the end of June 2009, China's five vessels were confirmed to have engaged in activity, seemingly military exercise in the water area around Okinotori-shima (island) which comes under Japanese territory. In terms of nuclear disarmament, China is still enhancing her nuclear arsenal and modernization in the current favourable atmosphere where US President Obama has showed a very positive stance towards a total ban of nuclear weapons in future and the summit meeting between US and Russia in July basically agreed to forward the negotiations on further reduction of nuclear arsenal.

The purpose for such military build-up in China has often been attributed to securing its own ocean interests, not to counter the USA, but at the same time, the lack of transparency of its intention is feared to trigger an arms race in Asia. Along with Japan's military budget decrease for more than 10 years, China's military rise is about to change the military power balance of the region including East China Sea and South China Sea, so much so that the kind of regional structure China intends to make is fast becoming Japan's concern. In the security field, Japan's viable responses are limited to strengthening the Japan-US alliance, urging China to take a positive stance to create bilateral schemes on conflict prevention and enhancing efforts to construct region-wide safety mechanisms.

Conclusion

The above discussions have enumerated the risks of China's rise and the pitfalls Japan-China relations could fall in, but the purpose of this chapter is, needless to say, not to emphasize China's threat. It showed the popular view on it among the Japanese based on the recommendations issued by Japan's leading think tank, the Institute for International Policy Studies (IIPS). For the Japanese, the risks surrounding China are not few and deemed serious, a view that may be possibly different from other Asian countries including Malaysia, let alone China herself who may not be so conscious of how she is reflected in the eyes of other countries. But there is no doubt that the gigantic presence of China has been overwhelming in Asia consistently from ancient times until now. Singling out global issues, there are still so many concerns such as nuclear proliferation and disarmament, global warming, energy, food security, ocean security, international finance, and ideology. In these matters, China will continue to be able to strongly influence, whether positively or negatively, on the international community.

It can be said that "threat" and "opportunity" are somewhat in the relationship of two sides of a coin. Japan is a country which has benefited greatly from the opportunities China has provided so far. Similarly, China's possible disorder would affect Japan most seriously. Japan, as a close neighbour and regional major power, is now forced to urge China to take an appropriate path that does not seek drastic changes in the regional and international order, which will lead to regional peace and stability. However, Japan's power to do so is limited, given the rising power of China. Therefore, a larger framework that includes USA in Japan-China relations and further multilateral frameworks that include ASEAN, India, South Korea, Australia and so on, are required to set a target of creating new relations based on collective security and the like.

The possibility of realizing this in the future is not small. Despite facing a lot of international issues, the Chinese authority is placing internal stability as its first priority at present. This can be seen by the fact that President Hu immediately returned to China right after the turmoil took place in Xinjiang Uyghur Autonomous Region in July, even though he had just arrived in Italy to attend the G8 Summit which was a good opportunity to display the mounting prestige of China. To secure its domestic stability, China needs, above all, a peaceful international environment. This coincides with the current world trend where it will be difficult to wage a war, due to many reasons such as the increasing number of democratic states, an enlarging network of free trade, and the mounting influence of international public opinion against a war.

If China can successfully channel its resources and wisdom for tackling various economic and social problems instead of arms buildup, it could further pursue economic development internally and advance "peaceful development" internationally. As the IIPS recommendations pointed out, it is impossible for any country to continue rapid economic growth forever. But if China were to carry out political and social reforms and succeed in enhancing the social safety network, the impact caused by an impending economic meltdown could be attenuated and a soft-landing could be possible. Stepping into the future with these measures in place, China naturally emerge as the leader of a harmonious region, a favourable situation which is resilient and sustainable for both China and each member nation.

As for Japan, its role within this region is considerably important, especially in its management of relations with China. The IIPS recommendations state that "Japan welcomed China's policy of reform and openness, which commenced in 1978, and has supported this policy through both public and private sectors – for example, Japan was among the first developed countries to provide financial assistance to China. The chief objective of this was to stabilize Cold War communist China politically by introducing a market economy, so as to mitigate the threat that it could pose to its neighbour Japan. It could thus be said that Japan adopted a policy of engagement towards China (involving measures such as aid and investment) and urged that China be gradually integrated into the international community." Now, Japan's role has changed in a sense that the emphasis should be on cooperation, mainly through provision of know-how based on Japan's experience to mitigate economic and social distortions which were brought about by rapid economic development.

For this region, although it has been said that the twenty-first century is the Asian era, a stable international environment is essential if Asia's current prosperity is to continue. Each country is expected to engage more positively in regional security including that of Japan-China relations, individually and collectively, being mindful of some sort of collective security. The sound development of Japan-China relations is crucial for the region in terms of building a new regional order. For a long time the hope that this relationship would mature has been growing among Asian nations, and their voices have successfully urged both Japan and China to improve the relations. In this information age, the collective voice of a region is becoming a strong soft power capable of influencing the thinking and actions of its regional members. This should also apply to the wish for China's sound development and her future orientation. The will and vision of the region in terms of what kind of order it is aiming for, could increase the opportunities of China and at the same time, decrease potential risks.

Notes

* Takashi Hoshiyama 星山隆 is Minister and Deputy Chief of Mission of the Japanese Embassy in Malaysia. He joined the Ministry of Foreign Affairs in 1982. His latest post abroad was the Economic Counselor of the Japanese Embassy in the Philippines (2001-2003). He was seconded to IIPS in 2005. He has an MA in Art & Science from Harvard University and is a member of the Japan Association for Asian Studies. The views expressed in this chapter are the personal views of the author and do not represent the views of the Japanese Embassy.

1. The Japanese government categorizes a foreign country as a "threat" in the case where a country has both the capability and intention of intruding Japan. In this definition, Japan officially does not regard China as a threat because it does not submit the latter.

2. IIPS was set up in 1988 as a private research institute by former Japanese Prime Minister Yasuhiro Nakasone who is presently its chairman. The institute deals with a broad range of international affairs and was selected as one of the 30 most influential international research institutes in 2007 and 2008 according to a survey made by Pennsylvania University in the US. The author was seconded to IIPS from 2005 to 2008.

3. IIPS homepage <http://www.iips.org>; "A New Chapter in Japan-China Relations – towards co-existence and co-development that overcomes history –".

4. The author details historical issues in the paper "New Japan-China Relations and the Corresponding Positioning of the United States", *Asia-Pacific Review*, Volume 15, Number 2, November 2008.

5. A survey of public opinion has been annually conducted by the Cabinet Office of the Japanese government since 1980.

6. A joint survey of Genron NGO (Japan) and *China Daily* conducted in 2008 <http://www.tokyo-beichingforum.net>.

7. Japanese government's provision of Yen-Loan to China for new projects/programmes has been suspended since 2008 through bilateral agreement.

8. 18th July 2008 evening edition of *Nikkei Shinbun* (newspaper).

Chapter 5

Vietnam-China Relations and Building the "Two Corridors, One Economic Belt"

Do Tien Sam* and Ha Thi Hong Van**

Introduction

Vietnam and China are neighbours, and the cultural, economic, social and political characteristics of the two countries are similar. Since the normalization of relations in 1991, political relations between the two countries have been developing rapidly; however, development in economic relations has not matched with political development, and the two countries have not explored their potentiality efficiently. Hence, building "two corridors and one economic belt" is not only significant to both sides but also to the development of relations between the two countries in the future

Vietnam-China Relations – Looking Back to the Last 18 Years

Achievements

Since the normalization of relations in 1991, relations between the two countries have been developing rapidly and gained historical great achievements in the last 18 years.

First, official meetings between the two countries' leaders have been conducted regularly. These meetings have strengthened mutual friendship and trust, enhanced friendship exchanges and mutual benefit cooperation, created motivations to boost the development of relations between the two countries. The two countries' leaders have defined cooperation guidelines and direction in developing the relations in the 21st century: "friendly neighbourliness, comprehensive cooperation, long-lasting stability, and looking forwards to the future" and "good neighbours, goods friends, goods comrades and good partners". Particularly, during the official friendship visit to Vietnam in November 2006, the General Secretary of the Communist Party and President of China Hu Jintao expressed the structures of the relations between the two countries as: "Rivers and mountains connect together, culture resembles each other's, ideology is similar, fortune is related to each other". The two countries have established Bilateral Cooperation Committee, laying foundation for the two countries' development of relations oriented towards "stability, wholesome and auspicious". During Vietnamese Communist Party's General Secretary Nong Duc Manh's visit to China recently, the two countries agreed to develop "comprehensive strategic cooperation partner" relations, based on the above-mentioned 16 words and four good spirits, to raise the relations to a higher plane.

Second, in terms of economic cooperation, the two countries have also gained remarkable achievements. In 2008, the bilateral trade volume was US$20 billion, having increased 610 folds compared to 1991, and surpassed the target set for 2010, and China has become a leading trade partner of Vietnam continuously for 5 years.

Figure 5.1 China-Vietnam Trade Relations (1991-2007)

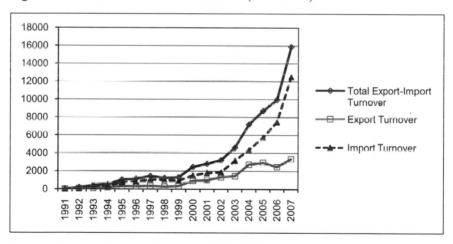

Source: *Vietnam Statistic Yearbook* (1992-2008).

Vietnam exports to China crude oil, agricultural products, seafood, mineral products, forest products, textile products etc. China exports to Vietnam gasoline, iron and steel, material for textile and shoes industries, fertilizer and equipment and machinery etc.

In terms of investment, up to May 2008, China has had 561 projects (excluding Hong Kong) in Vietnam with the total capital of US$1.87 billion, ranking 11th among 82 countries and regions investing in Vietnam. Chinese FDI in Vietnam has been increasing rapidly recently. In 1991, there was only 1 Chinese FDI project in Vietnam; up to 1995, there were about 10 projects with investment capital about US$60 million. In 2004, cumulative Chinese investment projects in Vietnam were 391 projects. In the period 1996-2000, there were about 13 Chinese investment projects in Vietnam per annum; there were about 80 projects per annum in the period 2002-2006.

Table 5.1 China's FDI in Vietnam by Sector

Industry	Number of Projects	Total Investment Capital	Disbursements
Industries and Construction	319	861,234,569	154,365,481
Agriculture-Forestry-Aquatic	61	113,317,157	38,439,307
Services	54	206,835,869	51,164,546
Total	434	1,181,387,595	243,969,334

Source: Foreign Direct Investment Bureau of Vietnam's Ministry of Planning and Investment, *Report on China's FDI in Vietnam*, April 2007.

Chinese enterprises invested in fields such as: restaurants, electrical goods, assembling motor bikes, shoes industry, processing food and fruit, toys, cattle-feed industry, ceramic industry, building infrastructure for industry zones (Linh Trung Industry Zone), building supermarkets (Cho Sat supermarket).

Regarding Chinese ODA in Vietnam, the total ODA from China to Vietnam was about US$312 million. Among this, non-payment assistance was US$50 million; non-interest loan was US$262 million. Non-payment assistance was concentrated on projects such as: building Vietnam-China Cultural Friendship Palace, improving Bac Giang Fertilizer factory, Thai Nguyen Iron Factory, building dormitory for the Ho Chi Minh National Politic Academy. Non-interest loan was used in projects such as: Rao Quan Hydroelectric Plant, Da Nang Textile Factory, Hanoi-Hadong railway project, Quang Ninh Thermo-electric Factory, Dac Nong Bauxite project etc.

In terms of tourism, China is the largest tourist source of Vietnam, and accounts for one third of the total foreign tourists visited Vietnam. Vice versa, Vietnamese tourists visiting China have also increased gradually, and about 20 thousand tourists visited China per annum.

Third, cultural, education cooperation and cooperation in other sectors have also gained a new development. In terms of education, there have been 7,000 Vietnamese students studying in China. In addition, there are about 40 universities of Vietnam having established cooperation and education relations with more than 20 universities and institutes of China.

Fourth, in terms of territory issues, the two countries have solved two out of three outstanding issues. In 1999, the two sides signed an Agreement on Land Border and in 2000, signed the Tonkin Gulf Demarcation Agreement and Fisheries Cooperation Agreement. The work of demarcation and landmark planting has made remarkable progress, and two sides are striving to finish the delimitation and demarcation by 2008 and will sign a new instrument on the rules of border management in order to build Vietnam-China border into a "peaceful, friendly and cooperational" area. The two sides will implement the Tonkin Gulf Demarcation Agreement and Fisheries Cooperation Agreement in the Gulf of Tonkin and carry out joint inspection in the joint fishing zone, joint survey of fishery resources and joint naval patrols. The two sides will accelerate the implementation of the "Framework Agreement on Oil and Natural Gas Cooperation in Agreed Zones in the Gulf of Tonkin". The two countries will make efforts in gaining achievement in joint inspection, joint exploration for oil and gas in waters over its continental shelf; remaining fishery manufacturing order normally; fishery cooperation, environmental protection cooperation in the Gulf of Tonkin. The two sides also agreed to continue to speed up negotiations to delineate waters beyond the mouth of the Gulf of Tonkin, exchanged ideas on cooperation development issues, started conducting joint inspection in this region early. In terms of the East Sea (South China Sea) issue, the leaders of the two countries agreed to follow strictly the consensus of maintenance of stability in the East Sea, continue to maintain negotiation mechanism on sea issues. The two sides agreed to seek a mutually acceptable basic and durable solution through peaceful negotiations, and at the same time, conduct research and discuss positively on the cooperation development to find out appropriate model and region. Above consensuses will have a positive role in maintaining stability in the East Sea.

Mutual trust and progress in the above-mentioned sectors will create a premise and condition for cooperation between the two countries, and raise the cooperation between the two countries into a more comprehensive and deeper state in the next few years, in order to achieve the goal of Vietnam to become an industrialized nation and China's goal of building a well-off society in 2020.

Outstanding Issues

Vietnam-China relations have gained remarkable achievements. However, the relation between the two sides is not comprehensive and harmonious among sectors. In fact, economic relations have not matched with development in political relations, potentialities of the two countries have not been fully exploited, and close geographical position and political and cultural similarity advantages between the two countries have not been promoted.

In terms of trade, bilateral trade volume has increased rapidly. However, Vietnam has seen constantly increasing deficit in trade with China. According to the Chinese custom's statistics, in 2007, the volume of deficit of Vietnam in trade with China was US$8.6 billion. In terms of investment, Vietnam's investment to China reached a very small volume, China's FDI to Vietnam are also modest and the quality of investment project is not high.

Hence, it is necessary and important to conduct surveys and find out appropriate solutions to strengthen and enhance economic relations between the two countries. The initiative of "two economic corridors and one belt" in the Gulf of Tonkin was raised by the premiers of the two countries and it has important political, economic and social meanings.

Figure 5.2 Map of the Two Economic Corridors and One Economic Belt

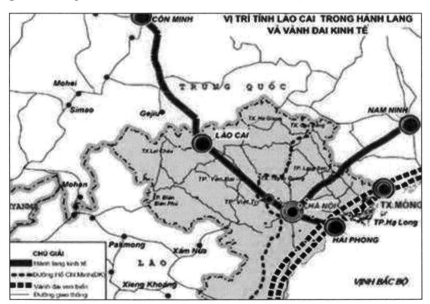

Source: Vo Van Thanh, 2006.

"Two Economic Corridors and One Belt" Development Cooperation

The "two economic corridors and one belt" initiative was raised by the Vietnamese prime minister during his official friendship visit to China in May 2004 and it was supported by Chinese premier. The two sides signed the Memorandum of Understanding on 16th November 2006, which clearly defined the sphere, key cooperation sectors and preferential sectors of the two economic corridors and one belt.

Table 5.2 Kunming-Lao Cai-Hanoi-Hai Phong Economic Corridor

Order	Province of Vietnam	Square Kilometre	Population ('000 people)
1	Lao Cai	6357.0	602.3
2	Yen Bai	6882.9	750.2
3	Phu Tho	3519.6	1364.7
4	Vinh Phuc	1371.4	1014.5
5	Hanoi	921.0	6116.2
6	Hung Yen	923.1	1167.1
7	Hai Duong	1648.4	1745.3
8	Hai Phong	1526.3	1845.9
	Total	23149.7	14606.2

Source: Vietnam General Statistic Office. <*http://www.gso.gov.vn*>

Table 5.3 Nanning-Lang Son-Hanoi-Hai Phong Economic Corridor

Order	Province of Vietnam	Square Kilometre	Population ('000 people)
1	Lang Son	8305.2	759.0
2	Bac Giang	8322.7	1628.4
3	Bac Ninh	807.6	1022.5
4	Hanoi	921.0	6116.2
5	Hung Yen	923.1	1167.1
6	Hai Duong	1648.4	1745.3
7	Hai Phong	1526.3	1845.9
	Total	22454.3	14284.4

Source: Vietnam General Statistic Office. <*http://www.gso.gov.vn*>

Table 5.4 Tonkin Gulf Economic Belt

Order	Province of Vietnam	Square Kilometre	Population ('000 people)
1	Quang Ninh	5899.6	1109.6
2	Hai Phong	1526.3	1845.9
3	Thai Binh	1545.4	1872.9
4	Nam Dinh	1641.3	1990.4
5	Ninh Binh	1383.7	936.3
6	Thanh Hoa	11,116.3	3712.5
7	Nghe An	16487.4	3131.0
8	Ha Tinh	6055.6	1307.3
9	Quang Binh	8051.8	857.8
10	Quang Tri	4745.7	635.7
	Total	58483.1	17399.4

Source: Vietnam General Statistic Office. <*http://www.gso.gov.vn*>

To realize this MOU, the two countries' expert group, research institutions and scholars held some science workshops on this topic. For example, from 2005 to 2007, the Vietnam Academy of Social Sciences coordinated with Lao Cai province and Hai Phong city to hold three international conferences, which focused on discussing cooperation in developing the Vietnam-China "two economic corridors and one belt". In this chapter, we would like to mention some individual points of view on this issue:

1. In terms of politics, this is a transnational economic corridor; it has been proved that the mutual political trust between the two countries has made realistic progress, and overcome obstructions of the traditional security concept.

   In terms of economics, economic corridors play a certain role in the economic development of each country and economic relations between the two countries. If this economic corridor is established, it will contribute to strengthen Vietnam-China economic cooperation.

   Particularly, it has an effect on the transition process of economic composition in the area referring to the service field such as transporting, warehouse, port and foreign exchange and so on.

   In the social category, the economic corridor will have "pervasive" and "radiative" impacts which can foster the process of labour division, creates more jobs, and reduce poverty in the area.

Therefore, in the field of politics, economics and society, the Vietnam-China corridors and economic belt will create a lot of benefit and satisfy basic and long-term expectation of two countries' people who rely on friendship and development, and the world trend of peace, cooperation and development.

2. Some thoughts agreed that the establishment of the Vietnam-China economic corridors is important and meaningful; however, the two corridors are lack of capital and socioeconomic infrastructure.

We argue that this is an objective fact. The main solution is we can make use of available advantages to solve the above difficulties. For example, we can connect the economic corridors with other development programmes including the economic corridors in the cooperation programmes of Greater Mekong sub-region (GMS), Zhujiang open economic corridor (9+2) and so on. As a result, we can utilize and develop many different resources from both two countries and other countries.

3. Regarding win-win policy and sharing interest, we would like to suggest some thoughts to develop the "two corridors, one economic belt" as follows:

Firstly, on infrastructure, the two countries need to improve roads connecting Youyi Guan with Hai Phong and Lao Cai in which they can become highways. Along with traffic roads, Vietnam should also improve railroads in the area of the corridors according to the world standard. This is to advance trading exchange between two countries. Moreover, port system in Hai Phong, Quang Ninh, Lao Cai and so on needs to be improved and re-built. The capability of these ports in transporting goods should also be increased.

Secondly, on policies, the two countries shall cooperate in the following fields: exit and entry, custom, trade procedure; and provision of good conditions to transport goods and people through the border gates. Economic corridors go through two countries, but it shall have one policies system, i.e. to implement the single-stop customs inspection model like the Shenzhen-Hong Kong border gate.

Thirdly, to develop the two economic corridors and one belt, we should cooperate on science and technology, particularly social science. For example: in the economic field, the two sides should cooperate in researching the impacts of the two economic corridors on nearby areas and cooperation mechanism for border economic areas; in the field of sociology, we should cooperate to research the economic corridors' role in the poverty reduction process and social issues occurring in the process of developing the economic corridors; in the legal field, we should cooperate to research the role of the laws related to the two economic corridors in settling conflicts appearing in the process of economic cooperation between the two countries; in the field of human sciences, we need to cooperate to research trans-border ethnic issues and problem of cultural identity protection for ethnic minority groups; in the field of environmental protection, we should research problems of environmental protection in the process of the "two economic corridors" cooperation. In general, science and technology play important roles in the development of the two economic corridors. Therefore, we should cooperate in the various fields of science and technology.

Conclusion

Vietnam-China relations have been developing well. This is an important factor to build the "two economic corridors and one belt". On the other hand, when the two corridors are completed, they will promote the development of the two countries' economic relations and consolidate the two countries' political relations. In the construction process of the two economic corridors and one belt, improving and completing the traffic infrastructure system play *important roles*, cooperating in the "single-stop inspection model" custom policies plays a *breakthrough role* and developing tourism is considered as an "early harvest".

The prospect of the Vietnam-China economic cooperation and the "two economic corridors and one belt" cooperation is bright. This is not only beneficial for each country's economic development but will also contribute to the building of the ASEAN-China Free Trade Area (ACFTA).

Notes

*   Associate Professor Do Tien Sam is Director of the Institute of Chinese Studies, Vietnam Academy of Social Sciences (VASS), Member of the Science Board of VASS, Member of the Committee of Vietnam-China Friendship Association, Editor-in-Chief of the *Chinese Studies Review*. He obtained his Bachelor of Chinese Language from Hanoi Foreign Language University and Bachelor of History from Hanoi National University and PhD of History from Vietnam Institute of History. Dr Do Tien Sam's research interests include China's politics, China's history and Vietnam-China relations.

**   Ha Thi Hong Van is a researcher of the Institute of Chinese Studies, Vietnam Academy of Social Sciences (VASS). She obtained her Bachelor of Economics from National Economic University (Vietnam) and MA of International Studies from University of Washington (USA). Her research interests include China's SOE reform, China's economic reform and Vietnam-China economic relations.

References

Do Tien Sam (2005), "Vietnam and China Strengthen to Cooperate and Develop Together", *Chinese Studies Reviews*, Volume 1.

Doan Cong Khanh (2008), "China-Vietnam Trade Relations: Achievements and Problems", *Chinese Studies Reviews*, Volume 4.

Gu Xiao Siong (2005), "Building the Tonkin Gulf Economic Belt, the Depth of Vietnam-China Friendship Cooperation", *Chinese Studies Reviews*, Volume 6.

Nguyen Xuan Thang (2005), "The Economic Corridor Kunming-Lao Cai-Hanoi-Hai Phong", *Chinese Studies Reviews*, Volume 6.

Nguyen Van Lich (2005), "Opening to Develop the Economic Corridor Nanning Lang Son-Hanoi-Hai Phong", *Chinese Studies Reviews*, Volume 6.

Nongli Fu (2005), "The Idea of Building the Economic Corridor Kunming-Lao Cai-Hanoi-Hai Phong", *Chinese Studies Reviews*, Volume 2.

Phan Kim Nga (2007), "China-Vietnam Trade Relations: Current Situation, Prospects and Analyzing the Reason of Unbalance in Trading", *Southeast Studies Reviews* (China), Volume 10.

Vietnam Academy of Social Sciences and the People Committee of Lao Cai (2006), "Cooperating in Building the Economic Corridor Kunming-Lao Cai-Hanoi-Hai Phong: the Roles of Lao Cai", Hanoi: Khoa hoc Xa hoi Publisher.

Vietnam Academy of Social Sciences and the People Committee of Hai Phong (2007), "Developing the Vietnam-China Two Economic Corridors and One Economic Belt within the Framework of ASEAN-China Cooperation", Hanoi: Khoa hoc Xa hoi Publisher.

"Vietnam-China Joint Declaration", Beijing, 1st June 2008. <*http.//vietnamnet,vn/chinhtri/2008/06/786117*>

Vo Van Thanh (2007), "Developing Vietnam-China Two Corridors and One Economic Belt: Will Form Chance of Border Gate Cities?", Tienphong Online. <*http://www.tienphong.vn*>

China's Dilemma:
Rural and Urban

Chapter 6

Whither China's Agriculture and Rural Sector? Some Thoughts on Changes in Rural China and Possible Effects on ASEAN[+]

John A. Donaldson* and Forrest Zhang**

Introduction

What changes are currently occurring in the mode of production in China's agriculture? In what forms are agribusiness companies entering agriculture and interacting with farmers? How are land, labour and capital now controlled by corporate and individual actors, and then organized into agricultural production? How does such control and organization shape relationship among the actors? How do these profound changes in China's agricultural system, especially the scale of agricultural production, affect China's neighbours, especially ASEAN?

In this chapter, we document various forms in which agribusiness companies are transacting with individual agricultural producers, and in doing so, transforming the household-based agriculture in rural China. We argue that the presence of these distinct forms and the diverging relations between agribusiness and producers show the central importance of China's collective land rights. China's unique system of land rights – featuring collective ownership but individualized usage rights – has acted as a powerful force in shaping interactions between agribusiness and direct producers. It provides farmers a source of economic income as well as political bargaining power – albeit to various degrees – and restricts corporate actors from dispossessing farmers of their land. As would be expected, the shift of China's massive agriculture system has important implications for the global economy and especially its neighbours in Southeast Asia.

The first part of this chapter documents the effects of the modernization of China's agriculture on China itself, and considers what pitfalls and prospects China will encounter as a result. The second part of the chapter reflects briefly on the implications of this for the Southeast Asian region.

China's Agriculture: The Social and Political Impacts of Agribusiness

The Household Responsibility System (HRS) started by Deng Xiaoping in 1978 brought land use rights to rural households, providing more leeway for farmers to select crops and market surplus production (Kelliher, 1992; White, 1998; Zweig, 1997). This new institution is credited for bringing, nearly single-handedly, hundreds of millions of poor farmers out of poverty – the fastest rate of rural poverty reduction in world history. At the same time, this move also returned Chinese agriculture to household-based production of miniscule scale and low level of mechanization.[1] Although in the years immediately following the reform, production already began to exceed the strict boundaries of the household in some cases – with some families hiring outside labour and renting the land of others, for instance (Unger, 2002a) – the presence of large-scale production and the role of agribusiness in the process of growing crops has been quite muted. To be sure, firms were involved in the processing and distribution of agricultural products, but by-and-large, in the vast majority of China, production was contained largely within small and scattered plots of land and carried out by members of rural households with severely constrained capital.

Subsequent stagnation in agricultural production led to widespread calls for new measures to further increase agricultural output. Proposed solutions include further developing and disseminating agricultural technology, securing farmers' land rights or even privatizing farm land to enhance farmers' incentives, and, more importantly and of the most interest to this study, scaling up production to achieve economy of scale and introducing large enterprises and modern technologies into agriculture. Other East Asian governments such as Japan, South Korea, and Taiwan, in order to reduce productivity loss caused by land reform, all resorted to some efforts to consolidate the overly parcelized land resulting from their policies of land reforms (Bramall, 2004).[2] Two decades after the HRS reform, the Chinese government also found itself battling the negative legacies of that reform.

Clearly, some changes were in order for agriculture and rural China to transcend the limitations of the HRS reform. Interestingly, in the road map for China's rural development, the central leadership under Deng Xiaoping already identified the next step. In 1990, Deng articulated his vision as the following:

> The reform and development of China's socialist agriculture, from the long-term perspective, requires two great leaps (*liangge feiyue* 两个飞跃). The first leap is dismantling peoples' communes and implementing the Household Responsibility reform. This is a great advance and should be kept in the long term. The second

leap is meeting the needs of scientific agriculture and socialized production, properly developing scaled-up operation, and developing the collective economy.

(Deng, 1993: 355)

These "Two Leaps" have since become the guiding vision for the central government's agricultural policies. Deng further elaborated that, "the rural economy eventually needs to become collectivized (*jitihua* 集体化) and coordinated (*jiyuehua* 集约化) ... agricultural modernization is impossible if each household works on its own." (Deng, 2004: 1349-1350) Since Deng had completed the first leap, for Deng's successors, the assignment was clear: the time has come to make the second leap.

The irony, however, is that the two leaps implied apparently contradictory directions: the first decollectivizes and sets agriculture back to household-based, small-holding operations, while the second tries to re-collectivize and scale up operation beyond the household boundaries. Thus, China's central government had to walk a fine line in order to start the second leap without undoing the first. At the core of the first leap, the HRS, is the household-based land use rights system that restored farmers' incentives and protected their interests. This would therefore remain a central institution in China's agricultural modernization programme.

The policy shift from HRS to the second leap started in the mid-1990s. While Deng only vaguely mentioned "agricultural modernization" as a part of the long-term goals of Four Modernizations, the central leadership under Jiang Zemin started to articulate "agricultural modernization" in more concrete terms and propose policy measures through a series of policy statements, starting from the Ninth Five-Year Plan passed in 1996, to Jiang's report to the 15th Party Congress in 1997, and culminating in the 1998 document of "Decisions by the Central Committee of the Chinese Communist Party on Several Key Issues in Rural and Agricultural Works." The central leadership clearly stated the goal of agricultural modernization (*nongye xiandaihua* 农业现代化) as to make the transition from traditional agriculture to modern agriculture and from uncoordinated and low-scale operation (*cufangshi jingying* 粗放式经营) to coordinated and large-scale operation (*jiyueshi jingying* 集约式经营). The central government characterized a modernized agriculture as commercialized (*shangpinhua* 商品化), specialized (*zhuanyehua* 专业化), scaled up (*guimohua* 规模化), and furthermore, standardized (*biaozhunhua* 标准化) and internationalized (*guojihua* 国际化).

The central leadership also identified agricultural vertical integration (*chanyehua* 产业化) as the main venue to achieve agricultural modernization.[3] Vertical integration here means two parallel processes: First, it means the scaling-up of production of a crop in a region, because without a large enough volume of harvest of a crop, further processing and marketing of it will not be economically viable.[4] Second, it means integrating cultivation of a crop with the processing and marketing of it and its derivatives. The central government believes vertical integration helps to bring farmers into markets and bring modern technologies into farming. At the centre of the government's vertical integration campaign is to promote "dragon head" agribusiness companies (*longtou qiye* 龙头企业) as the main vehicle for vertical integration (Waldron, 2006; Waldron, Brown and Longworth, 2003). Central and local governments bestow "dragon head" status to agribusiness companies. The designated dragon head enterprises can receive some forms of government support, such as easier access to loans from state banks. But as the criteria of designating dragon head enterprises become more lenient down the administrative hierarchy, local dragon head enterprises often receive nothing more than just the title. As a result, agribusiness companies have proliferated in recent years.

The second leap has indeed started and China's agricultural development has entered a new phase – one could say the fourth revolution since 1949, if we trace back to the land reform, the collectivization, and the HRS. Yet, this major change in rural China has barely been discussed in English-language literature. As Waldron (2006) points out, the fast growth of agribusiness is "one of the most important but unreported developments in Chinese agriculture in recent years." (Waldron, 2006: 292) This chapter intends to start the discussion on this new phase of rural development by first investigating a central force in this process of agricultural modernization through vertical integration: agribusiness. We should also point out that before the central government made it a policy priority, a spontaneous process of transforming the household-based agriculture already emerged through the rise of entrepreneurial farmers, who hired labour and rented land to expand their specialized commercial farming beyond the household boundary. Here, however, we will focus on the growth of agribusiness, including the role of agribusiness in the rise of agrarian capitalism in China, the multiple pathways it takes, and the changes it brings to rural society. It is based primarily on fieldwork conducted in 2007 and 2009, as well as insights from previous fieldwork in other provinces and secondary sources.

With this typology (see Table 6.1), we find variations along two dimensions. First, the control over – and use of – labour and land changes. Across these forms, agribusiness firms have varying degrees of control over labour and land *vis-à-vis* direct producers. Second, with changes in the control over land and/or labour, social relationship between actors also change. Most

Table 6.1 Relationships between Agribusiness and Farmers in China: A Typology

Form	Role for agribusiness	Role for direct producers	Harvest	Class relations
1. Commercial farmer	Purchase product, training	Work independently on allocated family land	All for commercial exchange	Direct producers can be dominated by purchasers through unfair terms of trade.
2. Contract farmer	Form purchasing contracts, provide technical support	Work on allocated family land to fulfill company contracts	Sold to contracting companies	Direct producers are dominated by the company, but retain some flexibility.
3. Semi-proletarian with Chinese characteristics	Form bases through leasing village farmland, hire villagers	Work on collective and rented to companies as company employees	Belongs to the company	Direct producers are dominated by the company but enjoy a degree of entitlement.
4. Semi-proletarian farm workers	Form bases through leasing wasteland, hire migrant labourers	Work on company land as company employees, but have allocated land at home	Belongs to the company	Direct producers are dominated by the company, but have family land as fall-back option.
5. Proletarian farm workers	Form bases through leasing wasteland, hire landless labourers	Landless, work on company land as employees	Belongs to the company	Complete domination by the company over direct producers

notably, the power relationship between rural resident (whether acting as a contractor or a farm worker) and agricultural firm is strikingly different in these five forms. Because this shifting power relationship is based on the agribusiness's varying degrees of control over land and labour – but primarily land, the institution of land rights plays a crucial role in shaping such relationship. We argue that the collective land rights system in rural China allows rural residents to resist agribusiness from acquiring more control over farm land and greater domination over them. With this in mind, we sharply disagree with growing calls to eliminate this institution and privatize farm land in China.

Form 1: Commercial Farmers

One of the first types of expanded production, that of "commercial farmer", emerged within a few years of reform (Unger, 2002b). While, as we noted earlier, commercial farming is not new in China (Huang, 1990), commercial farming by rural households was eliminated under collectivization. Its re-emergence depended on the marketization of agricultural products, without which the commercial households could then neither sell their crops nor buy grain. Although many rural households participated in product market by selling their surplus grain or the economic crop they grow in addition to subsistence grain, their subsistence is not commercialized – they relied on their own land and grain for subsistence needs and used commercial farming to earn cash income which supplemented their livelihoods.

By commercial farmer here, we refer to rural households who grow crops (mostly non-staple, economic crops) predominantly for commercial exchange, and satisfy their basic needs through buying grain on markets instead of growing it. The commercialization of the satisfaction of subsistence brings important changes to the peasant households. While still relying on family labour and contracted family land, these households derive their subsistence from markets, which often link them directly with remote actors and social processes that lie beyond the local community. They may still be dominated by outside actors through unfair terms of trade, but they are usually not directly subjected to the domination of local actors, such as an extractive local state.

Mr Chen, a commercial farmer living in the rural areas of Simao Municipality, Yunnan province, is one of many examples. Mr Chen has shifted from growing corn on his farmland to exclusively growing coffee beans. He and his family's shift from growing corn to growing coffee beans occurred over a series of steps. At first, while Chen and his family tended the corn on their own plot, Chen himself worked in an *ad hoc* manner at Beigui, a local coffee producing TVE, where he earned essential cash to supplement subsistence farming, and also learned the skill of growing coffee. Soon afterwards, just as Nestle became active in the area as a buyer of coffee beans, Chen switched from working for Beigui to growing coffee beans on his family's land. Soon, the family, like most of its neighbours, switched completely out of growing corn, and now exclusively grows coffee beans on its 20 *mu* of land[5]. Then, as now, the family sells exclusively to Nestle, which has proven to be a dependable buyer, purchasing coffee beans at the international price (some computer savvy farmers even check the international price on the Internet).

By completely given up subsistence farming, Chen and his family have accepted numerous risks, many of which are out of the family's control, such as the price of coffee which is based on global markets. However, while the fluctuation of the price of coffee beans reportedly has hurt the economic interests of other coffee farmers, Chen reports that such fluctuation does not hurt him much, since he makes at least some money each year – enough to purchase grain and other needs. Chen's family has now invested in preliminary processing equipment, with which they shell, clean, dry and split coffee beans before delivering them to Nestle. Cash from coffee sales allows the family to send their two children to boarding school in the municipal seat.

In order for them to shift out of grain production into an commercial crop, most rural families, like the Chens, require some type of outside impetus to help them learn how to grow new economic crops, provide needed capital and most of all secure a market that mitigates risk. In some cases, when roads (even humble dirt roads) link local areas to marketing towns and beyond, middlemen can come in to purchase such crops, inducing households to increase their production. Oftentimes, however, entrepreneurs and companies provide the needed access to skill, capital and market. Private enterprises, whether domestic companies or foreign ventures, represent channels through which subsistence peasants can shift into commercial farming. However, sometimes, especially for very poor farmers, the state is the only actor with the capability and resources to serve as an outside impetus shifting peasants to commercial farmers. With commercial farming, agricultural production, although still relying on the household as the unit of production, changes from self-reliance and subsistence-based production to market-oriented and commercialized agriculture. These commercial farmers also enter into new sets of relationships with individual, corporate, and state actors, who often mediate their interactions with markets. In such relations, agribusiness firms exert no control on land or labour that belongs to the direct producers.

The commercial farmers are usually not under any direct domination or exploitation, other than the unfavourable terms of trade they may endure on the open market.

Form 2: Contract Farmers

In dealing with independent commercial farmers, agribusiness has to face the uncertainty of fluctuating supply caused by farmers' shifting in and out of a commercial crop – sometimes dramatically – when prices for that crop change. One solution to that problem adopted by many companies is to formally establish contractual relationship with farmers, usually in a contiguous area. In this relationship, the company typically provides farmers with technology, training, service, and in many cases start-up capital. Although the farming households *retain control over their household land* and their own labour, in return for company support, they sign a contract, generally locking them into a selling price, with the promise to sell their entire harvest to the company. We call these the "contract farmers".

One of the many examples that we discovered of this type of production is Xinchang Foods, the Shandong poultry meat processing company, whose story we relayed at the beginning. In addition to the poultry processing facilities, this company also has two plants for processing microwavable food, such as TV dinners. Established in 1988, the company now reportedly employs more than 8,000 people, and has revenue in excess of Rmb800 million. As mentioned earlier, the company estimates that about 40 per cent of its production comes from such a base formed through contracts directly with the farmers.[6] In doing so, the company contracts out with approximately 10,000 households in the surrounding areas. The company guarantees a minimum, or "protective" price (*baohu jia* 保护价), pays the farmers immediately upon delivery and has overall established a solid relationship with the farmers over the course of the previous decade.

Farmers who produce under contract with this company confirm much of the company's point of view, agreeing that the company provides inputs such as animal feed and technical and safety training (in part to combat bird flu). For instance, Mr Zhao's farmland contains three duck coops and more than 8,600 ducks which he husbands, selling the full-grown ducks (after 46 days, he notes) back to the company. Through his association with the company, Mr Zhao reported that he can earn Rmb1500 on average each month. However, he argues that the company, because of its size and market position, holds the preponderance of the power, which it uses to hold down the purchasing price to Rmb1 for each grown duck Mr Zhao and his family raise. Mr Zhao lives in an urbanizing area and his family land has shrunk from 1.7 *mu* per capita to about 0.3 *mu*, due to land expropriation by the state for urban expansion (which he has only been inadequately compensated for, he adds). Now, instead of growing grain as they had previously, Mr Zhao and his family dedicate most of their land to raising ducklings, retaining a small plot for growing melons and other self-consumed vegetables. In fact, given their limited land, animal husbandry might be one of a few viable options in the agriculture sector that the Zhao family has left. In his relationship with Xinchang Foods, although farmers like Mr Zhao still retain their entitlement to land use rights provided by the village collective and are not subjected to personal domination in the labouring process, they nevertheless have relegated much of the control over the production and its final products to the company, as the company now sets the parameters of production and has the monopsony over their products. The company also facilitated the specialization and scaling-up of agricultural production by organizing tens of thousands of formerly scattered and isolated farmer households into specialized, coordinated, and standardized production.

Like the commercial farmers who have departed from subsistence agriculture and now rely on production of commercial crops, these contract farmers usually grow economic crops exclusively for commercial exchange, transact with outside actors, and depend for their subsistence on the market. The two differ, however, on one key aspect: due to their lack of access to capital, market or skill, contract farmers have to enter into formal contractual relationship with a more powerful and resourceful corporate actor. By providing them with the needed capital, skill, and/or market access, the corporate actor is thus able to reduce contract farmers' negotiating power and profit margin. The farmer commits legally to selling his product only to the contracting company. In such a relationship, farmers only provide labour and land. In contrast, commercial farmers enjoy a market-set price for their products, instead of one dictated by the contracting company, and have the flexibility of selling to the highest bidder at harvest time. Theoretically, contract farmers do enjoy one advantage: they can shield themselves from market risks by obtaining from the company the protective price for their products.[7] In our fieldwork, we routinely found farmers, sometimes even the local governments, try to obtain protective prices from the contracting company, often to no avail.

Due to their domination by corporate actors, although contract farmers like Mr Zhao's are probably better off economically than they were under subsistence farming, they are typically not as well off as independent commercial farmers. Partly in response to their unfavourable position *vis-à-vis* the companies, contract farmers have often neglected the contract and sold their harvest to other purchasers who, without bearing production costs the contracting company incurred, offered higher prices. This has created a phenomenon known as the "middleman problem" – referring to itinerant middlemen who drive around and secretly purchase products from companies' production bases. In other cases, according to one report, contract farmers tried to deflate cost by cutting corners in the production process, resulting in product defects (Li, 2008). Due to these difficulties, we believe that contract farming as a form of agrarian capitalism is unstable and likely to be transient, changing to either commercial farming or to the form we discuss next.[8]

Form 3: Semi-proletarian Farm Workers with Chinese Characteristics

From a contracting company's perspective, a long-term solution to the middleman problem can only come from gaining greater control over the growing and harvesting process and changing farmers' incentive structure. In practice, agribusiness firms establish production bases by renting the land (use rights) from the collective owner, the village, and hiring village residents, who, as members of the collective, are entitled to land use rights, as company employees to work on the land. In some cases, rural households still work on the piece of household land allocated to them by the collective – although now rented to the company base – growing whatever the company asks them to grow. In other cases, land is consolidated and household boundaries erased, farmers simply work for the company on company land. Even when farmers continue to work on the allocated household land, a profound change has happened: they are now only providing labour in the production process, while the land use rights – and the right to dispose of harvest from the land – are controlled by the company.

To this form, we add the appendage "with Chinese characteristics" because we argue that without the unique institution of collective land ownership and individualized land use rights in rural China, this form might not come to pass. The companies that are forming the base typically establish the contractual relationship with the village collective authorities, not with the individual farmer as is the case with the contract farmer. Because the collective land ownership restricts village authorities from disenfranchising rural residents from their land, it also restricts companies from denying rural residents jobs on company production bases. Without such a restriction, an enclosure movement led by these companies could easily have thrown many farmers off their land and into the army of reserve labour. In this way, farmers become semi-proletarian, in that they still have an entitlement to collective land (and in fact often receive rent for renting out this means of production to the company), yet at the same time, they have to sell their labour to the company for wages. In a sense, these farmers trade their land use rights for jobs. Their entitlement to collective land gives them entitlement to company jobs, and thus, in one sense, they "own" or have rights to their jobs in a way unlike proletarianized workers.

One of the examples of this form, Taiwan's Qianhui Flower Company, based in Chenggong County, Yunnan, rents 70 per cent of its land from collectives through contracts of at least seven years. It then pays members of the household a monthly wage to grow and harvest the flowers on their own land. This company currently has 10 such bases throughout Yunnan, giving it different environments in which to grow a wide variety of flowers. This company emphasized that once the household is contracted, the farmer cannot individually withdraw their land from the arrangement, because the land is contracted through the village committee to the base. Qianhui does not have a big problem with middlemen. Considering selling the product to outsiders to be a criminal issue, Qianhui works with local law enforcement to enforce their contracts with farmers.

Although these semi-proletarian farm workers with Chinese characteristics do benefit economically from this type of arrangement, they clearly lose autonomy and the greater economic benefit that commercial or contract farmers have. Compared to contract farmers, semi-proletarian farm workers not only have relinquished use rights over their collective land (although they often receive rent for that), they are also subjected to tighter company control in the production process. As a result of both, unlike contract farmers, they totally lose control over the harvest. While the company pays wages to farm workers, it also takes profits from the surplus that would otherwise belong to the farmers. Farmers are also largely deprived of the opportunities to undercut company's domination by selling to middlemen for higher margins. Despite these shortcomings, when rural residents lack capital and know-how, and will often benefit financially by making this sort of arrangement with agribusiness. From the company's point of view, this form is a relatively painless way to obtain control over farm land and overcome the middleman problem. However, companies have also found other ways to obtain even greater control over their employees, the production process and the harvest.

Form 4: Semi-proletarian Farm Workers

Under this form the company owns or otherwise controls the land of its production bases, and hires rural workers. The farm worker, who migrated to the company's production base, still possesses use rights over his or her own land, but their land is elsewhere – and has usually been rented out to relatives, neighbours or entrepreneurs. Hence, the labourer is classified as "Semi-proletarian Farm Workers": they sell labour for wages, yet still retain access to some means of production, although not directly used.

The Dahongpo Coffee Plantation in western Yunnan province controls a base of some 7,000 *mu*, of which 4,500 *mu* is currently cultivated with coffee plants. The company leases land that was previously classified as wasteland – mostly on mountain slopes – for its base with long-term leases that expire in 2030. The company got capital support from the Bank of Agriculture and an ear-marked World Bank loan to invest in infrastructure building. The local government was also involved in the early years in attracting poor peasants to come and grow coffee on the base. The entire process of growing and harvesting is tightly controlled by the company. Like most others of its kind, this company provides land, training, fertilizer, pesticides, seeds and other inputs. The company has a hierarchical organizational structure in place to supervise farm workers. The company passes down orders through this hierarchy to farm workers on every production procedure, ranging from when to apply fertilizer and pesticide to when to start harvesting. Materials such as seeds, fertilizers, and pesticides are also distributed from the company, through the teams and down to each worker family. The company does not charge rent from the workers, but establishes a production quota for each *mu* of land. The company and farm worker split the within-quota harvest on a 6:4 ratio, and 100 per cent of the sales from above-quota harvest belongs to the farm worker. Company representatives acknowledge that the harvest belongs to the company, but argue that the company chooses to give workers a share in the harvest – in lieu of wage – in order to attract workers. The company's control of land and close monitoring of the entire production process means that farm workers here have much less flexibility in comparison to the contract farmer, who work on their own land. Farm workers not only have great difficulties in "stealing" the harvest and sell it to middlemen for higher prices, as the company can relatively easily determine the output from each household's plot, they also face dire consequences if caught doing so – the company considers such selling to outsiders theft of company assets and will kick the workers off the farm as punishment.

This company leaves the impression of a benevolent employer. Not only it gives farm workers a generous cut in the proceeds from the harvest, it has also provided land for migrant farm workers to build their own housing (this is also out of necessity, so that workers can live in the field and tend the crops more closely). The easy availability of "undeveloped land" in the area and the relative tight labour supply (the area has a large minority population, who are less receptive of the idea of becoming hired employees) means that the company has to offer better terms to attract migrant labourers, whose access to entitled collective land at home also serves to strengthen their bargaining power. Many companies that operate production bases in this form are constrained in a similar way: the large area of land they can gain control of is rarely prime farm land, but reclaimed wasteland of various sorts, located in remote areas, another legacy of China's collective land system. During interviews, company representatives repeatedly stressed that had they had access to better farm land that is not burdened with a population of entitled villagers, they would not have bothered with the wasteland they currently used. When facing the choice of renting collectively owned land and then hiring villagers versus opening up wasteland and hiring migrant labourers, many companies eschewed the former for the complex relations it creates between companies, village authorities, and villagers. From the farm worker's point of view, however, while the company provides job opportunities that would not otherwise exist, their power base is quite constrained, resting in the form of escape clause the land back home that the worker retains.

Form 5: Proletarian Farm Workers

The final form discussed here that has emerged in China is similar to the previous type, except that the farm workers are landless labourers without major viable alternative livelihoods. The Beigui Coffee Company started off in the 1980s as a TVE under the prefecture Supply and Sales Cooperative (SSC, *gongxiao she*) in Yunnan's Simao Prefecture (now Pu'er Municipality), and reformed to a stock-holding company in 1998, with the SSC holding the majority stake, and workers each holding shares. Of the 10,000 *mu* base that the company controls, half is rented from farmers and half was previously classified wasteland that the company leased long-term (50 years) from the village collective. The operation involves 2,000 farmers, most of whom are stable farm workers who move their entire families from poor areas, primarily Zhaotong Municipality in northeastern Yunnan, one of China's poorest regions.[9] However, unlike the previous forms, the company encourages peasants to give up their land rights in their home villages and to obtain a local permanent resident permit, which, however, does not grant them any entitlement to collective land. These re-located migrant workers thus become second-class citizens in their adopted villages–they are members of the villages, their children can go to local schools, they have most of the political rights of any other villager, but do not have access to collectively-owned land.

This arrangement makes the farm workers closely dependent on the company. Workers can earn income from three sources: first, for each *mu* of coffee shrubs under their cultivation, they earn a labour wage of Rmb15; second, as a bonus to give workers more incentive, the company also pays a weight-based purchasing fee for the coffee beans workers yield; and third, workers can also earn a picking fee during peak harvesting season if they are hired to do picking for the company. Like Dahongpo, at Beigui, the company also takes total control over the production process. Given the larger size of Beigui (2000 workers in 600 households, compared to 600 workers in 168 households at Dahongpo), the company organizes their production in a three-tiered hierarchy: company – farms – teams. While team leaders are selected from farm workers, managerial staff at the farm level is full-time employees of the company. Overall, the company is supervised with more than 30 salaried staff, managing the production process in a top-down manner.

The company argues that the farmers as a result are far better off than they were. Given that these farmers are from one of China's poorest areas, and that they do migrate to Baoshan voluntarily, that is likely to be true. The company estimates farm workers earn between Rmb20,000-30,000 per household, which is far higher than the net rural income of any county in Zhaotong prefecture. While these poor farm workers likely benefit financially to some degree and even emerge from poverty, in terms of political and social power, they are the weakest among the forms that we have highlighted here. Since land acts as a type of insurance policy on which poor farmers can often fall back as they migrate or take other risks in order to improve their livelihoods, the fact that Beigui asks farmers to switch their household registrations, in effect giving up their rights to land, makes them unusually dependent on the company and base. On the other hand, the company's need to attract farmers to work on the base limits the extent to which they can exploit this dependence.

More interestingly, these migrant farm workers are relocated in villages where farmers have their own land usage rights. Therefore, in that same village, we find two classes of farmers live right next to each other, yet in contrasting conditions. Most of the relocated landless farm workers live at the centre of the village in houses built by Beigui, with some living sparsely in the field – also in company built housing. Other residents, on the other hand, who have become wealthy growing vegetables and other commercial crops, live in self-built houses on their own land, surround by coffee groves. Although these two groups of villagers do socialize with each other, a sense of distinction between the two is palpable through our conversations with both.

Agribusiness, Scaling-up and the Modernization of China's Agriculture

In some rural areas in today's China, the central government's vision of a "second leap" into a modern agriculture has become a reality. The household-based, small-holding agricultural production reinstated by the HRS has been transformed into specialized, commercialized, vertically integrated, and larger-scale agriculture that is competitive on export market. Shouguang County in Shandong province, for example, boasts the largest vegetable production base and vegetable trading market in the country, with hundreds of long-haul trucks departing daily to ship vegetables to all corners of the country. The entire county's farmland is fully covered by greenhouses for growing vegetables. Chenggong County in Yunnan, where agriculture has shifted entirely to commercial flower and vegetable production, now houses the largest flower trading and auction market in Asia, ships fresh cut flowers to markets in neighbouring Asian countries as well as the United States, and is projected to become in 10 to 15 years the biggest flower producer and exporter in Asia, if not in the world (Bradsher, 2006).

The diverse ways agribusiness enter agriculture and interact with direct producers, as we documented above, show how distinctive characteristics of China's rural institutions create unique patterns in China's path toward agrarian capitalism. The relationship between agribusiness – representing capital from local, urban, or even international origins – and direct producers will become the most important relationship in the new scaled-up, vertically integrated, modern agricultural sector and the relationship that shapes China's rural society in coming years. Our research underscores how this relationship is shaped by the system of collective land ownership and individualized land use rights of rural China. This system has proven to be not only adaptable, but in fact, conducive to development of rural markets and agricultural modernization. The separation of individualized land use rights from collective ownership has allowed land rental markets to develop rapidly. Land rental markets then facilitate the circulation of land and consolidation of parcelized land into larger operations, paving the road for scaled-up production needed by agribusiness.

On the other hand, the collective ownership protects agricultural producers – to various degrees – against the domination, exploitation and dispossession by outside capital. Nearly all of the companies that we interviewed expressed a desire to expand their production bases. While China's paradoxical lack of skilled and educated labour constrains to a certain extent the ability of companies to achieve this, the primary barrier to expanding bases is the lack of land – or, put in another way, the difficulty in wresting control over collective land from rural households. In fact, many companies and entrepreneurs that have formed bases have to do so on previously unproductive land that they themselves have opened up. For many companies however, the lack of undeveloped space means that they must expand through using land that is currently farmed by small rural households. In many other countries, in such battles pitting powerful corporations against unorganized small farmers, the rise of agrarian capitalism proceeded in a *Grapes of Wrath* fashion, with capital owners consolidating land through dispossessing smallholding farmers. In China, farmers' protected land rights under the collective ownership provide them nearly the only piece of political power over the companies. As a result, agricultural modernization in rural China so far has progressed in the more equitable ways as we described above and has not created an expanding army of landless vagabonds.

To be sure, there were cases of companies throwing around their political weight. For instance, village collectives can commit farmers to renting out their land to company bases, one pathway (Form 3) to the creation of semi-proletarian farm workers. One entrepreneur used his pull with local authorities to have forested land reclassified as wasteland, allowing him to purchase it from the village and create a privately owned and operated commercial orchard. He then used help from his brother-in-law, who was the village head, to form the base on favourable terms. Despite the use of company power, however, in no case did we encounter land grabs in order to form production bases, even though this would solve the shortage of farmland, a major constraint for companies and entrepreneurs, who would doubtlessly benefit from it. Some companies in Yunnan, unhappy with the restrictions they faced under China's collective land system, have in fact ventured into Laos, Vietnam and Myanmar to acquire land and expand their production.

Thirty years ago, the Household Responsibility reform established the institution of household-based land use rights under collective ownership, giving Chinese farmers an economically inalienable entitlement to land – a crucial resource that is denied farmers of most other countries. Indeed, this institution was so important and effective in restoring farmers' incentives that within a few short years after the reform started, poverty rates plummeted. Today, even as many farmers turn to – and even prosper from – off-farm jobs, most manoeuvre to maintain their land rights back home, for these rights provide a type of insurance policy that diversifies income and protects against misfortune. However, critics worried that Deng Xiaoping's reforms would permanently condemn China and her farmers to inefficient, low-tech, small-scale, traditional agricultural production. Indeed, these shortcomings of the household responsibility system, together with policy changes unfavourable to the agricultural sector, have resulted in rural stagnation in the 1900s. As a result, the government seeks ways of expanding production through vertical integration and other forms of modernization. At their base, these plans and approaches require an increase in scale of production. In this process, China's central government faced a crucial dilemma: the productive potential of these small plots of land have apparently been reached, but how to modernize agriculture without taking away farmers' household-based land use rights? This chapter has revealed one of China's solutions to this dilemma, one that allows agricultural production to expand and modernize without eliminating the crucial institution that benefited hundreds of millions of farmers. The collective land ownership has proven to be a flexible system that allows agribusiness and scale production to grow through a variety of forms, while maintaining a modicum of rights and material benefits for China's farmers.

Implications for ASEAN

How will the nations of ASEAN be affected by the increase in scale and involvement of agribusiness in China? One thing is certain – that these changes in China will affect in a number of ways the agricultural sections in Southeast Asia. Economic ties between China and ASEAN have never been stronger. Last year, despite the global financial crisis, trade volume between the two partners shot past the US$230 billion mark, raising expectations that ASEAN will soon replace Japan as China's third largest trading partner.[10] Whether these changes in China will have an overall positive or negative impact on ASEAN is much less certain. Below, we discuss a number of aspects of this issue.

One implication for ASEAN relates to food safety. Last year's Sanlu milk scandal sparked widespread concerns about the quality of China's food exports – not just milk. The modernization of the agricultural sector has created a number of links in a production chain from farmer to middle-man to processors to manufacturers to distributors. Each link in this chain must be monitored, a matter that would be daunting for any economy, let alone one a large and complex polity that is rapidly reforming and struggling to meet the challenges of institutionalizing for a market economy. The problem is multifaceted and has occurred through a number of channels. To be sure, some farmers who are squeezed between fixed contract prices and rising production costs have resorted to using cheaper, substandard inputs in the production process. More importantly, however, some unscrupulous firms that purchase from these farmers either turn a blind eye to these dodgy practices as they are more concerned about getting the supply to meet the surging demand, or are actually responsible for the problem, as they struggle to compete in a context of little to no effective regulatory oversight. The increased involvement of sometimes unscrupulous middlemen, difficult to monitor and often fly-by-night operators, is another vexing problem.[11] China's regulatory regime, meanwhile, has struggled to keep pace with the modernization and privatization of industry. The distance – both actual and symbolic – between central regulators and local authorities in a rapidly decentralizing context also contributes to this problem. Endemic corruption has also worsened the command-and-control issues that China faces. Until China is able to enforce its own regulations on the agricultural sector, ASEAN nations may be compelled to initiate its own regulatory measures on food-related imports from China, in order to assuage the concerns of its populace. This can be difficult, particularly in nations with weak regulatory and monitoring institutions. For such developing countries, stricter regulations may also further increase the price of food. Even relatively more developed nations will need to be wary about imposing more stringent regulations, as China may view such policies as protectionist or discriminatory in nature.

Another implication is that Chinese agribusinesses, frustrated with the institution of land usage rights, and the consequent restrictions on the acquisition of land, are increasingly setting their sights on Southeast Asia for expansion. The Chinese government, anxious about the need to satisfy the country's growing demand for food, commodities and natural resources, has also been encouraging Chinese companies to invest in land and natural resources acquisition overseas. These include such Southeast Asian nations as Laos, Cambodia and Vietnam. While such capital investments, particularly in the developing nations in Southeast Asia, have brought about some agricultural modernization and higher crop yields in the receiving countries, they come at a price in terms of social and environmental costs. In Laos for example, there have been allegations that small-scale farmers are selling away their lands to private investors at "inconceivably low fee rates".[12] Chinese investments in the timber trade in Cambodia and Myanmar have also been accused for the large-scale deforestation in these two countries.[13] The social and political impact of China's investment in these areas requires further research. How to weigh these costs and benefits of Chinese investment also remains an open question.

Many other potential implications remain to be explored. Will modernization in rural China open the floodgates to allow mass migration of Chinese farm workers and agricultural entrepreneurs to Southeast Asia, and if so, to what effect on society and politics? Will such investments provoke a backlash against China's economic policies in Southeast Asia, and put political pressure on governments to reform the administration of rural land and natural resources? This is but a partial list of questions. Further research will be needed to cast more light on the complex relationship between China's agricultural developments and its impact on ASEAN.

Notes

+   The authors acknowledge the research grant support from Singapore Management University's Office of Research. We thank Professor Cheng Housi of Yunnan University of Nationalities for facilitating fieldwork in Yunnan. The authors also thank Phoebe Luo Mingxuan for her assistance on this paper. Much of this paper is based on Qian Forrest Zhang and John A. Donaldson (2008), "The Rise of Agrarian Capitalism with Chinese Characteristics: Agricultural Modernization, Agribusiness and Collective Land Rights", *The China Journal*, Issue 60, July, pp. 25-48.

*   Dr John Donaldson, Assistant Professor of Political Science at Singapore Management University, studies local rural poverty reduction policies in China, as well as central-provincial relations. His research has been published in journals such as *World Development*, *International Studies Quarterly*, *China Journal* and *China Quarterly*. John received his PhD from George Washington University.

**   Dr Forrest Zhang, Assistant Professor of Sociology at Singapore Management University, studies social change in contemporary China. His research focuses on rural development, especially stratification and mobility. He is currently working on a project using family histories to study mobility patterns over the past 50 years under the People's Republic during a period of dramatic social change. Forrest's articles have appeared in *China Quarterly*, *China Journal* and *Journal of Marriage and Family*. Forrest graduated with a PhD from Yale University.

1. There are numerous areas in China, especially in wheat growing areas, where mechanized farming still prevails.

2. It is, however, a debatable issue as to whether land consolidation really leads to productivity gains. If farm size increases, but not to the extent of allowing mechanization and not associated with increased labour input, land productivity may actually decline due to reduced per unit labour input and a lower intensity of land-use. Land consolidation has to be carried out in certain specific ways – e.g., moving land to more efficient users – to increase productivity. See Q. Forrest Zhang,, "Retreat from Equality or Advance Toward Efficiency? Land Markets and Inequality in Rural Zhejiang", *China Quarterly*, 2008, 195, pp. 535-557, for a discussion.

3. Throughout this chapter, we use "agricultural modernization", or "modern agriculture", to refer to the mode of agricultural production as described by the set of policy goals stated in the above, including specialization, vertical integration, corporatization, commercialization, and large scale. We, however, refrain from

making claims about whether this modernized agriculture is necessarily more efficient, which is an empirical question that needs to be answered with data.

4. The scaling up here, however, does not necessarily mean production needs to be done at a supra-household level. It could simply mean more households in a region shift to growing a certain crop, so the scale of production for that crop increases in a region.

5. 1 *mu* 亩 = 0.0667 hectares.

6. A further 40-50 per cent of their production comes from a more formal contract with village governments, Form 3 in our typology. Thus, this case, as with many others, produces through multiple forms.

7. In their survey, Guo, Jolly, and Zhu (2007) found that only 27.3 per cent of contracts in their survey featured a price floor, with 23 per cent based on a fixed price. The remaining 44 per cent of these contracts were based on the market price, offering farmers little protection.

8. This is consistent with a survey conducted by China's Ministry of Agriculture that reveals among the different types of relationships between farmer and firm, the proportion of contract farming relationships dropped from 70.8 per cent to 49.0 per cent. See Niu (2002), also reported in Guo, Jolly, and Zhu (2007).

9. Mr Chen, described above, is an exception, having worked for years for Beigui as a temporary worker.

10. CCTV, "China-ASEAN Trade Tops US$230 bln", 10th April 2009 <*http://www.cctv.com/english/20090410/109563.shtml*>, downloaded 18th April 2009; Xinhua, "MOC official: ASEAN likely to become China's third largest trade partner", 11th April 2009 <*http://english.peopledaily.com.cn/90001/90776/90884/6634770.html*>, downloaded 18th April 2009.

11. Q. Forrest Zhang, "How Melamine Entered the Food Chain", *The Straits Times*, p. A22, 13th December 2008; Austin Ramsy, "China's Tainted-Milk Scandal Spreads", *Time*, 26th September 2008 <*http://www.time.com/time/world/article/0,8599,1844750,00.html*>.

12. Jeff Rutherford, Kate Lazarus and Shawn Kelley, "Rethinking Investments in Natural Resources: China's Emerging Role in the Mekong Region", International Institute for Sustainable Development, 2008.

13. Hing Vutha and Hossein Jalilian, "Environmental Impacts of the ASEAN-China Free Trade Agreement on the Greater Mekong Sub-Region", Cambodia Development Resource Institute, September 2008. <*http://www.atimes.com/atimes/Southeast_Asia/GJ20Ae01.html*>

References

Bradsher, Keith (2006), "Bouquet of Roses May Have Note: 'Made in China'", *New York Times*, New York.

Bramall, Chris (2004), "Chinese Land Reform in Long-Run Perspective and in the Wider East Asian Context", *Journal of Agrarian Change*, 4, pp. 107-141.

Deng, Xiaoping (1993), *Deng Xiaoping Wenxuan* [Collected works of Deng Xiaoping], Vol. 3, Beijing: Renmin Chubanshe (The People's Publishing House).

Deng, Xiaoping (2004), *Deng Xiaoping Nianpu, 1975-1997* [Chronicles of Deng Xiaoping, 1975-1997], Beijing: Zhongyang Wenxian Chubanshe (The Central Archives Press).

Huang, Philip C.C. (1990), *The Peasant Family and Rural Development in the Yangzi Delta, 1350-1988*, Stanford CA: Stanford University Press.

Kelliher, Daniel (1992), *Peasant Power in China: The Era of Rural Reform, 1979-1989*, New Haven and London: Yale University Press.

Li, Hongbin (2008), "Zai Nongye Chanyehua Fazhan zhong Peiyu he Tigao Nongmin Zuzhihua Chengdu Yanjiu" [A study on nurturing and strengthening the organization of farmers through developing agricultural vertical integration], *Nongye Jingji Wenti* [Issues in agricultural economy], pp. 99-102.

Unger, Jonathan (2002a), "Chapter 5: Disbanding Collective Agriculture", in J. Unger (ed.), *The Transformation of Rural China*, NY: M.E. Sharpe, pp. 95-118.

Unger, Jonathan (2002b), *The Transformation of Rural China*, Armonk, NY: M.E. Sharpe.

Waldron, Scott (2006), "State Sector Reform and Agriculture in China", *The China Quarterly*, 186, pp. 277-294.

Waldron, Scott, Colin Brown and John W. Longworth (2003), *Rural Development in China: Insights from the Beef Industry*, Aldershot: Ashgate.

White, Lynn (1998), *Unstately Power*, Armonk, NY: M.E. Sharpe.

Zhang, Forrest Q (2008), "Retreat from Equality or Advance Toward Efficiency? Land Markets and Inequality in Rural Zhejiang", *China Quarterly*, 195, pp. 535-557.

Zweig, David (1997), *Freeing China's Farmers: Rural Restructuring in the Reform Era*, Armonk, NY: M.E. Sharpe.

Chapter 7

Finding a Home in China's "Restless Urban Landscape"

Kate **Hannan***

Introduction

In China, well-heeled permanent urban residents with market power have been able to purchase and occupy the new housing situated in the most desired urban locations, while less favoured residents have found that they must relocate to more distant parts of the city. Those who have been obliged to relocate have also found that the compensation they have been paid for vacating their central urban homes under pressure from developers and urban planners, is often insufficient to access a comparable residence in a different location. At the same time, a substantial number of those who have been living at the urban/rural margin have been able to negotiate with developers and so improve their "life-chances", while others living in a similar location have had their land unfairly acquisitioned by self-interested developers and local administrators. In parallel with this situation, rural-to-urban migrants who have found wage-paying employment in cities have been obliged to accept hostel accommodation that is often crowded (eight, ten or twelve bunks or more to a room is usual in female factory accommodation), to live in temporary dwellings erected on construction sites, or find relatively cheap low quality urban housing where-ever they can. In this chapter I will discuss a number of issues related to finding a home in China's "restless" and ever-changing urban landscape[1].

In China's cities the use of centrally located urban land for industrial purposes is a practice that has passed. Centrally located land now accommodates the apartment buildings, town-houses, office-blocks and shopping centres that provide the accommodation, work environment and services required by China's better off permanent urban residents. Office blocks and retail outlets have "clustered in places of high accessibility and formed new commercial centres". At the same time, the development of an effective housing market has led to the establishment of desirable urban neighbourhoods. These neighbourhoods are located away from industrial areas and the immediate noise and other pollution, including some aspects of the air pollution that accompanies them. They are also a long way from the older "socialist"/ centrally administered Chinese experience of state-owned enterprise owned housing that surrounded manufacturing plants and was available to administrators and factory workers. The latter older and now superseded form of housing had a status component with the best and most convenient housing going to the most senior and best connected personnel, but all enterprise employees lived in the same general geographic area. The housing and the factories and other amenities were often contained within a wall that denoted the boundaries of the enterprise "kingdom". This form of housing was usually a better standard than directly government owned housing occupied by local administrators, teachers, medical staff and others. Today, the walls that surround specific urban areas surround housing compounds. They are marking out the boundaries of many gated, up-market urban apartment and town house developments. The well established practice of marking out the geographic boundary of communities continues.[2]

The post-reform redevelopment of China's cities that began in the 1980s and continued to pick up pace until the present global economic crisis (the crisis has led to "property prices going down by big margins everywhere"), has been attended by significant problems. The self-regarding interests of developers, their financiers and local urban administrators has been attended by considerable resentment among urban residents who have been closed out of much of the urban property market due to the high cost of purchasing newly constructed urban apartments. It has, of course, also been resented by the residents of housing that has been demolished to make way for the up-market town-house, apartment, office-block and shopping complex developments.[3]

Under Communist Party policy and centralized administration residential mobility had been low until the process of economic reform reached the point of offering a market for housing. The system of residential registration combined with urban residents' housing needs attached to their employment by state-owned enterprises or by local and central government administrations led to a security of housing tenure that some would describe as not only extremely stable, but also stultifying (it was not unusual for adult children to inherit their parents' jobs when they retired and some also inherited their parents' apartments as well). Now, after almost three decades of economic reform the rights that had been associated with a worker's or even a family's occupancy of a particular job and a government- or enterprise-owned apartment have been overtaken by the right of individuals to find employment in the market-place and to purchase their housing needs. However, China's urban housing market has increasingly favoured better-off urban residents. As I have been arguing, today urban housing is recognized as being "out of reach for many of the lower- and middle-class residents". It is noted that "after experiencing a 10-year rosy growth, the unit price of commercial houses is now far beyond the purchasing capability of the majority of urban dwellers". At the same time, the construction of urban housing that would be sold providing healthy profits for developers and their connections continues to depend on connections in combination with market measures. Just as the practice of marking the boundaries of communities with walls has continued, the entrenched Chinese practice of *guanxi* (social connections) that continued and was much used during the period of centralized administration has been carried over into the present period of marketization. Under economic reform and particularly during the most recent redevelopment of China's cities, connections have been essential when accessing the resources, particularly financial backing, access to urban land, and compensation and urban planning approvals required to construct apartments, office blocks, shopping plazas and other prestigious projects in sought after urban areas.[4]

Developers, Local Administrators and Relocated Urban Residents

In the early stages of the most recent wholesale redevelopment of China's cities state-owned enterprise managers were quick to take the trade in land use seriously. In the 1980s, in the early stages of the process of developing a market for land use, state-owned enterprise managers were particularly inventive when converting industrial and enterprise residential and land assets. They traded in kind, quite often becoming partners in new ventures where they had contributed land use rights that had previously been exercised by "their" enterprise. The need for effective government control over land use soon became both apparent and acute and it is now well recognized that in terms of redevelopment practices government policies over first land use acquisition and then housing were inadequate. Moreover, current unsatisfactory practices in relation to land and housing reform in China's urban spaces are a direct consequence of both the government's initial and on-going "failure to control the flow of capital into property markets". A significant "urban sprawl", an "overheated real-estate sector", and housing that can only be accessed by those who have considerable market advantage relative to their fellow urban citizens, are all a result of inadequate regulation of urban development and the remarkable level of self-interested and short-term profiteering that has persisted. While there were a range of extenuating circumstances that have fed China's fast-paced urban development (including substantial foreign funds some in the form of so-called "hot money" – speculative capital), there can be little doubt that China's urban land and housing reform has depended on (and has promoted) the group of self-interested domestic players who, alongside their foreign counterparts, have not only ensured that their own interests with respect to their land and housing dealings have been met, but have also quite often gone "beyond their legal and budgetary limits [in order] to tap profits ..." These speculators and developers have also had what some commentators aptly describe as an "excessive dependence on [continued] national economic growth".[5]

Though state-owned enterprise managers had already been bartering enterprise land use for alternative assets, the market became the principle formal medium of land use exchange after Beijing had separated land ownership from land use rights. However, connections (*guanxi*) and the profit and status stakes that property developers, their financial backers and local officials had in city construction, development and renewal immediately infected this system. As property owners, Chinese families are formally "entitled to land use rights for up to seventy years after they buy their home". However, government administrators, central and local, subsequently awarded themselves the right to override this claim to the point where it is worthless. Administrative override of the seventy year land-use claim is valid when:

(1) the land is to be used for the public interest;
(2) the transfer goes through legal procedures; and
(3) reasonable compensation is provided.

Given that the above three caveats were adopted in the context of established groups of profit seeking government, financial and private development players, it is not at all surprising that housing demolition and rebuilding proceeded apace in China's cities. Matters were then made worse when the Chinese government saw fit to issue an edict that was aimed at preventing residents of existing housing stock from objecting to their relocation and/or level of compensation. Residents were obliged to act in a manner that did not "threaten the construction of public projects". While residents may file a lawsuit in opposition to relocation and other related matters, in practice this ill-conceived government directive against residents' objection to redevelopment projects "denied citizens the legal right to protect their homes".[6]

The government's attempt to stop resident opposition to relocation has not stopped homeowner resistance. Many cases of resistance have been documented. While individual homeowner resistance cannot be expected to be effective in blocking redevelopment projects, collective action has certainly been used to delay relocation. Developers and local authorities have denied homeowners the right to negotiate and so homeowners have sought help from different government agencies. They have appealed to the Ministry of Construction in Beijing, going over the head of local government departments and administrators to central government agencies. Residents facing relocation expected their grievances to be listened to in spite of the edict decreeing that they cannot "threaten the construction of public projects". For their part Beijing administrators indicated that they were concerned over the problems associated with urban resident relocation with the central government's State Council urging "prudent handling [of] urban housing demolition". Home owners also presented their grievances to provincial complaints bureaus and to the standing committee of the Provincial People's Congress. In addition, they used legal avenues to block developers and/or to seek a higher level of compensation for the homes they would loose. They have even used physical patrols, including night patrols, to ensure that a developer cannot simply send in machinery and begin the process of demolition. It is clear that "collective action has made it more difficult for the developer to violate the homeowners' rights arbitrarily".[7]

The equation between local government, financier and real estate developers' interests and those of China's urban home-owners has obviously been unequal. It is clear that "intensified commercialization and commodification … and breakneck economic growth" have prevailed and at least until the last quarter of 2008 when the global economic crisis hit the Chinese economy, the development of China's cities has obviously primarily benefited developers, local administrators, financial speculators and those members of an increasingly well-heeled urban elite who could afford to purchase the most desirable urban housing.[8]

The most cynical Chinese commentators have argued that what happened in their country as economic reform delivered a functioning property market was that "powerful urban interests in China's opaque political system are [were] scurrying to extract their share of wealth before a more stable, transparent system [of governance] emerges". There is no doubt that local government representatives have been prominent among those who have been "scurrying to extract". City officials have seen both land sales and the redevelopment of housing stock as a means of "shoring up shrinking tax bases".[9] There were substantial profits to be made by both financiers and developers. The latter often bought existing housing stock at very reasonable prices. At the same time there was a range of local government taxation opportunities (both formal and informal) attached to land sales and to new residential apartments. There was also status to be gained when public infrastructure such as "a city square, a fly-over area, metro mass-transit, and a development zone" became a part of the new built environment of the city. Merit-based promotion of administrators within the institutions of local government can reasonably be expected. It is also useful to note that while residents do move willingly with a housing market giving much greater choice of housing type and place, the downside grievances of resident relocation were less visible than the "benefits" to be gained by local officials and commercial interests from the promotion of a new, modern city environment. In other words, "the misery of dislocated farmers and [urban] residents … [was and is] not as visible as a city's physical transformation".[10]

Another aspect of the situation I have outlined above is that even before the global economic downturn there were large projects undertaken by city developers that proved to be financially risky. When local government funds were used alongside the lure of increased taxation revenue and civic status it is obvious that local administrators would be tempted to participate in projects that have the potential to become a public "debt burden". This situation clearly exacerbated an already amply demonstrated keenness among local administrators to maximize profit from a redevelopment project by keeping compensation payments to relocated residents as low as possible. Local administrators sought to do this even though compensation payments are to be paid on the basis of a market evaluation of the floor area of an apartment or house that is to be demolished, rather than on the previous measurement of household size. Any negotiation of the purchase price of a property is closed out and importantly, compensation is only provided for property owners. None is usually available for property tenants. It is also the case that if property owners have constructed an illegal space – a space that lacks building approval and this has been common practice – no compensation will be paid.[11]

While there has been much criticism of members of the powerful triumvirate of real estate developers, their financiers and local government officials, at least one section of this opportunistic cabal have been very satisfied with their own "progress". Until recently, real estate developers considered themselves to be very successful market entrepreneurs. Even while the Chinese government in Beijing was expressing urgent concern over problems associated with China's urban real estate market, particularly with respect to the relocation of urban residents and illegal operations that have been associated with the alienation of arable land, real estate interests were boasting that they had been major drivers of modernization, development and economic growth. Their representatives were arguing that China's first-tier or primary cities – Beijing, Shanghai, Guangzhou and the Hong Kong/Mainland border city of Shenzhen – have been "a huge success" in real estate terms. They then insisted that "savvy businesses" should turn their attention to China's second and third tier cities where rising prices would ensure the continuation and expansion of healthy real estate profits. The real estate developers pointed out that they had based their assessment of a city's potential, on a city's "evolving commercial geography", on whether the city hosts major international companies, on the number of companies that can be considered hi-tech companies, on the number and position of retail mall developments and the number of retail banks in residence. Cities such as Tianjin, Hangzhou, Nanjing, Wuhan, Qingdao, Dongguan and Shenyang and Xi'an were promoted as suitable venues for further real estate speculation and development. The residents of these cities, many of whom have already had to face relocation, should have been concerned and so should a government that was still in the process of drafting a long-term land usage programme. The latter was intended to last until 2020.[12] What was unforeseen in terms of this expectation of future profitable real estate speculation was that China's "real estate boom" would "peter out". In 2008, particularly in the last three months of the year, foreign real estate investment declined sharply. By the end of 2008 foreign acquisitions totaled 16 billion yuan, "down 26 per cent from 2007". As well-known companies (among them the worst effected by the global economic contraction, companies such as Morgan Stanley that put its Shanghai properties on the market – "including Infiniti Plaza, Donghai Plaza, and Anxin Business Plaza" and its Jinlin Tiandi Residences) were seeking buyers for their holdings, investors were becoming ever more wary of "making large-ticket investments". Property prices were slashed and what is described as a "gloomy economic period" has followed with a Shanghai paper published at the end of April 2009 reporting that rents for retail plazas (including the Infiniti Plaza) had dropped by 8.7 per cent in the first quarter of the year.[13]

Together with the description and criticism I have offered above, I must make an important *positive comment* in relation to the property development that has most recently rebuild China's cities. In defence of the recent role in urban redevelopment played by real estate developers their financiers and local government administrators it should be pointed out that the often poor state of housing and infrastructure in the inner areas of Chinese cities has been very greatly improved. I should underline the point that "urban redevelopment has improved the quality of the built environment". I am visiting Shanghai as I finish writing this chapter and I am once again struck by the interesting and attractive architecture that dominates the city's sky-line. Urban development has overtaken the often "poor living conditions in the central areas in Chinese cities" and this means that an extremely important point must be stressed. *It is not a question of whether or not China's cities should be extensively redeveloped. They should be. It is a question of how this redevelopment is undertaken.*[14]

The Decline in China's Speculative Property Market

Notwithstanding the boasting of real estate developers over their entrepreneurial expertise, by the end of 2008 it was clear that China's cities were hosting "an ailing property sector". China's leaders and policy-makers immediately recognized that they must address this situation, particularly as they were also obliged to recognize the likelihood that "property investments [would] continue to decline in 2009". Concern was expressed by China's leaders and planners over the situation where after a number of China's city governments (including the Shanghai municipal government) had implemented policies aimed at boosting their property markets the urban property sector continued to experience a substantial drop in demand. The measures implemented by local governments included "raising the ceiling on government funding or subsidies for home-buyers, cutting taxes and extending the time limit for property firms to develop land parcels". Restrictions on owning second houses were also relaxed, though this measure applies more to rural and peri-urban property ownership than the up-market urban properties that I have focused on in my discussion above.[15]

China's leaders and planners, together with local administrators and policy-makers, have now noted that "if property investments continue to decline through 2009, increasing infrastructure investment alone would not be enough to push China's growth rate above 7 per cent". (Real estate investment had reached the point where it accounted for as much as 9.2 per cent of China's gross domestic product).[16] They have concluded that China's real estate sector must be "propped up" by both central and local government policy initiatives. Nevertheless, the global financial crisis has spelt the end of projects such as Shanghai's themed suburbs. These suburbs were constructed under the title of "one city, nine towns". They were intended to "echo the architectural and urban planning sensibilities of nine foreign cultures". The "nine towns" project prompted "an immense" construction binge on the urban/rural margin of Shanghai. Most of the theme towns were satellite towns. There is a German town – Antig that accommodates 30,000 people and forty kilometres away an olde English town – Songjiang. In a Shanghai suburb (Pujiang) the theme is "an Italian dreamscape" and there are French,

Dutch, Spanish, Swedish, and Canadian themed centres included among the nine sites. Altogether these Disney type mostly European themed towns are intended to accommodate no less than 500,000 people and, "of course, the developers of these satellite towns wanted to build luxury homes that they can make a lot of money on". There were reported to be high sales rates of residencies in these towns which were recognized to be "some of Shanghai's most comfortable neighborhoods". The Shanghai themed towns are certainly eye-catching and they have served to underline the luxury, indulgent and money-making nature of urban development and in spite of their often distant location from the city-centre, they under-score the drive to profit from "the high-end residential property market". The global financial crisis has exposed the extent and the vulnerability (even what some may now see as the folly) of this approach to China's urban development. Excesses such as themed satellite cities with "themed pubs and Tudor-looking architecture concealing high-rise blocks" and "tidy Tudor cottages, cobbled paths, a giant castle and a garden maze" ("ye olde England"/Thamestown which opened in October 2006) can be expected, ironically, to be a thing of the past.[17] By the end of 2008 Australia's Macquarie Group was obliged to slash the selling price of City Apartments in downtown Shanghai by 25 per cent from the price fetched three years earlier. By this time real estate sources were talking of "the stark reality of buyers keeping away". They were also noting that several factors had played into the crisis they were facing. Beijing's concern over the effect of hosting "hot money" and measures taken to discourage this short-term speculative capital from investing in China had had some effect and then "global factors such as the overall lack of liquidity in credit markets around the world" took a considerable toll. High end residential housing in all Chinese cities was affected and investment in shopping plazas and office blocks has been curtailed by sluggish sales and heavily reduced prices for both retail space and goods and services sold. In Beijing real estate personnel and developers have been left to lament the point that the "fat year-end bonuses and other rewards" they had come to expect would no longer be a part of their income while real estate companies in Guangzhou were reporting that they had retrenched 40 per cent of their staff. Commentators are now advising that the "risk-taking that had been allowed with big-budget, high-profile projects, will not be repeated in the future". They recognize that not only will high-end residential complexes and towns be hard to justify, but "the construction of glass-and-aluminum fortresses that serve only the privileged few" will no longer be favoured. China's leaders and administrators are promoting the view that since the on-set of the global economic crisis "the agenda has [had to be] changed".[18]

By the end of the first quarter of 2009, the Chinese government's change of agenda was affecting the private sector, not only in the housing sector, but also in the retail sector. For example, the owners of Shanghai shopping plazas have employed consultants who have advised them to use assets such as the Infiniti Plaza to promote down-scaled retail ventures. Infiniti Plaza has now been gutted and redeveloped. The consultants advised that rents for retailers should be significantly reduced and that the product to be sold should appeal to not only the very well heeled residents of the city, but also those they are referring to as "middle-end customers". They say that their clients should now promote "trendy shopping experiences, particularly catering to the needs of middle-end customers".[19]

Promoting Affordable Housing in China's Cities

Having already increased government spending on housing for the poor, central government administrators decided that the government must add the promotion of "mass-market commercial housing" to Beijing's policy brief and as I note above, they expect to effect a significant change in direction in terms of the manner in which Chinese cities are to be developed. The particularly narrow self-interested behaviour (entrepreneurship) of real estate developers, financiers and local administrators is now to give way to sustaining national economic growth through the promotion of housing consumption that should include middle and lower income urban residents. At the same time as government administrators have advocated measures that promote "mass-market commercial housing" central government sources are making it clear that they expect local government administrators to "unveil more creative measures, including preferential land policies, to match the central government initiatives". Central government administrators are also pointing out that the policies adopted should exert a positive demand for construction materials including steel and cement.[20]

The approach to urban development now promoted by Beijing is being touted as an approach that will provide a more stable economic system for the future. It is to be based on China's "great consumer potential". This is the "potential" of many consumers, not just the particularly well-heeled urban market elite. The changed approach to urban development is also consistent with the Chinese leadership's vow to use funds spent to stimulate the country's economy (in the name of making up for "external demand insufficiency and containing a possible further sliding of the national economy") on projects that will improve people's lives. Central government sources have stressed the twin points that "housing incurs the largest spending for most people" and that "how to solve the housing problems and activate the latent potential of domestic spending remains a pressing task". For his part, Chinese Premier Wen Jiabao has explicitly called for "a healthy development of the country's real estate market" while his government has urged the nation's banks to "lend to developers of low-price apartments". Central government administrators have also demanded that local government administrators "keep a close eye on the real estate market ... and step up supervision over the use of subsidies and [over the] quality of construction." The central government has charged the National Audit Office with "investigating projects backed by the 4-trillion-yuan (US$586 billion) stimulus package". The watchdog is to ensure that funds are "properly used". A total of 280 billion yuan has been specifically allocated for low-income housing projects.[21]

The central government's intention to oversee the spending of its stimulus package funds, including spending on real estate and a wide range of infra-structural projects must be welcomed by all except those who have long been "bending the rules" and are now being "condemned for their greed". With China's urban real estate industry seen to no longer be a sector generating dependably large profits (a sector where "where there will be less investment ... in the foreseeable future"), the time is ripe for a change of course. The view is now widely held that China's real estate market will change "from an investment-driven market to a consumption-driven one". However, a number of Chinese commentators are also noting that this change will not happen when, as at the present, "housing prices in many local property markets (continue to) remain high above the levels affordable to the majority of consumers". While the government's stimulus funds that have been marked for housing are destined for the lower reaches of China's housing market (this tranche of funding is to be spent on housing projects for low-income families, particularly for the development of "low-rent and affordable apartments" with both central and local government initiatives currently underway),[22] it is the middle market ground that is most likely to generate consumption led relief from the real estate development problems promoted by the present global economic crisis.

The advice that Chinese commentators concerned with the issue of urban development, investment and housing are providing is that "developers should adopt a proactive attitude" toward the changes that will "transform" their sector of the economy from an investment-driven to a consumption-driven sector. They are told that while the government is fulfilling its role in providing social housing for lower income earners, they should be "making housing properties affordable to the majority of residents". It is recognized that it is only by reducing the price to be paid for middle-range housing that

China's property market will "sustain stable development and become a driving force behind China's economic growth". Real estate developers and those who have been supporting their boundless development enthusiasm are now being told that they have a crucial role to play in ensuring the stable economic development of their sector through courting China's middle-income earners. The consultants providing advice to the managers of Shanghai's Infiniti Plaza and other prestigious retail complexes have, as I have noted, told their clients that price reductions and paying attention to "the needs of middle-end customers" is the best way to address the substantial drops they are experiencing in their income streams. The advice these consultants have offered to shopping mall investors would be very useful to those managing China's urban real estate development.[23]

Land at the Urban/Rural Margin

Before leaving the subject of finding a home in China's restless urban landscape I would like to add one further, relatively short, discussion. In April 2008, before the full-force of the global economic crisis was felt in China's urban property market, Chinese authorities had proudly announced that in a period of just four months (from September 2007 to January 2008) almost 32,000 cases of "unlawful land seizures" had been identified. The authorities also determined that a massive sixty per cent of land was estimated to have been "used before obtaining government approval". The remainder was "either illegally rented or misappropriated". After the identification of illegal land dealings "unlawful buildings" were confiscated or demolished and a campaign was mounted targeting local governments where administrators had "illegally transferred land from rightful owners to property developers or industrial parks". National regulations were also revised. It was intended to make local leadership responsible for serious case of illegal land use. By 2008 Beijing had been obliged to implement what one Chinese media commentator described as "a slew of measures to prevent arable land being lost to urbanization". Apart from making local administrators more accountable for land use, the central government was advising that "no water, power or gas shall be provided to these [illegal] projects, and no financial institutions shall be permitted to offer them loans".[24]

The central government's zeal in prosecuting "illegal land grabs" was not only driven by the social unrest promoted by rural land owners who made it very clear that they felt that their rights have been trampled, but also by the rapid loss of arable land (an estimated 8.3 million hectares has been lost in the decade 1996-2006 and more has been alienated in the following period.

An estimated 40,700 hectares of arable land is estimated to have been lost in 2007 with China's arable land shrinking by 4.6 million *mu* between 2006 and the end of 2008).[25] There had been well publicized protests by villagers who were keen to point out that they had been subject to illegal, heavy-handed and unfair dealings which had alienated them from their land. There are many reported cases of developers, often "well connected developers", who failed to pay villagers for their land or who inadequately compensated for land. Developers had also been accused of physically forcing villagers from their land. It is in this context that there have been and there continue to be "frequent confrontations" between villagers and the police and/or the army. In the same manner as urban residents who had been forced to relocate had petitioned central government authorities, villagers petitioned government agencies, central government and sometimes provincial government agencies as well, and they engaged lawyers to act on their behalf. They also demonstrated. Some blocked roads and took up Luddite behaviour in order to obstruct developers or in order to gain adequate compensation for alienation of their land.

As China's urban expansion continued unabated local officials and developers alike were described as acting in a "rapacious" manner. As in the case of urban housing relocation, developers, local administrators and financiers were accused of "pushing the boundaries" of legality and of "decent" behaviour. When developers came knocking and village land was slated to be re-allocated so that it is within city boundaries, local village cadres often stood to gain much from accessing permanent urban residency and from their locality's rise in status. With urban status local cadres and administrators "can become state officials with retirement pensions and much higher salaries ..." Moreover, if they do act "fairly" it is possible that "the entire village can benefit". The move from rural to urban household registration has been much sought after and it is difficult for a single family or person to negotiate. An urban "chop"/stamp denoting the right to reside in a particular city increases status and is attended by improved social provision, including improved access to education and employment opportunities. Villagers and their leaders have also negotiated other deals. When their land has been used for manufacturing purposes they have demanded jobs and when their land has been used for housing they have gained access to new housing for themselves and their families and sometimes second houses or apartments that they have rented out for income. There have been reports of villagers "trading" relatively large (in terms of the square footage) rural houses for several urban apartments. They can then live in one and rent the others and so provide their household with a substantial and steady income. Some villagers have also taken over the process of urbanizing their land themselves. Some of these projects have been legally approved and there are a range of projects (for example accommodating migrant workers in hastily constructed and often sub-standard urban fringe accommodation that may well be unsewered, etc.) that are more questionable. However, *there are large numbers of villagers who loose their land and this "disappearance of their land causes their world to spin out of control".*[26]

A number of commentators have recognized that villagers would be greatly advantaged if they had "strong independent civic organizations which could help them deal with the negative effects of development".[27] However, civil organizations such as this would have to tread carefully. They would not be allowed to overtly challenge government policies and possibly even decisions made by local government administrators. When villagers have chosen to oppose the sale of their land they have often engaged in what many see as "rightful resistance". This form of action is expected to "stop short of violence", though trouble-making (such as blocking entry for construction machinery or demonstrating in a manner that draws attention to an unsatisfactory situation) can be, and is quite often, tolerated. A more formal and legal avenue for villagers to protest their treatment is through the use of lawyers and/or petitions. When petitions are used they are intended to plead with those who hold official authoritative positions to take up their cause and they are also intended to draw on public sympathy or outrage.[28]

Chinese villagers who have complained over their treatment in relation to administrators and developers acquiring land have won payments and compensation and in some cases they have been instrumental in having government officials dismissed from their positions. However, there are most villagers who have been alienated from use of their land against their will and without what most would consider fair compensation. The disappearance of China's near-city agricultural land under a layer of urban development is obviously a complex and vexed issue.

The question now is: What will happen at the urban/rural interface as China's urban real estate market is transformed from a market for the urban elite to a market for the middle reaches of society and one where "low-rent and affordable apartments" are made more widely available? At the moment relatively little is being said in official circles about what we can expect to be at least a continuing and quite likely an increased growth in urban housing and infrastructure spilling out into the country-side devouring agricultural land and often rural livelihoods in the process. (In the fifteen years to 2007 it is estimated that Shanghai grew faster than any other global city. The physical size of the city is estimated to have grown sixfold, "as people sought more space and the city government rushed to develop nearby areas, such as Pudong").[29]

Conclusion

The anger of many land owners at the ever expanding area of urban/rural interface of China's cities is clearly evident. The taking of land on the basis of what are considered to be unfair arrangements is the most usual source of this anger. Unfair arrangements range from inadequate compensation to expulsion from land that has been occupied for a long period of time without any compensation to issues such as the future use of land that has been assumed. A mixture of these situations is demonstrated by a recent case reported in the Shanghai media. The case does not relate to Shanghai or any other major Chinese city, but it does clearly illustrate the urban/rural interface issue and the development problems I have been discussing in this chapter. A substantial package of land (153 hectares) had been "bought" from rural land-holders by developers. The Shaanxi land-holders held out against the developers even though their land was slated to be used for a park – a public good. The land-owners only moved when the project developer cut off their power and water supplies. Local administrators had told the villagers that their land would be used to build an Olympic-themed park on the edge of their town. The park would benefit the local economy. The villagers now find that 400 villas have been built on "their" land. It is intended that the villas will be sold to the well-heeled in the community for considerable profit. In the course of negotiations with the villagers local administrators had halved the land acquisition fee and had "also exempted the developer from having to pay compensation to the villagers because the company was [said to be] in financial difficulties". Finally, local administrators had decided "to help the developer" by agreeing that the company would only have to pay 20 per cent of the already halved acquisition fee.[30] The scene I outline immediately above is one that has been repeated in many settings. Villagers have been aggrieved and urban residents who have been obliged to relocate have similar grievances and an endless catalogue of shared stories to tell.

In the wake of the effects of the present global financial downturn reaching China's real estate market, change will obviously take place. While real estate developers, their financiers and local government administrators continue to do favours for each other (now with local administrators taking action "to help the developer" in tough economic times), their consistently demonstrated self-interest is likely to be curbed. Beijing is keen to "transform" China's urban real estate market from one driven predominantly by land and home developers, financiers and local administrators who have demonstrated considerable ability to promote their own "greed, disregard for safety rules and environmental quality" to one where middle-range urban consumers ("middle-end customers") not only experience "trendy shopping experiences", but also wider market access to desirable urban housing. At the same time, central government funding of low-cost/low-rent apartments under the relatively generous funding of Beijing's stimulus packages is expected to offer greater housing opportunity for lower income urban residents. The question then is – Will these lower income urban residents include the migrant workers who have provided the labour-time for the construction of China's very impressive (and architecturally interesting) landscape? While I have been staying in China I have been interviewing migrant workers and a significant proportion are returning home to their rural villages, or they are at least considering returning home. They are taking this action as the volume of construction and factory work they have accessing has decreased and because they have either lost their jobs or they are now not earning enough to make it worthwhile living in the city. If their employers do not offer accommodation, they cite the problems associated with accessing suitable accommodation as a central difficulty. This is the case even when some migrant workers have been traveling to cities for employment for three, four, five and even ten years. The difficulties and problems associated with finding a home in China's restless urban landscape are clearly evident and we can expect that these problems and difficulties cannot be immediately solved, even if China's urban property developers change tack and offer housing that can be afforded by a wider range of urban residents. However, alongside the description and criticism I have offered in this chapter, there is the point that in the final analysis *it is not a question of whether or not China's cities should be extensively redeveloped. They should be. It is a question of how this redevelopment is undertaken.*

Notes

*   Dr Kate Hannan is Associate Professor at the School of History and Politics and Research Fellow at the Faculty of Arts of the University of Wollongong, Sydney, Australia. She has published books, chapters and papers on contemporary industrial relations in China. Her most recent research has focused on the effect of China's fast-paced development on the use of urban space. She has also been engaged on research on the effect of the present global financial crisis on the employment opportunities and working conditions of China's rural-to-urban migrant workers.

1.   See Wu *et al.* (2007: 2-4).

2. Wu *et al.* (2007: 233-242). See also Hannan (1998). The gated housing communities of the present are particularly obvious in Shanghai where I have written part of this chapter while involved in another research project. Some compounds with the most expensive housing have gated and guarded entrances and several strands of electrified wire on top of the housing complex boundary walls.

3. "Property Sector Needs to Adapt to Changes", *China Daily*, 12/01/2009.

4. Beech (Shanghai-based correspondent) (2005) and "Govt Should Not Rush in to Aid Housing Market", *China Daily*, 08/10/2008.

5. Wu *et al.* (2007: 118-119). Since 1989 the City Planning Act had given municipalities the power to issue urban land use and building permits. See *ibid.* See also "China Warned of Sudden Retreat of Hot Money", *China Daily*, BIZCHINA, 18/03/2008; "Govt Should Not Rush in to Aid Housing Market", *op. cit.*, and "Shanghai Property Boom Fading Away", *China Daily*, 09/01/2009.

6. Cai (2007: 179-180).

7. See *ibid.*, p. 184, and Wu *et al.* (2007: 241).

8. See Wu *et al.* (2007: 255) and "Central Government Backs Property Moves", *China Daily*, 20/10/2008. As I have argued, it has been increasingly reported that in China's large cities "house prices are [now] way beyond the reach of [the majority of] residents". Middle earning Chinese urban residents, and more particularly low-income urban residents, were those who were obliged to relocate when developers and local administrators and planners decided their existing housing should be replaced by luxury apartments, shopping malls and office blocks. Another way to express this equation is to observe that "active relocation" where residents choose to move their residence has been much more common in households with higher than average levels of education and income than in households who belong to lower urban socio-demographic groups. See *ibid.*

9. Zweig (2000: 119-120).

10. Wu *et al.* (2007: 227-228, 254). Wu *et al.* also argue that competition between cities (or more correctly between city governments and administrators) has played a significant role in promoting a high pressured approach to urban redevelopment. They talk of "competitiveness-building" between cities that is the province of two elite groups (i) "local government – especially top government officials" and (ii) commercial interests – financiers and developers. They are also keen to note the "inherently speculative" nature of much that has been undertaken. See *ibid.*, p. 229.

11. *Ibid.* p. 229, p. 241 and pp. 255-256.

12. "Real Estate Focus Turns to China's Secondary Cities", Xinhua, 29/06/2007, and "Arable Land Reserves Continue to Decline", *China Daily*, 17/04/2008.

13. "Shanghai Property Boom Fading Away", *China Daily*, 09/01/2009; "Downturn Forces Malls to Reposition Image and Brand", *Shanghai Daily*, 29/04/2009.

14. Wu *et al.* (2007: 260-261).

15. "Economists: New Property Stimulus Key to Sustaining Growth", Xinhua, 18/12/2008, and "Central Government Backs Property Moves", *op. cit.*

16. "Economists: New Property Stimulus Key to Sustaining Growth", *op. cit.*
17. Beech (2005).
18. "China's Property Climate Index Declines in Nov", Xinhua, 12/12/2008; "China Warned of Sudden Retreat of Hot Money", *op. cit.*; "Shanghai Property Boom Fading Away", *op. cit.*; "Job Loss in Real Estate Sector on the Rise", *China Daily*, 09/01/2009; and "Mega No More", *China Daily*, 24/02/2009.
19. "Downturn Forces Malls to Reposition Image and Brand", *op. cit.* I visited the Infiniti Plaza building in May 2009 and found it gutted and undergoing a substantial refit. By the time I visited again in August the refit had been completed.
20. *Ibid.*
21. "Premier Calls for Healthy Development of Real Estate", Xinhua, 18/12/2008; "Wen: More Stimulus Push if Needed", *China Daily*, 1/03/2009; "Govt Plan Signals Shift From Growth-first Policy", *China Daily*, 17/11/2008; "Auditor Vows to Closely Monitor Stimulus Projects", *China Daily*, 27/03/2009; and "Economic Stimulus Package to Improve People's Livelihood", *op. cit.* Government sources estimate that by May 2009 420 billion of the total 1.18 trillion in government stimulus monies to be spent by 2010 had been allocated. In addition, by May 2009 commentators were noting that the stimulus package was "having a significant impact" on the Chinese economy. See "Stimulus Package Has Started Bearing Fruits", *China Daily*, 07/05/2009.
22. See "Economic Stimulus Package to Improve People's Livelihood", *op. cit.*, and "Govt Should Not Rush in to Aid Housing Market", *op. cit.* In addition to Beijing's stimulus package measures that will fund low-income housing projects "at the end of last year, the Shanghai municipal government took out 2 billion yuan ([US]$293.49 million) from the returns of its public housing fund to build houses for low-income people". In addition, "some local governments have ... built ... government-subsidized apartments to accommodate white-collar employees". They have done this in order to attract skills to their areas. See *ibid.*
23. "China Housing to Recover in 2 Years", *China Daily*, Hong Kong edition, 21/11/2008; "Property Sector Needs to Adapt to Changes", *op. cit.*; "Economists: New Property Stimulus Key to Sustaining Growth", *op. cit.*; "Downturn Forces Malls to Reposition Image and Brand", *op. cit.*
24. "China Punished Thousands of People for Illegal Land Grabs", Xinhua, 14/04/2008, and "Arable Land Reserves Continue to Decline", *op. cit.*
25. *Ibid.* See also "Arable Land Reserves Continue to Decline", *op. cit.*, and "Govt Urged to Reform Land Expropriation Policies", Xinhua, 09/03/2009.
26. Zweig (2000: 120-122).
27. Zweig (2000: 131).
28. Urban residents who have been threatened with relocation have also used this avenue. Informed villagers have been known to cite laws and precedent that would support their case. However, even when they have raised funds and

employed a lawyer and even won a case in court, many have found it difficult to get officials to act in accord with the court's finding. See Chen (2007: 253-257).

29. "Property Sector Needs to Adapt to Changes", *China Daily*, 12/01/2009, and Schifferes (2007).

30. "Anger as Villas Built on Land Meant for Park", *Shanghai Daily*, 29/04/2009.

References

Beech, Hannah (2005), "Ye Olde Shanghai", *Time, Business and Tech*, 07/02/2005. <*http://www.time.com/time/magazine/article/0,9171,1025219,00.html*>

Cai, Yongshun (2007), "Civil Resistance and Rule of Law in China" (Chapter Eight), in Elizabeth J. Perry and Merle Goldman (eds), *Grassroots Political Reform in Contemporary China*, Cambridge, MA: Harvard University Press, pp. 174-195.

Chen, Xi (2007), "Between Defiance and Obedience" (Chapter Eleven), in Elizabeth J. Perry and Merle Goldman (eds), *Grassroots Political Reform in Contemporary China*, Cambridge, MA: Harvard University Press, pp. 253-281.

Hannan, Kate (1998), *Industrial Reform in China: Economic Restructuring and Conflicting Interests*, London: Routledge.

Ho, Peter (2000), "Contesting Rural Spaces: Land Disputes, Customary Tenure and the State" (Chapter Four), in Elizabeth J. Perry and Mark Selden (eds), *Chinese Society*, 2nd edition, London: RoutledgeCurzon, pp. 93-112.

Lee, Ching Kwan (ed.) (2007), *Working in China*, New York: Routledge. See particularly Sian Victoria Liu's Chapter Three.

Liu, Sian Victoria (2007), "'Social Positions' Neighborhood Transitions After Danwei" (Chapter Three), in Ching Kwan Lee (ed.), *Working in China*, New York: Routledge, pp. 38-55.

Naughton, Barry (2007), *The Chinese Economy*, London: MIT Press.

Perry, Elizabeth J. and Mark Selden (eds) (2000), *Chinese Society*, 2nd edition, London: RoutledgeCurzon. See particularly Peter Ho's Chapter Four and David Zweig's Chapter Five.

Perry, Elizabeth J. and Merle Goldman (eds) (2007), *Grassroots Political Reform in Contemporary China*, Cambridge, MA: Harvard University Press. See particularly Yongshun Cai's Chapter Eight and Xi Chen's Chapter Eleven.

Schifferes, Steve (2007), "Can Shanghai Turn Green and Grow?", BBC Report, 17/05/2007. <*http://news.bbc.co.uk/2/hi/business/6683103.stm*>

Wu, Fulong, Jiang Xu and Anthony Gar-On Yeh (2007), *Urban Development in Post-Reform China*, London: Routledge.

Zweig, David (2000), "To the Courts or to the Barricades: Can New Political Institutions Manage Rural Conflict?" (Chapter Five), in Elizabeth J. Perry and Mark Selden (eds), *Chinese Society*, 2nd edition, London: RoutledgeCurzon, pp. 113-135.

Chinese Media Sources

"Real Estate Focus Turns to China's Secondary Cities", Xinhua, 29/06/2007.
"China Warned of Sudden Retreat of Hot Money", *China Daily*, BIZCHINA, 18/03/2008.
"China Punished Thousands of People for Illegal Land Grabs", Xinhua, 14/04/2008.
"Arable Land Reserves Continue to Decline", *China Daily*, 17/04/2008.
"Government Should Not Rush in to Aid Housing Market", *China Daily*, 08/10/2008.
"Central Government Backs Property Moves", *China Daily*, 20/10/2008.
"Govt Plan Signals Shift from Growth-first Policy", *China Daily*, 17/11/2008.
"China Housing to Recover in 2 Years", *China Daily*, Hong Kong edition, 21/11/2008.
"China's Property Climate Index Declines in Nov", Xinhua, 12/12/2008.
"Economists: New Property Stimulus Key to Sustaining Growth", Xinhua, 18/12/2008.
"Premier Calls for Healthy Development of Real Estate", Xinhua, 18/12/2008.
"Shanghai Property Boom Fading Away", *China Daily*, 09/01/2009.
"Job Loss in the Real Estate Sector on the Rise", *China Daily*, 09/01/2009.
"Property Sector Needs to Adapt to Changes", *China Daily*, 12/01/2009.
"Mega No More", *China Daily*, 24/02/2009.
"Wen: More Stimulus Push if Needed", *China Daily*, 01/03/2009.
"Govt Urged to Reform Land Expropriation Policies", Xinhua, 09/03/2009.
"Auditor Vows to Closely Monitor Stimulus Projects", *China Daily*, 27/03/2009.
"Downturn Forces Malls to Reposition Image and Brand", *Shanghai Daily*, 29/04/2009.
"Anger as Villas Built on Land Meant for Park", *Shanghai Daily*, 29/04/2009.
"Stimulus Package Has Started Bearing Fruits", *China Daily*, 07/05/2009.

China's Future:
International Milieu,
Ethnoterritoriality and *Realpolitik*

Chapter 8

China after Thirty Years of
Reform and Open Policy: *Quo Vadis?*

Im-Soo **Yoo***

Introduction

At the beginning of the nineteenth century the Western powerful nations descended upon the Chinese mainland. China during that period was in malaise. The once formidable empire of the mainland nation was close to collapse. The West labeled China the Eastern Sick Tiger or Sleeping Tiger. It was deemed a "Sick Man" on the Asian continent who was feeble and debilitated. In the nineteenth century, there was rampant corruption, rampant poverty and widespread disease. It was during this period of time that China exposed its vulnerabilities to the Western conquerors. The Opium War (1839-1842)[1] led to China's surrendering of Hong Kong to Great Britain.

After World War II, Civil War tore China into two conflicting factions, the Nationalists and the Communists. The Nationalists retreated from the mainland, took refuge in Taiwan and became a country of its own until today. Meanwhile, the Communist state was under the command of Mao Zedong. This year, 2009, marks the 60th year of Communist rule in China. Mao's legacy of communist ideology was the foundation of China's solid political and economic developments today. This year is also the 30th anniversary of China's "Reform and Open" policy of Deng Xiaoping. Deng's model of reform and open-up of China was the second historical epoch of modern Chinese history.

Now his successors, state political leader Jiang Zemin and Hu Jintao have developed tremendously the economy and diplomacy of China as well as the military solidarity of China's defense. With the solid historical setting and the modern stewardship under current successors, China has gained tremendous developments and has high vision that in the thirty years to come, China will become a strong nation in industry, trade, finance and diplomacy in the world. Before the rise of China, there was only the *Pax Americana*. Now, China will bring the *Pax Sinica* to the world.

This chapter aims at reviewing China's past sixty years of the socialist model, its thirty years of "Reform and Open" policy and its continued rise in another thirty years in future. In comparison with Russia, the former USSR, the question of whether the Chinese socialist model could or could not survive will be a debatable reality. But China has already insisted that its socialist model will not be changed. It is very interesting to note in the world history that never has there been a single country which could thrive on a socialist model. Now, the question which has drawn considerable attention is whether both the contradictory policies of the Chinese model of one-party socialist central rule with its pragmatic open-market basis for an economy could sustain in the years to come. It is well known that under the socialist model, political decision is primary while economics is normally secondary. Most of the time, political decision overrides economic advantage. Will this model of China be sustainable and become the exemplary model for the rest of the aspiring countries in the world? Or will there be fallout and if there is this possibility, will China fall on its back and relapse to the olden days of historical torpidity?

Six Decades after 1949

This year, China will celebrate the 60th anniversary of its founding of a socialist nation since 1949 which marked the birth of the first major socialist country in Asia after World War II. It has been six decades since the founding father of Chinese socialism, Mao Zedong succeeded in unifying the whole nation which contributed to today's unity and nationhood in China.

The first and second generation of Chinese socialist leaders like Deng Xiaoping adopted a pragmatic position by introducing more market-based economic policies while at the same time retaining the one-party political system. The Chinese experience from the "Reform and Open" policies introduced in 1979 was quite different from that of the Soviet Union's Perestroika and Glasnost[2]. Its more pragmatic and flexible approach compared to the USSR's in times of the Cold War had achieved remarkable development, especially after the collapse of communism. In the same year, China established diplomatic relations with US, breaking its old policy of political and economic alignment with the Soviet bloc.

The third and the fourth generation of the Chinese socialist leaders led by the head of the Communist Party, Jiang Zemin and Hu Jintao, have inherited the country's impressive records from their predecessors. This year, two anniversaries, i.e. 60 years of socialism and 30 years of economic "Reform and Open" policy mark an important event, which was reflected in China's ambition to host the Olympic Games in 2008. The event can be regarded as a sign of political harmonization to bridge cultural gaps that had formally existed between East and West. On the other hand, China is striving to turn into a world leader in science and technology, while carrying out its military and space programmes based on high-tech industrialization. For China to achieve these two ambitious goals, it is of importance for the nation to develop a sense of its cultural identity and common values.

These goals will certainly not be achieved overnight. It will take a tremendous effort for either this generation of Chinese leadership or the next one to live up to this new Chinese vision of a global power. China's position in the international order is still considered to be inferior to the US due to many factors. This allows China to upset its Western counterparts every once in a while. But once China reaches a level of equal line of sight with the US or even becomes superior in the long run, the country has to be prepared to face challenges and attacks from other countries, be it in the economic or political arena. The ability of China to achieve this stronger position will depend on the Chinese people, both the political leadership as well as the population.

Critical Factors in China's Sustainability

The following six arguments may serve as a summary of my personal views on this issue, based on my experience and research that I have accumulated and conducted in the era of the Cold War. During that era, I collected ideas and came up with a set of analytical tools for examining the rise and collapse of a global superpower.

1) Every country should adopt a long-term vision for the future. China is no exception in that regard. It should prepare a national long-run strategy, as the basis of a strong nation and as a powerful country in the next thirty years. It should learn from history – how the Anglo-Saxons, the European nations and Japan had managed to build up their regional as well as global power capacities. These are the areas that China needs to look at, comparing its own experience with those of other strong nations which have managed to rule the world in the last century. China will be a powerful country in the second half of the 21st century – an era of *Pax Sinica*.

   The current financial crisis that was triggered by the US mortgage subprime bubble has produced worldwide economic turmoil and recession. There is a lot of discussion regarding whether this will eventually lead to a paradigm change, away from casino capitalism towards a more stable system. At this moment, in the socialist sphere, the Chinese way is the only system that seems to bear justifiable results. Comparing the failure of the USSR model with the Chinese system leads to the conclusion that the latter system is unique. No one knows whether the system will continue to work or not. It depends on the Chinese people to make it work. Otherwise, the global capital market system is at stake. No one can say whether it is only a single case of operational failure and whether the world economy will recover after this slowdown according to the business cycle theory.

But it could also be a failure of the entire global economic system as such. In that case another new paradigm should be adopted. However, many people believe that the capitalist system can work as a whole and therefore needs only minor adjustments. The comparative system analysis states that in socialism, political decisions for the allocation of resources take a prioritized stand over the principle of economic efficiency. In market economies, however, the opposite is true. This means that market efficiency is a primary goal, with the political decisions merely functioning as a tool to achieve these objectives. The US and China represent this contrast in theory and can be regarded as good examples to support that theory.

2) In the context of this current financial crisis, the concept of a new bipolar order of the global system is enshrined by the idea of the G2 as well as G20. These are in the forefront that will play increasing role in global decision-making in the world economy. The G2 – consisting of China and the US – has gained importance as a concept during the course of this crisis. Both countries are no longer seen so much as antagonists, but are in fact complementing each other. The interdependence between China and the US is very strong in terms of trade flows and financial entanglement as well as political cooperation in many regions of the world. Despite pressured by the Congress for the US to condemn China on the manipulation of the currency, President Barack Obama's administration has chosen not to do so. It is the same position as the one taken by the Bush administration. The main reason behind this motive is that the US heavily depends on China's purchase of its treasury bonds. In many aspects, the US needs China's help to tackle the current and also the future economic turmoil. Therefore, the timing is not really right for the US to provoke China. In addition, US have also stated that China had already taken steps to enhance its exchange rate flexibility and confirmed its commitment for greater flexibility. As such, the decision by Obama's administration for not condemning China is predictable.

In year 2007/2008 when the US subprime mortgage crisis occurred, it created another big shock in world economy after the Great Depression in 1929. Until now, there is no equitable solution on how to overcome the problem. There are a lot of these questions in the US regarding what the cause is and how they can find the solution.

In Wall Street, there is an interesting saying among the financial analysts as well as the economists that the Chinese people are exporting lead-coated toys which are dangerous and hazardous for the American children, while the US financial managers are also exporting toxic derivative financial products, e.g. bonds in the market. In this picture, we do not know who the winner is. Maybe China makes use of this chance in this circumstance to bring up its name in the international power games.

On the political side, US needs China's cooperation on several issues such as North Korea, Iran and Darfur conflicts. The US would also be looking into other areas of cooperation which include global climate change and clean energy resource.

North Korea's recent statement to withdraw from the negotiation on the denuclearization of the Korean Peninsula has highlighted stronger and inevitable participation of China to essentially revive the six-party talks, which also involves Japan, South Korea and Russia.

These two issues, i.e. the declination to label China as currency manipulator and the need for China's strong involvement in North Korea's denuclearization, do not indicate that there is a one-sided dependency. But in fact both countries are strongly and increasingly inter-dependent on one another. Nevertheless, it will not be an exclusive G2 or America-China affair as it is essential to include a combination of other strong political players, i.e. EU, Russia and Japan to solve the problems at hand.

The bipolar system being established will increasingly cover global issues that cannot yet be anticipated to reach their fullest extent today. In times of a fast changing globalized bipolar system, different coalitions between these players may form, leaving behind the static status quo of the Cold War times. This will lead to even greater interdependence that is subjected to political as well as economic preferences and power relations among the countries involved.

3) The human rights issue is a basic concept in any society that is based on common values in all countries throughout the world.

From the Chinese perspective, US is a country which is largely based on the concept of individualism. But China is striving for nationalism, collectivism and individualism at the same time. A good example for that contradiction is Jackie Chan's quote: "I'm gradually beginning to feel that we Chinese need to be controlled."[3] The Hong Kong movie star said that in a press conference in Boao, China. He made the remark referring to the experience of Hong Kong and Taiwan whereby people, according to him, enjoy greater freedom of speech and that from his point of view, chaos is the principal result of this kind of development. At the conference, he said that the society in Hong Kong and Taiwan might be "too free" in this sense. This statement has brought about great controversy and argument in China and especially in Taiwan and Hong Kong in which legislators and lawmakers expressed their anger over his freedom remarks, saying that he failed to understand the meaning of freedom and democracy despite having enjoyed the freedom, democracy and economic gains of capitalism[4].

This remark can be regarded as a turning point for China, considering that China may now be at a crossroad in terms of its social development. While the economy is growing rapidly, there is a huge demand for greater freedom of speech and expression. But for a huge country like China with a population of 1.3 billion, too much freedom could pose a threat to the established order of the one-party system and the communist nation.

Western countries have always stressed that China should improve the state of its human rights within its territory, as well as outside China proper, such as in Tibet. That is to say that China should give more freedom of speech to the citizens. Human rights problem is a serious issue. Chinese authorities have always been strict on the freedom of expression and have never really given such freedom to the people. On top of that, the recent statement made by Jackie Chan goes in line with what the Chinese authorities have proclaimed. Only when China becomes a more developed country in terms of its sustained economy, then more freedom of expression could be granted to its citizens.

This year the People's Republic of China celebrates the 60th anniversary of the establishment of the socialist country while Taiwan, the Republic of China, has for as long separated itself from Mainland China and until now there are persistent confrontation and disputes between them. The Beijing government wants Mainland China to be integrated with Taiwan so that China's Chinese will eventually come to the stage of full integration to form a great China.

Comparing the political integration on the matter is not easy. Both China's and Taiwan's economic sectors are starting their integration in terms of mergers and acquisitions (M&A). Their connected economy started to gradually grow up. The Beijing government directs financial aid to buy the Taiwanese companies especially those in electronics, IT and mobile industries. This is because Taiwan has more managed skilled-labour and technology for the world market. China wants to be competitive in the world market. In recent years, China has become more interested in mining for steel and iron in which such industry is expanding.

There is more intensive work in this field such as ship-building for the freight and passenger ships as well as for the aviation industry. This is one of the reasons that China will sooner or later become a strong country in the marine aspect.

4) Chinese economic development brings about an increased ambition to become a stronger military and naval force. It is essential for China to secure the seaway for exporting products and to guarantee the smooth flow of imports of raw materials. In the conference at Boao, President Hu Jintao expressed China's ambition for a new trade area called CEAGPOL – Central East Asia Growth Polygon, consisting of Philippines, Hong Kong, Macau and the Chinese provinces. China had expressed its feeling to be a strong player by controlling the sea transportation along the area, and become a competitor to Japan's initiative of economic zone in the East Asia, i.e. the Economic Partnership Agreement (EPA).

This area is also very important to be China's frontline and as a gateway for China to enter East Asia via sea. Until now, Japan has been the strong sea power in the region, and therefore China should now take more initiative to build up its naval force as a stepping stone in the future as a sea power. It can be seen that China is building up its naval force to strengthen and develop its first regional power as it is more interested in Southeast Asia and South China Sea. The recent demonstrations of China's naval forces in which the military vessels are equipped with nuclear power have shown the world that China has hidden all this while its naval strengths. This means that China will be competent at the regional level as a strong force and will aspire to be a sea power in the world in future.

This intention of China to build up its naval force is also because of the conflicts of the Spratly Islands, Paracel Islands and Scarborough Reef. These islands and reefs are situated in the South China Sea and are under territorial dispute between China and neighbouring countries i.e. Malaysia, Philippines, Brunei, Vietnam, Taiwan, etc. According to C.G. Monique, these islands' are probably the most sovereignty-disputed areas on the planet for its oil resources, fisheries and strategic sea lane[5]. But China has a strong position and has built its watching control facilities at Mischief Reef to look at the disputed archipelagos in the 1990s. Neighbouring countries fear of the dominance of China power in the areas, which contain a lot of economic potentials, i.e. in fishing and oil and gas reserves. In addition, it can also be a territorial or sea line for marine transportation. On the other hand, when China becomes a strong naval force, it will pose a challenge to the US and Japan.

We understand that a strong nation such as the US has the capability and potential to develop the space and astronomical programmes as well as to compete in marine affairs. In this case, China sought to gain more proportion in regional market power in the sea in order to acquire greater sea-power. As such, they need to build up vessel capabilities including nuclear submarines.

As early as in the 15th century in the Chinese marine history, there was a mariner named Cheng Ho who expanded the mission of China's naval expedition and maritime might in the regional area. Hence, whether it is possible or not for China at this point of time to regain the potential and impress others of its sea-power would depend primarily on the Chinese leadership.

Recently, a US observation ship passed by the area of South China Sea. It clarified that it was just a normal surveillance conducted in international seas. China said that US has intervened in its territory while the US argued that it was a typical international observation at international seas. However, there was no confrontation between the two powers in the sea. This was one showcase of a small incident but we could anticipate that there will be more similar incidents between China and the US in the area as well as in other seas in the future. This serves as a lesson and signal for the two countries in tolerating their future interests in that the best way is through consultation and not direct confrontation.

5) China is striving to become a strong nation on a par with other super-powers, especially with the US, EU and Japan. Rapid and successful economic development is not enough to qualify China as a developed country. This country has a huge population with wide disparity between rural and urban population in terms of income, education, technology, facilities, economy, social welfare, etc. China should narrow the gap. Perhaps this is the best way to develop its science and technology sector by stressing more on equal distribution, while at the same time not to compromise its long-established cultural identity.

Another area that China needs to focus on is its cultural heritage. China has a very long history of traditional culture. The Chinese people are proud of their civilization. In this sense, China should export its culture beyond the Asian region to the global level for "China-ization" of the world. It is time for the Chinese to spread and propagate their culture and language globally. English is an international language and widely spoken all around the world. From the last century until now, the developed nations e.g. the

Anglo-Saxon and the French have managed to export their culture. History shows us that the strong countries could not sustain for long time without exporting their civilization. They need to create a cultural domination, which can be regarded as a challenge faced by the new Chinese generation of leadership.

China also needs to develop its human capital. Education, being part of the social capital, should be even more emphasized in the national development. In this regard, more resources and infrastructure need to be directed and invested in this area, especially in technology and science. China has developed basic and applied science for the national building and defense system. China will have to invest in education by putting in place the necessary facilities that will promote and enhance the knowledge based industries i.e. in science, technology, etc.

The Beijing government has also identified its long-run strategy and development of the nation, i.e. to be a dominant industrial country and a strong trade nation. Also, China has a wish to be a financially strong nation which could self support on its own development of the nation as compared to the US and EU. China could reach this stage only with strong background in domestic banking, capital market and foreign exchange.

This is not a simple task for China. Even though it had succeeded in the real economy, the financial business is not easy due to its more traditional background, skill, manpower and capital accumulation. The technical knowhow is also necessary to be developed in order for China to become a financial hub and the next step for China in the future would be to include all other Chinese-based countries, including the Chinese financial hubs in the ASEAN countries.

6) Even though China has made remarkable development, especially in the economic sphere, its political system has not picked up this pace yet. It will be very crucial regarding which path of development, either political or economic, that the country will choose in the future. Even if the economic development can be sustained, the question of distribution of wealth and disparity of welfare will have to be addressed by the nation's leadership.

In addition to that, human rights and democratic participation must be granted to the Chinese people if the country wishes to achieve the level of a "truly developed" country as we understand it today.

Certainly, the rise of China in recent years has triggered different responses and opinions on whether it would really pose a great challenge to the US as the existing global superpower in economics and science and technology and become itself a global leader that overrides or stands shoulder to shoulder with the US in the future. It is *bona fide* to say that

China does have the potential to develop to be a global superpower due to its strengths in low cost of production, abundant labour force, huge market and competitive exchange rate. However, much effort is required to bring China to a greater height as it loses its first-mover advantage compared to the world's giant nations.

The Way Forward

After discussing the many factors and aspects that may cause China to rise or stumble and fall, to further the discussion, I would also like to cite a few projections and anticipations on the economic, political, social and cultural arenas of China in the eyes of the world in the next 30 years to come amidst the pre-emptive measures taken by China.

1) China had in the last decade achieved more than 10 per cent economic growth until last year[6]. This means that China's reform and open policy was effective and extensive economic growth policy is possible. To be a developed nation, it is a necessary strategy for China in the future to improve its productivity and its industry structure together with human capital via innovation and education.

   First, industry structure should be changed from labour-intensive to technology-based or capital-oriented. In the beginning of industrialization, China was quite successful by remaining a low-wage, low-skill and labour-intensive economy. Retaining this mindset without transforming into a high-value economy will only produce low growth in the country. As such, there is an urgent need to address critical economic issues, particularly those related to human capital, technology and innovation as well as the pricing system.

   Enhancing human capital is a strategic move but it must also look beyond education and into the labour market policies. If the supply of human capital is mismatched with industrial need, there will be unemployment and underemployment.

   Technology and innovation are essential for an economy to move up the value chain. Hence a culture of innovation is essential if competitiveness is to be improved. Many measures to develop technological capacity have been introduced with only modest success. China needs to also combine technology and market-driven innovation approaches to be ahead of the other countries, lead in strategic technologies and capture market shares in products and services growth. This economic achievement is based on intensive productivity strategy.

Apart from that, domestic consumption and demand must also be boosted in order for China to be a strong nation. According to the Chinese media, the national commission for reform and development is cutting income taxes and will introduce a new stimulus package of over 4 trillion yuan to be spread over two years (2009-2010). A stock market injection of at least 400 billion yuan has also been allocated in its measure to increase investors' confidence[7]. Since mid-September 2008, the Central Bank of China has cut interest rates for three times. Besides, anticorruption measures have been announced, to prevent the extra funds from enriching local officials.

Premier Wen Jiabao pledged to stimulate domestic consumption by improving the rural circulation network, increase the availability of various commodities in rural markets, improve urban community service facilities, promote the upgrading of durable goods, support development of circulation companies, stimulate holiday consumption through exhibitions, and to step up supervision over product quality and safety (after the crises of tainted milk and hazardous colourants in toy products).

In addition, to facilitate external trade, China plans to improve current financing services for importers and exporters by urging the banks to provide more export credits. Trade between Guangdong, the Yangtze River Delta and Hong Kong and Macao, and that between Guangxi, Yunnan and members of the Association of Southeast Asian Nations (ASEAN) will be settled in renminbi on a trial basis.

Furthermore, China will increase the imports of products that are needed in its market, particularly hi-tech products, critical equipment and elements, energy products and raw materials.

Besides, China and Japan are regional big power in terms of politics and economics powerhouse, but in 1972, China also established diplomatic relationship with the US. China's economic development was aided by the Japanese, as Japan used to have economic cooperation with China and now the interdependence is to become stronger, following the relationship that both countries developed from the past.

Also, since 1992, China has also established diplomatic relationship with South Korea. China becomes one of the largest trade partners of South Korea, with investment and capital flow since the last decade. Two-way trade with China hit a high record of more than US$200 billion last year despite the global economic crisis. Both sides will strive to raise that figure to US$250 billion by 2010 while gradually balancing two-way trade.

We can see that things have changed over years. The US was used to be the most important partner of Japan and South Korea in terms of economy, trade and military alliance. Today, it is pretty much different. The rise of China has surpassed the importance of the US to become the most influential trade partner of Japan, South Korea as well as the Asian region[8].

Other than that, China also formed economic cooperation with the ASEAN countries for economic priority in the form of trade, investment and capital flow. The more China has economic relations with ASEAN, the better it is for implementing security policy and influences.

China has a number of companies in private sector and joint venture production. These are joint ventures with Chinese diasporic people in the region. One of the main tasks is to help them to look for business opportunities in ASEAN. Most Chinese companies have businesses in ASEAN and some of them are doing very well.

China has an aggressive influence towards ASEAN. In the past, Asia was worried about its tributary system in the time of the Dynasties, which gave China strong influence towards Asia. China has signed treaty of amity and cooperation with ASEAN. China used more soft power with ASEAN nations. In this case, China gains the regional advantage of market penetration and economic cooperation with most of the countries in the Asian region as compared to the US government, which has also considered the treaty of amity and cooperation with ASEAN countries.

Take Malaysia-China diplomatic relationship which was long-established back in 1970s for an example. These two nations will further strengthen their bilateral relationship in order to foster future development of the two countries in trade, economy and regional peace. It can be seen from the visit of Malaysia's premier Datuk Seri Najib Tun Razak to China in June 2009 when he pledged to negotiate the territorial disputes so that they would not hamper the cordial Sino-Malaysian ties[9].

However, 30 years down the road, China is anticipated to still lose to the US in terms of technology development. It is intensively export-oriented and FDI would still be the major capital and financial support to develop local industry and financial market.

At the moment, China has underdeveloped domestic banking, financial and capital market system. It should be more developed and expanded towards neighbouring countries, i.e. ASEAN and Shanghai Cooperation countries, at the regional and global levels, including the US and Europe.

China should develop their infrastructure and market access as well as efficient networking of city and airport, and reliable public transportation, electric supply, telecommunication access, frequent flights to other financial centres and major cities should be more convenient, more connected with other countries. China has a development plan in Southern area, for example, the industrial and financially connected triangle linking Hong Kong-Macau-Guangzhou. It is a platform for China to build a better connection with Beijing in order to become a strong financial nation.

There are many obstacles to overcome in its way to become a strong financial nation. In terms of finance and capital aspects, the modern history of its banking and finance is not long but it has always been using its own system during the socialist times. Under the socialist system, it does not work the Western style but the Chinese way. Now with the open policy, for China to become a strong financial system, there should be more systematic and competitive system acceptable by the Western standard.

Also, China's financial institutions, both in structural and operational terms, are not very well developed in comparison with the Western institutions. China should develop its capital and money institutions. It needs to develop its capital institutions in order to be competitive. The status of China's financial market depends firstly on the strength of the Chinese economy. Financial institution depends on two dimensions. One, it should be profitable and with assumed risks, and at the same time since it is a public affair, it needs to be transparent and devoid of moral hazards. Chinese financial authority focused on the development of financial market and strengthening financial supervision, consistent with Chinese ambition to become a strong financial nation. In the global world, M&A (Merger and Acquisition exercise) is frequent in industry, banking and financial institutions. China is not very experienced in M&A and there is an urgent need to develop that.

2) After the G20 conference in 2009, China is now a major partner in an international effort in combating crisis by contributing an unofficial amount of US$40 billion into the US$1.1 trillion package of measures agreed in the summit to boost the current sluggish world economy[10]. Since 2003, US and China have met and consulted each other on the economic level and currency issues, but they have lots more expectations beyond economic issues. The two countries have decided to expand and to enlarge many fields beyond economic issues such as diplomatic issues, climate change and terrorism. This also means that the US cannot readily accept China as a shoulder-to-shoulder partner on all major issues.

The Chinese government believed that the instability of the US dollar is one concern for Chinese dollar reserves in US financial market. If China pulls out all its money reserves from the US financial market, then the dollar will plunge and will set off jitters in the world currency exchange. Chinese government believes that the US is one big country and could also prove useful for China's advantage in the future. However, according to R.N. Cooper, the dollar is likely to remain the dominant international currency for many years due to its widespread and convenient use in foreign exchange transaction, having relatively low risk and highly liquid securities[11].

Furthermore, US demands China to develop its domestic market for import and China should improve its quality of life in that social safety net should be guaranteed, besides creating more employment for all people. In this way, US could have more options in China's economy. US believes that China has a great potential for their economic penetration and expansion in the Asia-Pacific region and would expect China to join in rank in major trade blocks with US as a member.

On top of that, China has dominant sea power in the South China Sea. This is the seaway to ASEAN in terms of trade, security and cooperation. US is interested and perceived this seaway as important to US as the Indian Ocean and the Pacific Ocean. In recent years, US marine had harboured for observatory in these areas and Chinese marine had in direct confrontation with the American Marine. This could be one main reason for ongoing political conflict in the future.

From the political perspective, China could not remain as a socialist political party-ruled country. Also, China should not terminate the relationship with Russia and the latter's former satellite countries that are now independent from Russia and located in the neighbourhood of China. In fact, China has also cooperated with Russia against US. China founded Shanghai Cooperation Organization in Beijing in 2001 consisting of 6 members[12]. It is aimed at cooperation at the international level in mutual economic interest and combating terrorism and drug trafficking. But all in all, the main common interest is the guarantee of energy supply. This will form one strong group against NATO by establishing cooperation, first, in economy, and later, in defense system in the region. In the future, this will stimulate a convergence of major unipolar power which is now enjoyed by US alone. China and Russia will cooperate to counter US prevalence and hegemony.

Another political tension faced by China would be the dispute against legal ownership of the Spratly islands, Paracel islands and Scarborough Reef among the surrounding neighbour countries in the Asian region. China would consistently be strangled unless the issue is resolved for the good sake of all the nations involved.

China being a huge country with a large diversified population will definitely have its own political issues. But until now, China is still ruled by the socialist Communist Party of China in a one-party system. This is a supreme organization, which decides on everything, compared with Western democracy represented by every state of citizens. China also has many surrounding autonomous entities, who are continuously claiming independence, such as Tibet and Taiwan. These issues are unresolved and therefore such political instability and non-consolidation of democracy will be an obstacle to lure Western investors into the country.

As an extension to that, China has also often been stroked by challenges related to the international relations issue. Tibet was invaded by the Chinese government fifty years ago and the Tibetan leaders left for India into seclusion there. Dalai Lama and his followers have staged protests and operated from there. But China has had its control over the Tibetan government. This is an ongoing conflict between Tibet and China and will take some time to resolve. US has been keen on showing strong support for the Tibetan government-in-exile.

Also, the July 5 protest in Urumqi, the Xinjiang regional capital, which involved ethnic riots between the Han, China's largest ethnic group, with the Uighurs, the minority ethnic group, also poses a challenge to China's government in looking for the best solution to resolve the issue without creating much dispute in the country amidst the judgment of the nations worldwide. Certainly, China's approaches in dealing with the riots have met much condemnation and dissatisfaction. One of it is the death toll of Uighurs revealed by the government. It was deemed to be suppressed while Uighurs expressed their disbelief claiming that many Uighurs had died in the riots.

It further relates to the issues of human rights and freedom of expression which were always sensitive and controversial in China. Recent action of the Chinese authorities to shut down blogs, internet forums and social media sites such as Twitter[13] had faced much criticism claiming that the action was inconsistent with the right to freedom of speech and expression. It might be out of a concern to prevent further inflammation of the situation, but the intention of the government to suppress political and public discussion of the 20th anniversary of the Tiananmen Square pro-democracy protest was clear and vivid.

Perhaps adopting more capitalist ideology, and attention on granting more human rights and freedom of expression to create a more democratic China would be a difficult task to be accomplished in a short period of time. But with sheer will and determination, and in order for China to gain more respect from global nations, such move is inevitable. History shows no nations could become a global superpower by oppressing basic human rights and freedom of speech and expression. Certainly, China would not be an exception.

3) China is ever ready to extend and direct its foreign aid from the Asian region to Africa and South America. China has also vowed ambitiously to the rescue of the Third World nations. China is boosting aid and assistance to the Third World in a bid to regain its diplomatic clout as a major donor. China's initiative comes at a time when the Third World nations have just started to see strong economic growth in their countries, nevertheless unfortunately marred by recent price hikes for the continent's rich natural resource, i.e. oil.

As a way to expand the Chinese cultural heritage to the world, China should have invested more by providing training for the Third World's population to propagate and inculcate the learning of the Chinese language and also more comprehensive Chinese cultural heritage. This is the best way to globalize the cultural components of China.

With over 1.3 billion Chinese population in China and more residing overseas, there stands a bright opportunity for China to spread its culture-full heritage and history to the world to create and form an "Oriental" value with the well-known serenity, tranquility and decency. In fact, the widespread use of Chinese language and cultivation of Chinese traditional values worldwide would ensure the greater forge of China in the international platform and more entrenched it would become.

From the social aspect, infrastructures such as the transportation, electric and communication structures are not well developed. Also, a big portion of its population is not well educated. The high illiteracy rate is a big obstacle for China, in its attempt at industrialization. Also, there are many who receive low income and many who live in hardcore poverty. In comparison to the Western countries, Chinese population is also not well exposed to the banking system and this could cripple the development of the financial market.

As such, China needs to develop the human and social network. The government should cultivate more qualified personnel who are equivalent to international standards with good command of the English language as well as highly motivated. China should also develop its infrastructures adhering to the international standard.

In short, even though China has seen pleasant outcome from its transformation from socialism to more capitalism, it is still on the way, and the transformation is not full and complete yet. China needs more time and effort to complete this transition as it needs also to develop its industry and trade market which serve as a strong foundation and essential basis for China in order to become a financial hub not only in the region, but also globally.

However, the progress of development could be marred by several issues that if not given appropriate concern, could cause further malaise for China in the next 30 years. First is the integration of all regions and provinces in China especially of those autonomous regions such as Tibet in terms of culture, economy, politics, ethnicity and religion. It is crucial that China needs to be united internally and domestically before proceeding to the international arena to be a superpower or it is susceptible to great criticism which jeopardizes the image as a great leading country. Often, China has been reported to suppressed human rights and freedom of expression via propaganda and media blockage. Unless China could tolerate such liberalization, it will not gain respect from the free developed countries of the world.[14]

This in fact was ironical if compared to America. Way back in 1835, a French political thinker and historian, Alexis de Tocqueville, in his famous book *Democracy in America* had written about the success of democratic practice in America compared to other countries while China at this moment is still under great condemnation of its one-party political system and its suppression of human rights and freedom. At times, China shows no appetite in urging for political liberalization. A solid example would be the permanent scar of China marked by the crackdown on pro-democracy protestors around Tiananmen Square 20 years ago.

Apart from responding aggressively to the possible threats and resolve them in a proper manner, China should grab the opportunities and the privileges it has to expand the country in the international arena. China has huge markets luring investments from developed countries while at the same time, invested in other countries in the region. In this case, China could be a stakeholder as one of the world leaders with extended relationship with countries in the region. China's firm and well-established cooperation with Asian countries in terms of trade, economics and politics as well as diplomacy together with strengthening military forces patrolling and playing more vital role in the East and South China Sea would definitely stand to be an advantage to outrage US's hegemony in the region. To achieve this, continuous close rapport among all countries in the region with China must be maintained and China should also focus more on R&D in technology to further empower its military forces.

On top of that, together China and America could form a "Chimerica" alliance that would emerge to be a great power economically. Only then, the real Pax Sinica could be achieved by China.[15]

However, with great power come great responsibilities. Once established as a global leader, China must be prepared to support and provide aid and help to its less developed counterpart countries. Furthermore, once it becomes a great power, China must also be ready to react to any criticism raised by other countries, just like the US, EU and other international organizations always being blamed and criticized by the developing nations now. It must also play a vital role in global issues such as climate change, world politics, human rights, food and clean water supply and national conflicts, etc. in order to maintain its status as a strong nation.

This year marks the 30th anniversary of China's economic reform and open-door policy. China has already achieved noticeable success in becoming a strong nation of trade and industry. The next step is for China to become a strong financial nation in the next thirty years. This will be China's second achievement in the reform of its open policy.[16]

We have discussed China's model of economic development and political orientation, but discussion on the future direction and austerity of China is certainly difficult. While there is a lesson from the failure of USSR model and the new Russia, we have limited understanding on China's sustainability. The above discussion represents my personal opinions.

Conclusion

China is a unique case worthy of investigatory research. At most times, it seems that China is capable to resolve its own obstacles and prove its resilience. China hardly falls from external shock and pressure from international watchdogs. In the Cold War time, there were no complicated external shocks yet from the multilateral angle, unlike today's China which faces more obstacles than ever. If in the old days China was safe under the protection of the socialist bloc like USSR, now in this globalization period, this kind of protection no longer exists and it is left in direct confrontation with US power.

China is now in many fields running parallel with US. It is now underway catching up with US pace of advancement in technology, capital and human resource and military defense. China should be ready to handle the pressure of criticism on its aggressiveness and assertiveness in world agenda when its impact of advancement is observable and felt by the competing nations around the world.

To conclude this discussion, I think that there is no ideal model for ruling the people and the question remains that which system is better. It depends on the people and the nation as such. In the past, the world was not as integrated as today. In today's world, however, globalization has resulted in a closer relation among nations with increased interdependencies. Anyhow, it is hard to predict what role will today's world superpowers play in the future.

The progress of China would certainly be dragged by its Communist Party ruling system and practice, and unless more liberalization is granted, China will not be able to achieve the same level as in Western countries in all aspects. If it would be impossible for China to relax its political ideology of Communist one-party rule, a certain level of political as well as social freedom must be provided, regardless of the political system.

I believe that 30 years is a long way down the road, and China certainly has enough time to develop its economic, political, social, cultural and financial sectors while at the same time resolve the existing and emerging domestic woes to stand proudly as a global leading country.

Notes

*   Dr Im-Soo Yoo 유임수 / 劉壬洙 is Professor Emeritus at the Department of Economics, Ewha Womans University, Seoul, Republic of Korea. He obtained his Bachelor of Arts and Master in Business Administration from Yonsei University, Korea, and holds a PhD in Economics from University of Cologne, Germany. Dr Yoo has been teaching for the past 30 years. He has been Visiting Professor at various universities throughout Europe and Asia including University of Munich, University of Potsdam and University of Paris III. Dr Yoo served as Visiting Professor at the Faculty of Economics and Administration, University of Malaya, Kuala Lumpur, Malaysia, and currently he is a Senior Research Fellow at the Institute of China Studies, University of Malaya. Dr Yoo was advisor to the Board of Audit and Inspection of Korea and also several other government and corporate organizations. He was President of Korean Association for Contemporary European Studies and currently President of Asia-Europe Perspective Forum. His current research interests include international economics, trade, economic development and global finance especially for economic integration between European Union and East Asian community.

1. *<http://historyliterature.homestead.com/files/extended.html>*.
2. *<http://www.soviethistory.org/index.php?page=subject&SubjectID=1985perestr oika&Year=1985>*.
3. *<http://ca.news.yahoo.com/s/capress/090418/entertainment/china_people_jackie_ chan>*.
4. "Anger over Jackie's Freedom Remarks" (Hong Kong (AP)), *New Straits Times*, 20th April 2009, p. 22.
5. *<http://www.ebookee.com.cn/Sovereignty-over-the-Paracel-and-Spratly-Islands_ 167407.html>*.

6. *<http://www.publications.parliament.uk/pa/cm200607/cmselect/cmtreasy/90/9006. htm>*.
7. *<http://www.asianews.it/index.php?l=en&art=13834>*.
8. Frank Ching, "Lee on Mission to Strengthen Ties with China", *New Straits Times*, 12th June 2008, p. 23.
9. Celeste Fong, "Accord to Talk on Claims", *The Star*, 6th June 2009, p. 2.
10. Martin Khor, "Realities behind the G20 Hype", *The Star*, 6th April 2009, p. 43; Mohamed Ariff, "Can G20 Fix the Broken World Economy?", *New Straits Times*, 31st March 2009, p. 17; I.S. Kim, "China Economy Paradigm Shift", *Korea Export Insurance News*, Exciting Export, March/April, 2008, pp. 8-11.
11. Cooper, R.N, "The Future of the Dollar", *The Korea Herald*, 4th June 2009, p. 10; M. Vatikiotis and H. Holland, "Thinking the Unthinkable", Asia Financial Union, 8th April 2004, p. 40.
12. *<http://www.trcb.com/news-and-society/international/shanghai-corporation-organization-sco-a-new-platform-2531.htm>*.
13. "China Cracks Down on Media" (Beijing (AP)), *The Korea Herald*, 4th June 2009, p. 15.
14. "Quiet Mourning at Tiananmen" (Reuters), *New Straits Times*, 5th June 2009, p. 33.
15. Frank Ching, "The Interdependence of China and the US", New Straits Times, 23rd April 2009, p. 17; Thierry De Montbrial, "The Time Has Come to Rebuild the World Order", *New Straits Times*, 5th April 2009, p. 20.
16. "Thirty Years of Reform", *The Star*, 9th December 2008, p. 38; Matthew Lee, "Star Power Fuels Clinton Trip to Asia", *New Straits Times*, 24th February 2009, p. 16.

References

"Beijing Tries to Stimulate Domestic Consumption, against Unemployment and Revolts", Asianews, 24th November 2008. *<http://www.asianews.it/index. php?l=en&art=13834>*

Buckley, Chris, "China Raises Xinjiang Death Toll, Adds Ethnic Detail", 11th July 2009. *<http://thestar.com.my/news/story.asp?file=/2009/7/12/worldupdates/2009-07-11T215343Z_01_NOOTR_RTRMDNC_0_-409658-5&sec=Worldupdates>*

Chang, Chun (2003), "Progress and Perils in China's Modern Economy", Federal Reserve Bank of Minneapolis.

Chemillier-Gendreau, Monique (2009), "Sovereignty over the Paracel and Spratly Islands". *<http://www.ebookee.com.cn/Sovereignty-over-the-Paracel-and-Spratly-Islands_167407. html>*

"China to Take Measures to Spur Consumption Stimulates Foreign Trade", *PLA Daily* (China Military Online Daily), 25th December 2008. *<http://english.pladaily.com. cn/site2/news-channels/2008-12/25/content_1597085.htm>*

"China's Financial Market – A Future Global Force?", Deutsche Bank Research, 16th March 2009.

Ching, Frank, "Lee on Mission to Strengthen Ties with China", *New Straits Times*, 12th June 2008, p. 23.

Einhorn, Bruce and Theo Francis, "Asia Breathes a Sigh of Relief", *Businessweek*, 22nd September, 2008, p. 32.

Feldstein, Martin (2009), "Lessons of China's Economic Growth: Comment", prepared for 2009 January Meeting of the American Economic Association.

Giles, Herbert Allen (2006), "The Civilization of China". *<www.gutenberg.org>*

"Globalisation in Recent Years". *<http://www.publications.parliament.uk/pa/cm200607/cmselect/cmtreasy/90/9006.htm>*

Mehran, Hassanali and Marc Quintyn (1996), "Financial Sector Reforms in China", *Finance and Development*, IMF, March. *<www.imf.org/external/pubs/ft/fandd/1996/03/pdf/mehran.pdf>*

"Quiet Mourning at Tiananmen" (Reuters), *New Straits Times*, 5th June 2009, p. 33.

Schearf, Daniel, "China Marks Thirty Years of Economic Progress", *Voice of America News Online*, 2nd December 2008. *<http://www.voanews.com/english/archive/2008-12/2008-12-02-voa50.cfm>*

"The History of China". *<http://www-chaos.umd.edu/history/toc.html>*

Tschang, C.C., "Chinese Banks Head for the U.S.", *Businessweek*, 5th November 2007, p. 28.

Waterton, James, "Thoughts on China's Future", 5th January 2006. *<http://www.samizdata.net/blog/archives/008435.html>*

Wu Xiaoling, "New Frontiers for China's Financial Sector", *Caijing Magazine Online*, 7th October 2008. *<http://english.caijing.com.cn/2008-10-07/110017990.html>*

Chapter 9

Emerging Threats in South, Central and West Asian Regions: China's Strategy and Responses

Mutahir Ahmed*

Introduction

Keeping its economic, political and security interests in perspective, China is strengthening and establishing relations with the power centres of global actors – the US, Russia, Europe and India. In the post-Cold War era, China has secured the status of a major player of international politics, by identifying three areas of development. First, focusing primarily on economic development, China acquires the largest foreign exchange reserves in the world more than the worth of four trillion dollars. Second, in order to sustain its growth, China has to become an active player of international politics. A major proportion of oil and other natural resources and raw material that China needs to feed its growing economy is imported from Latin America, Africa and Central and Southwest Asia. These regions are the emerging markets for Chinese products, making them profoundly valuable. Finally, sustained economic growth within China depends on a stable security and peaceful environment in its neighbourhood.

The State policy of China does not have hegemonistic design in or outside Asia. With the passage of time, Chinese security concerns have also changed. Moreover, the threat level is also not the same as it was in the decades of 50s, 60s and early 70s when Chinese policy makers were convinced that war with superpowers was inevitable. But, if anybody had the ability to challenge Chinese territorial integrity in late 90s, it was the United States (Breslin, 2009). China worried about a stronger US military presence in Southeast and Central Asia. Furthermore, after the event of 9/11, the United States had pursed aggressive diplomacy in Afghanistan, by convincing its NATO allies to deploy troops in Afghanistan, acquired military bases in Central Asia and pressurized Pakistan to aggressively start operation against Taliban and its allies. All these developments in the region have a direct impact on Chinese security concerns. The Chinese ambassador to Pakistan Luo Zhaohui showed concern on the "outside influence" in the region. He stated that China was worried about the US policies and the presence of a large number of foreign troops in neighbouring Afghanistan. While reiterating China's support for the fight against terrorism, he declared that the US strategies needed some corrective measures (Symonds, 2009). Ambassador Luo's remarks came just one day after the meeting of President Barack Obama with his Chinese counterpart, President Hu Jintao. The statement of the Ambassador shows the Chinese concern over growing US influence in South Asia. China, having longstanding ties with Pakistan, is obviously disturbed by these developments. A far as the economic interest of China is concerned, 60 Chinese companies are involved in 122 projects in Pakistan, and more than 10,000 Chinese engineers and technical experts are working in Pakistan (Symonds, 2009).

China regards Pakistan as a crucial partner in its own regional strategy. In this regard, China is keenly developing Pakistan's infrastructure in order to counter India especially after the 1962 Sino-Indian border war and later on India's nuclear testing in 1998 which according to Indian officials was directed towards China rather than Pakistan. Moreover, Pakistan is the largest purchaser of Chinese arms. According to a Pentagon report, 36 per cent of China's military exports went to Pakistan between 2003 and 2007. Chinese technical assistance was critical to Pakistan's nuclear weapons and ballistic missile programmes. In return, Pakistan has permitted China to build a major naval/commercial port facility at Gawadar, a coastal town in Baluchistan. The port is the linchpin of Bejing's "string of pearls" strategy to establish access for its expanding Navy to a series of ports along key sea routes across the Indian Ocean and at the same time to protect civil and gas supplies from the Middle East and Africa. The US which regards China as a rising economic and strategic rival is determined to maintain its military, including naval predominance (Symonds, 2009).

Besides China's strategic strategy, its policy in existing international order is based on four pillars of its foreign policy: 1) a commitment to multi-lateralism and supporting central role of the UN as the guarantor of global security; 2) a commitment to consultation and dialogue rather than force as means of settling disputes; 3) a commitment to global economic development with the developed world taking a greater share of responsibility for promoting growth; 4) a spirit of inclusiveness, recognizing all societies and cultures as coexistent and equal stakeholders in the global order (Breslin, 2009).

Elaborating these four points, it is clear that China supports existing international order and reflecting uni-polar hegemony of the *Pax Americana*. Moreover, China respects the state sovereignty and does not seek to impose values and policies on others. Moreover, situation in and around China is more challenging and alarming. First, the nuclear testing of North Korea has a far reaching implication in the region involving regional and extra-regional powers. Second, Indo-US civil nuclear deal has also created ripples in South Asia and directly affected China's security. Third, NATO's presence in Afghanistan has also seen an active and negative role in the region. Finally, the presence of the US in the Central Asian region and at the same time violent religious extremists threaten not only the Southwest Asian regions, but also affect the Xinjiang Uighur Autonomous Region (XUAR) of China.

The focus of this chapter is to analyze the role of international actors in these regions, commonly known as the "Great Game", and the responses coming from these regions in the shape of ethno-nationalism and violent religious extremism. Attempt are made to analyze the role of regional and extra-regional powers, which affect China's economic, political, and security interests as well as China's response to these threats.

Emerging Developments in South and West Asian Regions

The Great Game

In the late nineteenth century the British Empire in India and the Tsarist Russia were in competition and tried to influence Afghanistan and the Central Asian region (Rashid, 2001). Moreover, the centrality of interests of both powers was Afghanistan. The British feared that a Russian thrust on Heart from the Turkmen region could threaten British Baluchistan, while the Russians feared that the British would undermine them in Central Asia by supporting revolts by the Muslim tribes and the rulers of Bukhara and Kokand (Rashid, 2001). After the disintegration of the Soviet Union its successor Russia wanted to take the Central Asian region as its area of influence for the flow of Caspian oil through pipelines that link Russia. In this context, Russian Federation had formulated the Commonwealth of Independent States (CIS) in which all Central Asian republics are the members. Moreover, Russian Federation proposed a policy of "Near Abroad"; it means that the last soldier of the Russian army was deployed in Tajikistan. In other words, Russian territory has been stretched to Tajikistan under the banner of CIS. It shows the importance Russia has given to the Central Asian region. On the other hand, the US is also interested in the region because of its resources. The US proposed an oil pipeline which would bypass Russia. Iran, Turkey and Pakistan are also building their own links with the region. However, China remains the most affected and also most active party among all powers. Religious extremist forces pose a threat to Chinese authority in the Xianjiang Autonomous Region. Massive riots took place during the 90s causing ethnic tension and instability (Tara, 1996).

The background of this violent instability can be seen in the context of the Soviet presence in Afghanistan. Moreover, the violent phase of Chinese Muslim unrest has a direct correlation with the US-China-Pakistan-Saudi Arabian axis to support the Mujahideen's Jihad and to bleed the Soviets in Afghanistan. Later on, when the Soviets withdrew from Afghanistan, Mujahideen infighting started in order to gain control of Afghanistan. However, the division among the Mujahideen and the spill-over effect of their infighting could easily be visible in the neighbouring countries including China's Xinjiang Autonomous Region.

The Xinjiang Uighur Autonomous Region occupies a pivotal position in the region with its borders touching Mongolia, Tajikistan, Kyrgyzstan, Kazakhstan, Afghanistan and Kashmir. In Xinjiang, the Han Chinese are 37 per cent and the Uighur Muslims are 47 per cent. Increased trans-border trade and traffic between Xinjiang and the adjourning regions of Kazakhstan, Kyrgyzstan and Pakistan via KaraKaram highway passing through Azad Kashmir had resulted in greater interaction between the Turkic speaking Uighurs and their ethnic counterpart and co-religionists in Central Asia, Pakistan, Turkey and Saudi Arabia (Warikoo, 1996). Furthermore, the exposure which they got during Afghan Jihad with full support of the Chinese state and later on when Taliban took control, these Uighur Muslims tasted a new phenomenon of life which revolved around a particular brand of religion. Historically, the Uighur Muslims were the single largest community constituting about 7.2 million of China's 18 million Muslims and they mainly concentrated in Xinjiang Autonomous Region (Sawran Singh, 2002: 409).

As it is stated above, China encouraged Uighur Muslims to fight in Afghanistan against the Soviets. But when the Soviets decided to leave Afghanistan in 1989 these well-trained and well-equipped Uighurs were unable to return to China and continued to fight for various Afghan factions including the Taliban (Stobodon, 1999).

Chinese Nationalism

Presently, the dominant western view of Chinese nationalism is revolving around party propaganda constructed by the Chinese Communist Party to legitimize its rule. However, the matter of fact is that the pride in the superiority of the five thousand years of Chinese civilization is central to nationalism in China today (Triandafyllidov, 2006: 290). The five thousand years are central to the dream of a prosperous country and a strong army, which still inspires Chinese nationalists over a century after it was first promoted by the late Qing-dynasty reformers (*ibid.*: 491). However, there are "two Chinas": the Chinese people's "motherland" and the ruler's "State". State nationalism is propagated and tied to socialism, while popular networks are challenging the State's hegemony over nationalism, threatening to rupture the Chinese nation-state (*ibid.*: 496). The ethnic issue of Xinjiang between Uighurs and Han can be analyzed in this context.

Linkage between Taliban and Uighurs

During the Soviet presence in Afghanistan, Uighur Muslims along with other fellow Mujahideen from different Muslim countries built strong relations with the locals. Moreover, the Uighurs had also developed relations with other powerful groups called the Islamic Movement led by Tahir Yuldashev who came from Uzbekistan and based in Afghanistan (Gangadharan, 2000: 62). All these forces were closely associated with the Taliban.

The matter of fact is that Uighurs got political, moral and material support from Afghanistan during the Afghan Jihad. The young generation of Uighurs is more militant, aggressively inspired by the international Islamic resistance Jihadist movement centred in Afghanistan during Taliban rule. This young generation of Uighurs represented ethnoreligious nationalism and they cornered the old generation which was secular nationalists. As a result, ideologically tough Uighurs inspired and fought the Afghan war and brought violence inside China's Xinjiang Autonomous Region. However, China deliberately sent the Han ethnic group into Xinjiang Autonomous Region in order to create balance in the region, but this was not taken as a positive step. Uighurs are of the opinion that the Han would create problems at two levels: first, identity crisis for Uighurs and second, economic competition. Han control job market and would create economic competition for Uighur Muslims.

Ethnic Riots

Violent riots took place in the region during the decade of nineties. It has been reported with concern that the activities of some two hundred activists of Pakistani religious parties were engaged in propagating their brand of religion in Xinjiang. The Chinese authorities describe this phenomenon as interference in its internal affairs (Mutahir, 1992: 80). Moreover, China also claimed that the Taliban had trained Islamic fundamentalists and provided them arms.[1]

Since the beginning of the 90s availability of small arms and light weapons had been accessed through different routes and sources. Weapons began to move into China causing ethnic tensions and instability in Xinjiang. Violent clashes took place and left more then eighty people dead and hundred injured (Moonis Ahmar, 1997). In this connection ethnic riots again broke out. On 5th July 2009, at least 197 people were killed and 1,600 were wounded in ethnic riots in Xinjiang. Hundreds of rioters had been arrested after the Uighurs took to the streets of the regional capital Urumqi, burning and smashing vehicles and confronting anti-riots police. According to Chinese authorities the unrest was the work of extremist forces abroad. They blamed the violence on the World Uighur Congress and other separatist groups to split Xinjiang from China. Highlighting the severity of the crisis, President Hu Jintao had cut short his trip to Italy for the G8 Summit – observers said it was an unprecedented move – to tackle one of China's worst spikes in ethnic tensions in decades.[2] But exiled Uighur groups adamantly rejected the Chinese government's claim of a plot. They said the riots were an outcome of the policies of the Chinese government.

Xinjiang has long been a tightly controlled hotbed of ethnic tension, fostered by an economic gap between the Uighurs and the Han Chinese, and government controls on religion and cultural activities. Additionally, Han migrants are the majority in urban centres and control the markets. Strategically, Xinjiang, bordering Russia, Mongolia, Kazakhstan, Kyrgyzstan, Tajikistan, Afghanistan and Pakistan, has abundant oil reserves and is China's largest natural gas producing region.[3] Thus, it is natural that Chinese authorities would deal with the matter with an iron hand.

Regional Reactions

The exiled Uighurs in Kazakhstan and Turkey reacted sharply. Officially Turkey called on China to show restraint in dealing with unrest in Xinjiang saying it cannot "remain indifferent" to the plight of the region's Turkic speaking Muslim Uighurs. Addressing a Press Conference, the Turkish Foreign Minister, Ahmet Davutoglu said, "The Uighurs are a community of ethnic brothers whose fate concerns us … there is humanitarian situation there that requires the world's attention … it is out of the question for Turkey to remain indifferent."[4] Moreover, in a written statement, the Turkish foreign ministry said it hoped that Chinese security forces would "act in accordance with international human rights norms and principles" and give priority to the safety of civilians.[5]

Moreover, the Prime Minster of Turkey, Recep Tayyip Erdogan, urged China to stop the "assimilation" of its Uighur minority and termed it "genocide" and said that "suffering of the Uighurs is ours".[6] Turkey has been angered by the plight of Turkic-speaking Muslim Uighurs at the hands of the Chinese authorities and the Han Chinese. Prime Minster Erdogan asks the UN Security Council to discuss ways of ending the violence. The call was rejected by China, one of five permanent members of the Council which can veto its actions.[7]

In Kazakhstan thousands of ethnic Uighurs rallied in the Kazakh city of Almaty to protest against a crackdown against Uighurs. Around five thousands Uighurs gathered in the city to express their anger against the crackdown on Uighurs in Xinjiang. Kazakhstan is the home of the largest Uighur community outside China and many more are scattered around the rest of the Central Asian region where Uighurs want to set up their own state. The violence in Xinjiang has brought internal tensions among Kazakhstan's Uighurs and created a broad-based instability in the vast region of Central Asia particularly in Afghanistan.

Al-Qaida Connection

According to the London-based risk analysis firm Stirling Assynt, Al-Qaida had vowed to avenge the deaths of Muslim Uighurs killed in Xinjiang by targeting Chinese workers in North Africa. It was the first time the Osama bin Laden network has directly threatened China's interests.[8] However, China issued security alert to its citizens in Algeria after Al-Qaida's threat. Foreign Ministry spokesman said that Beijing would take all necessary measures to ensure the safety of overseas Chinese institutions and people.[9]

Shanghai Five

In order to resolve the crisis, China proposed a regional solution to its Uighur problem in the shape of the Shanghai Five forum. The focus of this forum is to reduce and resolve outstanding disputes to consolidate confidence building in the military sphere and to increase mutual trade and economic cooperation. It is a strategic arrangement framed in Shanghai in April 1996. The original members are China, Russia, Kazakhstan, Kyrgyzstan and Tajikistan. The group agreed to counter the threat of religious extremism and to form a joint anti-terrorist centre to fight cross-border incursions by guerillas and drug traffickers. The treaty was a continuation of the 1990 agreement formulated between the former Soviet Union and China for the principles of mutual reduction of armed forces and confidence building in the border areas.

On a larger scale, the formation of this group has to counter the United States and its allies in Europe and the Far East who wanted to encircle Russia and China. The European experience of the Cold War perceived Russia as a potential adversary and the alliance got support from the US. While in the East, the US security perceptions in the Asia-Pacific region have focused on the potential threat from China. Thus Shanghai Five had been viewed to contain the United States in the Far East and the Southwest Asian regions (Maqbool, 2000). However, the US under Obama is pursuing a policy to contain China particularly in Southeast Asia. In this regard, Secretary of State Hillary Clinton signed a friendship pact with ten countries of the ASEAN. The purpose of this treaty is to re-establish the role of the US in the region and give no room to China in the region. In other words, the Obama Administration wanted to establish cordial relations with ASEAN countries in order to revive the traditional relations with the regional bloc as well as to contain China and North Korea in the region.[10] Initially, the Shanghai Five is confined to security-related issues, but later on, it has broadened the definition of security by including religious terrorism, arms and narco-terrorism. The group agreed to ban "the use of territories of their states for activities causing damage to the sovereignty, security and the social order of the member states".[11]

It is in the line of the Chinese concern regarding subversive activities of dissident elements in Xinjiang. The group has established its credentials as an alternative paradigm for cooperative security and opened its doors to other states (Sawran Singh, 2000). Besides, the forum strengthened China's bilateral ties with neighbouring countries particularly Russia. The two countries formed common interests to contain terrorism and extremism in the region. Later on in 2001, the Shanghai Five officially transformed into Shanghai Cooperation Organization (SCO) in an "institutionalization of a regional organization work for a cooperative security arrangement".

Impact of 9/11 on the Region

The event of 9/11 changed the chemistry of international politics and directly affected the South and West Asian regions. International players had endorsed the United States' war against terrorism. Though SCO was also against any form of religious terrorism, the involvement of the US and NATO in the region has been considered as extra-regional forces thus posing economic and security threat which is dangerous for regional stability. However, the military engagement of the US in Afghanistan by removing the Taliban regime from power had helped China to cut off the external linkage to the Uighur separatists in Xinjiang. However, on a broader scale permanent pressure of the US in Afghanistan strengthened the fear of the "New Great Game" in the region which would not be tolerated by China and Russia.

New Great Game

The concept of "New Great Game" was taken from the traditional power rivalries between Czarist Russia and British Empire during the nineteenth century. However, today several new actors emerged, representing regional and extra-regional powers. These are China, Central Asian States, Russian Federation, Iran, Turkey, Pakistan, India, United States and European Union.

In order to contain extra-regional forces, emphasis has been made to strengthen regional economic bloc which further strengthen the political and security environment. In the line of this strategy, Chinese leadership has accelerated economic pace so that rewards of growth benefited if not all segments of the population then at least most of them (Shahid, 2009).

Russia and China have signed energy deals worth 100 billion dollars in 2009. According to the Russian economy ministry, China overtook Germany and the Netherlands as Russia's biggest trade partner in first four months of 2009. In a joint statement, Chinese President Hu Jintao along with Russia's Dmitry Medvedev called for a greater role of emerging economies on the world financial stage and a bigger use of national currencies in bilateral trade, focusing on the "creation of favorable conditions for widening the sphere of settlement in rouble and yuan". Both countries have also criticized the US on the political front, saying no country should base its defense on expanding military alliances and building missile defenses.[12]

Moreover, at SCO meeting held in Russia in June 2009, China extended ten billion dollar loan to a regional group of four Central Asian states. Chinese President Hu Jintao stated that the loan was intended to strengthen economies of its members amid the global financial crisis.[13] In this connection, the first summit of emerging economies BRIC (Brazil, Russia, India and China) was held in Moscow. The purpose of this summit was to strengthen the economies of its members. The Russian economic advisor stated that ruble, yuan and gold should be the part of revised basket of currencies to form the valuation of the IMF's special drawing rights. He further stated that new currencies should help to distribute the global wealth more fairly and also encourage economic leaders to pursue a more balanced economic policy. The talk about the new global currency has been prompted by concerns in China and Russia that soaring US budget deficits could spur inflation and weaken the dollar, debasing the value of their holdings.[14]

Chinese Interests in South Asian Region

In the context of South Asia, the poorest as well as strategically important region of the world, India and Pakistan are two neighbouring nuclear countries while China, though not geographically located in the region, is a very important player in South Asian politics. Thus, there is a triangle in South Asia, politically and strategically dominated by these three states. However, the US also has a great influence in the region. The South Asian region confronted mainly with two problems. First, the war against terrorism has been fought in the region. Second, extra-regional actors are directly involved in the region which has further radicalized the politics of the region. Moreover, India and the US have developed their relations in the field of nuclear technology. An agreement was signed between India and the US. According to it, the US will transfer civil nuclear defense technology to India. Pakistan and China have criticized this deal on the ground that it would disturbed the balance of power in the region (India supported the National Missile Defense announced by the then President George Bush in May 2001) (Mutahir, 2002: 23). It shows the intentions of India and the US to counter the influence of China in the South Asian region.

Moreover, China also reacted sharply to the extension of the US military assistance to Taiwan. China has reason to be concerned over the deployment of the US National Missile Defense for its allies (*ibid.*). In this backdrop China sees the civil nuclear agreement with great concern. But on the economic front, China follows the policy of engagement with India. Sino-Indian trade now exceeds 52 billion dollars a year (Pak-China bilateral trade is around 7 billion dollars a year). China has also engaged the US companies which have established more than 20,000 joint ventures in China, while 100 of the top US-based multinationals have agreed to develop projects in China (Furukh, 2009).

On the other hand, Pak-China relations have strategic importance. China also uses Pakistan to contain India's geo strategic ambitions. China invested 198 million dollars in Gowadar port in order to create a balance in the Indian Ocean. Moreover, China also seeks Pakistan's help in containing the East Turkistan Movement based in Xinjiang. For Pakistan, China is a major supplier of military hardware, nuclear reactors and counter leverage to the

US. For this purpose, China adheres to "military strategy of active defense". However, Beijing needed to boast its military capabilities to counter security threats and support its commitments to help ensure peace and stability.[15]

On the other hand, element of insecurity prevails in India because of China's close relations with Pakistan, its supplying weapons to Sri Lanka and improving relations with Myanmar and Nepal. This leads to the Indian fear of strategic encirclement. Historically, border clashes between India and China in 1962 ended after China captured over 3,500 km borders of Arunachal Pradesh area from India which China still holds. This traditional distrust of India against China and Pakistan has led to an atmosphere of enmity and insecurity in the region. An intended function of China's support for Pakistan was the *de facto* confinement of India in strategic affairs in the sub-continent. Sensing such apprehensions, India was quick to exploit China's desire for a strategic dialogue, though it has been possible to resolve some of the longstanding disputes over territory and sovereignty. India now recognizes Chinese sovereignty over Tibet, and China recognizes Indian sovereignty over the former princely state Sikkim. However, besides taking these measures both are suspicious of each other.[16] By and large, Chinese concerns about India's emergence as an American bulwark rationally exhibited a disinclination to be used in an instrumental manner by other powers. However, it seems that they will continue to regard each other with some caution.[17]

Conclusion

The South, Central and West Asian regions are confronted with severe threats in the shape of the direct involvement of extra-regional powers, nuclear proliferation, ethnic tensions, and religious extremism. In other words, these three regions are becoming the hub of the above-mentioned turmoil which poses challenges to the security of these regions. In this scenario, China has to act and react because of its economic and political interests in these regions. Moreover, from Chinese point of view, all these regions are bordering China thus posing security challenges. At present, China has taken a very soft line and its foreign policy is not reactive. But if situation in and around China has been radicalized then China has to act actively in the future.

Notes

* Dr Mutahir Ahmed is Professor at the Department of International Relations, University of Karachi, Pakistan. He was a Visiting Fellow at Henry L. Stimson Centre, Washington, US, and Asia Fellow at the University of Malaya, Kuala

Lumpur, Malaysia. His areas of research interest are religious extremism, State-society relations, arms control and disarmament in South, Central and West Asian regions.

1. *Newsline* (Karachi), March 1997, p. 55.
2. *Dawn* (Karachi), 9th July 2009.
3. *Dawn*, 20th July 2009.
4. *Dawn*, 9th July 2009.
5. *Dawn*, 9th July 2009.
6. *The News* (Karachi), 12th July 2009.
7. *The News*, 12th July 2009.
8. *Dawn*, 16th July 2009.
9. *Dawn*, 16th July 2009.
10. *The News*, 24th July 2009.
11. *The News*, 24th July 2009.
12. *Dawn*, 18th June 2009.
13. *Dawn*, 17th June 2009.
14. *Dawn*, 17th June, 2009.
15. *The News*, 23rd May 2009.
16. *Strategic Survey*, The ISS Annual Review of World Affairs, London: Routledge.
17. *Ibid.*: 284.

References

Breslin, Shoun (2009), "Understanding China's regional rise: interpretations, identities and implications", *International Affairs* (London), Vol. 85, No. 4.

Furukh Saleem (2009), "Peeking Man", *The News*, 31st May.

Kanta, Tara (1996), "Light Weapons Proliferation and Regional Instability in Central Asia", *Strategic Analysis* (New Delhi), December.

Maqbool Ahmed Bhatti (2000), "Role of Shanghai Five", *Dawn* (Karachi), 16th July.

Mutahir Ahmed (1992), "Prospects of Islamic Fundamentalism in Central Asia", *Pakistan Horizon* (Karachi), July.

Mutahir Ahmed (2002), "Missile Defense and South Asia: A Pakistani Perspective", in Michael Krepon and Chris Gagne (eds), *The Impact of US Ballistic Missile Defenses on Southern Asia*, Report No. 46, Washington, July.

Moonis Ahmar (1997), "Ethnic Assertion in Xinjiang", *The News* (Karachi), 6th March.

Rashid, Ahmed (2001), *Taliban Militants: Islam, Oil and Fundamentalism in Central Asia*, London: Yale University Press.

Sawran Singh (2000), "India and Shanghai Forum", *Strategic Analysis* (New Delhi), Vol. XXIV, No. 6.

Sawran Singh (2002), "China's Afghan Policy: Limitations versus Leverages", in K. Warikoo (ed.), *The Afghan Crisis*, New Delhi: Bhavana Books.

Shahid Javed Burki (2009), "Causes of State Failure in Asia", *Dawn*, 16th July.

Stobodon, P. (1999), "China's Central Asian Dilemma", *Strategic Analysis* (New Delhi), June.

Surya Gangadharan (2000), "The China-Taliban Equation", *Aakrosh* (New Delhi), January.

Symonds, Peter (2009), "Pakistan War Fuels International Tensions". *<http://wsws. org/articles /2009/ may/2009/pers-m11.shtml>*

Triandafyllidov, Anna (2006), "Nation Migrants and Transnational Identifications: An Interactive Approach to Nationalism", in Genard Delanty and Krishan Kumar (eds), *The SAGE Handbook of Nations and Nationalism*, London: Sage Publications.

Warikoo, K. (1995-96), "Ethnic Religious Resurgence in Xinjiang", *Eurasian Studies* (Ankara), Winter.

Chapter 10

China and Spain:
Critical Junctures, Ethnoterritoriality and
Paths of Reform and Devolution

Emile Kok-Kheng **Yeoh**

Introduction

> *Atado, y bien atado.* [Tied-up, well tied-up.]
>> – Generalísimo Francisco Franco (*El Caudillo*),
>> prior to his death on 20th November 1975

Hage, Hanneman and Gargan (1989: 89-91) remarked that theories of the determinants of public spending should not only be problem specific but also period specific. The historical dimension – the timing of State[1] involvement is a crucial factor.[2] Levi-Strauss (1967: 281-3) perceived time not solely in mechanical, cumulative or statistical terms, but also in social terms – deriving its properties from concrete social phenomena. Complementing his view of ethnicity as a special case of stratification, an analytical perspective concerned with conflict and power (the Weberian approach), Katznelson (1971: 69-70) emphasized the importance of the notion of "critical structural periods" – historical periods when "critical structural decisions" are made. Citing Schattschneider's remark that "organization is the mobilization of bias" (1961: 71), Katznelson noted that critical structural decisions are those that define the "structured relationships" which not only limit but also shape the direction of behavioural choice. In other words, *social time* rather than *historical time*, which can be misleading, is the crucial variable.[3]

Traditional Chinese mystical beliefs see great natural calamities as omens of tumultuous dynastic changes. Probably one of the deadliest wraths of nature in modern times – the official death toll stood at around 242,000, one third of some unofficial estimates – the Tangshan 唐山 earthquake on 28th July, in an ominous turn of events during the "Curse of 1976", was preceded by the death of Zhou Enlai (Chou En-lai)[4] 周恩来 on 8th January and that of Zhu De (Chu Teh) 朱德 on 6th July, and followed by Mao Zedong (Mao Tse-tung) 毛泽东's passing on 9th September that brought his ten-year Great Proletarian Cultural Revolution (*wuchan jieji wenhua da geming* 无产阶级文化大革命) to a close. The so-called Gang of Four (*si ren bang* 四人帮), led by Mao's widow Jiang Qing (Chiang Ch'ing) 江青, were arrested on 6th October in what amounted to a palace coup, paving the way for the return of the twice-purged pragmatist and reformist Deng Xiaoping (Teng Hsiao-p'ing) 邓小平 to the government and party in the following year, who was to deal the *coup de grâce* to Mao's failed autarkic collectivist utopia.

Just a year earlier, in 1975, on the other side of the globe, in Spain which constitutes 85 per cent of the Iberian Peninsula, Generalísimo Francisco Franco y Bahamonde[5] (the *Caudillo*) died. While repeatedly expressing confidence that he would leave Spain *atado, y bien atado* ("tied-up, well tied-up")[6], Franco's death in 1975 was followed within two years by the dismantling of the structure of the whole Franquist regime, and the first free parliamentary elections in over 40 years were held on 15th June 1977. One of the most remarkable developments under the democratic transition had been the political decentralization of the State. The issue of regionalism in fact became the most contentious political issue during the post-Franco transition to democracy, with almost one-tenth of the Constitution devoted to the regional matters. The three main ethnolinguistically non-Castilian regions of Catalonia, the Basque Country and Galicia were given a special status as being "historic regions" – a recognition of the former Statute of Catalonia (1932) which established the *Generalitat*, Statute of the Basque Country (1936) and the putative Galician statute which was approved but never enacted before all three were crushed by the Franquist regime – which entitled them to the fastest route of all to autonomy. Although the *Comunidades Autónomas* project is not designed solely to resolve the ethnic or socioracial[7] problems facing the Castilian centre stemming from the "historic regions" of Catalonia and the Basques Country (and to a less extent, Galicia), hence the creation of seventeen instead of two or three such Communities, it cannot be denied that it is the real or potentially centrifugal pressure from these ethnic regions (rendered even more explosive after the long years of Franquist repression) that provided the first and main impetus behind the will to decentralize after the restoration of democracy in 1975.

The case of China is rather complicated. Deng Xiaoping's return to power signalled China's entry into a new age, with his pragmatism paving the way for the rise of Hu Yaobang 胡耀邦 and Zhao Ziyang 赵紫阳 whom Deng entrusted to plan and implement China's market-oriented economic reforms from 1980 to 1989. These reforms were nothing less than revolutionary, whose origin could be traced to Zhao's successful experimental reforms – during which Zhao laid the foundation of his key reform framework of the coming years[8] – from 1978 in Sichuan, where Zhao was the Party's First Secretary, before Hu and Zhao entered the politburo respectively in 1978 and 1979 and the Standing Committee in 1980 when Hu was appointed the Secretary General and Zhao later the Deputy Premier and then Premier (Bao, 2009: 28-29). In terms of political culture and atmosphere, this was also a period of limited political liberalization, an aspect of reform where the tug-of-war between the reformist and conservative forces was particularly acute, which eventually led to the downfall of, in turn, first Hu in January 1987, then Zhao in June 1989, when they overstepped the mark into the minefield of "bourgeois liberalization" where Deng who sanctioned full-scale economic reform was not prepared to bring China into.

Going back to the 1970s, what we are seeing here is that at their respective critical structural junctures three decades ago, in 1975 and 1976, fascist Spain and Marxist-Leninist China embraced different paths of reforms, with post-Franco Spain spurning overnight her fascist-corporatist past and embracing multiparty democracy and federalism, taking the risk of the disappearance of the central State, to hold the country together against potentially separatist ethnoregional conflicts, while post-Mao China has since followed a more cautious path that was to evolve later into an institutionalized relationship between the central State and the localities some would call "selective centralization" (Zheng, 1999).

This chapter will begin with an examination of the evolution of the Spanish *Comunidades Autónomas* project especially during its early stage in comparative perspective with the state of Chinese decentralization since the abovementioned critical junctures of the two countries in the 1970s. It will subsequently move on to scrutinize the impacts and implications of public policy decisions at the next critical junctures – Madrid's 1981 coup and the 1989 Tiananmen 天安门 demonstrations and hunger strikes of which this year 2009 carries the significance of being the twentieth anniversary. Finally, it will provide a detailed analysis of the impacts of such public policy development on the exigencies engendered in multiethnic societies[9] characterized by ethnoterritoriality, with special reference to the El Ejido riots in 2000 and the Ürümqi riots in 2009.

Decentralization in Spain and China: Comparisons and Contrasts

While nonconcentration in Spain can be traced back to very early days as until the early 18th century, Spain was formed by a set of kingdoms – some of which in fact had their own political and economic institutions very different from those in Castille – united under the monarchy of the king, a diversity later ended by the Borbon dynasty's policy of centralization (Vinuela, 2000: 1), contemporary regional decentralization in Spain is a product of the 20th century.

The most outstanding characteristic of the Spanish process of decentralization since democratic transition and the 1978 Constitution is undoubtedly the emergence of the Autonomous Communities as a new intermediate level of government with political self-governing capacity (Table 10.1), reflected in the growth in the proportion of regional government expenditure which increased from practically zero in 1980 to about a fifth of the total public spending of the country by 1992, while central government's control over public expenditure fell during the same period from almost 85 per cent (the rest are with the local governments) to less than 65 per cent (Figure 10.1). The ratios of both regional current and capital expenditures to those of the central government have been increasing steadily during this period (Figure 10.2). The growth of the ratio of regional to central government expenditure was particularly notable (Figures 10.1 and 10.2). The speed and degree with which this decentralization was accomplished have been an unprecedented phenomenon among the Western economies. This growth in regional expenditure took place in a scenario where the share of gross domestic product (GDP) devoted to total public expenditure (at all levels of government) was going up from around 30 per cent in 1980 to more than 50 per cent by 1992 (Figure 10.3).

To compare this with the case of China, one should first note that Chinese public expenditures or revenues as a proportion of GDP are actually relatively small (Figure 10.4) compared with the developed countries and even with other developing countries.

While China is not a federal country, it could be misleading to simply describe China's political structure as unitary. Nevertheless, with a system Xu (2008) called a "regionally decentralized authoritarian system", China is indeed far more centralized than a federal or fiscal federal system, especially in view of the central State's direct appointment of the main local personnel, e.g. provincial[10] leaders, and direct control on local political issues (Yeoh, 2009b: 244).[11]

Unlike the Spanish decentralization, China's reform is characterized unmistakably by the central government's tight control of the local governments, including those of the demographically Han-dominated provinces of China proper and the ethnic minority "autonomous regions" as well as a few province-level municipalities, in executing the central government's

Table 10.1 Spain*: *Comunidades Autónomas* (Autonomous Communities)

Autonomous Community (Region)	Language Use**	Date of Statute of Self-government	Official Title of Government
Euskadi (País Vasco)	Basque (30%), Castilian	18 December 1979	Gobierno Vasco
Catalunya (Cataluña)	Catalan (70%), Castilian	18 December 1979	Generalitat de Cataluña
Galiza (Galicia)	Galician (65%), Castilian	6 April 1981	Xunta de Galicia
Andalucía	Castilian	30 December 1981	Junta de Andalucía
Asturias	Bable, Castilian	30 December 1981	Principado de Asturias
Cantabria	Castilian	30 December 1981	Diputacion Regional
La Rioja	Castilian	9 June 1982	Consejo de Gobierno
Murcia	Castilian	9 June 1982	Consejo de Gobierno
Valencia	Valencian (Catalan) (49%), Castilian	1 July 1982	Generalitat Valenciana
Aragón	Castilian, Catalan (northeast border)	10 August 1982	Diputacion General
Castilla-La Mancha	Castilian	10 August 1982	Junta de Comunidades
Islas Canarias	Castilian	10 August 1982	Gobierno Canario
Extremadura	Castilian	25 February 1983	Junta de Extremadura
Islas Baleares	Catalan (71%), Castilian	25 February 1983	Gobierno Balear
Madrid	Castilian	25 February 1983	Gobierno de la Comunidad
Castilla y León	Castilian	25 February 1983	Junta de Castilla y Leon
Navarra***	Basque (9%), Castilian	10 August 1983	Diputacion Foral

Notes:

* The total area of Spain also includes five places of sovereignty (plazas de soberania) on and off the coast of Morocco – Ceuta, Melilla, Islas Chafarinas, Peñón de Alhucemas, Peñón de Vélez de la Gomera. Spain's total number of municipalities also include the North African enclaves of Ceuta and Melilla (2 municipalities) which are "self-governing" but not "autonomous" (to avoid being considered colonies on foreign land).

** "Castilian" also includes Castilian dialects. e.g. Riojano, etc.

*** Navarra was granted autonomy under the terms of an organic law on the rehabilitation and improvement of its Foral Regime.

Source: Heywood (1995); Castells (1990); Mansvelt Beck (1991); Brassloff (1989); Brunn (1992).

Figure 10.1 Spain: Total Expenditure, Current & Capital Expenditures –
Ratio of Regional & Provincial Governments to Central
Government (first two decades of decentralization)

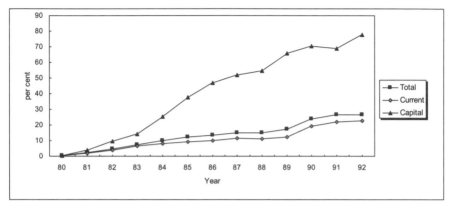

Source: IMF, *Government Finance Statistics Yearbooks*; *Anuarios Estadísticos
de España*, Instituto Nacional de Estadística/Ministerio de Economía y
Hacienda, Madrid.

Figure 10.2 Spain: Total Expenditure, Current & Capital Expenditures –
Growth of Regional & Provincial Governments to Central
Government Ratio (first two decades of decentralization)

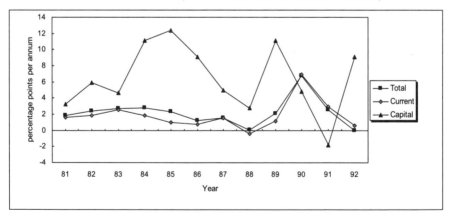

Source: IMF, *Government Finance Statistics Yearbooks*; *Anuarios Estadísticos
de España*, Instituto Nacional de Estadística/Ministerio de Economía y
Hacienda, Madrid.

Figure 10.3 Spain: Total Expenditure as Percentage of GDP at All Levels of Government (first two decades of decentralization)

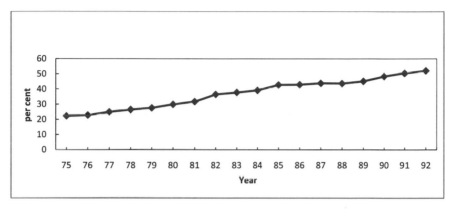

Source: IMF, *Government Finance Statistics Yearbooks*; *Anuarios Estadísticos de España*, Instituto Nacional de Estadística/Ministerio de Economía y Hacienda, Madrid.

Figure 10.4 China: Government Expenditure and Revenue as Percentages of GDP, 1990-2007

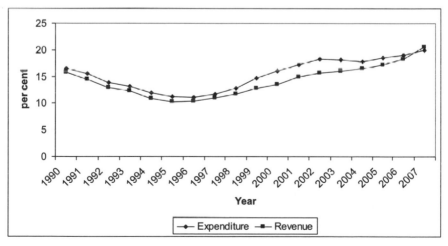

Source: Computed with data from *China Statistical Yearbook*, various years.

policy decisions through the instruments of appointment and promotion, even though there has been extensive decentralization in which various levels of local governments have participated intensively in economic reform and development (Yeoh, 2009b: 245-246). As Xu (2008: 187-188) noted, this is a characteristic that distinguishes China's decentralization from that of federal states where the provincial heads or mayors are produced through elections and hence are accountable to the citizens-voters who have elected them.

On the contrary, in Spain the determination to break with and reverse the repressive policies of the Franquist regime and to integrate the country into a prosperous and democratic Europe has made possible huge concessions to subordinate group aspirations in the country's decentralization process[12], as apparent in the following description of the priorities to design the process of decentralization at that critical juncture in Spain at Franco's death:

> First, the historical nationalities should get the top of self-government as soon as possible. They did not need to prove that the majority of their populations were really desiring to become autonomous. Second, for the rest of the regions, whatever they were, access to self-government involved fulfilling a set of requirements that showed clearly that their local governments, provinces and municipalities, were for becoming an autonomous community. Third, for these regions, which might need to build their institutional capacity to manage effectively certain policies, the powers they could assume, during a transitory period of five years, should be much lower than for the historical nationalities. Fourth, to prevent that some of these regions may felt discriminated relative to the historical nationalities, it was necessary to leave a door open for them to get to the top of self-government without waiting the period of five years, but fulfilling such stringent requirements than the possibilities of success were practically null. Five, it was necessary to avoid an excessive fragmentation of the country by restricting the possibility that a province could accede to self-government, what could prevent an efficient provision of regional public services. But it was necessary again to leave a door open to solve special cases, such as Madrid, the capital of the country, and Navarra, which has historically had an exceptional status very similar to that of Pais Vasco, even during the autocratic period. The result of having to comply with all these priorities was necessarily a great complexity of this part of the constitution.
>
> (Vinuela, 2000: 3-4)

The fear of a return to the old regime, as to many was vindicated by the August 1981 coup, served only to convince the post-coup administration of a need to speed up the policy change and to turn the subordinate groups further away from particularism to universalism in orientation, as illustrated in van Amersfoort's typology[13] of dominant-subordinate relations (van Amersfoort, 1978) in Figure 10.5. The combined result of such changes in dominant and

Figure 10.5 Van Amersfoort's Typology of Dominant-Subordinate Relations

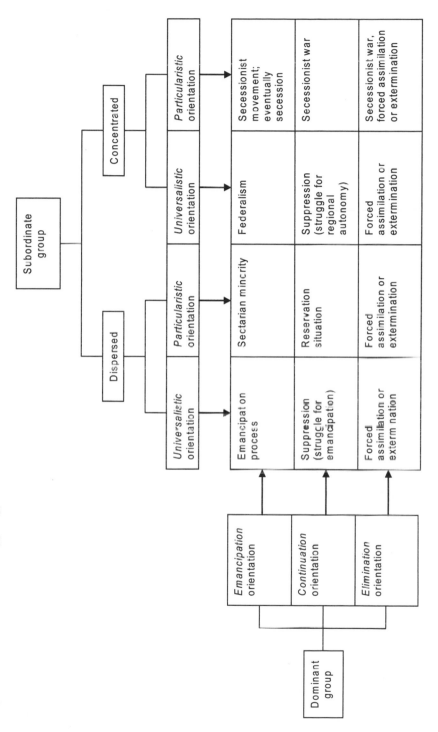

subordinate groups' orientations has, as van Amersfoort's typology shows, led to and facilitated the adoption of federalism as a solution to ethnic conflict. The territorial nature of ethnic division and the legitimacy of territorial claims on the part of the subordinate homeland groups (see Figure 10.6) have also, on the other hand, made political decentralization and fiscal federalism a feasible option.

Figure 10.6 Spain: The Autonomous Communities and Non-Castilian
     Ethnolinguistic Distribution (native languages in brackets)

On the other hand, besides the uniqueness of the Chinese local governments' control over the major part of China's economic resources[14], another distinctively Chinese feature is that the proportion of her local public spending has since the mid- and late 1980s been steady at about 70 per cent of her total national public spending (Figure 10.7), a percentage much higher than those of the major federal countries around the world, e.g. the US, Germany and Russia where the proportions of local public spending in total national public spending are only respectively 46 per cent, 40 per cent and 38 per cent (Xu, 2008: 188). China's scope of economic decentralization in fact goes far beyond decentralization in public finance, but even in terms of

Figure 10.7 China: Local Government Expenditure and Revenue Respectively
as Percentages of Total Government Expenditure and Revenue,
1990-2007

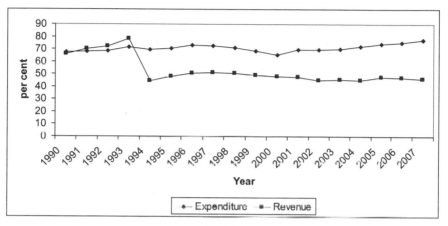

Source: Computed with data from *China Statistical Yearbook*, various years.

the latter alone, according to Xu, China can be said to be the world's most *economically* decentralized country

Just like that of Spain, China's decentralization has its root lying in the long history of the country. Although ancient imperial China was character-ized by centralism and authoritarianism, with local officers appointed by the central imperial court, since early time, the emperor had never directly managed local economic matters, but delegated control over all local affairs to the local governments, and the central government was only holding the power over the appointment of local officers and military affairs (Yeoh, 2009b: 260). Hence, in this regard, China's unique combination of high degree of political centralization and high degree of economic regional decentralization can be traced back to ancient time, and, according to Xu (2008), had continued to form the theoretical basis of the Great Leap Forward (*da yuejin* 大跃进), the people's commune (*renmin gongshe* 人民公社) movement and the Great Proletarian Cultural Revolution; hence when the Open and Reform (*gaige kaifang* 改革开放) policy began in 1978, the major economic resources were already concentrated in the hands of the local governments (*ibid*.: 191-192), albeit contemporary China's decentralization has never been institutionalized, and is found neither in the country's constitution, nor in her administrative laws, nor in the constitution and programme of the Chinese Communist Party (CCP)[15].

Just like the major federal countries cited above, the proportion of local and regional expenditures in total national public expenditure of Spain is nowhere near the Chinese figures. Nevertheless, the growth of the Spanish regional expenditure (Figure 10.8) has been remarkable due to the *Comunidades Autónomas* project. While this occurs at the expense of central government expenditure, it is also a source of overall public sector expansion in the longer term.

Figure 10.8 Spain: Decentralization of Government Expenditure
(early years of decentralization)

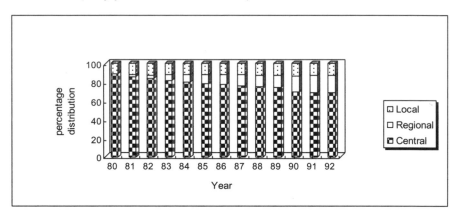

It is true that the Autonomous Communities project is not designed solely to resolve the ethnic problems facing the Castilian centre stemming from the "historic regions" of Catalonia and the Basques Country (and to a lesser extent, Galicia), hence the creation of seventeen instead or two or three such Communities. Nevertheless, it cannot be denied that it is the real or potentially centrifugal pressure from these ethnic regions (rendered even more explosive after the long years of Franquist repression) that provided the first and main impetus behind the will to decentralize after the restoration of democracy in 1975. The primary importance of the ethnic regions (which extend beyond the three "historic regions") can be observed in Figure 10.9 which shows the interregional distribution of public sector resources in 1985, during the early phase of decentralization. The top six regions in 1985 which accounted for 74 per cent of the seventeen regions' total resources were Andalucía, Catalonia, the Basque Country, Galicia, Madrid and Valencia. Out of the six, Catalonia, the Basque Country, Galicia and Valencia (which together accounted for 44 per cent of the total regional resources) are ethnolinguistically distinct

Figure 10.9 Spain: Distribution of Public Resources by Autonomous
Community, 1985 (early phase of decentralization)

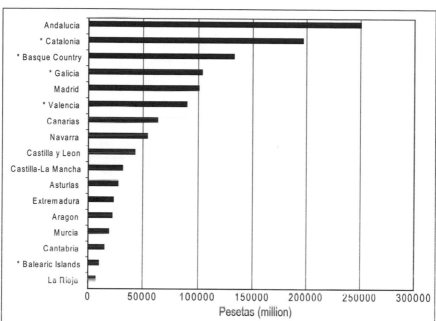

Note: * Ethnolinguistically non-Castilian regions.
Source: Resource use figures from Ortiz Junquera and Roldán Mecanat (1988).

from Madrid, the Castilian centre. In terms of resource utilization, these six
regions accounted for 75 per cent of the total, with Catalonia, the Basque
Country, Galicia and Valencia alone accounted for 48 per cent of the total
(Figure 10.10). The privileged position of Catalonia, the Basque Country and
Galicia in the decentralization process is a clear reflection of this concern.
The creation of the other "grade one" (the special route) or "grade two" (the
slower track to autonomy) Communities can be seen as an outgrowth of this,
while decentralization as such is said to aim at creating a new form of State
structure bringing the tax-payers closer to the providers of public services
their contributions pay for.

The case of China shares with the multiethnic Spain the fact that the
State is principally under the control of a dominant group which struggles
to maintain or perpetuate such control in the presence of subordinate group
aspirations not only for equality but also for cultural and politico-economic

Figure 10.10 Spain: Distribution of Public Resources by Ethnolinguistic
Region, 1985 (early phase of decentralization)

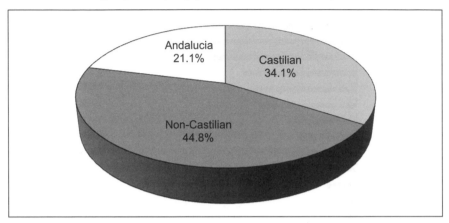

Note: * Non-Castilian Regions: Catalonia, the Basque Country, Galicia, Valencia,
the Balearic Islands; the case of the Andalucian ethnogenesis will be
examined later.

self-determination and autonomy. Public finance is in this case not so much
an instrument of State power that the ethnic factions freely compete for,
but a tool with which the dominant group perpetuates its political control
and at the same time maintains the survival of the Party-State. Despite the
Chinese local governments' alleged control over the major part of China's
economic resources, it is not easy to measure the extent of local autonomy
given the present complex structure of the Chinese politico-economic system,
especially the unusual political centralism amidst economic noncentralization,
though we have observed the tight grip of the central government over local
governments via its control over personnel appointment and promotion.
Nevertheless, according to Schneider (2003), one of the ways to gauge the
degree of administrative decentralization – one of the three core dimensions of
decentralization he hypothesized, the other two being the fiscal and political –
or "local administrative autonomy" is by examining the control exercised over
local revenue. Besides this, according to Schneider, subnational autonomy can
also be measured by looking at the percentage of total grants and revenues not
accounted for by transfers.[16] In this regard, Chinese official statistics for 2008
show a central-to-local tax revenue rebate to all transfer ratio of 0.428:1.866
or the former as about 23 per cent of the latter amount. On the other hand,
non-earmarked transfers were 46.6 per cent of total transfers. Central-to-

local tax revenue rebate and transfers form local revenue and spent by local arrangement. An average 38 per cent of local government expenditure was funded by central government transfers, and in the case of the central and western regions an average 54.4 per cent of local government expenditure was funded by such central government transfers.[17] Overall local government revenue totaled 5.159052 trillion yuan for 2008, comprising local own revenue of 2.864491 trillion yuan and central-to-local tax revenue rebate and transfers totaling 2.294561 trillion yuan (Figure 10.11). A comparison of earmarked transfers and other local revenues including general transfers, central-to-local tax revenue rebate and local governments' own revenue shows that for year 2008 local revenues which were not earmarked transfers constituted 81 per cent of total local revenues (Figure 10.12). From the time-series perspective, it can be seen in Figures 10.13 and 10.14 that from 1999 to 2008 transfers from the central government always constituted just slightly below half of the total local government revenues. Figure 10.15 shows central-to-local transfers for year 2008 (actual) and 2009 (estimate). It can be seen that earmarked transfers are slightly larger than general transfers.[18] Hence, the present state of Chinese administrative decentralization does not seem to be encouraging in the existing structure of political centralism, an awkward coexistence with the remarkable degree of economic decentralization.

Figure 10.11 China: Local Government Revenue, 2008 (billion yuan)

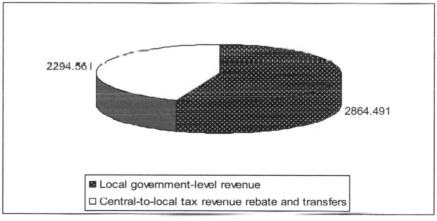

Source: Yeoh, Liong and Ling (2009: 170), Figure 11.2. Data from 关于 2008 年中央和地方预算执行情况与 2009 年中央和地方预算草案的报告.htm <*http://www.mof.gov.cn/mof/zhengwuxinxi/caizhengxinwen/200903/t20090316_122544.html*>.

Figure 10.12 China: Central-to-Local Governments' Earmarked Transfers and
Other Local Government Revenues, 2008

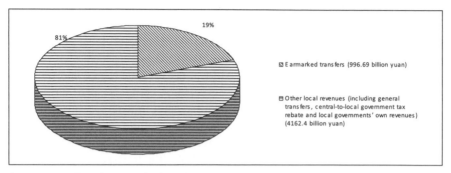

Source: Yeoh, Liong and Ling (2009: 175), Figure 11.3. Data from *http://www.
mof.gov.cn/mof/zhengwuxinxi/caizhengxinwen/200903/t20090316_
122544.html*

Figure 10.13 China: Transfers from Central Government and Sub-total Revenue
(i.e. Revenue which Are Not Transfers from Central Government)
of Local Governments, 1999-2008

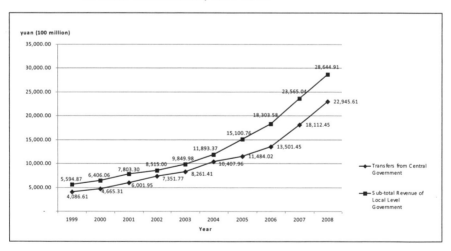

Source: Yeoh, Liong and Ling (2009: 175), Figure 11.4. Data from *Zhongguo
Caizheng Nianjian* 中国财政年鉴, various years; *http://www.mof.gov.
cn/mof/zhengwuxinxi/caizhengshuju/200807/t20080728_59019.html*;
*http://www.mof.gov.cn/mof/zhengwuxinxi/caizhengxinwen/200903/
t20090316_122544.html*

Figure 10.14 China: Transfers from Central Government and Sub-total Revenue (i.e. Revenue which Are Not Transfers from Central Government) as Percentages of Total Revenue of Local Governments, 1999-2008

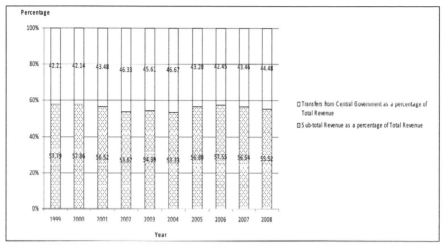

Source: Yeoh, Liong and Ling (2009: 176), Figure 11.5. Data from *Zhongguo Caizheng Nianjian* 中国财政年鉴, various years; *http://www.mof.gov.cn/mof/zhengwuxinxi/ caizhengshuju/200807/t20080728_59019.html*; *http://www.mof.gov.cn/mof/ zhengwuxinxi/caizhengxinwen/200903/t20090316_122544.html*

Figure 10.15 China: Central-to-Local Governments' Transfer Payments, 2008-2009

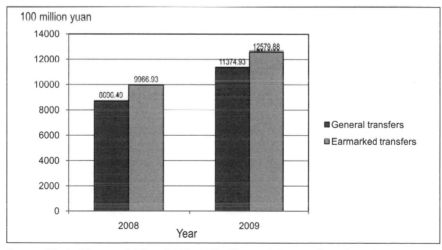

Source: Yeoh, Liong and Ling (2009: 178), Figure 11.6. Data from *http://www.mof.gov. cn/mof/zhengwuxinxi/caizhengshuju/200903/t20090319_124155.html*

The above situation has placed China is in marked contrast to contemporary Spain. Formerly under Franco's rule, bureaucracy had always been used as an instrument of central control over the periphery, with administrative, but not political, autonomy delegated to various bodies established at the provincial level[19]. Since the death of the *Caudillo*, with the transition to democracy and decentralization, many of the functions assigned to the *administración periférica* (as this whole system was called) have been transferred to the respective bureaucracies of the Autonomous Communities. During 1982-1986, the peak years of transfer, more than 360,000 civil servants, formerly employed by the central government, changed masters and a further 40,000 were recruited directly at the regional level. While such transfers steadily increased to reach a level of some 432,186 posts by February 1992, the central government had continued to retain more administrative staff than are required by its remaining powers (Hebbert, 1989; Alonso Zaldívar and Castells, 1992: 165; Heywood, 1995: 156). The result was a substantial increase in the total number of public service personnel since the creation of the Autonomous Communities, which in turn was reflected in the remarkable growth of public expenditure on wages and salaries over the period concerned (Figure 10.16). The phenomenon was particularly notable at the regional government level, while that of the central government, which had already burgeoned under Franco's *administración periférica* system, stabilized since

Figure 10.16 Spain: Expenditure on Wages & Salaries at All Levels of Government (first two decades of decentralization)

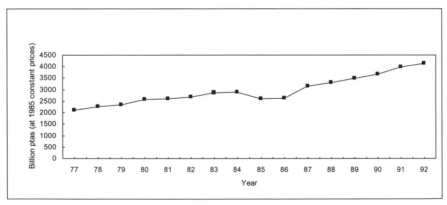

Source: IMF, *Government Finance Statistics Yearbooks*; *Anuarios Estadísticos de España*, Instituto Nacional de Estadística/Ministerio de Economía y Hacienda, Madrid.

Figure 10.17 Spain: Expenditure on Wages & Salaries – Central Government and Regional & Provincial Governments (first two decades of decentralization)

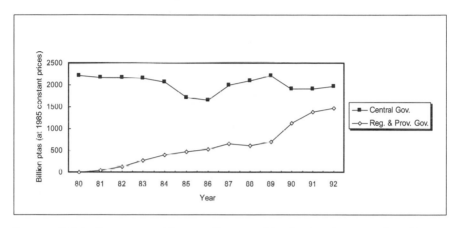

Source: IMF, *Government Finance Statistics Yearbooks*, *Anuarios Estadísticos de España*, Instituto Nacional de Estadística/Ministerio de Economía y Hacienda, Madrid.

the transfers of personnel occurred after the creation of the Autonomous Communities (Figure 10.17).

The separate development of reform and devolution in Spain and China, here shown to be two radically different paths, thus reflects fundamentally in Spain the response from the ruling echelon of the dominant group to the aspirations of the subordinate groups – mainly the Catalans, Basques and to a less extent the Gallegans, in contrast to the absence of such policy response to the demands of the much less influential ethnoterritorial groups in China. Such responses, or non-responses, would, by extension, also impact upon the mass of the dominant group itself.

Ethnic Diversity and Public Policy

In terms of the link between ethnic diversity and public policy, multiethnic Spain and the outwardly homogeneous China share in their common majority-minority ethnic configuration, as compared to, say, countries like the mainly bi-ethnic Belgium and Malaysia which are characterized by a "precarious balance" in intergroup relationship[20]. While the development of the Spanish political reform is influenced by the dominant group's reaction to subordinate groups' aspirations and that of Belgium or Malaysia is shaped more by intergroup competition and variations in the balance of power, China is unique due to her long-running absolute Han predominance in demography and political configuration, with her minority ethnic group – while large in absolute numbers – not even reaching a critical mass as a proportion of the country's total population. Yet Spain and China share much in terms of the territoriality of their ethnic divisions, homeland nature of all the major ethnic factions, though not level of economic affluence and political democracy, and any common strategy of adopting some form of political decentralization and fiscal federalism during the last few decades in response to the exigencies engendered by their respective patterns of ethnic conflicts.

As noted by Gladney (1991: 6-7), due to the interchangeability of the terms "ethnicity" and "nationality" in the literature, there is much confusion over minority nationality identity in China. The term *minzu* 民族 is used for both concepts of nationality and ethnicity (or *zhongzu* 种族) in China, the former being what the Chinese State has designated "56 nationalities". While "ethnicity" should more rightly refer to an individual's self-perceived identity, it is also often influenced by State policy. Gladney pointed out that in contrast to the limited term *minzu* ("nationality"/"ethnicity") used in China, Soviet ethnological vocabulary distinguished in Russian between *ethnos*, *nationalnost*, and *narodnost* ("ethnicity", "nationality", "peoplehood") (*ibid.*: Chapter 1, note 19). In China, "nationality" (*minzu*) is what the Chinese State has conferred upon the 56 ethnic groups identified mainly in the 1950s (*ibid.*: 6). This historical background explains a lot about China's "national" policy till today.

Leaving aside the Han-non-Han dichotomy, even the so-called "Han Chinese" as a homogeneous ethnic group, whether phenotypically or culturally, may not be what it has always been taken for granted. The great diversity of the mutually unintelligible regionalects is well known. The speakers of many of the Chinese regional languages are in fact simply too numerous for the word "dialects" to be used as an appropriate term to designate their languages. For instance, the number of speakers of either Cantonese/*Yue* 粤 or Hokkien/Fujianese/*Min* 闽 is larger than the number of speakers of either Polish or Ukrainian, the two East European/Slavonic languages with most numerous speakers except Russian, or the speakers of Dutch, Danish, Norwegian and Swedish combined. In China, regional differences, including the distinction between the wheat-eating northerners and rice-eating southerners, have always been observed, or as one observer noted, the *Hanjen* 漢人 and the *Tangjen* 唐人, plus "national minorities" who have to different extents been Sinicized:

The contradistinction between Han Chinese and national minorities repeatedly made [...] suggests that the Han Chinese constitute a homogeneous, discreet community from whom the national minorities are readily distinguishable. In fact, however, the cultural gap between "Han Chinese" and "minority" is often no greater than that between Han Chinese of different regions. There is an almost continuous ethnocultural spectrum extending from the northern, wheat-eating, Mandarin-speaking Chinese at one end to, at the other, the dark-skinned K'awa in the south who are primitive food-gatherers and speakers of a language of the Mon-Khmer family. In between are the more than 100 million "Han" Chinese of south-coastal China who speak dialects other than Mandarin and who, in fact, sometimes refer to themselves as *T'ang-jen* (men of T'ang, after the T'ang dynasty, seventh to tenth centuries) rather than as *Han-jen* (after the Han dynasty, third century B.C. to third century A.D.) and the more than ten million persons of the "national minorities" in south China who have been to varying extents acculturated to Chinese ways – to the point, in some cases, that they had no awareness of being different, of being a "minority," until they were informed of the fact by workers from the Chinese Academy of Sciences who came to their areas after 1949.

(Moseley, 1966: 8-9)

While ethnic diversity may affect the role of the State, whether in terms of the various aspects of decentralization or the trend and pattern of budgetary policy, it is not the ethnic composition *per se* but its interaction with the socioeconomic structure of the society concerned that really matters. The Weberian approach views ethnic group is being not "natural" (as kinship group is) but "rational" and primarily political:

Ethnic membership (Gemeinsamkeit) differs from the kinship group precisely by being a presumed identity, not a group with concrete social action, like the latter. In our sense, ethnic membership does not constitute a group; it only facilitates group formation of any kind, particularly in the political sphere. On the other hand, it is primarily the political community, no matter how artificially organized, that inspires the belief in common ethnicity.

(Weber, 1968 tr.[21]: 389)

Contrast the Weberian approach with Geertz's approach in his 1963 paper on the effect of "primordial sentiments" on civil politics:

By a primordial attachment is meant one that stems from the "givens" – or, more precisely, as culture is inevitably involved in such matters, the assumed "givens" – of social existence: immediate contiguity and kin connection mainly, but beyond them the givenness that stems from being born into a particular religious community, speaking a particular language, or even a dialect of a language, and following particular social practices. These congruities of blood, speech, custom, and so on, are seen to have an ineffable, and at times overpowering, coerciveness in and of themselves.

(Geertz, 1963: 109)

Today, studies on intergroup relations usually see ethnicity not as a "'given' of social existence", but a political construct linked directly to power relations and resource competition. The boundary marker of ethnicity is frequently mobilized to meet the rising need of identity investment for economic and political purposes (the "situation theories" of ethnicity, see Barth, 1969). Heiberg (1979) observed that for political purposes, descent has never been regarded by the Basques in Spain as a sufficient criterion for ethnic inclusion. "Basqueness" is measured instead in terms of the adherence to certain morally-loaded political and social prescriptions, or more specifically, whether one is a Basque nationalist.[22] Thus it is as an instrument for political mobilization that ethnicity often plays a key role in the interplay between group activities and public policy[23] which again is apparent in the case of Uyghurs' ethnic identity in Xinjiang, as lucidly described by Gladney (2003: 3-4):

> Chinese histories notwithstanding, every Uyghur firmly believes that their ancestors were the indigenous people of the Tarim basin, which did not become known in Chinese as "Xinjiang" ("new dominion") until the eighteenth century. Nevertheless, the identity of the present people known as Uyghur is a rather recent phenomenon related to Great Game rivalries, Sino-Soviet geopolitical manoeuvrings, and Chinese nation-building. While a collection of nomadic steppe peoples known as the "Uyghur" have existed since before the eighth century, this identity was lost from the fifteenth to the twentieth century [...] The Islamicization of the Uyghur from the tenth to as late as the seventeenth century, while displacing their Buddhist religion, did little to bridge their oases-based loyalties. From that time on, the people of "Uyghuristan" centred in Turpan, who resisted Islamic conversion until the seventeenth century, were the last to be known as Uyghur. The others were known only by their oasis or by the generic term of "Turki". With the arrival of Islam, the ethnonym "Uyghur" fades from the historical record.

The emergence of a modern "Uyghur" ethnic identity is thus basically a political construct:

> Competition for the loyalties of the peoples of the oases in the Great Game played between China, Russia and Britain further contributed to divisions among the Uyghur according to political, religious, and military lines. The peoples of the oases, until the challenge of nation-state incorporation, lacked any coherent sense of identity. Thus, the incorporation of Xinjiang for the first time into a nation-

state required unprecedented delineation of the so-called nations involved. The re-emergence of the label "Uyghur", though arguably inappropriate as it was last used 500 years previously to describe the largely Buddhist population of the Turfan Basin, stuck as the appellation for the settled Turkish-speaking Muslim oasis dwellers. It has never been disputed by the people themselves or the states involved. There is too much at stake for the people labelled as such to wish to challenge that identification. For Uyghur nationalists today, the direct lineal descent from the Uyghur Kingdom in seventh century Mongolia is accepted as fact, despite overwhelming historical and archeological evidence to the contrary.

(Gladney, 2003: 4-5)

Similarly, answering the question "Who are the Chinese?", Moseley observed that "Han Chinese" as an ethnic marker began with its use for political mobilization linked to the May Fourth Movement:

Psychologically, the Han Chinese only became a nation in response to Western imperialism; culturally, this movement was greatly reinforced by the literary reform movement led by Hu Shih and others. And nationalism has been a dominant feature of Chinese Communism. Yet much of China's heterogeneity – in speech, diet, and physical appearance – so often remarked upon by foreign visitors still remains. With reference to its ethnic component, being "Chinese" is a dynamic quality. "Chineseness" may be likened to a geographical zone, a blurred place on the map, through which an unending stream of peoples has filtered in a north-south direction [...] On the whole, this southern movement was gradual and piecemeal, being characterized by an influx of Chinese colonizers from the north who mixed with the local people [...] The indigenous populations that have remained unabsorbed sometimes live side by side in discreet communities with the Chinese, sometimes retreat back into the hills, and sometimes attempt to emigrate southward. Thus, in any given national minority region of south China today there is a whole range of comparative "Chineseness" among the inhabitants which altogether eludes the dichotomy, "Han Chinese"-"national minority."

(Moseley, 1966: 10-13)

The above description does not apply to Xinjiang – China's "wild west" – and Tibet, in contradistinction to the southern regions or, with Chinese colonization greatly facilitated by railroads built by Western powers, Inner Mongolia to the north and the northeastern region formerly being Manchuria. Incidentally, Inner Mongolia had already been overwhelmingly Chinese by the time the Inner Mongolia Autonomous Region was created in 1947, and in the case of the northeast "the Manchus disappeared and Manchuria became safely Chinese, dooming in advance the Japanese attempt to establish an independent 'Manchukuo'" (*ibid.*: 13). In this contradistinction lies the root of the Chinese government's present problem of Xinjiang and Tibet:

Outer Mongolia, Sinkiang, and Tibet retained their uniqueness: although held by successive Chinese dynasties, the imperial administration was always unstable because it lacked the ballast of a sizable Han Chinese community.[24] They were tied to China without ever becoming Chinese. Outer Mongolia broke away altogether and succeeded in establishing an independent state [...] With the modern transportation and communication facilities[25] developed by the Chinese Communists, the colonization of Sinkiang and Tibet is now proceeding, although it has encountered bitter resistance.

(ibid.)

While the democratization and federalization process (the latter refers to the *Comunidades Autónomas* project, as the term "federal" is not officially used) of the Spanish polity after the death of Franco has been looked upon by many countries with ethnoterritoriality problems undergoing political transition as a model to emulate, van Amersfoort's model suggests that a federal solution may be an exception rather than a rule among nations given the different objective realities facing different countries.[26] For instance, in China, unlike in Spain, the lack of a stable democratic political institution and the existence of economic deprivation can render intergroup compromise difficult or impossible. In short, variations in one or more of these socio-politico-economic parameters can result in a drastically different form of State response to the objective exigencies presented by a country's ethnic fractionalization and of societal reaction to State intervention.

Second Critical Juncture

Government, even in its best state, is but a necessary evil; in its worst state, an intolerable one.

– Thomas Paine (1737-1809), *Common Sense*, Ch. 1

Nineteen eighty-one could in a way be considered the year of a second critical juncture for Spain. The risk of the disappearance of the central State was by then getting real and that made the entire autonomy process rather controversial. The approval of the Statutes for Catalonia and the Basque Country in 1979 (the most sensitive moment in the process) – which effectively put no ceiling on their regional powers while limiting the powers of the central State to national defence, foreign affairs (with restrictions) and the national currency – provoked an outbreak of *fiebre autonómica* (autonomy fever) as all the other aspirant *comunidades autónomas* were eager to obtain the same level of autonomy as the Catalans and Basques. Fearful of the virtual disappearance of the central State, the government negotiated amendments to the Catalan and Basque Statutes in which the powers ascribed to the *comunidades autónomas* as "exclusive" should be "accepted as such without prejudice to the constitutional provisions which attributed the same exclusivity to the powers of the central state" (Brassloff, 1989: 34). Meanwhile, Andalucía followed the "exceptional" (grade one, under article 151) route to autonomy (by which a region could apply to receive the same high level of autonomy as the privileged regions of Catalonia, the Basque Country and Galicia) – the only one to do so – and some regions like Valencia and the Canary Isles were allowed an intermediate status between grade one and grade two (the latter involves a lengthy process and a "low" autonomous status). Navarra, on the other hand, was given its own special route in recognition of its historic "foral" rights (*fueros*), while ten other regions followed the "normal" (grade two, under article 143) route to autonomy. The controversy and confusion over the regional picture and the fear for the loss of Spain's national identity, as well as the continued attacks by ETA, the Basque separatist group, nevertheless continued to fuel right-wing discontent, led to a series of conspiracies against the democratic government and culminated in the almost successful military coup of 23rd February 1981. However, the result has not been to roll back reforms but to push the ethnoregional question even more firmly to the top of the political agenda.

From May Fourth to June Fourth

> Every Communist must grasp the truth, "Political power grows out of the barrel of a gun."
>
> > Mao Zedong (1893-1976), *Selected Works*, Vol. II,
> > "Problems of War and Strategy", 6th November 1938

> I told myself that no matter what, I refused to become the General Secretary who mobilized the military to crack down on students.
> > – Zhao Ziyang (2009a: 29; 2009b: 48; 2009c: 62)

Across the globe in China, since the demise of Mao, another critical juncture arrived in 1989, with the 100-day peaceful Tiananmen demonstrations and hunger strikes that received global sympathy probably other than those behind the high walls of Zhongnanhai 中南海. These poignant lines from Howard Chapnick's foreword to *Beijing Spring* (Turnley *et al.*, 1989: 15) speak of June Fourth as a historical milestone:

> [...] The martyrs of Tiananmen Square lie silent and still. They spoke for themselves throughout the tumultuous and chaotic weeks of the Beijing Spring of 1989. But now, in the aftermath of repression and intimidation, their symbolic

Goddess of Democracy has been shattered, their banners have been removed, and their voices have been silenced [...] We were incredulous spectators as the Chinese students dared to dream what became an impossible dream [...] But certain events are so monumental, so symbolic, so glorious, and speak so eloquently to our highest ideals that they transcend the immediacy of the news. History demands that they be preserved.

Exiled dissidents estimated the number of civilians, workers and students killed in the crackdown during the night of 3rd-4th June 1989 to be from 2000 to 3000[27], while the official death toll stood at four hundred and forty-three, 223 of whom were soldiers and police officers, plus 5000 soldiers and police officers and 2000 civilians wounded in the crackdown (Hutton, 2006: 27)[28]. While Spain's 1981 failed coup had put the decentralization plan into more urgency by highlighting the peril in the management of decentralization, the threat from conservative forces, and the threat from regional reformers and secessionists, the Tiananmen demonstrations had instead ended in the spill of innocent blood and arrested the maturing of the political system with the purge of Zhao Ziyang, the arrest of Bao Tong and the exile of other chief reformists and intellectuals who advocated democratization such as Yan Jiaqi and Fan Lizhi and the student leaders in the forefront of the mass protest. Aspects of political reform have since either been rolled back or stalled. In view of the close link between political decentralization and democratization,[29] the tragic end of the Tiananmen protests and democracy movement of June 1989 was a disaster for democratic pluralist development and ethnoregional accommodation. The post-June Fourth robust, even miraculous, economic growth has been used time and again rather successfully by the CCP for the *ex post* justification of the Tiananmen crackdown of 1989, that the brutal crackdown had been necessary to preserve China's stability and economic progress, but if the blood-chilling words attributed to Deng Xiaoping[30] – that it was worth killing 20 *wan* 万 (i.e. 200 thousand) people to ensure 20 years of stability for China – in ordering the brutal crackdown of June 1989 were truly his, then the continuing, even recently escalating, social unrest – including those more alarming incidents with ethnic or ethnoregional flavour – that culminated in Xinjiang's July Fifth deadly riots of 2009, just a month past the 20th anniversary of the Beijing-Tiananmen[31] massacre, look somehow like an omen that time might be running out.

The 1989 Beijing-Tiananmen massacre could be seen as a wake-up call for the CCP to embark rigorously on a path of continuing economic reform while rolling back the Hu Yaobang-Zhao Ziyang era of limited politico-cultural liberalization (a prominent symbol being the *He Shang* 河殇 [river elegy] documentary[32]) and the subsequent collapse of Communist Party-rule in USSR and Eastern Europe from the end of 1989 to early 1990[33] had seemed to reaffirm the correctness of such decision to crack down on the part of the CCP to ensure the survival of its one-party rule. June Fourth could also be seen as a catalyst for the single-minded determination to deliver on the economic front after Deng Xiaoping's "southern tour" (*nanxun* 南巡) later in 1992 to reaffirm the Party's policy of moving forward with economic reform and liberalization, coupled with more determined repression of political dissent. Nevertheless, as Bao (2009) noted:

> There are people who said that the crackdown has led to prosperity. What I know is: economic reform created prosperity. It is the people who have, with market economy, crushed the yoke of Mao Zedong to create prosperity. Now there are people who concluded that prosperity is the output of crackdown. Facing the global economic crisis, I do not know whether they are preparing to introduce the experience of crackdown to save the world economy. There are people who applause that a muzzled China – a China in Total Silence – has leapt forward to become the world's second largest economic entity – just after the United States; I believe this is true. Under the brutal rule of Kublai Khan, China has so early already been the prosperous paradise witnessed by Marco Polo [...] June Fourth opened up a new phase of Total Silence. After Deng Xiaoping's southern tour, the China in Total Silence reiterated economic reform and wealth redistribution. But who are the beneficiaries of such redistribution in a China in Total Silence?[34]

Such worries are not unfounded. There is indeed little unique for a politically repressive country to achieve economic miracles. Many authoritarian and neo-authoritarian countries have done it before, such as Chiang Kai-shek's Taiwan and Park Chung-hee's South Korea, or in a way even Augusto Pinochet's Chile and Socharto's Indonesia. In fact, many of such countries are among the models CCP's China, in its search for a way forward after 1989, found attractive to consider for emulation. This year 2009 is the 20th anniversary of June Fourth. It is also the 90th anniversary of May Fourth. There are indeed many similarities of between May Fourth of 1919 and June Fourth seventy years later – the passion for social reform and national rejuvenation, the resentment against contemporary socio-politico-economic injustice, the call for democracy, science, human rights and modernization (in 1989 very much symbolized by the hugely popular *He Shang* documentary), the forlorn challenge against the overwhelming power of a ruthless State. Like May Fourth of 1919 which, while inclusive of the liberal tradition, eventually turned Chinese intellectuals away from Western liberalism to Bolshevism, planted the seeds of Mao's ascending the Tiananmen on 1st October 1949[35] and of the contradictions between national rejuvenation, modernization and radicalism, June Fourth of 1989[36], which happened to coincide with the 200th anniversary of the French Revolution, 70th anniversary of the May Fourth Movement and 40th anniversary of Chinese Communist Party rule, in a way also sowed the seeds of escalating internal contradictions and tension in subsequent policy orientation. Even not seen in ethnic and ethnoterritorial terms, such social contradictions have manifested themselves in the alarmingly widening income gap, deteriorating socioeconomic inequalities[37] and proliferating social unrest. The following account in a sense captures the essence of the problem:

> China is a profoundly polarised society, with hundreds of millions of impoverished workers and peasants at one pole, and a tiny capitalist elite at the other. According to a Boston Consulting Group study, China had 250,000 millionaire households in 2005, ranking the country sixth in the world. These households accounted for only 0.4 percent of the total, but controlled 70 percent of national wealth.
>
> Chan (2007)

In addition, it was also alleged that almost 60 per cent of public revenue was used for the benefit of the 70 million-strong community of CCP cadres and apparatchiks who enjoyed a level of welfare – including healthcare, education and career opportunities – greatly higher than the ordinary citizens, and among the rich with wealth worth a hundred million yuan and above, 91 per cent or 2932 were the children of high-ranking CCP cadres and apparatchiks, possessing assets above 2.045 trillion yuan.[38]

The fact that 70 per cent of China's wealth was in the hand of 0.4 per cent of the people was confirmed by Cai Jiming 蔡继明, a Chinese People's Political Consultative Committee member, on the 6th Meeting of the 11th Standing Committee of the CPPCC, referring to an authoritative government department report.[39] Cai emphasized that with 0.4 per cent of the people in control of 70 per cent of wealth, China's wealth concentration was higher than that of the US. Proposing income tax and inheritance tax reforms, Cai emphasized that such wealth concentration in the hands of a minority of people has led to inadequate consumption and even distorted consumption. In fact, a recent report revealed that with luxury goods consumption reaching US$8.6 billion, i.e. 25 per cent of the world market, China superseded US to become the world's second largest luxury goods market by January 2009, ranked only after Japan.[40] Other data show that the degree of wealth concentration towards the rich in China is presently growing on average at an annual rate of 12.3 per cent which is double the world average growth rate. Such tendency is also reflected in sad state of the small and medium enterprises, with data showing the disappearance of 7,700,000 private businesses over the decade of 1994-2004 and the collapse of the middle class leading to an M-shape society.[41]

From Megaghost to Megastar: A Party Reborn?

[…] Not only is Peking a nightmare streetscape awash in atrocity and anguish; the nation at large has become a haunted land. This howling, lurching mega-ghost is the Chinese Communist Party. In one staggeringly brutal stroke, it shot itself through the heart. It will not recover. A regime that professes itself to be the distillation of popular will has turned on the Chinese people, committing the ultimate sacrilege of eating its own children. Hundreds of China's brightest, most idealistic sons and daughters, their movement commanding wide public sympathy, were nakedly sacrificed to the cause of preserving an élite.

(Asiaweek, 16th June 1989, p. 16)

As *Asiaweek* in its 16th June 1989 editorial "The Rape of Peking" lamented a Goya-esque landscape, these lines seems today, by hindsight, a gross underestimation of CCP's resiliency and the effectiveness of authoritarian power. Building upon the strong foundation set by Zhao Ziyang's audacious reformist programmes, Deng Xiaoping moved forward with the flirting with capitalist market economy by reinvigorating the post-Tiananmen chilling politico-economic milieu through his *nanxun* in 1992, culminating lately in China superseding Germany to become the world's third largest economy in early 2008, ranked only after the United States of America and Japan.[42] Also impressive was the country's poverty reduction achievements (see Table 10.2), with GDP per capita reaching today's US$2,000, though according to a report released in March 2009 by the Beijing's Ministry of Finance, the country's Gini coefficient which had leapt from 0.282 in 1991 to 0.456 in 1998 had further increased to 0.457 in 1999 and 0.458 in 2000, with more than 50 per cent of the national income in the hands of the richest 20 per cent of the population and only 2 to 4 per cent of the national income in the hands of the poorest 20 per cent.[43]

China has been adamant that each country has the right to choose her own path to development and the sanctity of national sovereignty must be at all costs protected from foreign intervention[44] – a position largely supported by most developing countries including most ASEAN members. While steering the country towards the status of an economic superpower, with the inevitable concomitant expansion in political and military might and prowess, the CCP, building on the foundations set by Hu Yaobang and Zhao Ziyang[45] under the auspices of Deng Xiaoping, also embarked on a remarkable process of internal

Table 10.2 China: Rural Poverty

	Year	1978	2006
Rural absolute poverty		250 million	21.48 million
Incidence of poverty		30.7%	2.3%

	Year	2000	2006
Low-income population[+]		62.13 million	35.5 million
Proportion of low-income		6.7%	3.7%
population in rural population[‡]			

[+] In 2006, the rural net income per capita of nationally designated focal poverty assistant counties reached 1,928 yuan.

[‡] In 2006, the rural absolute poor plus rural low-income population reached 13.7% of total rural population in the Western Region.

Source: Yeoh (2009b: 264), Table 10.7. Data from Fan (2008), pp. 14-19.

reform and rejuvenation. Many of these internal reforms have involved power succession or leadership transition which have been remarkably successful over the years and have definitely played a crucial role in maintaining intra-Party political stability and smoothing the path of economic reform and transition. These basically involve ideology restructuring, recruitment of new breed of élite into the leadership, construction of "political exit" channel for aging leaders and grooming of the core of future generation of leadership (see, e.g. Zheng and Lye, 2004). Besides, Beijing has also been emphasizing the democratization of rural governance since the National People's Congress passed the "Village Committee Organic Law of the PRC (Experimental)" in 1987 that introduced the direct election of the directors, deputy directors and members of the villagers' committees. At least theoretically, these grassroots government officials, being elected by the local people, could be more independent in their dealings with the higher authorities since their political legitimacy depends on popular votes rather than appointment by higher authorities (Zheng and Lye, 2004). The recent years saw the geographical expansion of such villagers' committee elections, with 929 counties across China covering Tianjin, Hebei, Shanxi, Inner Mongolia, Fujian, Jiangxi and Shaanxi holding such elections in the year 2003 (*ibid.*).[46] Nevertheless, such village committee elections should not be taken as a sign that China is taking the first step in political reform moving towards multiparty liberal democracy. In fact, the country's leadership has never made any pretension that this is so. In the sixfold typology of regime classification of Diamond (2002), China is classified as "politically closed authoritarian" (Table 10.3). When describing

Table 10.3 Diamond's Sixfold Typology of Regime Classification
(as at end of 2001)

Liberal Democracy	*Western Democracies* – 24 West European states, United States, Canada, Australia, New Zealand *Postcommunist* – Czech Republic, Hungary, Poland, Slovakia, Slovenia, Estonia, Latvia, Lithuania, Bulgaria, Croatia, Romania *Latin America and the Caribbean* – 8 Caribbean states (Bahamas, Barbados, Belize, Dominica, Grenada, St. Kitts & Nevis, St. Lucia, St. Vincent & the Grenadines), Uruguay, Costa Rica, Panama, Suriname, Bolivia, Peru, Chile, Dominican Republic, Guyana *Asia* (*East, Southeast, & South*) – Japan, Taiwan, South Korea *Pacific Islands* – 8 Pacific island states (Kiribati, Marshall Islands, Micronesia, Nauru, Palau, Samoa, Tuvalu, Vanuatu) *Africa* (*Sub-Sahara*) – Cape Verde, Mauritius, São Tomé & Príncipe, South Africa, Botswana *Middle East-North Africa* – Israel
Electoral Democracy	*Postcommunist* – Moldova, Yugoslavia, Albania *Latin America and the Caribbean* – Argentina, El Salvador, Jamaica, Mexico, Brazil, Ecuador, Honduras, Nicaragua, Trinidad & Tobago, Guatemala *Asia* (*East, Southeast, & South*) – India, Mongolia, the Philippines, Thailand, Bangladesh, Nepal, Sri Lanka *Pacific Islands* – Papua New Guinea, Solomon Islands *Africa* (*Sub-Sahara*) – Ghana, Mali, Namibia, Benin, Madagascar, Seychelles, Senegal, Malawi, Niger
Ambiguous Regimes	*Postcommunist* – Armenia, Georgia, Macedonia, Ukraine *Latin America and the Caribbean* – Venezuela, Paraguay, Colombia *Asia* (*East, Southeast, & South*) – Indonesia *Pacific Islands* – Fiji, Tonga *Africa* (*Sub-Sahara*) – Mozambique, Tanzania, Nigeria, Djibouti, Sierra Leone, Zambia *Middle East-North Africa* – Turkey
Competitive Authoritarian	*Postcommunist* – Bosnia-Herzegovina, Russia, Belarus *Latin America and the Caribbean* – Antigua & Barbuda, Haiti *Asia* (*East, Southeast, & South*) – Timor-Leste, Malaysia *Africa* (*Sub-Sahara*) – Lesotho, Central African Republic,

Table 10.3 (continued)

	Guinea-Bissau, Côte d'Ivoire, Gabon, the Gambia, Togo, Ethiopia, Kenya, Cameroon, Zimbabwe *Middle East-North Africa* – Lebanon, Iran, Yemen
Hegemonic Electoral Authoritarian	*Postcommunist* – Azerbaijan, Kazakhstan, Kyrgyzstan, Tajikistan, Uzbekistan *Asia (East, Southeast, & South)* – Singapore, Maldives, Cambodia, Pakistan *Africa (Sub-Sahara)* – Burkina Faso, Congo (Brazzaville), Comoros, Mauritania, Chad, Guinea, Uganda, Angola, Liberia, Equatorial Guinea *Middle East-North Africa* – Kuwait, Jordan, Morocco, Algeria, Tunisia, Egypt
Politically Closed Authoritarian	*Postcommunist* – Turkmenistan *Latin America and the Caribbean* – Cuba *Asia (East, Southeast, & South)* – Brunei, Bhutan, China, Laos, Vietnam, Afghanistan, Burma, North Korea *Africa (Sub-Sahara)* – Swaziland, Burundi, Congo (Kinshasa), Eritrea, Rwanda, Somalia, Sudan *Middle East-North Africa* – Bahrain, Oman, United Arab Emirates, Qatar, Iraq, Libya, Saudi Arabia, Syria

Source: Diamond (2002: 30-31), Table 2.

the Franquist regime as "authoritarian", Gunther (1980: 2) elaborated, "It was based upon the explicit rejection of mass suffrage as a means of elite recruitment and a basis of legitimacy [...] The concept of political conflict among social groups was formally regarded as illegitimate, and mass organizations which engaged in what the state regarded as conflictual political activities were vigorously suppressed." It is again interesting to compare this with the case of post-June Fourth China. While many authors inside and outside China have been lauding the country's "grassroots democratization" and intra-Party reforms as pointing to a promising path of de-authoritarian evolvement, the perception that China is moving out from this "politically closed authoritarian" category of regime type could prove to be as misleadingly whimsical as it is empirical unfounded. Furthermore, past record of mismanagement and repressive, often violent, response to dissent, including the excesses during the Cultural Revolution both in China proper and in ethnic regions like Tibet and Xinjiang, and the June Fourth atrocities, may not be encouraging for many, as a dissident astrophysicist, exiled after the 1989 Beijing-Tiananmen massacre, ruminated:

> [...] changes are not devoid of suffering. China has again shed fresh blood, blood which testifies to an oft-proved truth:
>
> – Without respect for human rights, there will be resorting to violence;
> – Without tolerance and pluralism, there will be resorting to prison;
> – Without democratic checks and balances, there will be resorting to armed coercion.
>
> China's history has long since proven, and continues to prove, that using violence and imprisonment and armed coercion to enforce upon a nation a single belief, a single point of view, a single superstition, will only lead to instability, poverty, and backwardness.
>
> (Fang, 1991: 259)[47]

Indeed, while promoting the rural elections in 1987, Peng Zhen 彭真 had argued that such elections could be used to help the Chinese Communist Party govern the country's rural areas and perpetuate the Party's rule (Zheng and Lye, 2004). Any perception that such electoral initiatives are implying that the Party is loosening its stranglehold over China's politics could be illusory as the signals conveyed by the ruling regime regarding the tolerance threshold for dissent remain unmistakable, not least highlighted in recent years by the arrest and jailing of civil rights lawyers Gao Zhisheng 高智晟 and Zheng Enchong 郑恩宠, the jailing of researcher Zhao Yan 赵岩, blind civil rights lawyer Chen Guangcheng 陈光诚 and *Straits Times* (Singapore) journalist Ching Cheong 程翔. Other cases included the arrest of Hu Jia 胡佳, an AIDS and environmental activist, in December 2007, on subversion charges, and Wang Dejia 王德佳, a cyber dissident, in the same month, also on subversion charges for criticizing the government over human rights abuses ahead of the Beijing Olympics (Lye, 2009: 239). On 8th December 2008, a prominent Chinese dissident Liu Xiaobo 刘晓波, who played a prominent role in the 1989 Tiananmen demonstrations and hunger strikes, was remanded in police custody for organizing the signing of "Charter 08" that managed to gather over 300 signatures on the eve of the International Human Rights Day. Charter 08 (*Ling-ba Xianzhang* 零八宪章), signed in December 2008 by over three hundred prominent Chinese citizens, was conceived and written in emulation of the founding of Charter 77 in former Czechoslovakia in January 1977 by over two hundred Czech and Slovak intellectuals, including the future Czech president Václav Havel. The number of signatories, local and overseas, later increased to about 7000 by March 2009.[48] After being taken away for half a year, Liu was "formally" arrested on sedition charges on 23rd June 2009 that carry a possible jail term of up to 15 years.[49] Besides, China's civil rights issues have also been thrust into the limelight again with the recent release of dissident Yang Zili 杨子立 after eight years of imprisonment for advocating political reform on the Internet, while his fellow dissidents Jin Haike 靳海科 and Xu Wei 徐伟 were still languishing in prison.[50] Yang, Jin and Xu, together with Zhang Yanhua 张彦华 and Zhang Honghai 张宏海, were members of the Xin Qingnian Xuehui 新青年学会 (New Youth Study Group) they set up in 2000 for the exploration of China's political and social reforms. The case of a former People's Liberation Army (PLA) soldier Zhang Shijun 张世军 who was taken away by the authorities, as the 20th anniversary of the massacre approached, after writing an open letter to President Hu Jintao 胡锦涛 through the Internet citing the "unspeakable atrocities" he witnessed committed against civilians and students twenty years ago on that fateful night of 3rd-4th June 1989 while serving in a unit that was involved in the bloody crackdown – a rare eyewitness account from inside the PLA – is another reference point for reading civil rights development in China.[51] Besides these high-profile cases, there are also many other little observed arrests and imprisonments that rarely raise an eyebrow beyond the border. According to the advocacy group Reporters Sans Frontiers (Reporters without Borders), there are more journalists in prison in China than anywhere else in the world.[52] A report of the International Federation of Journalists (IFJ) at the end of January 2009 accused China of reneging on her promise of press freedom during her bid for hosting the Olympics and called for the country to immediately release imprisoned journalists and halt the repression of journalists with the current national security and other laws – and this came amidst reports that a new series of rules and regulations would be launched in 2009 to strengthen the control on journalists and news reporting ostensibly for maintaining quality and authenticity in news reporting (Yeoh, 2009a: 10). Reporters Sans Frontiers ranked China number 167 out of a total of 173 countries in its 2008 Worldwide Press Freedom Index and considered the number of arrests and cases of news surveillance and control by China's political police and Department of Propaganda to be still very high, while Human Rights Watch asserted that China's extensive police and State security apparatus continued to impose upon civil society activists, critics and protestors multiple layers of controls that included "professional and administrative measures, limitations on foreign travel and domestic movement, monitoring (covert and overt) of the Internet and phone communications, abduction and confinement incommunicado, and unofficial house arrests [and] a variety of vaguely defined crimes including 'inciting subversion', 'leaking state secrets' and 'disrupting social order' [which] provide the government with wide legal remit to stifle critics" (Lye, 2009: 215, 237). The latest development saw the Foreign Correspondents' Club of China – an organization with more than 260 members from 33 countries – issuing a statement in August 2009 accusing China of reneging on her 2008 Olympics promise on freer foreign press reporting, based on a member survey in the previous month that reported 100 cases of driving away reporters at public places, 75 cases of tailing reporters, 16 cases of physical violence against reporters, 45 cases of threatening interviewees and 23 cases of calling in reporters for questioning.[53] Official policy towards dissent could be chillingly Orwellian, as related in Poole (2006: 203): "In June 2005, users of Microsoft's newly launched Chinese weblog service were banned from using words and phrases such as 'democracy' or 'democratic movement': attempts to type these terms invoked an error message that read: 'This item contains forbidden speech.'" The latest attempt by the Chinese government to enforce the compulsory installation of a *"lüba* 绿坝" (Green Dam)[54] Internet filtering software was widely interpreted to be yet another similar assault on dissent in cyberspace.[55] Further recent developments saw the government closing down the Open Constitution Initiative (OCI) (*Gongmeng* 公盟), a legal research centre set up in 2003 which has been involved in various sensitive cases in recent years – including the case of Chen Guangcheng, melamine-contaminated baby milk scandal, and various other civil rights and press freedom cases – and published critical reports on China's human rights and minority policies, on 17th July 2009 ostensibly for tax offenses, subsequent to the 5th July 2009 Xinjiang riots and with the 60th anniversary of the founding of the People's Republic approaching. This came after the revoking of the licences of 53 Beijing lawyers, many of whom being well-known personalities active in civil rights cases.[56] In the 2009 Freedom House's Annual Global Survey of Political Rights and Civil Liberties (ratings reflect events from 1st January 2008, through 31st December 2008), China was rated 7 (i.e. the worst rating) on political rights and 6 (next to worst) on civil liberties (see Figure 10.18), making her one of the 17 "worst of the worst" countries in terms of political rights and civil liberties (Puddington, 2009: 5), just marginally better than Burma[57], North Korea, Sudan, Libya, Somalia, Turkmenistan, Uzbekistan and Equatorial Guinea that were all rated 7 on both political rights and civil liberties (Freedom House, 2009).

Despite the much touted intra-Party and grassroots democratization, it is undeniable that China remains an authoritarian state, with party regulations on cadre selection still charging "local Party committees with nominating key officials in local governments, legislatures, and courts" (Minzner, 2006: 10):

Figure 10.18 China, Taiwan and ASEAN: Political Rights and Civil Liberties, 2008

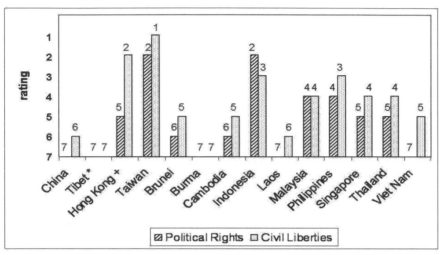

Notes: 1 is the best rating, 7 the worst. Ratings reflect events from 1st January 2008, through 31st December 2008.

    * Xizang (Tibet) Zizhiqu ("autonomous region"), China.

    + Hong Kong Special Administrative Region (SAR), China

Source: Data from Freedom House (2009).

Local Party committee control extends over the electoral systems that permit citizen participation in the selection of delegates to local people's congresses and village/residents committees. Selection of who may serve as a candidate is under the control of local election committees dominated, and sometimes chaired, by county and township Party secretaries. Election committees use non-transparent practices to narrow the list of acceptable candidates [...] Citizens who attempt to challenge Party-nominated candidates can find themselves unable to even get on the ballot. Chinese officials do permit a degree of citizen political participation, but only within channels that local Party institutions can control and monitor. Some non-Party members do win seats on local village committees. "Consultative" channels, such as the Chinese People's Consultative Conference, allow non-Party members to offer nonbinding input into policy formulation. Chinese authorities have also recently experimented with allowing citizen participation in the selection of local Party officials. These experiments, however, grant citizens only a limited voice in the nomination of potential candidates, allow Party committees to eliminate names from the nominee lists, and retain Party control over the final approval of the results.

(*ibid.*: 10-11)

O'Donnell and Schmitter (1986: 9) opined that a transition from authoritarian rule could produce a democracy, but it could also terminate with a liberalized authoritarian regime (*dictablanda*) or a restrictive, illiberal democracy (*democradura*).[58] As the above discussion shows, while shadows of the remnants of her ghostly past still linger to haunt the one-party State, there are already telling signs that the continuing transformation from a *dictadura* (dictatorship) into a *dictablanda* leading further to a highly restrictive *democradura* in the near future is the most possible direction the CCP regime is heading to and indeed planning to head to, given the fact that the Western, "bourgeois liberal" democracy (*democracia*) has already been ruled out of the cards.

Political Reform: Pax Sinica sine Trias Politica?

> Infidelity does not consist in believing, or in disbelieving, it consists in professing to believe what one does not believe.
> – Thomas Paine (1737-1809), *The Age of Reason*, Pt. I

While the establishment of village committees in rural areas through direct elections began in 1988, a year before the Beijing-Tiananmen massacre, the "Organic Law on Village Committees" – according to which, the director, deputy director, and members of the village committee are directly elected by villagers for a term of three years, and villagers who are at least 18 years old have the right to vote and to stand for election – was only officially promulgated in November 1998 (Bo, 2009a: 7), some years after the post-Tiananmen uncertainties, and grassroots elections were expanded to the township level in the same year and the county level in 2002 (*ibid.*: 7-8).

After the 13th Party Congress in October 1987, at which Zhao Ziyang – who became the Party's general secretary and first vice-chairman of the Central Military Commission – proposed the one and only political reform package in the history of the Chinese Communist Party which attempted to introduce reforms such as the separation of power between Party and State (Zhao, 2009a: 286)[59], and the successful experiment on the "permanent party congress system" in the Jiaojiang 椒江 district[60] of the prefecture-level city of Taizhou 台州, Zhejiang Province, in 1988-1989, such voting system on the appointment and removal of cadres was only promoted again by the Central Organization Department in 2001 (Bo, 2009a: 13-14), years after the post-Tiananmen uncertainties. Further intra-party democratization ensued, including the Plenum Voting System whereby the party's leading cadres are selected by the plenum of the party committee through secret ballot:

In April 2004, the CCP Central Committee promulgated a regulation on "methods of selecting and recommending candidates for chief leaders of the party committee and the government of the next lower level by voting in the party's local committee plenary sessions." The regulation provides that candidates for chief positions of the party and the government of the city, prefecture, league, county, district, flag, township, and neighborhood should in general be presented to the plenum of the party committee of the next higher level where the appointment will be decided through secret ballot. For chief positions of the party and the government at the prefecture and county levels, the standing committees of the provincial party committee and the municipal party committee should nominate candidates, respectively and the respective plenums will review them and make a decision by secret ballot.

(Bo, 2009a: 14-15)

In short, we are witnessing intra-party democratization picking up speed again after the historic political reform package introduced by Zhao Ziyang at the 13th Party Congress in October 1987 was temporary halted by the political repression immediately after the Beijing-Tiananmen massacre. With June Fourth as the watershed, CCP's élite political thinking has markedly progressed from Deng Xiaoping's complete dismissal of the North Atlantic democracy, especially the *trias politica* (tripartite separation of powers) for checks and balances[61], to affirmation at least in theory by Hu Jintao (a former protégé of Hu Yaobang) and Wen Jiabao 温家宝 (a former aide of Zhao Ziyang who was at Zhao's side during the latter's last public, heart-rending appearance in 1989 in Tiananmen Square) the notions of democracy, the rule of law, freedom, and human rights as universal common values of the humankind, which, as we have seen, has been accompanied by the remarkable pace of intra-party democratization.[62] However, as Minzner (2006: 21) noted, all the institutional reforms so far "share a common thread: firm commitment to the principle of centralized Party control":

Officials have curtailed social and political reforms when they appear to challenge this core principle of centralized Party control. Since the late 1980s, Chinese officials have allowed citizens to take part in local elections for village committees. But they have quashed local experiments aimed at expanding these initiatives to higher levels in the Chinese bureaucracy, and have maintained tight control of the nomination and selection of candidates to screen out individuals who might challenge Party control. Similarly, in the late 1990s, Chinese officials created a regulatory structure to govern the registration of civil society organizations with more attenuated ties to the state. But when a group of social activists attempted to use these channels in 1998 to openly register branches of the Democracy Party[63], Chinese officials rapidly suppressed the group and sentenced the leaders to lengthy prison terms. This unwillingness to alter core principles of centralized Party control appears to make it unlikely that officials will be able to address the institutional factors that drive social unrest.

(*ibid.*)

This is made absolutely clear in a the State Council's October 2005 White Paper on "Building Political Democracy in China" which stated that "Party committees serve as the leadership core over all [government and mass] organizations at the same level [...] and through Party committees and cadres in these organizations, ensure that the Party's policies are carried out [...] Party committees ensure that Party proposals become the will of the state, and that candidates recommended by Party organizations become leaders in the institutions of state power."[64]

In the process of maintaining a tight grip on political power in ensuring the CCP's perpetuation of its Party-State monopoly while delivering on the economic front and bringing prosperity and wellbeing to the long-suffering people of this giant country, the neo-authoritarian developmentalism followed since June Fourth could be leading the country on a path threaded before by various East Asian countries like Taiwan (Republic of China) and Singapore – a model sometimes termed "State corporatism". When the enraged and desperate Beijing citizens yelled "fascists" at the rampaging PLA armoured vehicles on that murderous night of 3rd-4th June 1989, when Chai Ling in hiding screamed "fascists" in her taped condemnation of the massacre shortly following that night of terror, when that lone individual[65] stood in front of and blocked a column of tanks signifying terrifying State power in that poignant image reminiscent of Pablo Picasso's *Guernica*[66], when melancholy and despair descended upon and the tune of *Xueran de Fengcai* 血染的风采[67] surrounded the hunger strikers in the Tiananmen Square, there was little telling of the course to come to pass in China's subsequent political evolvement. "Fascism" could eventually prove to be an overstatement – other than that night's slaughter and subsequent arrests and executions, nothing that came in this one-party state in the aftermath of June Fourth remotely approached Franco's repression against the defeated Republicans and their supporters in the dictator's "no-party" state[68] immediately following the end of the civil war, though the term could still be in certain way fitting if it is defined as the requirement for faith in and unquestioning loyalty to the one-party State (or in the case of Franco's Spain, in particular to the *Caudillo*). The post-June Fourth State corporatism, or referred to by some observers as "Leninist corporatism"[69], could provide a closer resemblance to Franco's *Nuevo Estado* (New State), and the "harmonious society" vision declared in recent years recalls Franco's vision of social cohesion and harmonious relationship between employers and workers via corporatism that would promote a close collaboration between them under the direction of the State and his corporatist policies to regulate the economy by controlling the conditions of work, wages, prices, production and exchange, though Gunther (1980: 3) somehow described Franquist Spain as "halfheartedly" corporatist:

> Labor unions were outlawed, and in their place were created 27 vertical syndicates, to which nearly all workers, technicians and employers belonged. "Representative" institutions (e.g. the Cortes and local government bodies) were organized along corporatist lines. Nevertheless, hundreds of economic and social organizations (which either were considered to be non-political by nature or were formed by groups supportive of the regime) remained completely independent of the state-dominated corporative structure.

While it is interesting to discern both similarities and contrasts between this and the case of post-June Fourth China, and corporatism, or State corporatism, might not be a grand theory that could adequately explain the new, emerging developmental paradigm in China's astounding transition, it may yet prove to be helpful in understanding the inevitable transforming political landscape which, as Unger and Chan (2001) argued, could be moving in a "societal corporatist" direction in incremental shifts instead of the introduction of any form of political democracy, and as Unger and Chan further observed, the exclusion from these corporatist structures of the peasants and most of the non-State-sector workers whose grievances would thus be devoid of such mechanisms for articulation does not auger well for social and political stability. Some aspects of State corporatism may indeed recall the classic analysis of Bonapartism as a basis of State autonomy. Being propelled into a leading position by a balance of class forces, combined with the inability of the subordinate classes to exercise control over their supposed representatives in the State apparatus, the government – or here the Party-State – uses the leverage gained to preserve both the status quo and the interests of the dominant class. The dominant class (or the bourgeoisie, as in Marx's (1852) original description of the Bonapartist regime in *The Eighteenth Brumaire of Louis Napoleon*), in turn, is willing to abdicate to a certain extent its opportunity to rule in exchange for other kinds of protection by the ensuing strong State (Stepan, 1985).[70] Therefore it is important to recognize that the State, or a Party-State, is neither necessarily a neutral nor a passive actor. It may be perceived as an autonomous body that possesses its own interests and objectives independent from the rest of the populace. It can be a potentially disinterested party that engages in mediation and crisis management. However, it can also negotiate to achieve goals based on narrower interests. The State can use its influence to establish, entrench or expand its power (Enloe, 1980). In a way, while June Fourth can be seen as a culmination of the unstable development of an early stage of State corporatism since reform began partly due to the liberalism of the Hu Yaobang-Zhao Ziyang administration, the 1989 tragedy can also be observed to be the catalyst of the subsequent authoritarian corporatist evolution and reaffirmation of the path of economic reform (after Deng's *nanxun*) and economic success as realization of the root causes of the tragedy had served to spur the CCP into attempting to reinvent itself as a strong, benevolent and enlightened ruler (i.e. a *dictablanda*), or as Thomas Hobbes referred to in his 1651 treatise, "the generation of that great Leviathan".[71]

Decentralization and Corruption

> Truth is on the march; nothing can stop it now.
>
> — Émile Zola (1840-1902)

In recent years, the "neo-corporatism" hypothesis emerged to claim that while the traditional Leviathan hypothesis from the school of public choice reappeared in Russia in the form of the "grapping hand" hypothesis, China is instead characterized by a "helping hand" (Krug and Zhu, 2004; Frye and Shleifer, 1997; Shleifer and Vishny, 1994, 1998; Oi, 1992, 1995, Unger and Chan, 1995, Nee, 2000; summarized in Krug, Zhu and Hendrischke, 2004).[72] Gu and Chen (2002) concluded on the results of their multiregional analysis: "[...] in the case of China, the corruption of the helping hand when taxes are decentralized can be socially preferable to the corruption of the grabbing hand when taxes are centralized." Ahlin (2000), based on a conceptual model, argued that though deconcentration has the potential to increase corruption, political decentralization has the potential to contain it due to interjurisdictional competition, while empirical evidence from Crook and Manor (2000) shows that political decentralization reduces large-scale corruption but increases the petty one in the short run, but both may decline in the long run, and Olowu (1993) considered political centralization a root cause of endemic corruption in Africa.[73] Huther and Shah (1998) also found that increased fiscal decentralization was associated with enhanced quality of governance, political and bureaucratic accountability, social justice, improved economic management and reduced corruption.

Figure 10.19 shows the results of a sample survey by the National Statistical Bureau conducted in early November 2007 in all 31 provinces

Figure 10.19 China: Most Concerned Social Problems (%), 2007

(a) All China

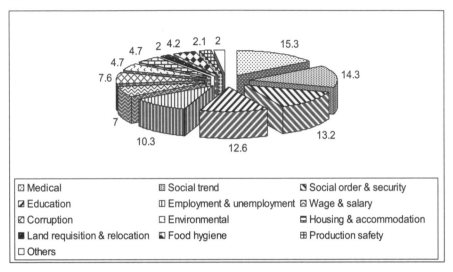

(b) Urban China

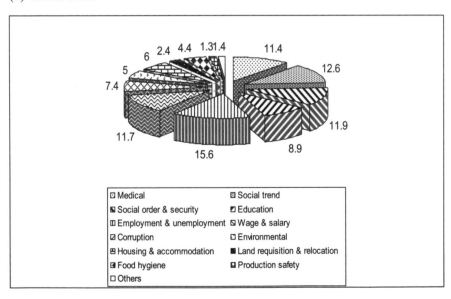

(c) Rural China

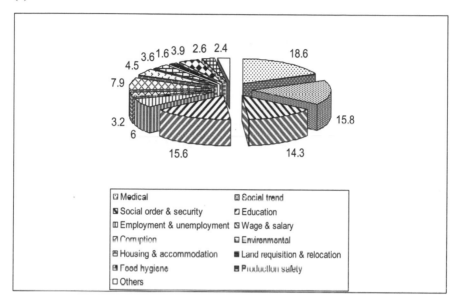

Source: *Zhongguo Shehui Tongji Nianjian 2008*, p. 412, Table 6.

(*sheng* 省) / *zizhiqu* 自治区 ("autonomous region") / *zhixiashi* 直辖市 (municipality with province status, directly ruled by the central government) covering 101,029 families regarding social problems the respondents were most concerned with. Out of the 13 types of social problems, the medical, those regarding social trend (social situation), social order and security, education and employment/unemployment are the top five, constituting 15.3 per cent, 14.3 per cent, 13.2 per cent, 12.6 per cent and 10.3 per cent respectively. Urban residents were most concerned with employment/ unemployment, social trend, social order and security and wage and salary, while rural residents were most concerned with the medical issue, social trend, education and social order and security. This shows that social trend and social order and security are the common concerns of both urban and rural residents, while the concern with employment/unemployment and wage and salary issues are more urban than rural and the medical issues and children's education are more the concerns of rural than urban residents.

It should be noted that many of these such as land requisition and relocation, wage, employment, housing and accommodation, environment and food hygiene and safety are closely linked in this country to the issue of corruption and government-business collusion (*guan-shang goujie* 官商勾结, here referring to the collusion between local government officials and businessmen or entrepreneurs in return for favours) and contribute to widespread popular resentment and constitute the source of most public protests – officially labeled *qunti shijian* 群体事件, literally "mass incidents" which take various forms "from peaceful small-group petitions and sit-ins to marches and rallies, labor strikes, merchant strikes, student demonstrations, ethnic unrest, and even armed fighting and riots" (Tanner, 2004: 138) – often against the police and the local governments.

After the crushing of the massive 1989 pro-democracy demonstrations which actually began with smaller-scale anti-corruption protests, this root cause of the protest has gone worse, not better. Citing Sun Yan in *Current History* (2005), Hutton (2006: 127) reminded us that "large-scale corruption is mounting. The average 'take' in the 1980s was $5000; now it is over $250,000. The number of arrests of senior cadre members above the county level quadrupled between 1992 and 2001 [...] In 2005 it was disclosed that a cool $1 billion had been misappropriated or embezzled in Gansu, one of China's poorest provinces, by a ring of forty or more officials." Hutton cited Hu's (2006) estimate that the annual economic loss due to corruption over the late 1990s alone amounted to between 13.3 and 16.9 per cent of GDP, while evidence provided by government departments revealed that the annual economic loss between 1999 and 2001 due to corruption averaged 14.5 to 14.9 per cent of GDP.[74] As Hutton (2006: 127) noted, "Every incident of corruption – smuggling, embezzlement, theft, swindling, bribery – arises in the first place from the unchallengeable power of communist officials and the lack of any reliable, independent system of accountability and scrutiny [...] the evidence of the depth of corruption at the apex of government, business and finance, mean that any paradoxical usefulness [of corruption in the early years of reform in providing flexibility to an otherwise highly bureaucratic system] has long since been surpassed. Corruption to this extent is chronically dysfunctional and even threatens the integrity of the state." This threat to the integrity of the State is most evident in the worrying frequency of incidents of social unrest which mostly stem from protests against local official corruption and abuse of power. For instance, in 2005 alone, such public order disturbances amounted to 87,000 cases, or an average of almost 240 a day, involving about 4 million people[75]. While social unrest among farmers and workers has long been observed since the early 1990s, as Lum (2006: "Summary") described, "recent protest activities have been broader in scope, larger in average size, greater in frequency, and more brash than those of a decade ago":

According to Chinese Communist Party sources, social unrest has grown by nearly 50% in the past two years, culminating in a particularly violent episode in December 2005. China's Public Security Ministry declared that there were 87,000 cases of "public order disturbance" – including protests, demonstrations, picketing, and group petitioning – in 2005 compared to 74,000 reported cases in 2004. In 2003, the PRC government reported more than 58,000 "major incidents of social unrest" involving an estimated 3 million to 10 million persons, of which 700, or less than 2%, involved clashes with police, while a Hong Kong-based labor rights group estimated that the number of labor demonstrations reached 300,000 that year. The December 2005 clash between villagers and People's Armed Police (PAP) in Dongzhou village (Shanwei city), southeastern Guangdong province, in which 3-20 villagers were killed, became a symbol of the depth of anger of those with grievances and the unpredictability of the outcomes of social disputes.

(Lum, 2006: 1 2)

According to official statistics, "illegal" *qunti shijian* nationwide increased from 10,000 to 74,000 cases over the decade of 1994-2004, with an average annual growth rate of 22.2 per cent, while the number of people involved in the *qunti shijian* went up from 730,000 to 3,760,000, with an average annual growth rate of 17.8 per cent (Hu, Hu and Wang, 2006). The figures continued to climb to 87,000 cases and about 4 million people by 2005 (Figures 10.20

Figure 10.20 China: Incidents of Public Protest (*Qunti Shijian*)

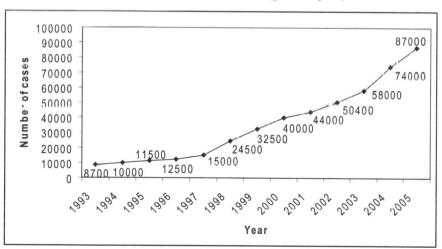

Source: Lum, 2006: 1-2; Tanner (2005), cited in Keidel (2005: 1), Table 1, data from *Liaowang* 瞭望 magazine and China Ministry of Public Security; Hu, Hu and Wang (2006).

Figure 10.21 China: Numbers of People Involved in Public Protests
(*Qunti Shijian*)

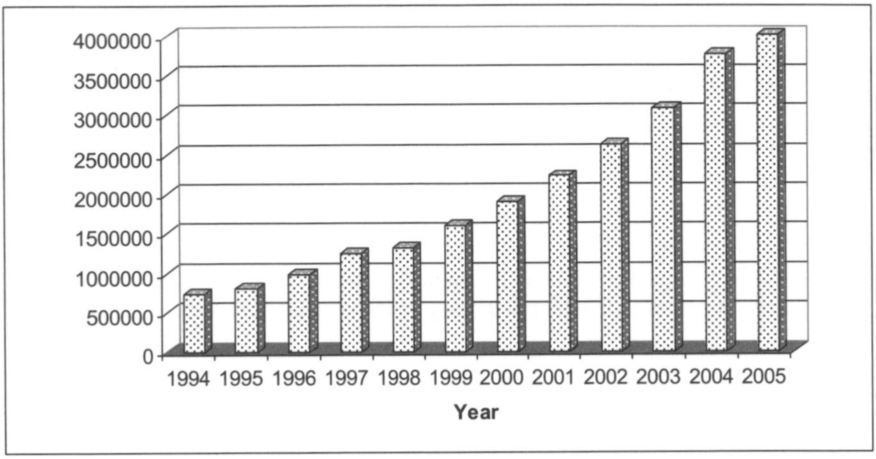

Source: Hu, Hu and Wang (2006); Yeoh (2009b: 284).

and 10.21). In general, the number of *qunti shijian* had been rising at an alarmingly increasing rate. From a growth of about 10 per cent from 1995 to 1996, *qunti shijian* was growing at an average annual rate of as high as 25.5 per cent from 1997 to 2004, i.e. higher than the average growth rate of 22.2 per cent during the decade of 1994-2004, with annual growth in certain years reaching as high as above 40 per cent; or with 1994 figure indexed 100, a steep increase of the index from 100 to 740 in terms of the number of cases during the decade of 1994-2004 (an increase of 6.4 times) and from 100 to 515 in terms of the number of people involved (an increase of 4.2 times) (*ibid.*).

More recent cases of such public order disturbance were alarmingly on the rise in a series of serious incidents including year 2008's high-profile conflicts of 28th June (in Guizhou), 5th July (Shaanxi), 10th July (Zhejiang), 17th July (Guangdong) and 19th July (Yunnan). Yet these constitute but just a small sample of the overall rise in social unrest across China in recent years, some of which involved ethnic conflicts[76]. Adding to these are the long-running Tibet conflicts including the March 2008 Lhasa riots and the March 2009 conflict in Qinghai's Guoluo 果洛 Tibetan *zizhizhou* 自治州 ("autonomous prefecture")[77], as well as the July 2009 Ürümqi riots. With the memory of the 1989 Beijing-Tiananmen massacre constantly hanging like the sword of Damocles, the ruling regime is again facing a dire dilemma:

[…] the struggle to control unrest will force Beijing's leaders to face riskier dilemmas than at any time since the 1989 Tiananmen Square demonstrations. Experiments with less violent police tactics, economic concessions to demonstrators, and more fundamental institutional reforms all risk further encouraging protest in an increasingly restive society. Nevertheless, these challenges must be navigated if the party wants to avoid the ultimate dilemma of once again resorting to 1989-style violence or reluctantly engaging in a more fundamental renegotiation of power relations between the state and society.

(Tanner, 2004: 138)

The ruling CCP has not been oblivious to this deteriorating situation. Anti-corruption measures have continued to constitute a main prong in the Party's political reform since the Jiang Zemin 江泽民 administration, as Jiang himself declared in 2002 in his last political report to the National Congress, "If we do not crack down on corruption, the flesh-and-blood ties between the party and the people will suffer a lot and the party will be in danger of losing its ruling position, or possibly heading for self-destruction."[78]

Having averted such a dire scenario for the Party in 1989 via a bloody crackdown, CCP was in full awareness of the root cause of the Tiananmen protests. The predominantly Chinese squeaky clean, efficient tiny state of Singapore – and her long-ruling People's Action Party (PAP) – has quite incongruently become a role model for the CCP to emulate.[79] To the Western accusation that China's so-called "political reform" is nothing but a ruse since political reform in an authoritarian state should mean democratization and that China is copying a bad Singaporean model to develop its own version of neo authoritarianism, combining free market economy with dissent-muzzling one-party rule, China's answer usually goes along the line like the West should recognize China's specific national conditions and give due respect before China could reach the Western standards in human rights and democracy. Whether the neo-authoritarian experience of the corruption-free tiny city state of Singapore could effectively be emulated by a huge country with one-fifth of humanity where corruption is endemic has always been a centre of debate, given the fact that China's growing social unrest indeed reflects deep institutional problems of the evolving local State corporatism after June Fourth, as Minzner (2006: 9) observed:

Particularly at local levels of government, control over all formal political and legal institutions is centralized in the hands of the local Party secretary and a few deputies. These individuals exercise extensive control over institutions such as local legislatures, courts, Party disciplinary committees, and the media. This concentrated power in the hands of a few individuals breeds numerous problems. First, it allows corruption to thrive. Second, it allows local leaders to choke off the flow of information to higher-level leaders regarding policy failures that might reflect poorly on local officials' performance. Third, it deprives citizens of effective redress of their rights through local legal and political institutions, particularly when the source of the violation is a local Party official. Chinese citizens appear to be increasingly resorting to mass protests and petitions directed at higher-level authorities as a means of circumventing the controls of local officials over legal and political institutions, and triggering the intervention of higher level officials in resolving their grievances.

Ultimately, as Fang (1991: 254-255) warned, "There is no rational basis for a belief that this kind of dictatorship can overcome the corruption that it itself has bred. Based on this problem alone, we need more effective means of public supervision and a more independent judiciary. This means, in effect, more democracy."[80] Nevertheless, the path towards a North Atlantic liberal democracy as envisaged by Fang has seemed increasingly forlorn as the CCP regime has in the post-June Fourth era led the country to economic miracle and hence, in the eyes of many, has successfully reasserted its legitimacy.[81] Describing China as "doubtless a post-totalitarian regime ruled by a ruthless Party", Béja (2009: 14-15) ruminated on the 20th anniversary of the Beijing-Tiananmen massacre:

> Twenty years after the 4 June 1989 massacre, the CCP seems to have reinforced its legitimacy. It has not followed the communist regimes of the Soviet bloc into oblivion. Its policies of elite cooptation, subtle response to social contradictions, and instrumental support for the "rule of law" have become major complements to its continued control over the press and the political system. It has made concessions to prevent discontent from crystallizing into social movements that might challenge its rule, and it has sent in the police to silence dissidents. Over the course of the same two decades, the opposition has had to wrestle with the trauma of the June 4 Massacre and the huge difficulties that it has raised for anyone who would challenge the CCP's primacy.

Successful it might seem to be, the CCP regime's reassertion of its legitimacy and unassailability has in reality not been immune to series of challenges, some rather severe and unexpected, since June Fourth.

From June Fourth to July Fifth

> *J'accuse.* [I accuse.]
> – Émile Zola (1840-1902), *L'Aurore*, 13th January 1898

Referring to Muslim marchers in 1989 protesting the publication of a Chinese book entitled *Xing Fengsu* 性风俗 [sexual customs] that they claimed denigrated Islam, Gladney drew an interesting picture of stark contrast in State responses between this case of "protest *to* the government" and the other case of "protest *against* the government" in those same days[82] staged by the students and workers and their supporters from all walks of life around Beijing and other Chinese cities who eventually paid dearly by blood:

> Just prior to the bloody suppression of the 1989 democracy movement in China, in the midst of the flood of protesting students and workers who, for a remarkably lengthy moment in history, marched relatively unimpeded across Tiananmen Square and the screens of the world's television sets, another comparatively unnoticed, but nevertheless significant, procession took place [...] the protest began with mainly Hui Muslim students who were joined by representatives of all 10 Muslim nationalities in China, including some sympathetic members of the Han Chinese majority [...] this procession was on its way to Tiananmen Square, the so-called "Gate of Heavenly Peace", which soon opened on to a hellish nightmare of indiscriminate warfare in the streets of the terrorized city. This procession to the Square also made its way along Changan Jie, "the Avenue of Eternal Peace," that shortly thereafter was to be renamed "Bloody Alley" by Beijing's citizens [...] Remarkably, and in another dramatic contrast to the crackdown on the student Pro-Democracy Movement, the state took the following actions in response to this Muslim protest over an insignificant Chinese book: The government granted full permission for all the Muslim protests, often despatching police to close streets, stop traffic, and direct the marchers [...] By stressing the legality of the Muslim protests, what Barbara Pillsbury noted as their "*protest to* the government," rather than *against* it – the fact that the Muslims had permission and were often escorted by police – the state-controlled press sought to juxtapose the legal Muslim protest with the *illegality* of the student protests.
>
> (Gladney, 1991: 1-5)

One of the most prominent student leaders who led the pro-democracy demonstrations in Tiananmen Square was Örkesh Dölet (Wu'erkaixi 吾尔开希), who together with his fellow student co-fighters Chai Ling 柴玲, Wang Dan 土丹, Feng Congde 封从德 and the rest against official corruption and political repression, had virtually launched the Tiananmen Square demonstrations that later evolved into the now well-known broad-based pro-democracy movement after being joined in by other demonstrators from all walks of life from Beijing to Hong Kong, from Chengdu to Shenzhen, and sustained it against all odds throughout the 100-day Beijing Spring[83] that tragically ended up with, *à la Asiaweek*, the Rape of Beijing on that fateful night of June 3rd-4th, 1989, when a besieged regime finally responded with a massacre to reclaim the capital from the unarmed peaceful protesters. It is interesting to note that Örkesh Dölet was then a Beijing Normal University student of the Muslim Uyghur nationality. However, unlike the protesters in the parallel State-permitted demonstration in Beijing at that time against *Xing Fengsu*, Örkesh Dölet's involvement in leading the pro-democracy movement since the Tiananmen days till today transcends ethnicity, and it was notable that his recent condemnation – jointly issued on 7th July 2009 with Taiwan's China Human Rights Association[84] – of perceived government repression in the July 2009 Xinjiang disturbance was issued, while not denying his ethnic identity, as a civil rights activist[85], in comparison with some pronouncements made by former Nobel Peace Prize nominee Rabiyä Qadir (Rebiya Kadeer), chairperson of the World Uyghur Congress[86]. Nevertheless, in the eyes of the Party-State during those turbulent days of 1989:

> The students [demonstrating on Tiananmen Square in 1989 against corruption and for democracy], as an unrecognized voluntary association, were considered unlawful, riotous, and a threat to the state's order. For that they were met by a military crackdown. The actions of the Muslims [marching against the book *Xing Fengsu*], as members of state-assigned minority nationalities and believing in a world religion approved by the state, were considered permissible. For that they were inundated with state-sponsored media and assisted in their demands. The difference, from the Chinese state's standpoint, was one of order and disorder, rationality and confusion, law and criminality, reward and punishment.
>
> (Gladney, 1991: 5-6)

If widening socioeconomic inequality and deepening corruption are the two most prominent manifestations of the internal structural contradictions of the path of policy development of the CCP post-June Fourth – not least of which is the authoritarian political centralism amidst *de facto* fiscal federalism and economic decentralization[87] – a third manifestation, as mentioned earlier, social and socioracial unrest, closely linked to the previous two, is becoming an increasing headache for the ruling regime, rapidly growing with worrying frequency and escalating scale. While social unrest in general has been so frequent that they have grown into almost a part of daily life, those with a socioracial flavour[88] should be the most worrying for the ruling CCP including the recent two ultra-serious incidents of ethnoregional disturbance – the 14th March 2008 riots in Tibet and the 5th July 2009 riots in Xinjiang, with the latter claiming almost 200 lives, mostly Han, according to the Beijing government or at least 500, mostly Uyghur, dead[89] and nearly 10,000 Uyghur "disappeared" as alleged by Rabiyä Qadir[90].

Whether the riots and racial attacks had been triggered by the police and army firing on unarmed Uyghur protesters – in other words, a mini-Tiananmen – as alleged by Rabiyä Qadir and Örkesh Dölet or simply Uyghurs going on a rampage against Han interests as claimed by the government, the ethnoregional content of this latest, probably the most deadly, incident of social unrest is unmistakable. Here, a parallel can be drawn between this and the El Ejido violence that rocked Spain's southern province of Almería of the *comunidade autónoma* of Andalucía in 2000.

El Ejido Burning

Just like the July Fifth riots in Ürümqi was triggered by the June 26th Uyghur-Han brawl – which was in turn triggered by the alleged rape of two Han female factory workers by six Uyghur workers which the government condemned as an ill-intentioned rumour – at a Shaoguan 韶关 (Guangdong province) toy factory involving hundreds and ending up in the death of two Uyghurs, violence erupted in El Ejido – the centre for fruit and vegetable production on Spain's southern coast that relies heavily on cheap immigrant labour – in early 2000 when a Moroccan man was arrested on suspicion of stabbing to death a Spanish woman in a local market, which came two weeks after another Moroccan man was arrested in connection with the stabbing to death of two people. Although the police had said that there was no evidence that the immigrant community was committing more crimes than anyone else, hundreds of local people began marching through El Ejido shouting racist slogans, and proceeded on the rampage, burning cars and shops belonging to Moroccans – a minority that constituted just one-tenth of the local population, who mainly worked in agriculture, picking and planting fruit and vegetables – low-paid and back-breaking work which Spaniards shun. While several thousand people went on the worst rampage of racial violence in the recent history of the country, wrecking businesses, shops and bars owned by immigrants, and beating up Moroccan workers, the local police, under the control of the populist mayor Juan Enciso, did not seem to try to stop the rioters. Six hundred police reinforcements were sent from Madrid two days later, and it took several days to restore order. The mayor, meanwhile, resisted pressure from the prime minister, Jose Maria Aznar, to condemn the violence, vetoed a plan for the Red Cross to set up a camp for the immigrants whose shacks had been destroyed in the riots and helped provoke the resignation of the liberal labour minister, Manuel Pimental, who had spoken out in support of the immigrants.

While details might differ, such resentment towards immigrants or settlers is equally familiar in the ethnic homeland regions of China, typically Tibet and Xinjiang. Such resentment of the local ethnic communities against large-scale migration of the country's Han majority into her ethnic regions is nothing peculiar. Such outburst of resentment, long suppressed under authoritarian rule, has become more and more a rule rather than exception in the major formerly Communist Party-ruled countries including the former Soviet Union and those in Eastern Europe. Similar conflicts, albeit with differing characteristics, are also witnessed all over the post-Cold War World, whether in Darfur or in Irian Jaya, whether stemming from the rise of ethnoreligious bigots or on the contrary, the demise of authoritarian rule that makes way for the spread of free market democracy (see, e.g. Chua, 2003)[91].

While ethnic conflict in El Ejido clearly did not arise from the existence of a market-dominant minority (Chua's protagonist, which befits better the Han minority in China's ethnic regions), it could only be understood by taking into consideration the complex ethnic mosaic of Spain. Historically, the Spanish State has always endeavoured to impose a rigid ethnic, religious and cultural homogenization, not least by expelling the two most important minorities – the Jews were exiled by the Catholic Monarchs in 1492, and the Morescos were banished by Felipe II in 1609. Until the emergence of Basque nationalism in the late nineteenth century, the ethnolinguistic and ethnoreligious homogeneity of the Spanish people has never been questioned in the country. The small immigrant minorities – African slaves brought into the country in the sixteenth and seventeenth centuries and Germans who settled in the Sierra Morena in the eighteenth century – were easily assimilated. However, even under this façade of homogeneity, several ethnic groups in Spain have always kept a separate identity, culturally and linguistically: the Catalans (16 per cent of the population), mainly in the northeast of the country and on the eastern islands; Galicians (7 per cent) in the northwest; Basques, or Euskal-dun (2 per cent), mainly around the Bay of Biscay; and the nomadic Gitanos (Gypsies) who are dispersed all over the country, with the greatest number found in Madrid, Barcelona and the larger southern cities. Besides, there are also some less significant but somewhat differentiated groups like the "agotes" in Navarra and the "vaqueiros de alzada" in Asturias (with the distinctive local language called "bable"). Recent immigration, however, is adding a new element to the ethnic mosaic of the country, the "new minorities". While there are hardly any incorporation problems for the European immigrants and not much difficulty in the assimilation of Latin Americans given their Hispanic cultural and linguistic background, the integration of Africans and Asians has proven to be much more problematic.

According to official statistics, there are at present between 2.5 and 3 million foreigners in Spain, of which only about 1.8 million have a residence permit. That is to say, those who are "*sin papeles*" (without permit) total more than one million. Besides EU nationals (mainly Britons, Germans and Italians), these foreigners are mainly from Latin America (about 32 per cent, mainly some 190,000 Ecuadorians and 120,000 Colombians) and Africa (about 25 per cent, mainly the more than 350,000 Moroccans). The majority of the immigrants (about 90 per cent) are in the capital and the region of Catalonia. There are about 300,000 immigrants living in Madrid today, with around the same number in Catalonia. The remaining 10 per cent of immigrants are in the vast southern region of Andalucía, as well as Valencia and the Balearic islands. Both Valencia and the Balearic Islands are regions ethnolinguistically distinct from the Castilian centre. Half of the people in Valencia speak Valencian, a variety of Catalan; more than 70 per cent of the Balearic islanders speak Mallorquí, also a variety of Catalan. This means that besides Madrid, most of the immigrants actually end up either in the ethnolinguistically non-Castilian autonomous communities or regions with a strong ethnic movement.

In comparison with the other Western European countries, the percentage of immigrants in Spain (5 per cent) can be considered rather low.[92] Nevertheless, racism against these "new minorities", however subtle, is not unheard of. It can even take violent forms, as occurred in El Ejido in the southern province of Almería, Andalucía. Nor was El Ejido an isolated incident. Earlier in July 1999, there had been three nights of violence against North African immigrants in the north-eastern town of Tarrasa, near Barcelona, when hundreds of angry residents took to the streets shouting "Moroccans out" and "No more Moroccans" and attacked shops and cars of the immigrants.

A few things are readily observable in the pogrom in El Ejido – features that are common in such incidents elsewhere.[93] First is the role of politicians – in particular the populist mayor – and the local police, which the Spanish media blamed.[94] Van Dijk (2005) has highlighted the views expressed by conservative politicians in the historic autonomous regions who condone or flirt with xenophobic ideas. He noted the publication of a book by Heribert Barrera, former president of the Catalan parliament, with explicitly xenophobic remarks, in which the author declared himself in agreement with the right-wing Austrian politician Jörg Haider. Van Dijk also noted that the former Catalan leader Jordi Pujol, in his last major speech in the Catalan Parliament, declared on 2nd October that immigration was one of the most "problematic facts" of Catalonia. While insisting that it is a general problem for developed countries, Pujol emphasized that in Catalonia it has specific significance because immigration can affect "our identity". Van Dijk observed further that in a lecture for the Catalan Summer School in August 2004, Pujol defended the integration of immigrants in Catalonia, but without "going as far as miscegenation" because that would spell the "end of Catalonia". Other similar statements of Pujol in 2004, according to van Dijk, essentially repeated the same theme of the alien "threat" to Catalan language and culture and the all-importance of maintaining the Catalan national 'identity' for if Catalonia should have a "central" or "dominant" culture, this culture should be Catalan culture.

On the treatment of the "new minorities" by the "peripheral nationalisms" in Spain, van Dijk (2005) observed that being both associated with nationalist values, the "autonomous-nationalist" and conservative attitudes towards immigrants tend to be based on related ideologies – a resemblance that exists paradoxically in the two opposed forms of centralist and regional nationalisms in Spain, respectively. While there is the official, hence often "tacit while presupposed", nationalism of the Spanish State that opposes any infringement on the unity of Spain – a centralist nationalism that represents a continuation of the Franquist-Falangist tradition that had emphasized the unity of Spain, and repressed any form of linguistic diversity and political autonomy of the nations of Euskadi or Catalonia – van Dijk observed, on the other hand, the existence of "peripherical nationalisms" in the historic autonomous regions, especially those that are ethnolinguistically distinctive from the Castilian centre, such as Catalonia, Euskadi and Galicia. Hence, he noted, for conservative nationalists in these regions, too many immigrants might jeopardize the delicate consensus of a system in which the autonomous project is dominant, for instance teaching and using Catalan in Catalonia, because both ideologies, especially their more radical conservative brands, have "the tendency to oppose multiculturalism, multilingualism, immigration or any other way 'national unity' or cultural or linguistic homogeneity are seen to be threatened".

The sentiment of the electorate is no less alarming. Van Dijk cited some 1990 statistics which suggest that less than half of the people who vote for nationalist parties in Euskadi and Catalonia accept the thesis that foreigners should have the same rights as the Spanish people, and research which suggests that voters of more radical autonomous-nationalist parties also tend to have less sympathy for Arabs, Blacks and Gitanos. As van Dijk pointed out, such reaction against immigrants in Spain's historic autonomous regions has a longer tradition, and was not only directed against immigrants from outside Spain, but also against migrants from other parts of Spain, especially from Andalucía.

Hence, as the above Spanish example shows, ominously, to add to the challenge posed by the resurgence of ethnoregionalism, the increasingly assertive ethnoregional groups' sentiment towards other minorities in their midst tends to add to the gravity of the issue of peripheral nationalism. Kendra Clegg, in her study of the Sasak people in Lombok, Indonesia, observed that while "[r]egional autonomy allows local communities to strengthen their cultures and identities ... it may also marginalise minority groups." She also found that "[p]oliticising Sasak identity has meant the promotion of a single cultural identity, which disguises the great diversity of understandings of 'Sasak'" (Clegg, 2004). In other words, while regional autonomy "gave Sasak the authority over their territorial homeland, previously controlled by a Javanese bureaucracy, as well as the opportunity to focus on the development of the local economy and the majority cultural identity" (Clegg, 2008: 172), it also contributed to "the over-development of awareness and regional sentiments within the community, and the emergence of arrogant superiority attitudes that may cross and have on occasion crossed established acceptable boundaries" (*ibid.*: 181) and government-led programmes implemented in response to the regional dominant community's aspirations "may lead to further ethnic and religious tensions developing between the dominant group and those under-represented minorities" (*ibid.*: 182).

Peripheral Nationalism and the Ürümqi Riots

The above account of "peripheral nationalisms" in Spain and Clegg's observation of Lombok serve to throw light on the Xinjiang situation. Similarly, recent years have witnessed increasing nationalist sentiment tacitly encouraged by the Han political centre – especially among the young, many born after 1989, very much encouraged by China's increasing international standing spurred by her new-found, astounding economic strength and political and military might – a "centralist nationalism" that serves the CCP well. The "hundred years of national humiliation" has been used time and again to explain or justify the upsurge of nationalism and the obsession over territorial integrity. Unity has been the greatest concern of the generation that holds dear to the conviction that China's shameful defeat at the hands of Western and Japanese colonizers would never be allowed to be repeated, and that, though not often explicitly stated, high degree of regional autonomy especially in the non-Han ethnic regions like Tibet and Xinjiang could be the prelude to separatism and pave the way to China's disintegration, as the cases of the former Soviet Union and Yugoslavia have amply attested to.[95]

To understand fully the Chinese central State's unwavering position regarding such ethnoregional separatist sentiments, it is inadequate to attribute it, as quite often done, to "China's obsession with national security and the integrity of its historical borders" (Cook and Murray, 2001: 147). Instead, one needs to go back to the fundamental tenets of Marxism-Leninism:

> Marxist-Leninist theory on the national question defines a methodology for dealing with specific questions concerning the status of communities called nations or nationalities [...] According to Communists, the fundamental cleavages of world society are along class rather than national lines. "Nations" are artificial units which came into being with the rise of capitalism and which are destined to disappear when capitalism is replaced with Communism; nationalism is a club used by capitalists to keep the world proletariat divided and subdued. When the proletariat seizes power throughout the world, then, according to the theory, nations and nationalism will vanish [...] when one realizes that more than half the population of Russia at the time of the October Revolution consisted of peoples other than the Great Russians, and that more than half the territory of China "liberated" in 1949-1950 was inhabited by peoples other than Han Chinese, it will be appreciated how immensely important the national question was to the success of both revolutions. The national question has been central, not peripheral, to the revolutions in both countries [...] In concrete terms, what "Marxist-Leninist theory on the national question" as applied in Russia and China really means is that claims for national independence on the part of minorities in socialist countries is [sic] counter-revolutionary, and only in capitalist and colonial countries are such claims correct. Once the Communist Party, the vanguard of the proletariat, seizes power, then the oppression of one nationality by another is impossible; anyone still demanding independence, therefore, can only be an agent, witting or unwitting, of world imperialism and therefore an enemy of "the people." By similar arguments it is demonstrated that national minorities do not need their own Communist parties, since their interests are abundantly guaranteed by the unique Communist Party of the country.
>
> (Moseley, 1966: 4-7)

A correct perspective on the issue of ethnoregionalism and the root cause of ethnoregional secessionism and the accompanying "peripheral nationalisms" – long regarded by the Party-State as irrational, ungrateful and unfathomable not unlike the sentiments of the Tiananmen demonstrators of 1989 – free from the preconceived bias of "centralist nationalism" is important to understand the complexities of Xinjiang, Tibet, Taiwan and other chasms. For instance, Mikhail Gorbachev may be a sinner blamed for the disintegration of the Russian-dominated Soviet Union in the eyes of the Russians, but could be remembered in history as the person who liberated the many long-tortured subordinate nationalities from the "prison of nations", especially from the perspective of the non-Russian citizens of the Soviet Union, who have long languished under Leninist-Stalinist totalitarianism, not to mention particularly the horrors of the Stalin years, ever since the days their quest for national self-determination was hijacked by the Bolsheviks:

> According to history, the Empire of the czars was a 'prison of the peoples' and Lenin opened it. But history is never quite that simple. At the start of the twentieth century the empire was already showing signs of weakness; all its subject peoples were beginning to resent its domination and looking for ways to escape from it. Lenin's genius lies in having grasped the breadth of these desires for emancipation, and in having understood that by utilizing those desires – which had nothing to do with the working class – he could assure the victory of the workers in his own country.
>
> (Carrère d'Encausse, 1979: 13)

Similarly, the whole idea of the Confucian grand unity in the Cultural China construct should not be taken for granted without paying due consideration to the will of all groups, whether dominant or subordinate, in the People's Republic of China. This so-called "grand unity" emphasized in the Cultural China construct, far from being a voluntary federalization by amalgamation, has always been a top-down arrangement in the millennia of China's history, shaped mostly by conquest and domination. As Mikhail Gorbachev pointed out in the case of the former Soviet Union, the dis-integration of such an entity represents the dissolution not of a country, but of the command structure that has long gone against the genuine will of the constituent nationalities of the empire (Gorbachev, 1991).[96]

According to the 2000 census, Uyghurs are but only 45 per cent of the population of Xinjiang although the region was organized as a "Uygur Autonomous Region". Even if we add on the Kazakhs (7 per cent) and the Hui (5 per cent), Uyghurs and their Muslim co-religionists contribute only to about 57 per cent of the population. Lin Hueisiang, writing in *Minquo* 25th Year (民國二十五年 i.e. 1936), provided the following information:

> Today's Huei 回 (Muslim) *zu* 族 (nationalities) are mainly found in Sinziang 新疆, Qansu 甘肅 and Shaansi 陝西 – and mostly in Sinziang [...] the Tuzve 突厥 (i.e. Turk) *zu* were earlier found to the north of the Siongnu 匈奴 (Huns), later moved southward into Mongolia. After the conquest of Hueiqe 回紇 by Siaziaseu 黠戛斯 (Kirghiz), they moved southwest into the regions of Sinziang and Qansu. After the suppression of the Muslim rebellion, Sinziang was changed into a province in the Eighth Year of the Reign of the Cing dynasty Emperor Quangsvu (清光绪八年 i.e. 1882). Today the Muslim population there still constitutes eighty per cent.
>
> (Lin, 1936: 42-43, tr.)

If Lin's data were accurate, today's Uyghur (and other Muslim) population in Xinjiang is a far cry from that in the 1930s. On another note, the history of Xinjiang is a history of continuous rebellion and imperial, often brutal, suppression. Lin (1936) wrote:

> Islam's entry into Sinziang 新疆 began in early 11th Century, but then it was limited to the southwest corner of the region. The expansion became rather rapid by the Yvan dynasty 元朝. By the time of early Cing dynasty 清朝 the southern part was completely populated by Muslims, who came to expand into the region's north after the time of Emperor Cianlong 乾隆 [...] Since the conquest of Hueiqe 回紇 by Siaziaseu 黠戛斯 (Kirghiz), Muslims had migrated southwest from the north to south of the Tianshan 天山 mountain. Since then the Tuzve 突厥 (Turk) people have been mostly residing in Sinziang. After the conquest of Weiwuer (畏吾兒 i.e. Uighur) by the Mongols, it belonged to Mongol's Chagatai Khan. During the Ming dynasty 明朝 located in this region were Hami 哈密, Huozhou 火州, Tulufan 土魯番 (i.e. Turpan) etc. which were semi-independent, among which the strongest being Tulufan whose population, other than Muslims, also consisted of Ciang 羌, Tufan 吐蕃 and Mongols [...] By the time of Emperor Cianlong, Amusana 阿睦撒納 of the Zhuenqeer 準葛爾部 (i.e. Dzungaria) rebelled against the Cing government; Muslim leader Hezhuomu 和卓木 took the opportunity to lead the Muslims to fight for independence from the Cing court but was defeated and killed. Hence the Muslim region again came under Cing rule in the 24th Year of the Reign of Emperor Cianlong (乾隆二十四年 i.e. 1759) [...] The next rebellion came in the 25th Year of the Reign of Emperor Ziacing (嘉慶二十五年) stemming from Cing officials' persecution of Muslim people. This revolt led by Zhangqeer 張格爾, offspring of Hezhuomu, was finally crushed by the Cing army in the 7th Year of the Reign of Emperor Daoquang (道光七年) [...] Muslim uprising occurred again in the 1st Year of the Reign of Emperor Tongzheu (同治初年) and Shaansi, Qansu and Sinziang almost all achieved independence. Shaansi's and Qansu's independence movements were crushed by Zuo Zongtang 左宗棠 who was sent in the 7th Year of the Reign of Emperor Tongzheu to the western region, who proceeded to crush the independence movement of Sinziang in the 2nd Year of the Reign of Emperor Quangsvu (光绪二年).
>
> (Lin, 1936: 37-41, tr.)

That said, the case of Xinjiang is much more complicated than a simple Muslim struggle for independence against Han colonizers, as Gladney (2003: 24-25) cautioned:

> The problems facing Xinjiang, however, are much greater than those of Tibet if it were to become independent. Not only is it more integrated into the rest of China, but the Uyghur part of the population is less than half of the total and primarily located in the south, where there is less industry and natural resources, except for oil [...] however, unless significant investment is found, Tarim oil and energy resources will never be a viable source of independent wealth. Poor past relations between the three main Muslim groups, Uyghur, Kazak, and Hui, suggest that

conflicts among Muslims would be as great as those between Muslims and Han Chinese. Most local residents believe that independence would lead to significant conflicts between these groups, along ethnic, religious, urban-rural, and territorial lines.

In fact, influx of ethnic Han into Xinjiang intensified only after the establishment of the People's Republic, with the numbers of Han settlers in Xinjiang rising from less than half a million in the early 1950s to 7.5 million by 2000 and 8.1 million by 2006.[97] On a historical timeline, Han Chinese colonization of the region has only been quite a recent phenomenon with large-scale Han migration into the region in the mid-19th century:

> [...] it was not until 1760, and after their defeat of the Mongolian Zungars,[98] that the Manchu Qing dynasty exerted full and formal control over the region, establishing it as their "new dominions" (*Xinjiang*), an administration that had lasted barely 100 years, when it fell to the Yakub Beg rebellion (1864-1877) and expanding Russian influence. Until major migrations of Han Chinese was [sic] encouraged in the mid-nineteenth century, the Qing were mainly interested in pacifying the region by setting up military outposts which supported a vassal-state relationship. Colonization had begun with the migrations of the Han in the mid-nineteenth century, but was cut short by the Yakub Beg rebellion, the fall of the Qing empire in 1910 [...]
>
> (Gladney, 2003: 4)

Such independence movements have not ended with the overthrow of the Manchu dynasty in 1911, as the ensuing warlord era dismembered the region and the nascent Republican China faced the danger of losing the territory on various occasions – the short-lived East Turkestan Islamic Republic in 1933 and East Turkestan Republic in 1944 which lasted till 1949 when the PLA entered Xinjiang ("peaceful liberation") and the region was incorporated as part of the new People's Republic, later established as the "Xinjiang Uyghur Autonomous Region" on 1st October 1955.

As the Uyghur population dwindled to just 45 per cent today (compare this with Lin's nineteen thirties figure of about 80 per cent) while large-scale Han Chinese settlement has caused the latter's proportion to burgeon to 41 per cent (see Yeoh, 2009b: 257, Figure 10.7)[99], Uyghurs' resentment against what they perceive as the Han Chinese empire's internal colonization and the exploitation of the region's rich resources by the Han Chinese central State is inevitable. Large-scale demographic transfer of members of a country's dominant ethnic group into a minority ethnic region of the country inevitably, for the ethnic minority, raises the spectre of internal colonization, plundering of local resources, dominant cultural assimilation, and unequal resource contest. In the case of Xinjiang, adding to such perception is the historical legacy left by China's use of Xinjiang as the testing ground for its nuclear weapons programme from 1964 to 1996, which according to recent Japanese research results by Professor Jun Takada 高田純, a physicist at the Sapporo 札幌 Medical University, have probably resulted in a "conservative minimum" of 194,000 deaths from related illnesses out of the 1.48 million people who were exposed to radioactive fallout from the testings, 1.2 million people afflicted with leukaemia, solid cancers and fetal damage, including 35,000 newborns who were deformed or handicapped. The 46 nuclear testings over the span of 32 years at Xinjiang's Lop Nur have been disastrous in particular for the ethnic minorities including Uyghurs and Tibetans as wind direction had brought nuclear dust to the Silk Road cities and townships in Xinjiang and Gansu, bringing about cross-generational legacy of cancer affliction – with Xinjiang's cancer rates allegedly 30 to 35 per cent higher than the national average – birth deformities and shorter lifespan.[100]

Similar phenomenon can be observed in Tibet. The Sinicization of Ürümqi is paralleled by the Sinicization of Lhasa 拉萨. The official population figures for Tibet differ much from certain unofficial ones. The official figures have been disputed by the Tibetan government-in-exile who claimed that "accelerating Han population transfer into Tibet ... has reduced the Tibetan people to a minority in their own land ... [and today] there are over 7.5 million non-Tibetan settlers in Tibet including Chinese and Hui Muslims, compared to six million Tibetans" (Cook and Murray, 2001: 141). However, such allegations of population transfer were rebutted by the Beijing government – according to whose official figures Tibetans constitute 93 per cent of the Tibet's total population (see Yeoh, 2009b: Figure 10.7) – who argued that "the only Han Chinese living in Tibet are specialists who have gone there voluntarily to help in the region's development ... [and they] make up less than five per cent of the population and many of the people are there for only a few years before returning home" (Cook and Murray, 2001: 141). The figure of 93 per cent Tibetans was one given by the 2000 Census. In fact, official data for the year 2005 gave the proportion of Tibetans as high as 95.28 per cent and that of Han as only 3.91 per cent of the total population of Tibet.[101]

The Inverted Paradigm: State Policy-Induced Ethnogenesis, Reethnicization and Polarization

Incidentally, Spain's southern province of Almería, where El Ejido is located, is in Andalucía, which is not supposed to be considered part of the ethno-linguistically non-Castilian "historic" regions with separatist sentiments. As a comparison with the case of China, let us look at an inverted paradigm in contrast to the discussion so far, using the case of Andalucía. Andalucía, of course, is Castilian. Nevertheless, what uneven development and public policy can do to fuel regional separatist sentiments is evident even in Andalucía where the population has little ethnolinguistic differences from the Spanish (Castilian) political centre, for while government responds to challenges from ethnic community organizations that seek to influence public policy, "within an inverted and complementary paradigm [...] ethnic communities take shape as response to stimuli which induce a process of ethnogenesis" (Gheorghe, 1991: 842-843). The shockingly rapid emergence since the late 1970s (with the advent of the *Comunidades Autónomas* project) of a politically disciplined and powerful regional cultural identity in Andalucía, which Greenwood (1985) argued to be as authentic as the Basque or Catalan ethnic movement, basically stems from the local people's grievances that they have been subjected to centuries of exploitation not merely by Andalucian capitalists, but by the Castilian political centre as well. This interesting phenomenon of public policy-induced ethnogenesis evident in the large southern impoverished region of Andalucía, which shares the linguistic identity of the Spanish (Castilian) centre, is the direct result of the post-Franco *Comunidades Autónomas* project. "The rapidity with which a politically disciplined and powerful regional cultural identity has emerged in Andalusia shocked everyone", commented Greenwood (1985: 222-223), "[...] the idea that the Andalusian movement is something qualitatively different from the 'true' ethnic movements in the Basque Country and Catalonia must be exploded."[102]

This phenomenon of public policy-induced ethnogenesis is also evident in the increasing support since the 1980s for Italy's *Lega Nord* (Northern League), whose leader has declared the aim to set up a state called "Padania" free from Rome's rule and from union with the poorer South.[103] Such centrifugal development in Italy, of course, reflects the increasing resentment of the more prosperous North for having to subsidize the poorer South and a tax revolt against Rome.[104] Although from the ethnolinguistic perspective the country is relatively homogeneous (with small Sard, Friul, German and Occitan minorities), Italy's late but rapid unification has left a legacy of widespread "pseudo-ethnic" sectionalism, which is no less ascriptive than that Greenwood found in Andalucía, across its numerous regions and compartments, partly reflected linguistically in the local *dialetti* or koinés.

In the case of China, such public policy-induced ethnogenesis is evident in, for instance, the most assimilated of minorities, the Zhuang whose ethnic consciousness was virtually created by the Han-dominated central Communist Party-State in the early 1950s[105], who have begun to press for preferential treatments from the central government, as the country's deadly race towards economic prosperity continue to widen economic disparities between the ethnic minorities and the Han majority, making it more and more challenging to manage ethnic nationalism and ethnoregionalism in the People's Republic (Figure 10.22).[106]

Figure 10.22 Interrelationship of Ethnic Fragmentation and State Policy

Ethnic fragmentation   State Policy

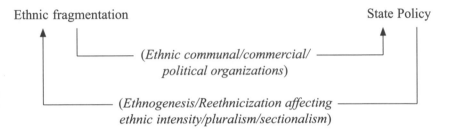

(*Ethnic communal/commercial/ political organizations*)

(*Ethnogenesis/Reethnicization affecting ethnic intensity/pluralism/sectionalism*)

It is a fact that Beijing has been intensifying efforts in developing the western region of China (Figure 10.23), including Xinjiang, in particular after the launching of the Western Regional Development Programme (*xibu dakaifa* 西部大开发)[107]. However, such heavy economic support and financing of disputed or ill-integrated regions for national territorial cohesion is nothing unique. For instance, ethnopolitical conflict brought about by the annexation of East Timor obviously had an effect on fiscal allocation in Indonesia in the years before Timor-Leste (East Timor) officially freed herself in May 2002 from more than two decades of Indonesian occupation and became a sovereign state. In fact, as Shah and Qureshi (1994) showed, the Indonesian "province" of Timor Timur (East Timor) received the highest per capita general-purpose central transfer among all Indonesian provinces (Shah and Qureshi, 1994: 62). Timor Timur, together with Irian Jaya (a province with strong secessionist sentiment), also received special preference in SDO ("subsidy for autonomous regions") grant allocation (*ibid.*: 65). It could of course be argued that Timor Timur was Indonesia's poorest "province" – both Timor Timur and Nusa Tenggara Timur had the lowest per capita non-oil GDP of just about 360,000 rupiah or US$180 (*ibid.*: 54, 254, Tables 3.8, A5.10). Furthermore, Timor Timur (and Irian Jaya) had the lowest proportion of own-source receipts in total current receipts and Timor Timur had the lowest proportion of aggregate own revenues of local governments in total current revenues and proportion of own revenue in total receipts (*ibid.*: 84, 86) that qualified the "province" for higher central transfers[108], but the continuing destitution of the poverty-stricken region was very much a result of the occupation and brutal military campaign against the independence movement.

It is also a fact that Xinjiang has not fared badly in development and modernization in recent years. In terms of Gross Domestic Product (GDP), Table 10.4 shows that Xinjiang has had a moderate performance among the provinces/zizhiqu/zhixiashi of the western region and fared much better than Tibet which has been the worst performer. In terms of GDP per capita, Xinjiang is the best among them. Rural poverty is still a serious problem for Xinjiang, with rural incidence of poverty in the bracket of 5-10 per cent but not as bad as Tibet and Qinghai whose rural incidence of poverty is above 10 per cent (Figure 10.24). In terms of urbanization, Xinjiang is also a moderate performer, ranking 17th among the country's 31 provinces/zizhiqu/zhixiashi, compared to the least urbanized Tibet (ranked 31st) (Figure 10.25). Other key indicators, shown in Figures 10.26-10.30, reveal a similar picture.

However, implementing the western regional development project within a cautious political framework is not without risks either. First, with strong constraints in the devolvement of central power, it could be difficult to coordinate the interests of the central and local governments over the power of authorization and permissions and to determine how far the right to independent development could go. Besides that, it may not be easy to adjust the interests of local governments over limited financial resources and projects to be implemented. Finally, there is the fact that 80 per cent of the ethnic minorities in China live in the western regions and national border areas where the new regional development strategy is targeted. Without accompanying decentralization of political power and the conferring of substantial degree of regional autonomy in the control and use of local resources, ethnic minorities may perceive the central State's projects as attempts at internal colonization – for instance, the mixed feelings of the Tibetans towards the Qinghai-Tibet railway – leading to their outright opposition to the whole regional development strategy itself, thus exacerbating the already simmering ethnoregional tensions, even culminating in repeated disturbances such as the deadly 14th March 2008 riots in Tibet and 5th July 2009 riots in Xinjiang. Paradoxically, further devolution in China that seems to be the logical extension of the already decentralist process of economic reform may yet be arrested by the lack of the will for political change – which is crucial to the maintenance of long-term stability – due to the illusory confidence brought about by the economic success itself.

While in Spain where ethnic division is territorial, the ethnic minorities are concentrated in Catalonia and the Basque Country which constitute the economic backbone of the country, in China, where the major ethnic

Table 10.4 China's Western Region: Major Economic Indicators, 2005

	GDP (hundred million yuan)	GDP growth (%)	GDP per capita (yuan)	Fixed capital formation (hundred million yuan)	Urban income per capita (yuan)	Urban income per capita growth (%)	Rural income per capita (yuan)	Rural income per capita growth (%)
Sichuan	7385.1	12.6	8440.1	3462.1	8386.0	8.8	2802.8	8.6
Guangxi	4063.3	12.7	8762.0	1775.9	8916.8	9.0	2494.7	8.2
Inner Mongolia	3822.8	21.6	16026.0	2687.8	9137.0	10.3	2989.0	14.7
Shaanxi	3674.8	12.6	9844.0	1980.5	8272.0	9.4	2052.0	6.9
Yunnan	3472.3	9.0	7833.0	1743.0	9265.9	4.5	2041.8	6.5
Chongqing	3069.1	11.5	10978.0	2006.3	10244.0	10.2	2809.0	11.9
Xinjiang	2609.0	10.9	13030.0	1352.3	8100.0	8.0	2482.0	10.6
Guizhou	1942.0	11.5	4957.0	1014.7	8147.1	10.6	1877.0	5.2
Gansu	1928.1	11.7	7341.0	874.5	8086.8	9.6	1980.0	6.9
Ningxia	599.4	10.3	10308.0	444.7	8093.6	12.1	2509.0	6.3
Qinghai	543.2	12.2	10043.0	367.2	8057.9	10.1	2165.1	8.0
Tibet	250.6	12.2	9098.0	196.2	8411.0	2.6	2078.0	11.7

Note: Rural poor for whole of China in 2004 totaled 26.10 million, with incidence of poverty 2.8 per cent.
Source: *Zhongguo Fazhan Shuzi Ditu, 2006*, p. 225, and *Zhongguo Xibu Jingji Fazhan Baogao (2007)*, p. 39, Table 5.

Figure 10.23 China: Three Economic Regions

Notes: Province/Zizhiqu/Zhixiashi in the officially designated Western Region
in bold italics.
━━━ Regional Boundary.
Source: Yeoh (2008a: 30), Table 1; Yeoh (2008c: 112), Figure 7.22.

Figure 10.24 China: Distribution of Rural Poor

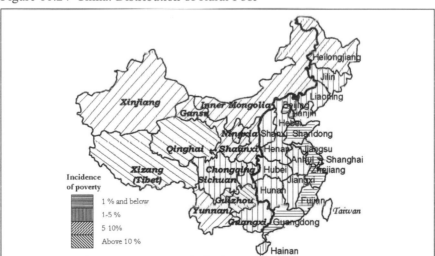

Source: Chen (2006: 176), Table 7-1. Data are for year 2003.

Figure 10.25 China: Urbanization in Ethnic Zizhiqu and Multiethnic Provinces
(Rate of urbanization; National ranking in rate of urbanization)

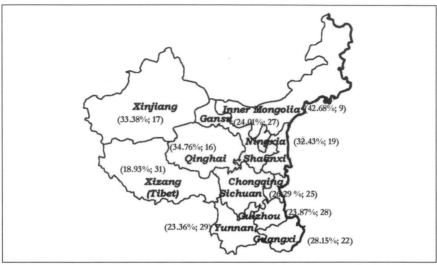

Source: *Zhongguo Minzu Fazhan Baogao, 2001-2006*, p. 232, Table 18 (original
source: *Zhongguo Renkou Wenhua Suzhi Baogao*, 2004).

Figure 10.26 China: Gini by Province/Zizhiqu/Zhixiashi

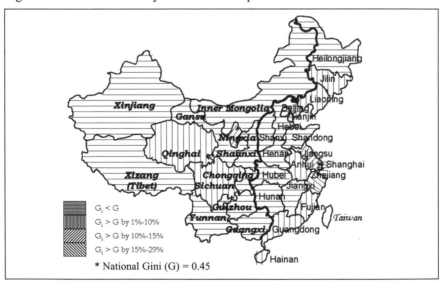

Source: Huang and Niu (2007: 161-162), Table 5-3(2).

Figure 10.27 China: Average Education Level in Ethnic Zizhiqu and
Multiethnic Provinces, 2000 (Years of schooling;
National ranking of education level)

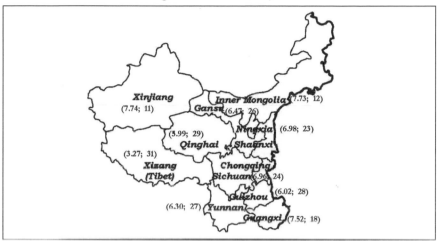

Source: *Zhongguo Minzu Fazhan Baogao, 2001-2006*, p. 231, Table 17 (original
source: *Zhongguo Renkou Wenhua Suzhi Baogao*, 2004).

Figure 10.28 China: Illiteracy in Ethnic Zizhiqu and Multiethnic Provinces,
2000 (Illiteracy rate; National ranking of illiteracy rate)

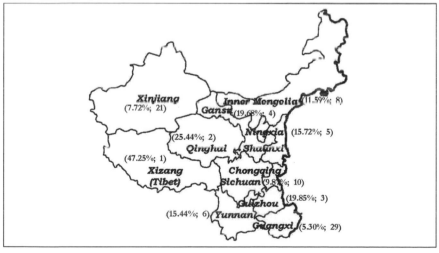

Source: *Zhongguo Minzu Fazhan Baogao, 2001-2006*, p. 230, Table 16 (original
source: *Zhongguo Renkou Wenhua Suzhi Baogao*, 2004).

Figure 10.29 China: Incidence of Absolute Poverty by Province/Zizhiqu/
Zhixiashi (2005)

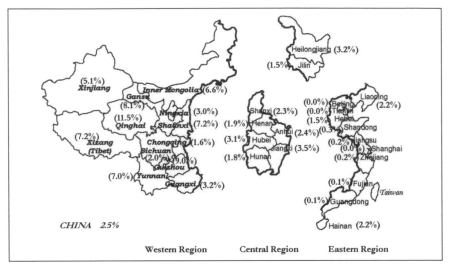

Source: *Zhongguo Fazhan Baogao 2007*, p. 39, Table 2.3.

Figure 10.30 China: Population Engaged in Agriculture in Ethnic Zizhiqu and
Multiethnic Provinces (Million people in 2000; Growth in million
1990-2000; Growth rate)

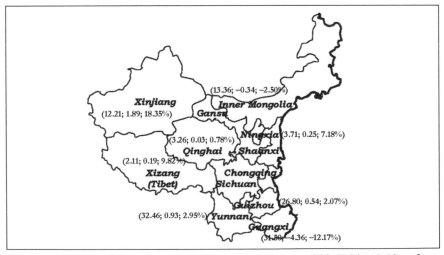

Source: *Zhongguo Minzu Fazhan Baogao, 2001-2006*, p. 232, Table 19 (data from
the 2000 Population Census).

division is also largely territorial, the country's major ethnic minority groups including the Uyghurs and Tibetans are concentrated in the resource-rich western provinces and zizhiqu.[109] It was forecasted that by 2010, the western region's coal, petroleum, natural gas and a whole range of abundant mineral resources will be adequate to guarantee China's economic development or exports, and hence the western region – being the major energy source for the whole of China, providing 34 per cent of the nation's coal, 78 per cent of hydroelectricity and 59 per cent of natural gas (Yeoh, 2008c: 16) – is poised to become the country's important reserve base of strategic resources.[110] The geographical demarcation of the western region for the *xibu dakaifa* programme was nevertheless not an easy process, since being incorporated as a part of the western region means that the regional government concerned would be entitled to receive various benefits, including priorities in obtaining projects funded by the central government and other fiscal subsidies. That explains why regional governments all over the country at that time of demarcation were swept into a frenzy trying to get their regions classified as "western" – in a course of events resembling the *fiebre autonómica* (autonomy fever) when the Spanish *Comunidades Autónomas* project was first introduced after the death of the *Caudillo* no matter how unconvincing their arguments were. However, given the fiscal constraints of the central government, continued fiscal help from the central government could be problematic. Hence, fund-raising would depend on the ability to attract domestic- and foreign-capital enterprises. That explains why many regional governments had raced to announce preferential policy measures as soon as the proposal was made for the *xibu dakaifa* strategy (*IDE Spot Survey*, 2001: 24). Such interregional scrambling for future benefits even at the early stage of the strategy can provide a glimpse into the potential resource contest between regions, especially given the understandable difficulty to coordinate and adjust the interests of regional governments over the distribution of the resources for the strategy.[111] Furthermore, the reassertion of old regionalisms and the development of new regionalisms in particular with an ethnic overtone have always constituted a challenge to countries facing an inevitable long-term prospect of decentralization and devolution, as we have seen in the *fiebre autonómica* (autonomy fever) that threatened to bring about the virtual disappearance of the central Spanish State when the country's *Comunidades Autónomas* project was first introduced after the death of the *Caudillo*. The undertaking of costly projects, such as the creation of regional public television networks, regional institutes for business development and promotion, the development of major infrastructures, etc., by the Autonomous Communities in a concerted effort to compete with each other in the levels of performance and achievement, for political legitimacy and consolidation, have served to further exacerbate the existing rivalry over public resources, the conflict between the Communities as well as between the centre and the periphery, with significant implications for the development of ethnoterritorial consciousness and interethnic relations. Even the fact that the Han command an unequivocal majority of 92 per cent of the total population of China needs not render the country immune to such threats.

From the discussions so far in this section, one underlying question, besides the State response towards minority aspiration after the critical junctures of 1976 and 1989 in China and 1975 and 1981 in Spain, is the impact on interethnic relations in the regions experiencing continuing large influx of migrants ethnically different from the existing local ethnic community who considers itself a "homeland" community with implication for relative ethnic intensity and legitimacy in claim to land. In looking at the case of Almería of the *comunidade autónoma* of Andalucía, we have discussed to some extent the case of the "new immigrants" of Spain. The following section aims to take this discussion a step further by analyzing the socioracial problems of China's ethnic regions, with particular reference to the case of Xinjiang, with regard to the possible theoretical implications of the impact of continued Han Chinese influx on interethnic relations which will in turn affect regional stability in the objective environment created by the State's ethnic and regional policies.

From Ürümqi to Lhasa: Superordinate-Subordinate Power-Size Configuration

One important aspect of the numerical structure of ethnicity refers to the role played by the relative size of ethnic groups in the societal power structure. The superordinate-subordinate relationship in a multiethnic society is related to the concept of "minority". It avoids some of the definitional problems accompanying the concepts of "race" and "ethnicity", especially those related to the nature and significance of different types of group markers. The concept of "minority", instead, focuses on the size and strength of the groups involved, in terms of variations in the economic, political and social balance of power. Wirth (1945: 347) defined a minority as "a group of people who, because of their physical or cultural characteristics, are singled out from the others in the society in which they live for differential and unequal treatment, and who therefore regard themselves as objects of collective discrimination". This definition has been criticized because it makes the existence of minorities completely dependent on the feelings of minority group members, despite his caveat that minorities "objectively occupy a disadvantageous position in society" (*ibid.*: 348). Wirth's emphasis on the disadvantageous social position of the minority leads to his neglect of the latter's numerical relationship to the wider society. For him, collective perception of their distinctive disadvantages is the decisive criterion that distinguishes minorities from other subordinate populations irrespective of their number, nature and disadvantage, as a people "whom we regard as a minority may actually, from a numerical standpoint, be a majority" (*ibid.*: 349).

Disregard for the numerical aspect, in addition to the importance attached to subjective definitions of the situation by the minority, leads to the view that every instance of group conflict in society is by definition, a "minority problem" (van Amersfoort, 1978: 219). Many researchers besides Wirth have shown the same disregard for the numerical aspect, e.g. Wagley and Harris (1967), preferring to emphasize the power dimension of the "minority" concept. Nevertheless, whether the concept of a minority group depends upon actual numbers, is more than a matter of definition, since power and numerical dimensions are ultimately linked to each other. As Stone (1985: 43-4) remarked:

> [...] this basic demographic fact [of actual numbers] will affect many different aspects of race relations, not least the question of the "costs" for the dominant group of promoting racial justice: whether such policies can be pursued in a relatively peaceful, evolutionary manner, or whether they are more likely to lead to persistent conflict and violence.

When analyzing the possible impact of public policy on ethnic conflict, such disregard for the numerical aspect diminishes any projected result. Smith (1987: 343-4) emphasized this numerical dimension in his critique of Wirth's definition:

> To lump together all disadvantaged populations irrespective of size without prior study of the relationships between their demographic ratios, organisation and differences of collective status, assumes in advance the irrelevance of these variables or the randomicity of their distribution. Such assimilation of demographic fractions and majorities is sociologically unsound because the situations of aggregates often differ as functions of their relative size and organisation or lack of it.

Relating the numerical dimension directly to the question of political power, van Amersfoort (1978: 221) noted that in a modern democratic state the "characteristic problem for a minority group is not so much that it is difficult to ensure formal rights, but that the numerical situation restricts the possibility of translating such rights into social influence". A useful redefinition of the concept of "minority" is that by Schermerhorn (1970: 14):

> Combining the characteristics of size, power, and ethnicity, we [...] use "minority group" to signify any ethnic group [...] that [...] forms less than half the population of a given society, but is an appreciable subsystem with limited access to roles and activities central to the economic and political institutions of the society.

For Schermerhorn only those subordinate ethnic groups that are numerical minorities of nation-states qualify as "minority groups". He thus implicitly endorsed all other criteria set by Wagley and Harris (1967: 10) to distinguish (ethnic) minorities, whose membership must be transmitted by rules of descent and endogamy, from other disadvantaged collectivities (whose disadvantages are due to social mobility, e.g. refugees, captives, and other disadvantaged categories such as women, slaves, proletarians and peasants). The "ethnic group" is defined by Schermerhorn as "a collectivity within a larger society having real or putative common ancestry, memories of a shared historical past, and a cultural focus on one or more symbolic elements defined as the epitome of their peoplehood", and the "dominant group" as "that collectivity within a society which has preeminent authority to function both as guardians and sustainers of the controlling value system, and as prime allocators of rewards in the society" (Schermerhorn, 1970: 12-3).

For a fundamentally bi-ethnic region like Xinjiang[112], it is apparent that the relationship between State policy and ethnic conflict and antagonism is influenced by the subordinate group's aspirations, the dominant group's orientations and their dynamic interaction. Figure 10.31 constructs a power-

Figure 10.31 Power-Size Configuration of Ethnic Groups

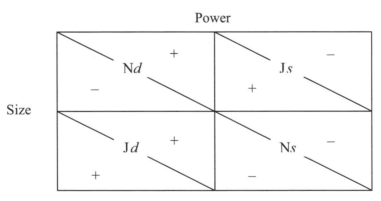

Notes: J*d* = dominant demographic majority (Schermerhorn's "majority group")
J*s* = subordinate demographic majority ("mass subjects")
N*d* = dominant demographic minority ("élite")
N*s* = subordinate demographic minority ("minority group")

Figure 10.32 Typology of Multiethnic Societies

Superordinate

		N*d*	J*d*
	N*s*	1	2
Subordinate			
	J*s*	3	4

Note: * Typology based on the paradigm presented in Figure 10.31.

size configuration of ethnic groups similar to Moscovici's diagram of group power-influence configuration (Moscovici, 1985: 26). Based on this paradigm, a typology of multiethnic societies can be constructed, as illustrated in Figure 10.32.

Excluding case 4 which is by definition not applicable in this typology, Figure 10.32 shows a threefold typology of multiethnic societies. Case 2 represents a J*d*-N*s* type of society which combines a subordinate demographic minority with a dominant demographic majority – a typical example is China as a whole with her demographically (92 per cent) and politically dominant Han Chinese majority. Case 3 is an N*d*-J*s* society in which the numerical majority is dominated by a demographic minority – the local Uyghurs and other real and exotic minorities in Xinjiang in relation to the minority Han Chinese settlers (around 40 per cent) backed by Han Chinese-dominated central State, hence as an extension of the Han Chinese-dominated central State power. The subordinate-superordinate intergroup relationship in a society with no obvious demographic majority (an N*d*-N*s* society) is represented by case 1 – the mainly bi-ethnic relations in Xinjiang between the Uyghurs (about 45 per cent) and Han Chinese (about 40 per cent) or if we take the estimates of the Tibetan government-in-exile, the relations between the Tibetans (about 44 per cent) and Han Chinese settlers (together with the minority Hui settlers totalling about 56 per cent). If we see the Han influx into Xinjiang as in a way an extension of the Han dominance of the central State, the Xinjiang society then belongs to the N*d*-N*s* category, while the continued influx of the Han following increasing economic prosperity of the region is moving the society towards a J*d*-N*s* configuration, or probably it could have already to a certain extent reached that stage, if some unofficial data on population composition are accurate. Indeed, if we look at cities – the centres of prosperity – while the populations of Kashgar/Qeshqer (Kashi 喀什) and Hotan/Xoten (Hetian 和田) are still in the main Uyghur, that of the capital city Ürümqi/Ürümchi (Wulumuqi 乌鲁木齐) is already almost 80 per cent Han.[113] Official data, in fact, show that Ürümqi's population is currently 12.62 per cent Uyghur and 74.70 per cent Han.[114] Similar situation is also apparent in Tibet and Lhasa.

Schermerhorn's concept of a minority mentioned above, which he re-defined as a variety of ethnic group, is part of the fourfold typology he developed to take account of the numerical and the power dimensions (Schermerhorn, 1970: 13):

Figure 10.33 Schermerhorn's Fourfold Typology of Dominant-Subordinate Relations

	Dominant Groups		
	Size	*Power*	
Group A	+	+	Majority Group
Group B	–	+	Élite

	Subordinate Groups		
	Size	*Power*	
Group C	+	–	Mass subjects
Group D	–	–	Minority Group

The fourfold typology illustrated in Figure 10.33 includes not only "majority group" and "minority group", which are dominant and subordinate respectively in terms of both size and power, but also "élite" and "mass subjects" where numerical superiority and power do not coincide. Societies that combine the subordinate numerical minorities ("minority groups") with dominant demographic majorities ("majority groups") (D+A, such as China as a whole), are contraposed as the structural opposites of those in which the numerical majority of "mass subjects" are dominated by a demographic minority, the "élite" (C+B, such as Xinjiang and Tibet, if one sees the minority Han settlers as an extension of the Han Chinese-dominated central State power). While it is undeniable that the typology provides a comprehensive picture of the dominant-subordinate relationship, the C+B case, other than cases of internal colonization of a country's ethnic regions, is rare in today's world after the demise of Western colonialism in the Third World and the end of White rule in Rhodesia (Zimbabwe) and South Africa. Nevertheless, the fact that such configuration is rare other than internal colonization does not imply its total disappearance – two obvious examples are Rwanda and Burundi where the Hutu majorities are still politically dominated by the Tutsi minorities.

Cases 2 and 3 in Figure 10.32 thus correspond to Schermerhorn's AD and BC configurations (1970: 13) respectively. However, since societies containing disadvantaged demographic minorities do not necessarily have the complementary majorities that Schermerhorn postulated (e.g. Niger, Nigeria, Liberia, Benin, see Smith, 1986), the inclusion of case 1 is necessary, examples of which as we have seen above are China's Xinjiang and possibly Tibet.

Such a typology can be considered exhaustive, since "race relations are essentially group power contests" (Baker, 1978: 316) wherein symmetrical power relationships among groups are rare and often transient:

> Whatever the power relationship (symmetrical, where both are equal, or asymmetrical, where one is dominant), each group may initiate action or respond to the acts, or anticipated acts, of others [...] Given changing circumstances over time, group power capabilities (measured in terms of group resources, additive resources, mobilization capabilities and situations) may alter, thereby transforming the character of group power relations. At any given moment in time (T1) the power of A may be equal to that of B (symmetrical), at a later period (T2) that of A may be superior to that of B (asymmetrical, with A dominant), or at another point (T3) that of A may be less than that of B (asymmetrical, with A subordinate).
>
> (Baker, 1978: 317 8)

The infrequency of a symmetrical power relationship was also noted by Hoetink in his study of slavery and race relations in the Americas:

> A race problem exists where two or more racially different groups belong to one social system and where one of these conceives the other as a threat on any level or in any context [...] One of the groups will commonly be perceived and perceive itself as dominant; the chances that two racially different groups within one society would attain an equilibrium of power, though not absent, are exceedingly small.
>
> (Hoetink, 1973: 91)

Hoetink (1973: 47-8) basically saw the multiethnic horizontally layered structure as a special form of *Herrschaftsüberlagerung* – "a stratification consisting of at least two layers of which the upper layer has, as it were, moved over the lower one (by military conquest, colonial usurpation, and so forth) or the lower layer has been pushed under by the upper one (by subjugation, the importation of forced labour, and the like)". In societies with such horizontal ethnic division, stimulation of solidarities based on economic or class position may have an aggravating, rather than an ameliorating, effect on ethnic conflict. By contrast, in those societies where ethnic division lines between the main population segments run vertically, it is likely that a functional relationship between economic differentiation and the increase of interethnic (horizontal) solidarities, such as those based on economic position, will emerge. These foster intercommunication and may serve to mitigate existing ethnic antagonisms. The two patterns of ethnic division are conceptually linked to the two different types of plural society – the hierarchic plurality (based on differential incorporation) and segmental plurality (based on equivalent or segmental incorporation). A society may combine both these modes of incorporation and form a complex plurality. Smith (1986: 198) noted that the segmental and differential modes of incorporation generate quite distinct ethnic tensions and problems. Hoetink (1973: 146-7) linked the two different patterns of ethnic division to the stability of multiethnic societies:

> It is interesting that the modern societies that often are put forward as examples of reasonably well-functioning cultural heterogeneity, such as Belgium, Switzerland, Great Britain, and the Soviet Union, all have vertical cultural boundaries, to the point that their cultural segments even have territories of their own with a certain degree of cultural and sometimes political autonomy. Although European history shows many cases of repression, expulsion, or political elimination of such territorially limited cultural minorities, and although it would be naïve to underestimate the still-existing cultural and political tensions in countries like Belgium or Great Britain, it is correct to assume that a minimum of horizontal interpenetration and communication gives these systems a certain viability.

To this list, Hoetink added Suriname, Guiana and Trinidad. However, symmetrical power relationship between groups in a society is rare and often transient. For various reasons ranging from demographic growth to economic ethos to social mobility, one of the groups usually achieves dominance in the long run, thus turning the vertical lines of ethnic division into horizontal ones, as illustrated in Figure 10.34.

Xinjiang and Tibet: Interethnic Power Shift in the Ethnic Regions

Hoetink (1973: 91) observed the infrequency of a symmetrical power relationship:

> A race problem exists where two or more racially different groups belong to one social system and where one of these conceives the other as a threat on any level or in any context [...] One of the groups will commonly be perceived and perceive itself as dominant; the chances that two racially different groups within one society would attain an equilibrium of power, though not absent, are exceedingly small.

In short, as mentioned in the preceding section, symmetrical power relationship between groups in a society is rare and even if it emerges, tends to be transient. One of the groups will ultimately achieve dominance in the long run through demographic growth, economic achievement or some other factors, thus pivoting the vertical line of ethnic division into a horizontal one, as illustrated in Figure 10.34 which represents the relative positions of ethnic and class categories, but not their relative sizes, and expresses a combination of the horizontal and vertical principles of social differentiation – similar to that presented by Warner (1936) in his caste-class configuration for the US Deep South.

Figure 10.34 Vertical *v* Horizontal Ethnic Division

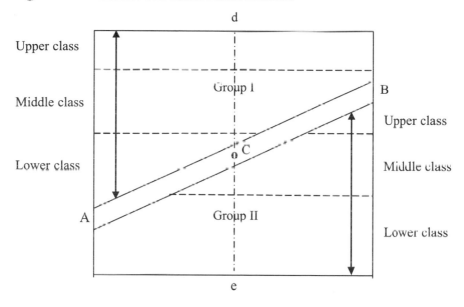

The diagonal boundary A-B incorporates the status gap and divide ethnic group I from ethnic group II (Warner's "castes"). The two double-headed vertical arrows indicate that movement up and down the class ladders within each group can and does occur, but there is no movement across the ethnic boundary A-B (Warner's "caste line"). Han Chinese penetration into Xinjiang and Tibet under the CCP rule would have at first created a temporary vertical ethnic boundary positioned at d-e, indicating a system of combined equality and separation – the upper class of one ethnic group (Uyghur/Tibetan) would be equivalent to that of the other (Han), while the lower classes in each of the parallel groups would also be of the same social status. However, the tilting of the ethnic boundary as shown in Figure 10.34 into the position A-B would have occurred somewhere along the timeline as, being an extension of the politico-economic power of the Han dominated central State, Han economic dominance in these ethnic regions grew due to various factors including political, economic and cultural environmental preconditions, initial endowments, long-established networks, etc.[115] With the ethnic line tilted in the way shown in the diagram, within each class level to which they have risen, members of group II (Uyghur/Tibetan) are thought of as socially inferior to members of group I (Han) of the same class, until as individuals they become assimilated (Sinicized) by the latter. It is a fact that the non-Han ethnic people are often looked upon as backward, dirty, lazy and superstitious by the dominant Han who pride themselves on assiduity and having a "5000-year culture". Marginalized by centuries of Han Chinese imperial expansion, China's ethnic minorities have historically been viewed as *manyi* 蛮夷, i.e. "barbarians", and it was only after the revolution that the "dog" radical 犭 – implying sub-humanity – in most of the Han Chinese names given to the ethnic minority groups was eventually replaced with a "human" radical 亻 (Yeoh, 2008d: 200). Paradoxically parts of the CCP's affirmative action policies for minorities such as exemption from the one-child policy, employment quotas and in particular legal leniency on minority offenders (in non-political cases) have added to the negative stereotyping of ethnic minorities in the eyes of the dominant Han population.

Returning to the configuration in Figure 10.34, it should be noted that a substantial degree of horizontal interpenetration and communication across the ethnic line is indeed possible and in fact necessary for the viability of the system, thus compromising the sharpness of the line A-B as a boundary. On the other hand, if the ethnic boundary is pushed further round its axis (C) towards a horizontal position, one group then becomes unequivocally dominant and the other, subordinate – the exact power distribution and extent of dominance depend on the skewness, i.e. the angle of slant of the ethnic boundary. The test of the existence of a superordinate-subordinate relationship is to verify a group's dominant behaviour towards the other within the same class.

Alternatively, as Marden and Meyer (1962: 42) did for the United States, the structure of differentiation can be comprehensively expressed by super-imposing the class pyramid of the subordinate ethnic group upon that of the dominant community (Figure 10.35). The former is then dropped less than a full horizontal segment to express the inferior position of each class segment of the subordinate group to others within the class. Such a representation could

Figure 10.35 Marden and Meyer's Model of Dominant-Subordinate Relations
and Class Structure

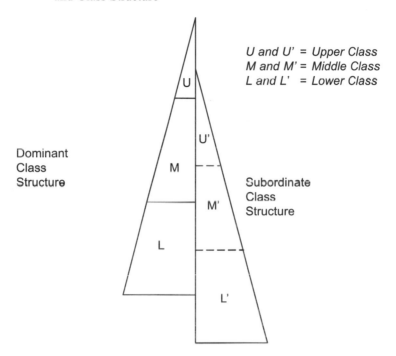

U and U' = Upper Class
M and M' = Middle Class
L and L' = Lower Class

Dominant
Class
Structure

Subordinate
Class
Structure

of course be just a simplification of a real world phenomenon, as the latter is
often complicated by the phenomena of class compromise and clientelism[116].
However, a rejection of race and class reductionisms should provide a more
rational theoretical foundation to analyze the complex relationship between
the variables of ethnic diversity, class structure, and the role of the State.

Seen from another angle, in contrast to the vulgar Weberian perspective
which argues that the increased ability of a bureaucratic State to realize
internally generated goals will reduce the power of all societal groups
"outside" the State, Poulantzian neo-Marxism posits that an "autonomous"
State, capable of wide ranging and coherent interventions in socioeconomic
relations, increases the social power of the dominant class, whose objective
and needs it necessarily functions to meet (Evans, Rueschemeyer and Skocpol,
1985). A dominant ethnic faction (Han) whose emergence in the ethnic regions
is depicted earlier as inevitable in Figure 10.34, thus, in line with the latter
theory, would be served by a powerful State (the country's Han-dominated
one-party central State) whose interests it concurs in.

Meanwhile, interethnic socioeconomic inequalities in ethnic regions like Xinjiang and Tibet are playing an important role in accentuating interethnic resentment and discord through expanding social distance, while contradictions, as illustrated in Figure 10.36, generated between incompatible class fractional identity and ethnic allegiance tend to breed discontent and instability.

Figure 10.36 Ethnic and Class Relations

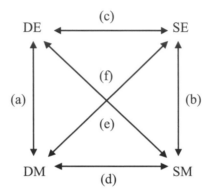

With D denoting the dominant ethnic group, S subordinate ethnic group, E élite and M masses respectively, the vertical division in Figure 10.36 shows the dominant-subordinate ethnic grouping, while the horizontal one indicates the élite-masses socioeconomic class grouping. Three types of relations are evident here: *vertical relations*, between dominant élite and their masses (a), and subordinate élite and their masses (b); *horizontal relations*, between dominant élite and their subordinate counterpart (c), and dominant masses and their subordinate counterpart (d); *diagonal relations*, between dominant élite and subordinate masses (e) and subordinate élite and dominant masses (f). Intra-ethnic relations are shown by vertical arrows, interethnic ones by the horizontal and diagonal. While intra-ethnic relations in Xinjiang between the dominant (Han) élite and dominant (Han) masses (DE-DM) represent an extension of the overall intra-Han relations of the country, the SE-SM relations are between the ethnic minority élite (Uyghur cadres and other Uyghur élites co-opted by the State) and the ethnic minority (Uyghur) masses who may perceive the former as cronies of the Han-dominated central State, as reflected in the Uyghur economics professor Ilham Tohti's accusation against Nur Bekri (Baikeli 白克力), chairman of the Xinjiang Uyghur Autonomous Region, in the former's blog "Uighur Online" before he was taken away on

7th July 2009.[117] On the other hand, relations between the dominant (Han) élite and the ethnic minority (Uyghur) élite (DE-SE) could be characterized by cronyism and clientelism[118], while those between the dominant (Han) masses and ethnic minority (Uyghur) masses represent a projection of the general biases, stereotyping and mistrusts as illustrated earlier in Figure 10.34. Similar configuration is also applicable to the case of Tibet.

The configuration presented in Figure 10.36 is in fact based upon Bonacich's (1979: 56-57) configuration of class and ethnic relations resulting from imperialism (Figure 10.37).

Figure 10.37 Bonacich's Model of Ethnic and Class Relations Resulting from Imperialism

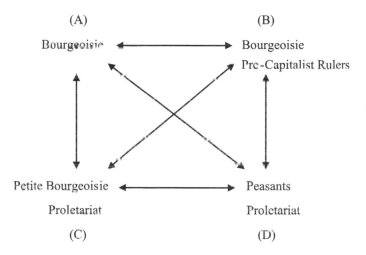

While segments A and C in Bonacich's model represent the "imperialist (white) bourgeoisie" and "workers in the imperialist nation" (and segments B and D refer to their non-white counterparts in the colonies and semi-colonies), in the present context they may well be the dominant ethnic bourgeoisie and proletariat whose existence is a direct consequence of internal colonialization and closely linked to the interests of the dominant central State and its ruling regime. While Bonacich's model refers to classes in the Marxian sense of the word, Figure 10.36 refers to "élite" instead. According to Brass (1985: 49), the term "élite" is not a substitute for "class", but refers to formations within ethnic groups (e.g. the aristocratic class) and classes (e.g. the secular élites) that often play critical roles in ethnic mobilization. Each of these élites may choose to act in terms of ethnic or class appeals. What determines their action is neither their ethnicity nor their class, but rather their specific relationship to competing élites in struggles for control over their ethnic group, or in competition with persons from other ethnic groups for scarce political and economic benefits and resources.

Bonacich's purpose was mainly to show how imperialism complicates class struggle by dividing classes along ethnic lines, and how her "split labour market theory" (Bonacich, 1972) could be invoked to explain such complications. However, the latter may not necessarily emerge in the form of conspicuous ethnic conflict. For instance, not only could élite members of the different ethnic groups who are appointed leaders of the ruling class share a desire to minimize conflict among themselves, but each group could also try to accommodate members from the other group into their respective spheres of predominance.

Dangdai Zhongguo Shehui Ge Jieceng Fenxi (2007: 6-7) observed the existence in China of an enormous set of "identity circles" encompassing the whole society (Figure 10.38) – "agricultural population" circle, "urban residents" circle, "workers" circle, "cadres" circle[119]:

1) Agricultural population: Those born into peasant families who have by informal procedure moved into other circles, even if having entered other classes or strata by work change or even having left the village the whole life, are still only considered peasants.
2) Urban residents: Broadly speaking, all non-peasants belong to this group of "urban residents". Formerly, "urban residents" narrowly defined refer to unemployed personnel – those without a fixed job. As "urban people", they had a status higher than peasants, but as people without work units, their status was below "workers". If they were formally employed by the labour department, even if they did work, they were just "temporary workers". This community of "temporary workers" no longer exists since the 1990s, but the concept is still alive in people's subconsciousness.
3) Workers: All workers in accordance with whether they are managed by the government's labour department or personnel department are divided into the "workers" and "cadres" sub-circles.
4) Cadres: From this sub-circle a further division can be made into "general cadres" and "leadership cadres". Civil organizations in China, schools, and even public enterprises and their personnel are all subject to the so-called "administrative stratification"[120].

Members of the society are unable to completely follow their own will in moving across these four circles between which exist different economic

Figure 10.38 China: Identity Circles

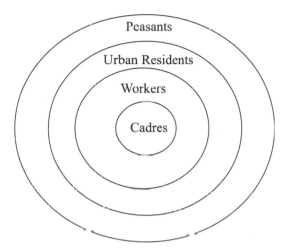

Source: *Dangdai Zhongguo Shehui Ge Jieceng Fenxi*, 2007, p. 6, Figure 1-1.

and political conditions. Hence, between these four circles there exists a high-low relationship in other words, this is not a multidimensional but a centripedal structure; moving towards the centre implies the raising of one's social status.

An editorial of a US daily[121] relates the tourists' perception of Lhasa, Tibet: roadside sellers are Tibetans, shopkeepers are Han; manual labours are Tibetans, clerical workers are Han; trishaw pullers are Tibetans, taxi drivers are Han; Tibetans or Hui might become mayor or chairperson of the "autonomous region" but the municipal or district secretary is almost always a Han; the Han people frequently get rich whereas the Hui people in the cities are mostly in the process of looking for a job or unemployed *nongmingong* 农民工 (rural-to-urban migrant workers). Seen in terms of such stratification and the rigidity in social mobility, the visibly ethnic patterns of employment and the strong identification of ethnicity with class as exist in China's ethnic regions could lead to a displacement of class-based frustrations by ethnic ones. Furthermore, while class mobilization may act to override ethnic distinctions, ethnic mobilization can obliterate internal class distinctions (Brass, 1985: 23):

> Elites who seek to gain control over or who have succeeded in gaining control over the state must either suppress and control [...] or establish collaborative alliances with other elites. When elites in conflict lack the bureaucratic apparatus or the

instruments of violence to compete effectively, they will use symbolic resources in the struggle. When elites in conflict come from different cultural, linguistic, or religious groups, the symbolic resources used will emphasize those differences.

(Brass, 1985: 29-30)

It is notable in this regard that the championing by former billionaire (China's number eight richest person in *Forbes'* list of 1995 with wealth worth two hundred million yuan) Rabiyä Qadir, who was once a CPPCC member, of the Uyghur cause has been doubted by some quarters of the exiled Uyghur community who regard her "being persecuted" to be in reality the result of uneven spoils sharing from government-business collusion (*guan-shang goujie*).

Observations have been made that members of China's ethnic minorities are appointed to leadership positions in the ethnic regions, for instance, the following comments by Tan (2004):

Contrary to the bash-China writers' portrayal, the minority policy of China is better than most countries, and in fact better than that of the U.S. (in relation to the American Indians) and Malaysia (in relation to the Orang Asli). China's constitution requires minorities to be represented in the local government. Thus, in a Yi majority area the county head has to be a Yi, and a Tibetan in the Tibetan autonomous region. In the one-person one-vote system of democracy practiced in Malaysia that is still largely ethnically based, it is almost impossible for an Orang Asli to be elected in a state or national election. Even where positions are bureaucratically appointed, it is rare, if any, for an Orang Asli to be appointed to such a position. In fact, the main officials of the Department of Orang Asli Affairs are not Orang Asli. Whereas in China there are many nationalities affairs commissions, these are mostly run by cadres who are minorities themselves, although in sensitive regions, government-trusted Han officials may hold the real power. Of course, China has more security concerns over certain minorities in certain regions, especially Xinjiang and Tibet.

To fully comprehend Tan's assertion in the context of the political economy of ethnic relations, it should be noted that the dominant group may perceive a subordinate group as "exotic" rather than "real" (Hoetink, 1973: 177-91). Another example of such an "exotic" minority in Malaysia, besides the Orang Asli (i.e. "aborigines") is the small *Gente Kristang* community (autoglossonym, from Portuguese "*Gente Cristã*") in the state of Melaka, descended from the 16th century Portuguese settlers and occupiers. Defined as "deviating in somatic and/or cultural respects, without being conceived subjectively as a menace to the existing social order" (Hoetink, 1967), "exotic" groups (or Cox's (1948) socioracial "strangers") are not perceived as "real", because they are not subjectively comprised within the "societal image" of the dominant. Thus they do not attract the latter's hostility, as do "real" subordinate groups viewed as a menace. The case of the Ainu アイヌ and the Burakumin 部落民 in Japan and that of the Amerindian natives and Afro-Americans in the United States today are good examples of these two polar subordinate situations – the Ainu and Amerindians being in some way viewed as "exotic" *vis-à-vis* the other two "real" minorities; instead of bitterness and hostility, they are met with "a mild benevolence, a condescending philanthropy" on the part of the dominant society (Hoetink, 1973: 179). Such distinction between the two types of subordinate groups was vividly described by DeVos in his study of the Burakumin: "The basic attitudes held [by the dominant Japanese society] toward the Ainu are not as pejorative as towards the outcastes [i.e. the Burakumin] [...] the Ainu have been treated ambivalently very much as the American Indians have been, in contrast to the caste distinctions which underlie the treatment of American blacks." (DeVos, 1972: 326) Paradoxically, China's largest minority, the Zhuang, could actually be more "exotic" than "real". Being the most assimilated of minorities, the Zhuang's ethnic consciousness was virtually created by the Han-dominated central Communist Party-State in the early 1950s (see, for instance, Kaup, 2000).

Whether members of an ethnic minority are appointed to leadership positions could ultimately be perceived by the ethnic community concerned as irrelevant, as it does not reflect the extent of autonomy and self-determination which the community may regard as crucial for the preservation of communal interests – be they political, socioeconomic or cultural – or in short, who holds the real power? For instance, while the chairman of the Xinjiang Uyghur Zizhiqu is Nur Bekri, a Uyghur, real power is allegedly in the hands of the Party secretary Wang Lequan 王乐泉, a Han.[122]

Rex (1986: xiii), in his remark that "what we call 'race and ethnic relations situations' is very often not the racial and ethnic factor as such but the injustice of elements in the class and status system", emphasized the economic, political and social balance of power rather than biological or cultural characteristics of groups. Differences in power and the dynamic change of power resources over time are seen as the key to explaining racial and ethnic conflicts. Such a perspective enables parallels to be drawn, for instance, between the "religious" conflict in Northern Ireland and racial violence in the British urban areas, which at first sight may not seem to share much similarity. As Stone (1985: 38) argued:

> It is true that the sectarian gunman who enters a public house in Belfast and demands to know the religion of the drinkers before deciding who to murder has

an identification problem not faced by the white racialist intent on attacking blacks in the streets of Brixton or Bradford. However ... [both] incidents of violence take place against a background of differential group power, perpetuated over the years in customary patterns of social relations and institutions, and both are to some degree a legacy of colonialism.

Such a focus upon power differentials and the conceptual problem associated with "race" and "ethnicity"[123] have led to the argument that the notion of "minority" is central to the analysis of race and ethnic relations.

It is useful to compare Rex's remark with Cox's thesis (1948) that perceives race relations as mainly proletarian-bourgeois, and hence political-class, relations. For Cox, racial prejudice is a weapon to exploit others rather than a defensive reflection of group solidarity. Racial categories exist in the social life of capitalist societies because they serve the interests of the ruling class; the contradictions in these economies have not yet reached the point at which the actual character of the underlying system is apparent to workers (Banton, 1983: 88). Such reductionist Marxist legacy of perceiving ethnic problem as class problem, coupling with the fact of the absolute demographic dominance of Han Chinese dwarfing the minorities out of a critical mass, could be clouding the CCP regime from effective understanding of China's ethnic problem, including that in the volatile ethnic regions of Xinjiang and Tibet. On the contrary, Wolpe, in his critique of reductionist Marxism which conceives classes as unitary entities, posited a different view:

> [...] classes exist in forms which are fragmented and fractured in numerous ways, not only by the division of labour and, indeed, the concrete organisation of the entire system of production and distribution through which classes are necessarily formed, but by politics, culture, and ideology within that division of labour, for example, gender, religion, the mental-manual divide and racial differentiation. Classes, that is, are constituted, not as unified social forces, but as patchworks or segments which are differentiated and divided on a variety of bases and by varied processes [...] Race may, under determinate conditions, become interiorised in class struggles in both the sphere of the economy as well as the sphere of politics.
>
> (Wolpe, 1988: 51-52)

Such a broadened understanding could serve to lead to a more balanced analytical framework on the trichotomy of polity, society and economy and in particular the political economy of State and ethnicity by taking into consideration both the two major dimensions of ethnopolitics – ethnic politics which includes both government responses to challenges from ethnic communities and the efforts of ethnic organizations seeking to influence State policy, and the politics of ethnicity which views ethnicity as a consequence of political action (Gheorghe, 1991), the latter "inverse paradigm" as we have observed earlier being exemplified by the waves of reethnicization in Eastern European countries after the fall of Communist Party totalitarianism and the phenomenon of ethnogenesis in Andalucía and among some highly Sinicized ethnic minorities of China such as the Zhuang and the Hui, as well as in the new-found ethnic intensity of the ethnoterritorial groups like the Uyghurs and Tibetans. Besides, in this regard, it is also instructive to compare Cox's thesis with the theories developed by Bonacich (1972) and Kuper (1974). Bonacich's "split labour market theory" is essentially a theory of ethnic relations which emphasizes the material bases of ethnic antagonism. It refers to labour markets which are divided along ethnic lines, so that higher-paid groups of workers are distinguished from cheaper labour by their ethnic characteristics. Although Bonacich described it as a "class" theory of race and ethnicity (Bonacich, 1979: 17) and located the origin of ethnic antagonism within the development of capitalism, her theory differs significantly from Cox's approach in that it attributes ethnic antagonism to the competition which arises from a differential price for labour, rather than to the strategy of the ruling class to keep two sections of the working class separate.

In his study of the revolutions in several African countries, Kuper (1974) found that, despite the existence of class differences, once revolutions started they developed along ethnic rather than class lines. Although class conflict is the source of revolutionary change in many societies, Kuper observed that in plural societies "it is the political relations which appreciably determine the relationship to the means of production, rather than the reverse, and the catalyst of revolutionary change is to be found in the structure of power, rather than in economic changes which exhaust the possibilities of a particular mode of production" (Kuper, 1974: 226). While Cox attributed the main forms of alignment and conflict, including ethnic ones, to the relation of groups (classes) to the means of production, political relations in plural societies, according to Kuper, influence relations to the means of production more than any influence in the reverse direction. Thus, conflicts developed in plural societies tend to follow the lines of ethnic cleavage more closely than class division. Such trend of development is apparent in the Eastern European countries after the collapse of Communist Party totalitarianism including the strife-torn Balkans as well as the increasingly the volatile ethnic regions of China exemplified by the troubled Xinjiang and Tibet, and the potential impact on the long-simmering peripheral ethnonationalism in Inner Mongolia from the recent rise of increasingly anti-Han-Chinese ethnocentrism of the neo-Nazis in the Republic of Mongolia, that first country in Asia to come under Communist Party dictatorship and also first country in Asia to release herself from that yoke. A relatively high-profile case related to peripheral ethnonationalism in Inner Mongolia, as highlighted by the Amnesty International, is that of Hada who was tried behind closed doors in the Inner Mongolia Zizhiqu in 1996 and sentenced to 15 years in jail for separatism and spying and his support for the Southern Mongolian Democratic Alliance that sought greater rights for China's ethnic Mongolians (Yeoh, 2007: 291).

Conclusion

> It was the best of times, it was the worst of times, it was the age of wisdom, it was the age of foolishness, it was the epoch of belief, it was the epoch of incredulity, it was the season of Light, it was the season of Darkness, it was the spring of hope, it was the winter of despair, we had everything before us, we had nothing before us, we were all going direct to Heaven, we were all going direct the other way [...]
> – Charles Dickens (1812-1870), *A Tale of Two Cities* (1859),
> Book the First: Recalled to Life, Chapter 1: The Period

Winston Churchill, in 1939, called Russia "a riddle wrapped in a mystery inside an enigma"[124]. This chapter has examined two no less enigmatic countries on two sides of the globe whose geographical sizes are massive, whose populations are complex, and whose modern blood-stained epics of a history are both momentous and torturous, harrowing yet monumental. In a sense, China as a self-contained East Asian land mass is comparable to Spain as a self-contained Iberian land mass. Both countries are more a continent than a country, both enjoying a sense of geographical isolation that feeds much the national psyche and popular subconsciousness of aloofness and conceit. Even the Chinese people's, both in China and overseas, unexpressed longing for the "lost" Mongolia is comparable to the Spaniard's unexpressed claim of Portugal as a part of herself (of which Galicia is a leftover). This chapter has placed the modern timelines of political and economic development in Spain and China in comparative perspective, focusing on a number of critical junctures where different critical decisions were made that have determined the subsequent course of socioeconomic and political development of the two countries. It has examined the diverse State responses at times of crisis – how the death of Franco had brought about overnight political democratization and decentralization while Mao's passing was followed by two-step forward, three-step back political liberalization and "selective centralization" in a system that could be perplexingly described as "regionally decentralized authoritarian". Both countries have come a long way, difficult and laudable, culminating in China superseding Germany to become the world's third largest economy (Yeoh, 2009a: 3) and the recent suggestion for Spain to replace Italy in the G8 among the other members of the club[125]. In the case of China, the student movement which snowballed into social protests of unprecedented scale is in many ways a return of May Fourth. While May Fourth of 1919 had eventually led to the triumph of Maoism-Leninism which in a way hijacked the early socialism of Chen Dusiou (Chen Duxiu) 陳獨秀[126], the violent suppression of the 1989 mass protests represented a prelude to the subsequent hijacking of the Hu Yaobang-Zhao Ziyang administration's initiative for politico-economic liberalization by the strengthening one-party authoritarian State corporatism preferred by Deng Xiaoping who once and again felt wary of and threatened by his protégés' "bourgeois liberalism". The conservative backlash had since worsened the uneasy coexistence of a highly decentralized economic structure with a highly centralized intolerant political regime which has, among other ramifications, stalled the more rational accommodation of ethnic and ethnoregional aspirations and precipitated the horrific events of 14th March 2008 and 5th July 2009.

In his iconoclastic 1985 study, Charles Tilly questioned the idea of a social contract in state making, where a society whose shared norms and expectations call forth a certain kind of government, and defined "those peculiar forms of governments we call national states" as "relatively centralized, differentiated organizations the officials of which more or less successfully claim control over the chief concentrated means of violence within a population inhabiting a large, contiguous territory" (Tilly, 1985: 170). Without going so far with Tilly in seeing nation-states as "quintessential protection rackets with the advantage of legitimacy", it is still impossible not to question the long taken-for-granted notion of the inviolable sovereignty of the nation-state and even the very essence of the nation-state itself. Benedict Anderson, too, defined a nation as a community socially constructed and ultimately *imagined* by the people who perceive themselves as part of that group and "regardless of the actual inequality and exploitation that may prevail in each, the nation is always conceived as a deep, horizontal comradeship. Ultimately it is this fraternity that makes it possible [...] for so many millions of people, not so much to kill, as willingly to die for such limited imaginings" (Anderson, 1991: 6-7). The sovereignty of a nation-state is imagined, according to Anderson, because the concept was born in an age in which Enlightenment and Revolution were destroying the legitimacy of the divinely-ordained, hierarchical dynastic realm, giving rise to the national dreams of freedom whose gage and emblem were the sovereign state. Similarly, other historicists (in contrast to the primordialists) like Ernest Gellner and Eric Hobsbawm also posited that nations and nationalism are products of modernity and have been created as means to political and economic ends, and the nation, assuming the nineteenth-century conceptual entity of a nation-state, is the product of nationalism – but not *vice versa* – through the unification of various peoples into a common society or community (Gellner, 1983; Hobsbawm, 1990). It is in this context of nation-state as imagined community that this chapter has proceeded to examine and analyze the causes and implications of the July Fifth Xinjiang riots against the backdrop of economic and political reforms and the intriguing question of China's centralism *v.* decentralization, which in turn brings us back in this concluding section to the issues raised earlier in the beginning sections of this chapter.

Decentralization: The Spanish Model

The Spanish system of decentralization has often been presented as a model for emulation by emerging democracies (Garcia-Milà, 2003: 19), including transition countries emerging from the ruins of failed Communist Party autocracies in Eastern and Central Europe, which are in a way "trying to approximate *first world countries* by applying decentralization processes" (Molero, 2001: 501) Spain's intergovernmental relations have indeed undergone a significant transformation over the last three decades, as Börzel summarized in the abstract of her 2000 article:

> With the transition to democracy, Spain has developed from a unitary-centralist into a quasifederal polity in which the 17 autonomous communities enjoy significant political autonomy. However, Spain is not only moving toward federal democracy, it is also approaching a cooperative model of federalism in which multilateral intergovernmental cooperation and joint decision-making supersede the bilateral negotiations and regional competition that traditionally characterized intergovernmental relations.
>
> (Börzel, 2000: 17)

The creation of the 17 Autonomous Communities – and linked to it 8,022 municipalities, 43 *diputaciones* (not counting the 7 uniprovincial Communities), *cabildos*, councils and other local entities, together with their own bodies and enterprises, as a response to the aspirations (long suppressed under the Franquist regime) of the ethnolinguistically non-Castilian communities with distinct historical, political and cultural separateness – the Catalans and Basques in particular – has unleashed a movement in which an intensified interregional rivalry over resources (though not outwardly as confrontational as, for instance, in the case of Belgium) is contributing to part of an increasing trend of public expenditure, with implications on related issues such as public sector employment and indebtedness. Moreover, even regions with less or no autonomist aspirations historically (the linguistically distinctive Galicia, Valencia, the Baleares and Asturias, or the merely administrative regions like Castilla y León, etc.), fearing that they might be left behind in the distribution of public resources in the decentralization process, suddenly find in themselves a previously non-existing autonomist consciousness, which in turn contributes further to the competition for public resources and the expansion of the public sector. Such an interesting phenomenon of public policy-induced ethnogenesis is particularly evident in the large southern impoverished region of Andalucía.

On the other hand, the new sources of interjurisdictional conflict created in the process (State *v* Autonomous Communities, *diputaciones v* Autonomous Communities, metropolitan bodies *v* Autonomous Communities, large municipalities *v* Autonomous Communities, etc.) are not always satisfactorily resolved, resulting inevitably in the multiplicity of personnel and competences, suspicion, resistance to cede functions or give way to other levels of government, all of which serve to give rise to an increase in internal inefficiency of the public administrative apparatus and to add to the cost of its functioning (Roig Alonso, 1987). The pressure exerted by the Autonomous Communities on the increase in expenditure especially through their indebtedness is set to grow given that those Communities which have already assumed the major competences during the transition phase of LOFCA (*Ley Orgánica de Financiación de Comunidades Autónomas*[127]) are going to claim even higher levels of competences, and those that have not are to demand gradual equalization with them. The undertaking of costly projects, such as the creation of regional public television networks, regional institutes for business development and promotion, the development of major infrastructures, etc., by the Communities in a concerted effort to compete with each other in levels of performance and achievement, for political legitimacy and consolidation, will further exacerbate the existing rivalry over public resources, the conflict between the Communities as well as between the centre and the periphery, with significant implications for the development of ethnoterritorial consciousness and interethnic relations.[128]

Uttering the "F" Word?: China's Future Path of Decentralization

The term "federation" was in fact never officially used in China or Spain. Such notwithstanding, post-Franco Spain has in reality evolved into an incipient federation, while in China, just like in Indonesia, the term "federal" is still very much a taboo[129], although the existence of the Chinese *de facto* fiscal federalism is irrefutable. In a sense, post-1981 Spain has outgrown the fear of both fiscal and political decentralization along federal lines being a prelude to territorial disintegration, but China and Indonesia have not. Nevertheless, the idea for the reorganization of a post-CCP China along federal lines has resurfaced amidst the anguish, agony and bitter frustration among the exiled Chinese intelligentsia in the aftermath of the 1989 Beijing-Tiananmen massacre (Yeoh, 2007: 296-297), in combination with the continuing cross-Strait tension, the "Handover" of Hong Kong and Macau to China respectively in 1997 and 1999, and the recurrent Tibet crises. Suggestions vary in arrangement details, including a prominent confederation proposal of a *Zhonghua Lianbang Qonghequo* 中華聯邦共和國 ("Federal Republic of China"), a "Third Republic" – the first republic being the *Zhonghua Minquo* 中華民國 (Republic of China) and the second, *Zhonghua Renmin Gongheguo* 中华人民共和国 (People's Republic of China) – proposed by Yan (1992) encompassing the "loose republics" of Taiwan, Hong Kong, Macau, Tibet, Inner Mongolia and Xinjiang (in an arrangement like that of the European Union) and "close republics" consisting of the rest of present-day China (in an arrangement akin to the US's). Yan obviously had in mind some sort of coexistence of federal and confederal systems within a single country – two systems such as those explained by Dorff (1994: 100): "[…] in a true federation, the central government can make decisions directly affecting individuals in the regional units without the formal compliance of the regional governments; in a confederation, the central government has authority over the regional governments, not over individuals, and hence must rely on the cooperation and support of the regions in order to exercise authority." In fact, asymmetric decentralization, according to Garcia-Milà and McGuire (2002: 1), could be justified from the economic perspective:

> Asymmetric fiscal decentralization, by which we mean different fiscal arrangements between the central government and different groups of, or individual, lower-level governments, may be justified from an economic efficiency perspective. As argued by Tiebout (1956), Oates (1972) and others, a decentralized system of regional and local governments is better able to accommodate differences in tastes for public goods and services. This efficiency argument calls for decentralization of fiscal authority to regional and local governments, but not necessarily asymmetric decentralization. However, when the differences in tastes for public goods and services arise out of differences in history, culture and language across regions of a country, asymmetric treatment may be justified. History, culture and language may influence how a group of people (a region) views autonomy, independence and fiscal authority. Some regions may have had experience with autonomous

government in the past, they may have a culture that is strongly reliant upon (or leery of) the central government, or they may be fearful of losing their separate languages if they do not have special arrangements. To accommodate differences in taste for independence, autonomy, and fiscal authority, it may be necessary to have different fiscal arrangements between the central government and the different regions comprising the country.

Such differential treatments in federal arrangement are common, for example during the Spanish federalization, among the *Comunidades Autónomas* (see, for instance, Castells, 1990), those financed under the foral provisions (*régimen foral*) – the Basque Country and Navarra which is often considered as part of the Basque Country – were at a higher level than those financed under the standard system (*régimen común*). Other Communities, especially the Catalans, tended to complain that the Basques and Navarrese had been given brandy to accompany their coffee (because of their favourable tax-raising regime), an allusion to the earlier description of "*café para todos*" ("coffee for everyone") when devolved powers, which were at first restricted to the "historic nationalities" ("champagne for the historic nationalities"), were generalized in the early 1980s to most regions (Brassloff, 1989: 48). The advantageous position of the Basque Country was due to the incorporation into its new statute the *concierto económico* (while its historic *fueros* as a whole were rejected as the basis of this new statute, including the claim to Navarra as part of the Basque Country) which allowed the Basque government to collect most taxes and hand over an agreed sum to Madrid (Keating, 1993: 219).

Political federalization has come under the limelight again in the case of China with the recent arrest of Liu Xiaobo for organizing the signing of "Charter 08" (Yeoh, 2009b: 279-280) that included an Item 18 "A Federated Republic" among its recommendations on national governance, citizens' rights and social development:

> A Federated Republic. A democratic China should seek to act as a responsible major power contributing toward peace and development in the Asian Pacific region by approaching others in a spirit of equality and fairness. In Hong Kong and Macau, we should support the freedoms that already exist. With respect to Taiwan, we should declare our commitment to the principles of freedom and democracy and then, negotiating as equals, and ready to compromise, seek a formula for peaceful unification. We should approach disputes in the national-minority areas of China with an open mind, seeking ways to find a workable framework within which all ethnic and religious groups can flourish. We should aim ultimately at a federation of democratic communities of China.[130]

While a nascent federalist structure has already been observed to be emerging in China as a result of rapid economic and fiscal decentralization, there could be inherent dangers to bring decentralization beyond the fiscal into the political along federal lines. Acute interregional economic inequalities could be viewed as incompatible with the very concept of federalism, and it is hence debatable as to whether federalization should come before or after sufficient interregional equalization in countries with high levels of interregional disparities such as contemporary China, taking into consideration the possibility of centrifugal forces triggered by interregional equalization efforts such as the tax revolts in modern federations like Begium or would-be federations like Italy (*ibid.*: 274). While the present taboo against a federal arrangement with high regional autonomy[131] has had deep roots from earlier times[132], it is currently being further enhanced by CCP's fear of losing its monopoly of power as federalization would inevitably tend to go hand in hand with democratization. Adding to that is the enigma of Taiwan[133] and the problem of Tibet with their perceived links with foreign, especially American and Indian, interests. With the disintegration of the Soviet Union[134] always hanging like the sword of Damocles to remind the present leaders and people of China of the peril of democratization and regional autonomy, and the fact that federalization or reaffirmation of federalism in whether former USSR, East European countries or post-Franco Spain both followed the disgraceful dethronement of dictatorial, authoritarian or totalitarian regimes, the present Chinese ruling regime's reservation against such federalization by devolution is plainly understandable. After all, the eventual disintegration of the Russian empire (the "prison of nations", or in its modern form, the Soviet Union) in December 1991 has left China to be the world's lone surviving former empire still remaining intact, having escaped that ignominious fate of dissolution that befell, besides the Russian empire, all in the 20th century, the Ottoman, Austro-Hungarian and the Western maritime empires (*ibid.*: 276-277). Incidentally, one ethnic region did escape from China, namely Outer Mongolia that formed the independent Mongolian People's Republic in 1924, with Russian support, though not recognized by China until 1946. Also, as we have seen earlier, the Uyghurs in fact established, with Russian help, a short-lived East Turkestan Republic in 1944, but it collapsed after the 1949 Communist victory in China's civil war, and the region was reincorporated into China as the Xinjiang Uygur Zizhiqu in 1955. Besides these, the island province of Taiwan has been *de facto* independent since 1949, regardless of the fact that it is not diplomatically so recognized by most countries of the world for *Realpolitik* reasons and that the government of the island state continues to technically consider itself the legitimate "Republic of China" government-in-exile with jurisdiction over all China.[135] Finally, adding to the federal taboo is the tendency to recycle the "black hand" (*heishou* 黑手) theory – the "shopworn conspiracy theories that blame mass protests primarily on the CCP's foreign and domestic enemies, reflecting the classic Leninist insistence that social protest in a Communist country cannot just happen, it must be instigated" (Tanner, 2004: 143) – which is unfortunately so apparent in the ruling regime's response to the recent Xinjiang crisis or last year's Tibet riots. For this "black hand" theory, Tanner gave an example from the 1989 Beijing-Tiananmen massacre:

> In the days after the Tiananmen demonstrations, this Leninist conspiratorial world-view was typified in a report on the protests issued by Gu Linfang, the Chinese vice minister of public security who was in charge of "political security." To document a conspiracy in 1989, Gu painstakingly listed dozens of allegedly nefarious contacts among protest leaders; reformist Communist officials; foreign academics; and, of course, Western and Taiwanese intelligence agencies. The vice minister railed against party reformers for coddling schemers who fomented rebellion. A Leninist to his marrow, Gu refused to concede any acceptance of what social scientists have known for decades, that whenever a society grows and changes as rapidly as China has, an increase in political protests is a normal development.
>
> (*ibid.*)

Similar State response can be observed following the recent July Fifth Xinjiang riots when Nur Bekri, chairman of the Xinjiang Uygur Zizhiqu, declared on 18th July 2009 the source of the riots being "the triumvirate of terrorist, secessionist and extremist forces"[136] and Wu Shimin 吴仕民, vice-chairman of China's State Ethnic Affairs Commission, stated on 21st July 2009 that the July Fifth riots had absolutely nothing to do with China's nationality (ethnic minority) policies. The ruling regime's inability to face domestic realities is further manifested in the continued repression including the arrest of ethnic Uyghur economics professor Ilham Tohti of China's Central Nationalities University and founder of the "Uighur Online" on 7th July 2009[137] and the revocation of licenses of civil rights lawyers who took up cases related to the Xinjiang riots.[138]

Without the courage to face up to domestic realities, any solution to the root problems leading to either June Fourth or July Fifth would remain illusive. The danger of fragmentation coming from democratization and federalization is real but not inevitable. One of the basic features of a federal system, according to Bakvis and Chandler (1987: 4), is that it provides "incentives for structuring group/class conflicts along territorial lines". When the territories concerned represent the centres of concentration of distinctive socioracial communities, ethnic conflicts are translated into territorial rivalries and the process of fiscal federalization becomes an arena of ethnic resource competition. Nevertheless, Dorff (1994) warned that federal *structures*, when not accompanied by federal *process*, could have contributed to the fragmentation of Yugoslavia, Czechoslovakia and the Soviet Union, and these one-party states' federalist structures, without federalist processes, initially used to suppress, not accommodate, ethnic differences, had actually helped to create a political environment ripe for disintegration via ethnic mobilization once decentralization began, as regional leaderships bent on protecting the interests of their territorial constituencies at the expense of other regions and the federation. It could hence be highly equivocal to keep seeing the disintegration of Yugoslavia, Czechoslovakia and Soviet Union as a sword of Democles warning against federal structures. On the contrary, the fate of these disintegrated nations could be a lesson to take heed of at this juncture of the 20th anniversary of June Fourth, in particular after the foreboding event of July Fifth, to begin early the federal process, before it becomes too late when eventually the moment of truth arrives for a China ripe for democratization[139] it turns out also to be the moment for a China ripe for disintegration. Definitely, a federal process is always full of pitfalls[140], especially for a country still facing the problems of high incidence of poverty, ethnoterritoriality, sectionalism and ethnoregional socioeconomic disparities. Inevitably, it is also a process abounding with right and wrong options and choices. The Chinese regional structure bears substantial similarity to the Spanish – for instance, only 3 out of Spain's 17 *Comunidades Autónomas*, comprising less than 30 per cent of the country's population, are non-Castilian ethnic regions, in contrast to countries like Belgium or the former Soviet Union, Yugoslavia and Czechoslokia where the state is composed of constituent regions each of which populated predominantly with a differentiated ethnic community. As Spain is pondering her options whether to move on from the State of the Autonomies to a full-fledged federation – through a whole spectrum of scenarios as summarized by Brassloff (1989: 41-45) into the evolutionist minimalist regional autonomist, radically revisionist neo-centralist, radically European regionalist, nationalist particularist, mixed federo-regional and, lastly, the federalist maximalist in which the presently evolving State of the Autonomies may develop all its potential and end up operating as a federal state – it could also be timely for a China in astounding transformation to ponder new options other than a *dictablanda* or even a *democradura* with the perpetually uneasy coexistence of economic decentralization with political centralism or, as a former vice-premier pointed out, being constantly trapped in the perennial "cycles of decentralization and recentralization"[141] that breed unending chaos and instability.

Notes

1. The term "State" with a capital "S" is used in this chapter (except in some quotations) to refer to the central body politic of a civil government – in contrast with the private citizenry or a rival authority such as the Church, whereas "state" with a lower-case "s" refers in general to other senses of the term, including a "country" or a political territory forming part of a country. The word "nation" in this sense is generally avoided since it has the alternative connotation of a community of common ethnic identity, but not necessarily constituting a state.

2. As Beard (1948: 220-2) noted: "[...] many of our neglects, overstresses, and simplifications are due to the divorce of political science from history [...] if political science, economics, law and sociology were cut entirely loose from history, they would become theoretical, superficial, and speculative, or what might be worse, merely 'practical', that is, subservient to vested interests and politicians temporarily in power."

3. For instance, the "critical structural period", when definitive State response to exigencies generated by a country's ethnic diversity, came in the year 1970 both in Malaysia (the implementation of NEP) and in Belgium (beginning of the federalization process), and at the end of the 1970s in Spain (the 1978 Constitution that saw the emergence of the Autonomous Communities, and the approval of the Statutes of Autonomy for all of these Communities from 1979 to 1983).

4. The Wade-Giles transliteration, the scheme commonly used before CCP's popularization of *Hanyu Pinyin*, in brackets. Note Wade-Giles's use of apostrophe – accurate though slightly clumsy – to indicate aspiration (further on transliteration in this chapter, see Appendix).

5. Born Francisco Paulino Hermenegildo Teódulo Franco Bahamonde in 1892 in the northwestern Iberian coastal town of El Ferrol.

6. Cited in Gunther, 1980: 285.

7. Barth (1969) noted that the "traditional proposition" that race = culture = language (= nation) is far removed from empirical reality. Hoetink (1975: 18) abstained from the use of the term "ethnic" – and preferred "socioracial" instead – because "ethnic group" suggested an absence of overlapping ascriptive loyalties. He noted that from the important ascriptive criteria of territoriality (ancestral homeland), notions of common descent ("race"), language and religion, the presence of only one of the four is necessary to create an "ethnic group" (Hoetink, 1975: 24). Since ethnicity may ambiguously subsume a variety of exclusive or overlapping loyalties, Hoetink preferred to analyze these in terms of their ascriptive content and their greater or lesser correlation. The term "ethnic" as used in this chapter should therefore be considered equivalent to Hoetink's term "socioracial". An equally important point to note is that there are other socioeconomic reasons behind ethnolinguistic and ethnoreligious divides. This is especially the case in Brazil and Spanish-speaking America where social

definition is relatively fluid, reflected in the Brazilian proverb: "A rich black man is a white and a poor white man is a black" (Mason, 1970: 122). It is probably in this light that Hoetink had chosen the attribute "socioracial", which reflects the concept of "social race" (*vis-à-vis* "biological race") expounded by Wagley (1959). Similar concerns are covered by Gordon's concept of "ethclass" as "the portion of social space created by the intersection of the ethnic group with the social class [which] is fast becoming the essential form of the subsociety in America" (Gordon, 1978: 134), and by Bonacich's "split labour market theory" as a "class" approach to race and ethnicity (Bonacich, 1972; Bonacich, 1979).

8. With the creation of the keywords of reform including "loosen", "devolve", "share profit", "reinvigorate" (*songbang* 鬆綁, *fangquan* 放權, *rangli* 讓利, *gaohuo* 搞活) etc.

9. The term "multiethnic" (or "polyethnic") is used often in this chapter in a less general sense of "consisting of *more than two* ethnic groups" (*vis-à-vis* "bi-ethnic"), though it is also used in a more general sense that includes "bi-ethnic". According to the "critical mass" theory (advanced, among others, by Semyonov and Tyree, 1981), societies are considered multiethnic only if minorities constitute more than ten per cent of their population; hence, China is strictly speaking not a multiethnic country. Nevertheless, it is obvious that the issue of "numerical significance" cannot be the sole criterion considered in the anomaly of China, due to the abnormal size of China's population and in particular the size of China's citizens of the Han ethnicity. The absolute numbers of minorities in this country are actually huge and definitely not negligible – about 110 million in total, including the 16 million Zhuang, 10 million Manchu, 9 million Hui, 8 million Uyghurs, 5 million Mongols and 5 million Tibetans, although they are practically dwarfed almost to invisibility by the sheer size of the Han population.

10. Referring to the 31 *sheng* (i.e. provinces of Anhui 安徽, Fujian 福建, Gansu 甘肃, Guangdong 广东, Guizhou 贵州, Hainan 海南, Hebei 河北, Heilongjiang 黑龙江, Henan 河南, Hubei 湖北, Hunan 湖南, Jiangsu 江苏, Jiangxi 江西, Jilin 吉林, Liaoning 辽宁, Qinghai 青海, Shaanxi 陕西, Shandong 山东, Shanxi 山西, Sichuan 四川, Yunnan 云南 and Zhejiang 浙江), *zizhiqu* (i.e. "autonomous regions" – each a first-level administrative subdivision having its own local government, and a minority entity that has a higher population of a particular minority ethnic group – of Guangxi 广西 of the Zhuang, Nei Monggol/Inner Mongolia 内蒙古 of the Mongols, Ningxia 宁夏 of the Hui, Xizang/Tibet 西藏 of the Tibetans and Xinjiang 新疆 of the Uyghurs) and *zhixiashi* (municipalities under the central government – Beijing 北京, Chongqing 重庆, Shanghai 上海 and Tianjin 天津). For details of administrative units below the provincial level, see Yeoh (2007: 237), Figure 12.4, and Yeoh (2009b: 247), Figure 10.6.

11. Despite strictures on paper delineating central *v.* regional spheres of competences (see Yeoh, 2007: 238, for details), in reality throughout the 1980s the devolution of authorities from the central government to the provincial governments was

substantial which sometimes ended up to be more beneficial to the provincial governments than the central. In fact, the guidelines of decentralization had given some subnational authorities rights for their own budgets and to manage their own finance, including the permission to experiment with a financial responsibility scheme, similar to the rural household responsibility system, given to Guangdong and Fujian in 1979. While the fiscal reforms since 1994 have largely been seen to be an attempt at recentralization and definitely weakened the limited autonomy of the provincial governments, it has also alternately been considered as replacing a negotiated system with a structure on which a decentralized system could be constructed (Bahl, 1998: 74)

12. Hence, the growth of the Spanish public sector since the end of the repressive rule (1939-75) of the *Caudillo* (see Figure 10.3) has thus coincided with, though not solely determined by, the process of political decentralization and fiscal federalism.

13. For a detailed explanation of van Amersfoort's typology, see Yeoh (2009b: 252-255).

14. This is unique as in most relatively mature market economies, as Xu noted based on his cross-national comparisons, the government usually is not in control of much economic resources, and even in those countries where the government is in control of these resources, the latter are usually in the hands of the central government, rarely the local governments.

15. Or more officially, the "Communist Party of China" (CPC).

16. Schneider (2003: 38-39) stated, "The percentage of local revenues from taxes provides an indicator of the degree of subnational control over resources. Taxes are different from the total amount of resources, which is more a measure of wealth rather than control [...] subnational revenues are a combination of taxes, transfers, grants, and loans. Taxes offer the greatest degree of autonomy, grants, and loans offer somewhat less, and discretionary transfers probably the least. Transfers, even supposedly automatic ones, can be withheld, and grants and loans generally arrive with conditions or with expenditures earmarked [...] the treatment of all revenues aside from transfers gives an indication of the degree to which subnational governments raise their own funds through taxes, loans, fees, or sales of assets."

17. 关于 2008 年中央和地方预算执行情况与 2009 年中央和地方预算草案的报告.htm <*http://www.mof.gov.cn/mof/zhengwuxinxi/caizhengxinwen/200903/t20090316_122544.html*>

18. For details of general transfers and earmarked transfers by items in 2008, see Yeoh, Liong and Ling (2009: 178-179), Figures 11.7 and 11.8.

19. The provinces, which were established in 1833, acted as agents of the central government and, until 1925, as controllers of the municipalities (Solé-Vilanova, 1989: 207; Heywood, 1995: 154).

20. As Lijphart (1977: 56) remarked, "The notion of a multiple balance of power contains two separate elements: (1) a balance, or an approximate equilibrium,

among the segments, and (2) the presence of at least three different segments." However, cooperation among groups becomes more difficult, as the number participating in negotiations increases beyond three or four. On the other hand, a moderately multiple configuration is preferable to a dual segmentation as the latter entails a constant tension between "a [majority] hegemony or a precarious balance [and it leads] easily to an interpretation of politics as a zero-sum game" (*ibid.*). Bi-ethnic states are thus a special, problematic type of multiethnic state. In a bi-ethnic state, a gain for one ethnic group is easily perceived as a loss for the other. By contrast, in societies with more than two major ethnic groups it may not be apparent who loses when one ethnic group improves its position. This can lead to a logrolling situation, in which each group cares primarily about its own gains and nobody is conscious of the possible costs of a policy decision. The scenario is outlined in Steiner's study on consociationalism in Switzerland (Steiner, 1974). It also implies that ethnic tension could be more easily aroused by preferential policies in bi-ethnic states than in those with more than two ethnic groups.

21. Year refers to publication date of English translation. Weber's original manuscript was written between 1910 and 1914.

22. Or in a different setting, take the case of Malaysia. According to Cheah (1984), the Malay ethnic identity (*bangsa Melayu*) was a creation after 1939 in response to the perceived threat from the increasingly politicized immigrants from China and India. The notion of a Malay race had therefore hitherto been absent, as Cheah elaborated: "[...] the Malays rose to confront what they considered threats posed by the immigrant races to their rights, but the Malays themselves had not been united as a race or a 'bangsa', and moreover they had not found a way to solve differences among themselves [... Such differences] were nurtured by the strong provincial feeling among the 'provincial Malays' (such as the Kelantan Malays, Perak Malays and so on), DKA Malays (those of Arab descent) and DKK Malays (those of Indian descent) [... There were also] tribal divisions, such as the Bugis, Minangkabau, Javanese, etc." (translated from Cheah, 1984: 83) The first open suggestion of a "Malay people" (*orang Melayu*) came only in 1939 when Ibrahim Yaacob (or I.K. Agastja by his Indonesian name) championed the notion of a unified Malay race across Malaya and Indonesia which he christened *Melayu Raya* (Great Malay) or *Indonesia Raya*. The boundary marker of ethnicity was thus mobilized to meet the rising need of identity investment for politico-economic purposes. An even more blatantly political ethnicization came after the 1969 riots in the creation of the "Bumiputera" race (*kaum Bumiputera*). *Bumiputera* (a term of Sanskrit origin meaning literally "prince of the land; son of the soil") became an official collective term grouping together the Malays, the aboriginals and the natives of Sabah and Sarawak (both on the Borneo island) after these two regions joined the Peninsula in 1963 to form Malaysia. It excludes "immigrant races" like Chinese, Indians and Europeans, but not Arabs and Malays from Indonesia.

23. See Yeoh (2008b: 81). While emphasizing the importance of the ethnic factor in understanding the role of the State does not diminish the significance of contention between social classes, it serves to avoid the pitfall of reductionist Marxism, in which, as Wolpe (1988: 15) remarked, ethnicity "becomes merely an external instrument for the reproduction of class interests which are assumed to be *entirely* defined by the economic relation of production".

24. This contradistinction in proportion is apparent in the fact that "while the Han population in Sinkiang and Tibet was nil, in 1949 Han Chinese comprised more than half of the total population of all China's national minority areas averaged together" (Moseley, 1966: 14).

25. Did the completion in 2006 of the Qinghai-Tibet (Qing-Zang) railway, said to bring modernity and economic progress to Tibet, also signal a new phase of Sinicization of Tibet? This is a fear that the 14th Dalai Lama's Tibetan government-in-exile has not been hesitant to voice.

26. Ethnic division may be territorial in some countries but not in others, thus making it difficult for federalization along ethnic lines. An ethnic faction can be a homeland group while the other or others may be immigrants, giving rise to imbalance in ethnic intensity, national legitimacy and power of negotiation.

27. *Dongfang Jeubao* 东方日报 (*Oriental Daily News*, Malaysian daily), 3rd June 2009.

28. Hutton's figures, drawn from Zhang, Nathan and Link (2001), were those of the General Office of the State Council reported to the Committee of Elders. Hutton also cited the estimates of Nicholas Kristof and Sheryl WuDunn, Beijing correspondents of the *New York Times*, that up to 800 unarmed people were killed and several thousands injured (Kristof and WuDunn, 1994, cited in Hutton, 2006: 364).

29. The structure of political party systems and more specifically their level of internal centralization have been argued to be the determinants of the fiscal structure of the State, i.e. the *degree* of decentralization, in the studies on decentralization as a means for democratizing political regimes and enhancing the efficiency of public policy, its implications for service delivery and democracy, and the political determinants of the process of devolving resources and policy responsibilities to subnational governments (Montero, 2001: 43). In her paper on the case of Latin America, Escobar-Lemmon (2001: 28) noted that at least there "the process of decentralization has come about in parallel to the process of democratization" and the "rationale is that strong subnational power centers will check the national government, consequently preventing the re-emergence of a strong, authoritarian leader nationally." Thus, according to Escobar-Lemmon, "decentralization becomes a way to avoid political crises and/or democratic breakdown. Given that political decentralization could increase opportunities for democratic participation, there is reason to believe that there is a systematic relationship between decentralization and democratization." Elaborating on his second fundamental characteristic of a

federal system – democratic pluralism both between and within the territorial components – Duchacek (1988: 16-17) drew attention to federalism being a territorial twin of the open democratic society: "Federalism is not compatible with authoritarian socialist and fascist one-party systems and military juntas. If a single party delegates some minor parts of its central power to the territorial components in which single-party rule also prevails, the result is a unitary and centralist system or, at best, an association or league of territorial dictatorships [...] a spatially sectorized unitary system or a confederation of [...] single-party territorial components [...] a territorial dimension of Lenin's "democratic centralism" – inter-territorial and inter-factional consociationalism of a special kind, but not a federal democracy."

30. The twice-purged pragmatist and reformist Deng Xiaoping is today one of the most enigmatic figures in the history of China who would both be remembered as the pragmatist saviour of modern China who dealt the *coup de grâce* to Mao's failed autarkic collectivist utopia in 1978 and the butcher of Beijing who unleashed his deadly wrath upon the "ungrateful" students and other denizens of the ancient capital in 1989.

31. "Beijing-Tiananmen" is a more appropriate appellation for the massacre than just "Tiananmen", as most civilian casualties occurred not in the Tiananmen Square but on Beijing streets leading to the square, especially Chang'an Avenue 长安街, when the People's Liberation Army clashed with Beijing residents and workers trying to protect the student demonstrators in Tiananmen Square during that fateful night of 3rd-4th June 1989.

32. Began airing on 16th June 1988, *He Shang*, a six-part television documentary produced by the China Central Television (CCTV), is characterized by its condemnation of China's isolation and admiration of and longing for the openness of Western civilization and modern democracy (Zhao, 2009b: 72, editors' notes # 81). After the June Fourth massacre, CCP denounced the documentary, blamed it for helping to inspire the demonstrations, and according to Zhao Ziyang, attacked him with the claim that he had supported its production, distribution and suppressed criticism against it (Zhao, 2009a: 267-268).

33. The 1989 Tiananmen demonstrations being the first uprising in a the whole series of similar events that led to the demise of authoritarian rule in Eastern Europe countries and Mongolia, the fact that most of these countries were Soviet satellite states with Communist Party rule virtually planted by the USSR rather the result of in the main part homegrown – though foreign inspired – mass revolutionary movement, and that their 1989-1990 protest movements came after the shocking Beijing-Tiananmen massacre all apparently played their roles in the diverse State response between China and these states, perhaps with the exception of Romania which took a popularly supported palace and army coop to overthrow the hated Communist dictator Nicolae Ceauşescu.

34. Translated from Bao Tong's introduction in Zhao (2009c), pp. 33-34.

35. Spontaneous as the 1989 Tiananmen protests, the "demonstrations that erupted on 4th May 1919 developed into a loose nationalist political movement that was one of the antecedents of the Communist Party's own official foundation in 1921" (Hutton, 2006: 7).

36. Notably too, this was just hardly a year after the anniversary of the posting by Wei Jingsheng 魏京生, the earlier vanguard of China's democracy movement and an electrician like the Polish labour union activist Lech Wałesa who was later elected president of Poland after the fall of the Communist Party dictatorship, of his manifesto "The Fifth Modernization" (i.e. democracy, in addition to the pursuit of the "Four Modernizations" of China's agricultural, industrial, national defense and science sectors declared by Deng Xiaoping) on the "Democracy Wall" on the morning of 5th December 1978 at a busy city intersection not far from the Tiananmen Square. The State responded by sentencing him to 15 years in prison.

37. See Yeoh (2008c) and Yeoh (2008d) for detailed accounts and analyses of China's problems of poverty, socioeconomic inequalities and interregional disparities.

38. *Dongfang Jeubao*, 17th February 2009; *Dongfang Jeubao*, 29th June 2009. The largest denomination of China's renminbi 人民币 ("people's currency", Rmb) is yuan 元 / 圆 (Latinized symbol ¥ or Ɏ), a term with cognates in the Japanese yen or en 円 (from 圓; Latinized symbol ¥) and Korean wŏn 원 / 圓 (Latinized symbol ₩). A yuan is equivalent to about US$0.146. Following the US (rather than British) convention, billion = 1000,000,000 and trillion = 1000,000,000,000.

39. *Dongfang Jeubao*, 23rd June 2009.

40. *Dongfang Jeubao*, 29th June 2009.

41. *Dongfang Jeubao*, 29th June 2009.

42. According to a report published on China's National Bureau of Statistics website on 14th January 2009, the confirmed 2007 Gross Domestic Product of China at current prices amounted to 25.7306 trillion yuan, an increase of 13 per cent from the previous year. While observed to be still short of a third of US's GDP, analysts have predicted China's GDP to overtake Japan's in three to four years, just as it overtook the United Kingdom and France in 2005 and now Germany.

43. *Sheuzie Jeubao* 世界日報 (*World Journal*) (US), editorial on 15th March 2009, reprinted in *Dongfang Jeubao*, 17th July 2009.

44. In principle, i.e. irrespective of whether a country's government is democratic, despotic like Burma, totalitarian like North Korea, or even genocidal like Sudan, the former Democratic Kampuchea or the murderous Serbian militia in a disintegrating Yugoslavia.

45. While still rudimentary, the rehabilitation and other *de facto* de-Mao programmes, or even the liquidation of the research office of the central Secretariat, and the closing down of left-wing magazines such as *Red Flag*, led the way to further internal structural reform of the CCP in coming days (MacFarquhar, 2009: xxi).

46. How effective are such elections as a means for rural governance democratization? Ann Thurston, who has followed such village elections since 1994, drew the following rather mixed conclusions (see Ann Thurston, "Village Democracy in China" <*http://www.chinaelections.org*>, cited in Yu, 2004): "First, the local emperors who came to power with the collapse of the communes still exist in some places. Usually they are able to exert control because they are also very rich, are in control of much a [sic] of a village's resources, and are able to influence higher levels in the government and party hierarchies. Second, many villages continue to exist in a vacuum of leadership. When, for instances, I have had the opportunity to visit Chinese villages with friends rather than through official sponsorship, it seems I invariably happen upon villages which are suffering crises of leadership, villages where elections, if they have been held at all are only pro forma, and the village leader is generally weak and ineffectual. Third, I have seen cases, too, where they local emperors are actually elected, ostensibly democratically. These are instances, for instance, where the second candidate seems to have been put there only for the sake of complying with election regulations and where the village chief who is running for re-election also controls a major portion of the village resources … Finally, and most important, I have also seen elections that by any measure anywhere in the world would be recognized as genuinely competitive, fair and democratic …"

47. From Fang Lizhi's letter accepting the Peace Prize jointly sponsored by the newspapers *Politiken* of Denmark and *Dagens Nyheter* of Sweden. Fang received the award in absentia in September 1989.

48. *Dongfang Jeubao*, 14th March 2009.

49. *Dongfang Jeubao*, 25th June 2009.

50. *Ibid.*

51. *Dongfang Jeubao*, 17th March 2009; *Dongfang Jeubao*, 22nd March 2009.

52. "Hong Kong Reporter Being Held By China", Washington Post Foreign Service, 30th May 2005. <*http://www.washingtonpost.com/wp-dyn/content/article/2005/05/29/AR2005052900986.html*>

53. *Dongfang Jeubao*, 9th August 2009.

54. Dubbed "*lüba* 滤霸" [filtering bully], this software was originally scheduled for compulsory installation by 1st July 2009 on all personal computers entering the Chinese market. The attempt was later temporarily postponed following domestic and international outcry, and finally declared on 13th August to be abandoned except for those computers for public access in schools, cybercafés and other public places. (*Dongfang Jeubao*, 10th June 2009; 15th August 2009)

55. *Dongfang Jeubao*, 2nd July 2009.

56. *Dongfang Jeubao*, 19th July 2009.

57. The military junta that rules Burma has officially changed the name of the country in the English language to "Myanmar". Nevertheless, the change has not been endorsed by the National League for Democracy (NLD) that won

a landslide victory (80 per cent of parliamentary seats) in the 1990 People's Assembly elections, yet prevented from governing the country to date by SLORC, or the State Law and Order Restoration Council. SLORC was formed when the Burmese armed forces seized power following the 8888 (8th August 1988) massacre of pro-democracy demonstrators. SLORC was reconstituted, essentially renamed, as the State Peace and Development Council (SPDC) on 15th November 1997.

58. Cited in Diamond (2002: 24).

59. Besides his declaration that China is at the "initial stage of socialism" which served to clear the way for further market transformations. See "A Brief Biography of Zhao Ziyang", in Zhao (2009a: 283-287).

60. The most successful among the 12 counties (cities, districts) in the provinces of Zhejiang, Heilongjiang, Shanxi, Hebei, and Hunan that the Central Organization Department chose to conduct the first round of experiments on the "permanent party congress system" (Bo, 2009a: 13).

61. "In developing our democracy, we cannot simply copy bourgeois democracy, or introduce the system of a balance of three powers. I have often criticized people in power in the United States, saying that actually they have three governments. Of course, the American bourgeoisie uses this system in dealing with other countries, but when it comes to internal affairs, the three branches often pull in different directions, and that makes trouble. We cannot adopt such a system." – Deng Xiaoping, "Take a Clear-Cut Stand against Bourgeois Liberalization", 30th December 1986. <*http.//web.peopledaily.com.cn/english/dengxp/vol3/text/c1630.html*>

62. See, for instance, Bo (2009a: 16).

63. Dissident Xie Changfa 谢长发, who was once arrested for his involvement in the 1989 Tiananmen demonstrations, was recently sentenced to 13-year imprisonment for his involvement in organizing the China Democracy Party since 1998. His was the fourth conviction of civil rights activitists, after Huang Qi 黄琦, Tan Zuoren 谭作人 and Guo Quan 郭泉, who voiced out on the alleged school building construction scandal following the 2008 Sichuan earthquake that resulted in huge number of student casualties due to the collapse of school buildings (*Dongfang Jeubao*, 3rd September 2009).

64. State Council Information Office, "White Paper on Building of Political Democracy in China", 19th October 2005 <*http://www.chinadaily.com.cn/english/doc/2005-10/19/content_486206.htm*>, cited in Minzner (2006: 9-10).

65. Later identifies as a young man named Wang Weilin 王维林, whose fate remains unknown to date.

66. Pablo Diego José Francisco de Paula Juan Nepomuceno María de los Remedios Cipriano de la Santísima Trinidad Ruiz y Picasso (25th October 1881 – 8th April 1973). *Guernica* (1937), arguably Picasso's most famous work, is his portrayal of the German bombing of Guernica during the Spanish Civil War.

67. Usually translated as "Blood-stained Glory" but literally "blood-stained

elegance", a song written in 1987 originally to commemorate those who died during the Sino-Vietnamese War, the melancholic tune came to be a hymn to their determined but forlorn struggle among the hunger strikers during Tiananmen Square protests of 1989.

68. Describing Franquist Spain, Gunther (1980: 2) stated, "The ultimate source of political authority was the Caudillo, himself. Officially a single-party authoritarian state, it can best be regarded as a no-party regime."

69. See, e.g., Hutton (2006: 8, 98, 144-148).

70. In the context of modern multiethnic societies, particularly those with an economy dominated by the minority, members of the demographically/politically dominant group are often willing to grant greater autonomy to a State (and its élite managers), which implements preferential policies in their favour.

71. "The only way to erect such a common power, as may be able to defend them from the invasion of foreigners, and the injuries of one another [...] is, to confer all their power and strength upon one man, or upon one assembly of men, that may reduce all their wills, by plurality of voices, unto one will [...] This is the generation of that great Leviathan [...]", said Thomas Hobbes in *Leviathan* (1651). Relating this to China's unitarism *v.* federalism, see Yeoh (2009b).

72. The "helping hand" and the "grabbing hand" were said to be the same "invisible hand on the left" described by Olson (2000). Gu and Chen's analysis with a multiregional econometric model found that "[w]hen local revenue share rises, the helping hand of local government becomes stronger and further leads to promotion in local economies and subsequently the national economy. When the centre increases its revenue share and adopts other recentralization measures, local governments become losers and switch from helping to grabbing hand."

73. These studies, including Huther and Shah's, were cited by Tugrul Gurgur and Anwar Shah of the World Bank (2000). Gurgur and Shah's study also confirmed that decentralization support greater accountability in the public sector and reduce corruption.

74. Hu Angang (2006), *Great Transformations in China: Challenges and Opportunities*, Oxford University Press, cited in Hutton (2006: 127).

75. Yeoh (2009b: 284); Yeoh (2006b: 224); *Dongfang Jeubao*, 18th March 2009.

76. Such as the bloody Han-Hui ethnic conflicts in 2004 and 2007.

77. *Dongfang Jeubao*, 23rd March 2009.

78. Cited in Hutton (2006: 126).

79. See, for instance, Professor Lü Yuanli 吕元礼's best-selling Chinese tome "Why Can Singapore Do It?" (2007).

80. "China's Despair and China's Hope", originally appeared in *The New York Review of Books* on 2nd February 1989, translated by Perry Link.

81. See, e.g. Bo (2009b). In an interesting attempt at refutation of Minxin Pei's (2006) claim of CCP's illegitimacy, Bo has set out to disprove point by point Pei's arguments which were based upon a series of international indexes which

the former listed in details: "China is one of the most authoritarian political systems in the world according to the Polity IV Project, is almost completely 'unfree' according to the Freedom House, and is one of the most corrupt countries according to Transparency International. China was ranked in the bottom third of the eighty countries surveyed in terms of 'quality of governance ranking' according to one group of the World Bank and was considered a weak state according to another group of the World Bank. China found itself next to the legion of failed states and most repressive countries in terms of 'voice and accountability' and also in the company of weak states such as Nicaragua, Cambodia, Papua New Guinea, Egypt, and Mali in terms of 'regulatory quality.' China was no better than Namibia, Croatia, Kuwait, and Mexico in terms of 'government effectiveness,' was comparable to Belarus, Mexico, Tunisia, and Cuba in terms of 'political stability,' and was in the company of Mexico, Madagascar, and Lebanon in terms of 'rule of law.'" (Bo, 2009b: 2)

82. Or paraphrasing *Yazhou Zhoukan*, "the hundred days of People Power that made one proud to be a Chinese" ("Preface", *Yazhou Zhoukan*, 1989: 4).

83. Unlike the Prague Spring of 1968 – which lent its name to the analogous Beijing counterpart a decade later and here again to foreign observers to describe the hundred-day Tiananmen demonstrations in 1989 – that was cut short by invading foreign troops, the crushing of the 1989 "Beijing Spring" was entirely a domestic affair, described by the Western journalists as the Rape of Peking (Beijing) in an insinuated analogy with the infamous Rape of Nanking (Nanjing 南京) by the Japanese troops in World War II.

84. 中國人權協會.

85. See, for instance, Örkesh Dölet's 8th July 2009 *The Guardian* article "A Declaration of Oppression". <*http://wuerkaixi.com/*>

86. 世界维吾尔代表大会.

87. See Yeoh (2009b) for a more detailed treatment of this contradiction.

88. One of the most notable of such incidents, before the more recent riots in Lhasa and Ürümqi was the Han-Hui conflict in October 2004 that occurred in the Nanren 南仁 village and two other nearby villages in Henan province's Zhongmou 中牟 county, which allegedly killed more than 100 people including at least 15 policemen, and injured more than 400 people. Though the conflict was probably triggered by a local traffic accident and rooted in strong historical-cultural factors including perceived overall Han dominance and backlash against certain preferential policies for the ethnic minorities, simmering tensions might have been exacerbated by China's economic success that led to a growing gap between rich and poor, especially in the countryside. Other than the Nanren conflict, there was also the unconfirmed news of another serious Han-Hui conflict in August 2007 in the Shimiao 石庙 township in Huimin 惠民 county of Shandong province, close to the Hui county of Shanghe 商河, that resulted in at least a death and more than twenty injured. This was not the first such open conflict in Shandong which earlier experienced the well-known "Yangxin 阳信

incident" in 2000 when six Hui were killed during a thousand-strong Hui protest against a "*Qingzhen Zhurou* 清真猪肉" [halal pork] shop sign.

89. *Dongfang Jeubao*, 9th July 2009.

90. *Dongfang Jeubao*, 30th July 2009.

91. Yale professor Amy Chua, in her highly controversial book *World on Fire: How Exporting Free Market Democracy Breeds Ethnic Hatred and Global Instability* (2003) contended that the spread of free market democracy breeds ethnic violence in developing countries by simultaneously concentrating wealth in the hands of the ethnic minority and empowering the impoverished majority that resents the former. "The global spread of democratization reflects the powerful assumption in Western policy and intellectual circles that markets and democracy go hand in hand", wrote Chua, "But in the numerous countries around the world with a market-dominant minority, just the opposite has proved true. Adding democracy to markets has been a recipe for instability, upheaval, and ethnic conflagration [...] As markets enrich the market-dominant minority, democratization increases the political voice and power of the frustrated majority. The competition for votes fosters the emergence of demagogues who scapegoat the resented minority, demanding an end to humiliation, and insisting that the nation's wealth be reclaimed by its 'true owners.' [...] As popular hatred of the 'outsiders' mounts, the result is an ethnically charged political pressure cooker in which some form of backlash is almost unavoidable." (Chua, 2004: 124)

92. In cities like Madrid and Barcelona it is about 10 per cent.

93. Elements that are not completely strange to Malaysians who had personal experience of the racial violence in 1969 or the boiling ethnic tension in 1987.

94. When violence erupted, although the story quickly reached the national news, pictures of the actual violence were few because, along with immigrants, journalists were also under attack by the mob.

95. The spectre of China's disintegration has never ceased to haunt the generation of Chinese who have had the first-hand experience of China's humiliation at the hands of the Western powers and Japan up to the Second World War, to whom the *bainian guochi* 百年国耻 (hundred years of national humiliation) is still crying out loud for redemption. This is the generation that today still makes up the leadership echelons in China, and leaders and respected intelligentsia in the overseas Chinese communities. This is the generation whose outlook having been shaped by their personal experience, among whom Beijing's stance that the benefits of stability under one-party rule far outweigh the risky endeavour of democratization and decentralization and that the human rights of the 1.3 billion-strong populace to be free from starvation and to be sheltered far outweigh the Western notion of freedom of speech and freedom of political choice would find resonance. This is a generation that the yearning and love for a great "Cultural China" (*Wenhua Zhongguo* 文化中国), and a China that could stand tall among the community of nations, a China that is fast becoming a superpower, is all

that counts in bestowing pride on one's Chinese ethnicity. Probably little else matters.

96. China's leaders, from Deng Xiaoping, Jiang Zemin to Hu Jintao have been vehemently against adopting Western liberal democracy for China, both for the fear that the Communist Party will lose its political dominance or China might disintegrate like the former Soviet Union. The nightmarish scenario of China's disintegration, and the most likely prospect of losing Xinjiang, Tibet, Inner Mongolia, probably also Qinghai and Ningxia, and of course Taiwan, and having China shrunk by half, alone is enough for the Communist Party leaders to convince many, not least among the overseas Chinese community leaders to shun the idea of democratization and regional political autonomy. The death of the Soviet Union hangs like the sword of Damocles to remind people that "[... when] Mikhail Gorbachev launched his radical political reform and initiated the process of political democratization in the former Soviet Union, scholars in the West argued that Gorbachev must be 'right' and China's Deng Xiaoping must be 'wrong.' [...] However, when Gorbachev's reforms eventually led to the collapse of the Soviet Union, Deng Xiaoping was proven 'right.'" (Zheng and Lye, 2004) The prevalence of such views that have fed into the collective fear somehow serves well in justifying the stance of China's current regime despite the value-loaded nature of judging right and wrong in this case. Soviet Union's disintegration is definitely wrong in the context of the preference for stability and territorial unity, but this is highly judgmental. Firstly, that a "nation" divided is destined to herald misery for the people might not be borne out by modern empirical evidence – the outstanding record of economic prosperity, political stability and human welfare of the many successor states of the former Austro-Hungarian empire, the Kalmar Union (the Danish empire) and, closer home, even the success of Taiwan. Of course, to generalize such successes could be as empirically unsound as to be consumed by the combination of ethno-national pride and the morbid fear of losing territorial domination, but sometimes, as the proverb goes, the best things might just come in small parcels. Schumacher, in his now classic *Small Is Beautiful* (1973) proposed the idea of "smallness within bigness" – a form of decentralization whereby for a large organization to work it must behave like a related group of small organizations. "Man is small, and, therefore, small is beautiful", Schumacher might just have a point. Secondly, the aspiration for a unified nation under the Han Chinese domination from the point of view of the Han Chinese should be indisputable, but whether this is true from the perspective of other non-Han Chinese people – "Chinese" as defined as "China's citizens" – especially those that are ethnoterritorial would deserve further investigation.

97. See *2000 Population Census of China* and *Xinjiang Statistical Yearbook 2007*.

98. It took a brutal campaign of ethnic genocide to deliberately exterminate the Dzungars and it has been estimated that more than a million people were slaughtered.

99. These data were from the *2000 Population Census of China*. Official data for the year 2006 gave the proportion of Uyghurs as 45.92 per cent and that of Han as only 39.62 per cent of the total population of Xinjiang. See *Xinjiang Tongji Nianjian 2007*, pp. 82-87, Figure 4-7, which gave the year 2006 figures of 9,413,796 Uyghurs and 8,121,588 Han out of a total population of 20,500,000 people of Xinjiang.

100. *Times* (UK), 19th April 2009; *Dongfang Jeubao*, 21st April 2009; *Scientific American*, July 2009; *Dongfang Jeubao*, 1st August 2009. Not allowed into China, Takada obtained his results based on estimation by extrapolating his model with Xinjiang's population density. Not allowed while in China to probe into the existence of disproportionate number of cases of malignant lymphomas, lung cancers, leukemia, degenerative disorders and deformed newborns, Enver Tohti, a Uyghur medical doctor who moved to Turkey 1998 ostensibly as part of his medical training and now works with Takada, claimed to have uncovered medical records showing Xinjiang's higher-than-national-average cancer rates with a team of British documentary filmmakers whom he smuggled back into Xinjiang as tourists.

101. See *Xizang Tongji Nianjian 2007*, pp. 33-34, Figure 3-4, which gave the year 2005 figures of 2,549,293 Tibetans and 104,647 Han out of a total population of 2,675,520 people of Tibet.

102. Reference should be made here to the controversial hypothesis of Rabushka (1974) that a larger public sector makes ethnic conflict more likely.

103. From its humble beginnings in the 1980s, the Northern League – complete name *Lega Nord per l'Indipendenza della Padania* (North League for the Independence of Padania) – has since been transformed from a marginal protest force to a national movement strong enough to bring down the 1994 Centre-Right coalition by withdrawing from it. While having had its ups and downs over the years, the real or potential political force it represents could never be totally counted out in the Italian political arena. "Padania" (the ancient Italian term for the Po valley), as proposed by the Northern League, would contain the most powerful industries of Italy, its best agricultural land, almost all its financial wealth and its greatest cities including Venice (the proposed capital), Turin, Milan, Bologna and Genoa.

104. It is exactly the same sentiment that is threatening the Belgian nation, driving Flanders away from Wallonia.

105. See, for instance, Katherine Palmer Kaup's *Creating the Zhuang: Ethnic Politics in China* (2000).

106. A challenge that the unprecedented 2004 Han-Hui conflict in Henan had amply attested to.

107. See Yeoh (2009b: 260), Figure 10.10.

108. Summarizing Shah and Qureshi's (1994) findings, Bird and Vaillancourt (1998: 18) noted: "[…] in Indonesia, Timor (one of the poorest provinces) has a per capita own-source revenue equivalent to 4 percent of Jakarta's […] however,

owing to transfer from the central government, Timor's per capita expenditures are 40 percent of those in Jakarta."

109. See Yeoh (2009b: 259), Figure 10.9. As Cook and Murray (2001: 126-127) succinctly summarized: "Three of China's four largest coal fields are in this area, as well as four of the most important oil fields. Some 140 kinds of mineral ores have been detected along with large reserves of bauxite for processing into aluminium, and gold. The Qaidam Basin in the middle of Qinghai Province, home to a large Tibetan population, for example, is described by local officials as the province's 'treasure bowl', containing proven oil reserves of 200 million tons, as well as 4.5 billion tons of mostly high-quality coal with low ash and sulphur content. Under the Kunlun and Qilian mountains are large proven caches of iron, manganese, chromium, vanadium, copper, lead, zinc, nickel, tin, molybdenum, antimony, mercury, gold, silver, platinum, beryllium and selenium. The iron reserves are estimated at 2.2 billion tons, and the province claims the country's largest lead and zinc mines, and is a primary producer of asbestos. The Hui people in the Ningxia Hui Autonomous Region, meanwhile, are sitting on large proven reserves of oil and natural gas, along with mineral resources such as copper, iron, silver, gold, aluminium and nickel. The growing prosperity of Xinjiang is being built on the back of developments in the vast and inhospitable Tarim Basin, where experts reckon there are reserves of up to 100 billion barrels of oil and 8,300 billion cubic metres of natural gas."

110. For details of these ethnic regions' resource-strategic importance, see Yeoh (2008c: 15-19).

111. For examples such interregional resource contest leading to local protectionism, see Yeoh (2009b: 282-283).

112. "Bi-ethnic" in terms of major power structure and socioeconomic relations, though the region's population consists of more than two ethnic groups.

113. *Shenzie Jeubao*, editorial on 16th July 2009, reprinted in *Dongfang Jeubao*, 18th July 2009.

114. See *Xinjiang Statistical Yearbook 2007*, pp. 82-87, Figure 4-7, which gave the year 2006 figures of 254,722 Uyghurs and 1,507,720 Han out of a total population of 2,018,443 people of the city of Ürümqi.

115. In another setting, for instance, in a country like Belgium, the tilting of the ethnic line is evident, with Flanders overtaking Wallonia economically since the 1960s and bringing with it increasing politico-economic leverage on the part of the Flemish community. It is Wallonia's fear of Belgium being slowly transformed into a Flemish-dominated country, coupled with the continued insecurity felt by the Flemish community over its new-found power, which is fuelling the interethnic discord of the country and threatening to tear the country apart.

116. Gunther (1980: 223) described public investment decision making in Spain during the Franco era as more closely conforming to the "clientelistic", rather than "corporatist", model. The higher positions in the rank-ordering of

clientelistic ties were occupied by those with direct contacts with political-level officials in the spending departments (directors general, subsecretaries and the minister concerned). At the apex of this hierarchy of clientelistic ties were those connected to the centre of the regime, especially those involving household members of the *Caudillo* himself. Gunther recorded one occasion when a family member of the *Caudillo* actively lobbied on behalf of a "client", as well as another example concerning "a well-known housing developer, who profited enormously by, first, securing a significant alteration in Madrid's master plan (rezoning his land from part of a green belt to 'high-density housing' status), then pushing for favorable state investment in the area, with the implicit or active support of the Franco household." (*ibid.*: 258) Besides, the recruitment to "political" posts within the State Administration (i.e. directors general, subsecretaries and ministers) also proceeded along clientelistic lines. It is true that clientelism exists to some extent in all political systems and the high degree Gunther found under the Franquist regime is not representative of such feature in expenditure decision making. However, given the explicit and formal bureaucratic and corporatist channels provided by the Franquist State, the far more frequent use of the clientelistic channels of interest articulation reveals it to be more than a passing phenomenon accompanying the allocation of public resources. The clientelist model was first developed when political instability in many Third World countries from the mid-1960s onwards increasingly attracted attention to the personalization of political relationships. Factional rivalries and ties of personal influence were increasingly perceived to be the predominant bases of politics behind the façade of the institutionalized State. The clientelist model explains how individuals with some access to scarce resources can use their control over resource distribution to procure various forms of political support from their clientele and use such support to promote their bargaining and rivalries with others. Rather than depicting ethnic groups as the component units of society and the wielders of State power, the clientelist model focuses on the role of individual patrons as leaders of clientelist networks (Brown, 1989). Clientelism can be defined as a relationship of exchange between unequals. Three strands are prevalent in the practice of clientelism. First, the relationship tends to become complex and multifunctional, with power relationships supplementing economic ones or *vice versa* and both of these being reinforced by personal ties. Secondly, while the patron-client relationship is inherently dyadic (involving two persons), it tends to lead to the formation of a chain of dyads, in which the same individual is simultaneously a client in relation to those above him in the hierarchy, and a patron to those below. Clientelism can be extended in this way through any large hierarchy, such as a national government. Thirdly, clientelism is by its nature competitive. Clients attach themselves to patrons in order to gain some special advantage over others at the same level as themselves in the hierarchy, in the contest for scarce resources, while the other would-be clients are then likely to retaliate by seeking to attach themselves either to the same patron or to another. The clients' services are sought by the patrons not only because of their value but also as a means to strengthen the patron's position as against other patrons, especially in political situations such as competition for office (Clapham, 1982: 6-7).

117. *Dongfang Jeubao*, 10th July 2009.

118. Brown (1989) was of the opinion that while in some types of clientelist systems the patron-client networks may serve to cut across and weaken ethnic communal ties (especially where the patron-client relationship arises out of the competition for individual goods such as contracts or jobs), clientelism may also promote the politicization of regional and ethnic communalism, where the focus of competition is on communal goods such as public amenities and development projects. Anyway, the politicization of ethnicity tends to become the more likely result of clientelism where leaders at the state-level seek to mobilize popular support so as to promote their political positions. Appeals to ethnic solidarity provide a useful basis for such mobilization, while at the same time cutting across and inhibiting class alignments. A notable impact of the personalized politics of clientelism is "to promote the politics of competitive ethnicity, in which inter-ethnic rivalry is pursued through the activities of entrepreneurs, patrons and brokers" (*ibid.*: 52). Factional instability which may ensue is minimized where one patrimonial leader and his entourage are able to acquire monopoly control of the State and thence of resource distribution, while ethnic communal clienteles are "politically mobilized by their communal influentials who act as brokers, delivering their communal group support to the patrimonial élites in return for the promise of state resources" (*ibid.*).

119. *Nongye renkou quan* 农业人口圈, *chengzhen jumin quan* 城镇居民圈, *gongren quan* 工人圈, *ganbu quan* 干部圈.

120. *Xingzheng jibie* 行政级别.

121. *Sheuzie Jeubao*, editorial on 16th July 2009; reprinted in *Dongfang Jeubao*, 18th July 2009.

122. *Dongfang Jeubao*, 8th July 2009.

123. There is a tendency in academic circles to distinguish between socially defined and biologically defined races – "ethnic" and "race". An ethnic or ethnic group is said to exist when three conditions are present – "a segment of a larger society is seen by others to be different in some combination of the following characteristics – language, religion, race and ancestral homeland with its related culture; the members also perceive themselves in that way; and they participate in shared activities built around their (real or mythical) common origin and culture [and] a nation [is] an ethnic group that claims the right to, or at least a history of, statehood" (Yinger, 1986: 22). In contrast with "racial groups" which are biological categories based on immutable, physical attributes fixed at birth, "ethnic groups" are defined by a much wider range of cultural, linguistic, religious and national characteristics, with a more flexible form of

group differentiation. Therefore, the term "racial" should more appropriately be used to describe group distinction on the basis of phenotypical (i.e. physical) characteristics, while "ethnic" refers to those based solely or partly on cultural characteristics (Yeoh, 2003: 26). The term "ethnic" can also be generalized to be a blanket concept (Hoetink's attribute "socioracial") to cover both the above distinctions. The term "cultural" here mainly covers the ascriptive attributes "ethnolinguistic" and "ethnoreligious". The emphasis on language and religion in empirical research is due mainly to the fact that they are the relatively less vague factors in the fourfold categorization of ascriptive loyalty (Hoetink, 1975: 23-4). While "racial" – meaning phenotypical – differences is only skin deep, ethnic boundary as a process (*à la* Barth, 1969) tends to be tenacious and uncompromising, the manifestation of the age-old fourfold ascriptive loyalty of race, territoriality, language and religion (Yeoh, 2006a: 224). However, racial and ethnic characteristics thus defined often overlap in any one group while extremely deep divisions are often found between groups whose racial as well as ethnic differences are actually imperceptible, e.g. the Burakumin, the so-called "invisible race" of Japan.

124. Cited in Lin (2009: 351).
125. *Dongfang Jeubao*, 9th July 2009.
126. In a way analogous to the French Revolution being hijacked by Maximilien Robespierre's Reign of Terror. Chen Dusiou's socialism was but one of the twin manifestations of the May Fourth spirit, the other being liberalism represented by Hu Sheu (Hu Shih) 胡適.
127. "Organic Law for Financing the Autonomous Communities".
128. While the cases of China and Spain could be used to analyze public policy and the role of the State in multiethnic societies with a numerically and politically dominant ethnic group *vis-à-vis* several minority groups, the situation can be very different in a bi-ethnic society without a clearly dominant ethnic faction, such as Belgium. Federalism in Belgium is equipped with "an array of institutional structures that are among the most complex found anywhere in the world" (Murphy, 1995: 73). The form of federalism developed in this country is unique and does not quite fit the classical federal model. Its uniqueness lies in the fact that it is not entirely territorial. The language regions do not correspond to the "communities", leading to a dichotomy between the former, with a territorial jurisdiction, and the communities, with personal jurisdiction. The French community has jurisdiction over persons living in Wallonia, the Walloon institutions and the French-speaking institutions in Brussels. The jurisdiction of the Flemish community covers persons living in Flanders and the Flemish institutions in Brussels. The German-speaking community has jurisdiction over persons and institutions in the German-speaking territory in the east of the country. The country, meanwhile, is still moving towards a further decentralization and the establishment of a confederal state (Mommen, 1994: 223). The centrifugal tendencies are reinforced by the continuing economic

decline in Wallonia and better performance in Flanders, and the latter's hope to stop further transfer payments to Wallonia through acquiring complete financial and fiscal autonomy.

129. For more details of this federal taboo, see Yeoh (2009b: 278-279).

130. Translated from the Chinese by Perry Link. <*http://crd-net.org/Article/Class9/ Class10/200812/20081210142700_12297.html*>

131. For instance, the 14th Dalai Lama's proposal for Tibetan autonomy has always been accused by Beijing as a disguise for his alleged Tibetan independence agenda.

132. One of the earliest proposals in China of decentralization along federal lines is probably that found in the oath of the Sing Zhong Huei 興中會 (Revive China Society, founded in 1894 by Sun Zhongshan 孫中山/Sun Wen 孫文/Sun Yisian 孫逸仙, leading revolutionary, founder of republican China, more popularly known outside China as Sun Yat-sen) – the establishment of a *hezhong* 合眾 government, i.e. government of a "union of many". In fact, with fourteen provinces proclaiming independence from the Cing 清 dynasty to reunite as the Republic of China/*Zhonghua Minquo* 中華民國 during the Sinhai 辛亥 Revolution, Sun Zhongshan in 1912 took the title "President of the Provisional Government of the United Provinces of China" – *liansheng* 聯省 ("united provinces") presumably suggesting a less regionally independent arrangement than *lianbang* 聯邦 ("federation") or the US-style *hezhongquo* 合眾國 ("united states"), partly reflecting reservation against earlier *liansheng zeuzheu* 聯省自治 ("united autonomous provinces") proposals since the 1920s, lest too much regional autonomy might jeopardize the country's badly needed ability at that time to resist foreign aggression as well as might legitimize the hated rule of the regional warlords. Regional autonomy has in fact not really always been a no-no as was usually presumed in the political discourse within the People's Republic of China. In fact, a soviet federal republic, modeled after the union republics of the Union of Soviet Socialist Republics, was obviously on the cards, with autonomous constituent republics planned for the ethnic regions like Inner Mongolia, Tibet and Xinjiang/Eastern Turkestan, at the time when a Chinese Soviet Republic was established in Jiangxi province and then during the *changzheng* 长征 ("Long March") a small autonomous republic for Tibetans was set up in Sichuan province. By the time of Yan'an 延安, such nationality policy had undergone a transformation, and in 1947 the Inner Mongolia "Autonomous Region", the first of its kind in China, was created, not "Autonomous Republic". Before the complete consolidation of power, the PRC which was established in 1949 consisted of six semi-independent "greater administrative areas". The central government in Beijing, just transferred from the People's Government of North China, in effect only had direct control of northern China and Inner Mongolia, while other "greater administrative areas" enjoyed a substantial level of autonomy, all of which but ended by 1954.

133. The Republic of China (ROC), controlling only the Taiwan 台灣 province, is today recognized by 23 mostly small countries. The ROC lost most of her diplomatic allies after she was expelled from the United Nations in 1971, as many countries dropped her to recognize the People's Republic of China (PRC), including Costa Rica, one of Latin America's most democratic countries, on 7th June 2007 – a bitter irony, according to Taiwan – within four days of the year's anniversary of the 1989 Beijing-Tiananmen massacre.

134. Judgement on the event, positive or negative, of course depends on from whose point of view, e.g. the Great Russians or the peoples of the captive nations of the former USSR (Yeoh, 2007: 280, 293-294).

135. For Taiwan's ratings on political rights and civil liberties *vis-à-vis* China, see Figure 10.18. En passant, probably also noteworthy is that with the collapse of the Qing Dynasty that led to the repatriation of the imperial troops from the region, Tibet (today China's Xizang Zizhiqu) was in every respect virtually on her own from 1911 to 1950.

136. *Dongfang Jeubao*, 20th July 2009.

137. After a storm of protest from Chinese intellectuals and academics against the arrest, Ilham Tohti was finaly released on 23rd August 2009 (*Dongfang Jeubao*, 11th September 2009).

138. *Dongfang Jeubao*, 10th July 2009, 15th July 2009, 17th July 2009.

139. Following Professor Zhou Tianyong from the Central Party School, China's authoritarian one-party political system will and should remain unchanged until at least 2037 (Zhou, Wang and Wang (eds), 2007: 2, 6, 45-46, see Bo, 2009b: 10-11).

140. For federal sustainability, see Yeoh (2009b: 276), Figure 10.15.

141. Bo Yibo, the former Chinese vice-premier, was in fact expressing the reformers' feeling towards the lessons of the multiple cycles of administrative decentralization and recentralization in China: "A [more] important and fundamental lesson of the [1958] attempt to improve the economic management system is: We only saw the vices of overcentralization of power, and sought to remedy the situation by decentralizing powers to the lower levels. When we felt too much power had been decentralized, we recentralized them. We did not then recognize the inadequacies of putting sole emphasis on central planning (and in particular a system dominated by mandatory planning) and totally neglecting and denying the role of the market […] As a result over a long period of time (after the 1958 decentralization) we were trapped within the planned economy model. Adjustments and improvements could only work around the cycles of decentralization and recentralization. Moreover the recipients of more powers are invariably the local governments, rather than enterprises." (Bo Yibo 薄一波, *Ruogan Zhongda Juece yu Shijian de Huigu* 若干重大决策与事件的回顾 [Looking back at some important decisions and events], 1993, p. 804, cited in Li, 2003: 1.)

Appendix to Chapter 10 – Transliteration*

HP	AT	PT	HP	AT	PT	HP	AT	PT	HP	AT	PT
a	a	a	dao	dao	tao	hou	hou	hou	lu	lu	lu
ai	ai	ai	de	de	te	hu	hu	hu	luan	luan	luan
an	an	an	dei	dei	tei	hua	hua	hua	lue	lve	luen
ang	ang	ang	deng	deng	teng	huai	huai	huai	lun	luen	luen
ao	ao	ao	di	di	ti	huan	huan	huan	luo	luo	luo
ba	ba	pa	dian	dian	tian	huang	huang	huang	lü	lvu	lvu
bai	bai	pai	diao	diao	tiao	hui	huei	huei	lüan	lvan	lvan
ban	ban	pan	die	die	tie	hun	huen	huen	lün	lven	lven
bang	bang	pang	ding	ding	tieng	huo	huo	huo	ma	ma	ma
bao	bao	pao	diu	diou	tiou	ji	zi	zi	mai	mai	mai
bei	bei	pei	dong	dong	tueng	jia	zia	zia	man	man	man
ben	ben	pen	dou	dou	tou	jian	zian	zian	mang	mang	mang
beng	beng	peng	du	du	tu	jiang	ziang	ziang	mao	mao	mao
bi	bi	pi	duan	duan	tuan	jiao	ziao	ziao	me	me	me
bian	bian	pian	dui	duei	tuei	jie	zie	zie	mei	mei	mei
biao	biao	piao	dun	duen	tuen	jin	zin	zien	men	men	men
bie	bie	pie	duo	duo	tuo	jing	zing	zieng	meng	meng	meng
bin	bin	pien	e	e	e	jiong	ziong	zveng	mi	mi	mi
bing	bing	pieng	ei	ei	ei	jiu	ziou	ziou	mian	mian	mian
bo	buo	puo	en	en	en	ju	zvu	zvu	miao	miao	miao
bu	bu	pu	ong	ong	eng	juan	zvan	zvan	mie	mie	mie
ca	ca	ca	er	er	er	jue	zve	zve	min	min	mien
cai	cai	cai	fa	fa	fa	jun	zven	zven	ming	ming	mieng
can	can	can	fan	fan	fan	ka	ka	kha	miu	miou	miou
cang	cang	cang	fang	fang	fang	kai	kai	khai	mo	muo	muo
cao	cao	cao	fei	fei	fei	kan	kan	khan	mou	mou	mou
ce	ce	ce	fen	fen	fen	kang	kang	khang	mu	mu	mu
cen	cen	cen	feng	feng	feng	kao	kao	khao	na	na	na
ceng	ceng	ceng	fo	fuo	fuo	ke	ke	khe	nai	nai	nai
ci	ceu	ceu	fou	fou	fou	ken	ken	khen	nan	nan	nan
cong	cong	cueng	fu	fu	fu	keng	keng	kheng	nang	nang	nang
cou	cou	cou	ga	qa	ka	kong	kong	khueng	nao	nao	nao
cu	cu	cu	gai	qai	kai	kou	kou	khou	ne	ne	ne
cuan	cuan	cuan	gan	qan	kan	ku	ku	khu	nei	nei	nei
cui	cuei	cuci	gang	qang	kang	kua	kua	khua	nen	nen	nen
cun	cuen	cuen	gao	qao	kao	kuai	kuai	khuai	neng	neng	neng
cuo	cuo	ouo	ge	qe	ke	kuan	kuan	khuan	ni	ni	ni
cha	cha	cxa	gei	qei	kei	kuang	kuang	khuang	nian	nian	nian
chai	chai	cxai	gen	qen	ken	kui	kuei	khuei	niang	niang	niang
chan	chan	cxan	geng	qeng	keng	kun	kuen	khuen	niao	niao	niao
chang	chang	cxang	gong	qong	kou	kuo	kuo	khuo	nie	nie	nie
chao	chao	cxao	gou	qou	kou	la	la	la	nin	nin	nien
che	che	cxe	gu	gu	ku	lai	lai	lai	ning	ning	nieng
chen	chen	cxen	gua	qua	kua	lan	lan	lan	niu	niou	niou
cheng	cheng	cxeng	guai	quai	kuai	lang	lang	lang	nong	nong	nong
chi	cheu	cxeu	guan	quan	kuan	lao	lao	lao	nou	nou	nu
chong	chong	cxueng	guang	quang	kuang	le	le	le	nu	nu	nu
chou	chou	cxou	gui	quei	kuei	lei	lei	lei	nuan	nuan	nuan
chu	chu	cxu	gun	quen	kuen	leng	leng	leng	nue	nve	nve
chua	chua	cxua	guo	quo	kuo	li	li	li	nuo	nuo	nuo
chuai	chuai	cxuai	ha	ha	ha	lia	lia	lia	nü	nvu	nvu
chuan	chuan	cxuan	hai	hai	hai	lian	lian	lian	ou	ou	ou
chuang	chuang	cxuang	han	han	han	liang	liang	liang	pa	pha	pha
chui	chuei	cxuei	hang	hang	hang	liao	liao	liao	pai	pai	phai
chun	chuen	cxuen	hao	hao	hao	lie	lie	lie	pan	pan	phan
chuo	chuo	cxuo	he	he	he	lin	lin	lin	pang	pang	phang
da	da	ta	hei	hei	hei	ling	ling	lieng	pao	pao	phao
dai	dai	tai	hen	hen	hen	liu	liou	liou	pei	pei	phei
dan	dan	tan	heng	heng	heng	long	long	lueng	pen	pen	phen
dang	dang	tang	hong	hong	hueng	lou	lou	lou	peng	peng	pheng

Appendix to Chapter 10 – Transliteration* (continued)

HP	AT	PT	HP	AT	PT	HP	AT	PT	HP	AT	PT
pi	pi	phi	se	se	se	tong	tong	thueng	yuan	yvan	yvan
pian	pian	phian	sen	sen	sen	tou	tou	thou	yue	yve	yve
piao	piao	phiao	seng	seng	seng	tu	tu	thu	yun	yven	yven
pie	pie	phie	si	seu	seu	tuan	tuan	thuan	za	za	za
pin	pin	phien	song	song	sueng	tui	tuei	thuei	zai	zai	zai
ping	ping	phieng	sou	sou	sou	tun	tuen	thuen	zan	zan	zan
po	puo	phuo	su	su	su	tuo	tuo	thuo	zang	zang	zang
pou	pou	phou	suan	suan	suan	wa	wa	wa	zao	zao	zao
pu	pu	phu	sui	suei	suei	wai	wai	wai	ze	ze	ze
qi	ci	ci	sun	suen	suen	wan	wan	wan	zei	zei	zei
qia	cia	cia	suo	suo	suo	wang	wang	wang	zen	zen	zen
qian	cian	cian	sha	sha	sxa	wei	wei	wei	zeng	zeng	zeng
qiang	ciang	ciang	shai	shai	sxai	wen	wen	wen	zi	zeu	zeu
qiao	ciao	ciao	shan	shan	sxan	weng	weng	weng	zong	zong	zueng
qie	cie	cie	shang	shang	sxang	wo	wo	wo	zou	zou	zou
qin	cin	cien	shao	shao	sxao	wu	wu	wu	zu	zu	zu
qing	cing	cieng	she	she	sxe	xi	si	si	zuan	zuan	zuan
qiong	ciong	cveng	shei	shei	sxei	xia	sia	sia	zui	zuei	zuei
qiu	ciou	ciou	shen	shen	sxen	xian	sian	sian	zun	zuen	zuen
qu	cvu	cvu	sheng	sheng	sxeng	xiang	siang	siang	zuo	zuo	zuo
quan	cvan	cvan	shi	sheu	sxeu	xiao	siao	siao	zha	zha	zxa
que	cve	cve	shou	shou	sxou	xie	sie	sie	zhai	zhai	zxai
qun	cven	cven	shu	shu	sxu	xin	sin	sien	zhan	zhan	zxan
ran	jan	jan	shua	shua	sxua	xing	sing	sieng	zhang	zhang	zxang
rang	jang	jang	shuai	shuai	sxuai	xiong	siong	sveng	zhao	zhao	zxao
rao	jao	jao	shuan	shuan	sxuan	xiu	siou	siou	zhe	zhe	zxe
re	je	je	shuang	shuang	sxuang	xu	svu	svu	zhei	zhei	zxei
ren	jen	jen	shui	shuei	sxuei	xuan	svan	svan	zhen	zhen	zxen
reng	jeng	jeng	shun	shuen	sxuen	xue	sve	sve	zheng	zheng	zxeng
ri	jeu	jeu	shuo	shuo	sxuo	xun	sven	sven	zhi	zheu	zxeu
rong	jong	jueng	ta	ta	tha	ya	ya	ya	zhong	zhong	zxueng
rou	jou	jou	tai	tai	thai	yai	yai	yai	zhou	zhou	zxou
ru	ju	ju	tan	tan	than	yan	yan	yan	zhu	zhu	zxu
ruan	juan	juan	tang	tang	thang	yang	yang	yang	zhua	zhua	zxua
rui	juei	juei	tao	tao	thao	yao	yao	yao	zhuai	zhuai	zxuai
run	juen	juen	te	te	the	ye	ye	ye	zhuan	zhuan	zxuan
ruo	juo	juo	teng	teng	theng	yi	yi	yi	zhuang	zhuang	zxuang
sa	sa	sa	ti	ti	thi	yin	yin	yien	zhui	zhuei	zxuei
sai	sai	sai	tian	tian	thian	ying	ying	yieng	zhun	zhuen	zxuen
san	san	san	tiao	tiao	thiao	yong	yong	yveng	zhuo	zhuo	zxuo
sang	sang	sang	tie	tie	thie	you	you	you			
sao	sao	sao	ting	ting	thieng	yu	yvu	yvu			

* HP – hanyu pinyin (Mainland China)
  AT – alternate transliteration
  PT – phonetic transcription
  For transliteration of terms and sources outside Mainland China, the experimental AT drops HP's unconventional "q", "x" and "r" initials (the first, a palatal, reassigned as an unaspirated velar; the last, a retroflex, replaced by "j") and employs "eu" for the empty vowel to enable double using "z", "c" and "s" for both palatals and dental sibilants. PT represents a more phonetic transcription (but not employing IPA, the International Phonetic Alphabet) by adding "h" (like Wade-Giles's aspirant apostrophe) to the phonemes of "p", "t" and "k" to indicate aspiration, and "x" to indicate the corresponding retroflexes. As a result, the consonants "b", "d", "g", "q", "x" and "r" would no longer be used as initials, though remaining useful in the transliteration of the Chinese regionalects. However, the aspirant "h" addition would make writing longer.

References

Ahlin, Christian (2000), *Corruption, Aggregate Economic Activity and Political Organization*, University of Chicago.

Alonso Zaldívar, Carlos and Manuel Castells (1992), *Spain Beyond Myths*, Madrid: Alianza Editorial.

Anderson, Benedict (1991), *Imagined Communities: Reflections on the Origin and Spread of Nationalism*, revised edition, London and New York: Verso (first published in 1983).

Anuarios Estadísticos de España, Instituto Nacional de Estadística/Ministerio de Economía y Hacienda, Madrid.

Bahl, Roy W. (1998), "China: Evaluating the Impact of Intergovernmental Fiscal Reform", in Richard Bird and François Vaillancourt (eds), *Fiscal Decentralization in Developing Countries*, Cambridge: Cambridge University Press (reprinted 2000), pp. 49-77.

Baker, Donald G. (1978), "Race and Power: Comparative Approaches to the Analysis of Race Relations", *Ethnic and Racial Studies*, Vol. 1, No. 3, July, pp. 316-335.

Bakvis, Herman and William M. Chandler (1987), "Federalism and Comparative Analysis", in Herman Bakvis and William H. Chandler (eds), *Federalism and the Role of the State*, Toronto: University of Toronto Press, pp. 3-11.

Banton, Michael (1983), *Racial and Ethnic Competition*, Cambridge: Cambridge University Press.

Bao Tong 鮑彤, "Zhao Zeuyang Luyin Huciyi de Lisheu Beizing 趙紫陽錄音回憶 的歷史背景 [Historical background of Zhao Ziyang's voice recorded memoir]", introduction in Zhao Ziyang 趙紫陽 (2009, posthumously), *Quozia de Cioutu: Zhao Zeuyang de Mimi Luyin* 國家的囚徒 —— 趙紫陽的祕密錄音 [Prisoner of the State: The secret voice recordings of Zhao Ziyang] (*Prisoner of the State*), edited by Bao Pu 鮑樸, Taipei: Sheubao Wenhua Chuban Ciye 時報文化出版企 業, pp. 23-35.

Barth, Fredrik (1969), "Introduction", in Fredrik Barth (ed.), *Ethnic Groups and Boundaries*, Boston: Little, Brown, pp. 9–38.

Beard, C. (1948), "Neglected Aspects of Political Science", *American Political Science Review*, Vol. 42, No. 2, April, pp. 211-222.

Béja, Jean-Philippe (2009), "China since Tiananmen: The Massacre's Long Shadow", *Journal of Democracy*, Vol. 20, No. 3, July, pp. 5-16.

Bird, Richard M. and François Vaillancourt (1998), "Fiscal Decentralization in Developing Countries: An Overview", in Richard M. Bird and François Vaillancourt (eds), *Fiscal Decentralization in Developing Countries*, Cambridge: Cambridge University Press (repr. 2000).

Bo Zhiyue (2009a), "The Future Development of China's Elite Politics", paper presented at the International Conference "China's Future: Pitfalls, Prospects and the Implications for ASEAN and the World", Institute of China Studies, University of Malaya, Kuala Lumpur, 5th-6th May.

Bo Zhiyue (2009b), "China's Model of Democracy", paper presented at the ICS Seminar, Institute of China Studies, University of Malaya, Kuala Lumpur, 11th June.

Bonacich, Edna (1972), "A Theory of Ethnic Antagonism: The Split Labor Market", *American Sociological Review*, Vol. 37, October, pp. 547-559.

Bonacich, Edna (1979), "The Past, Present, and Future of Split Labour Market Theory", in Cora Bagley Marrett and Cheryl Leggon (eds), *Research in Race and Ethnic Relations: A Research Annual*, Vol. 1, Greenwich, Connecticut: JAI Press, pp. 17-64.

Börzel, Tanja A. (2000), "From Competitive Regionalism to Cooperative Federalism: The Europeanization of the Spanish State of the Autonomies", *Publius: The Journal of Federalism*, Vol. 30, No. 2, Spring, pp. 17-42.

Brass, Paul R. (1985), "Ethnic Groups and the State", in Paul R. Brass (ed.), Ethnic Groups and the State, Totwa, NJ: Barnes and Noble, pp. 1-56.

Brassloff, Audrey (1989), "Spain: The State of the Autonomies", in Murray Forsyth (ed.), *Federalism and Nationalism*, Leicester: Leicester University Press, pp. 24-50.

Brown, David (1989), "The State of Ethnicity and the Ethnicity of the state: Ethnic Politics in Southeast Asia", *Ethnic and Racial Studies*, Vol. 12, No. 1, January, pp. 47-62.

Brunn, Gerhard (1992), "The Catalans within the Spanish Monarchy from the Middle of the Nineteenth to the Beginning of the Twentieth Century", in Andreas Kappeler (ed., in collaboration with Fikret Adanır and Alan O'Day), *The Formation of National Elites: Comparative Studies on Governments and Non-Dominant Ethnic Groups in Europe, 1850-1940*, Volume VI, Aldershot (Harts., England): Dartmouth, pp. 133-159.

Carrère d'Encausse, Hélène (1978), *L'Empire éclaté* (translated by Martin Sokolinsky and Henry A. La Farge as *Decline of an Empire: The Soviet Socialist Republics in Revolt*, Newsweek Books, New York, 1979).

Castells, Antoni (1990), «Transición democrática y descentralización del sector público», en José Luis García Delgado (dir.), *Economía Española de la Transición y la Democracia*, Madrid: Centro de Investigaciones Sociológicas (CIS), pags. 445-479.

Chan, John (2007), "An Explosion of Billionaires in China", World Socialist Web Site – published by the International Committee of the Fourth International (ICFI), 14th November. <*http://www.wsws.org/articles/2007/nov2007/chin-n14.shtml*>

Chapnick, Howard (1989), "Foreword", in David Turnley, Peter Turnley, Melinda Liu and Li Ming (1989), *Beijing Spring*, New York: Stewart, Tabori & Chang, pp. 15-17.

Cheah Boon Kheng (1984), "Perpecahan dan Perpaduan dalam Gerakan Kemerdekaan selepas Perang Dunia Kedua", dalam S. Husin Ali (ed.), *Kaum, Kelas dan Pembangunan/Ethnicity, Class and Development: Malaysia*, Kuala Lumpur: Persatuan Sains Sosial Malaysia (Malaysian Social Science Association), pp. 79-92.

Chen Jiansheng 陈健生 (2006), *Tuigenghuanlin yu Xibu Kechixu Fazhan* 退耕还林与西部可持续发展 [Defarming-reforestation and sustainable development in the western region], Chengdu: Xinan Caijing Daxue Chubanshe 西南财经大学出版社.

Chua, Amy (2004), *World on Fire: How Exporting Free Market Democracy Breeds Ethnic Hatred and Global Instability*, New York: Anchor Books (originally published in 2003 by Doubleday, New York).

Clapham, Christopher (1982), *Private Patronage and Political Power*, London: Frances Pinter.

Clegg, Kendra, "Ethnic stereotyping by politicians", *Inside Indonesia*, April-June (accessed at *http://www.insideindonesia.org/edit78/p19-20_clegg.html*, in 2004).

Clegg, Kendra (2008), "The Politics of Redefining Ethnic Identity in Indonesia: Smothering the Fires in Lombok with Democracy", in Nicholas Tarling and Edmund Terence Gomez (eds), *The State, Development and Identity in Multi-Ethnic Societies: Ethnicity, Equity and the Nation*, Oxford, London and New York: Routledge, pp. 172-184.

Cook, Ian G. and Geoffrey Murray (2001), *China's Third Revolution: Tensions in the Transition towards a Post-Communist China*, Richmond, Surrey: Curzon Press.

Cox, Oliver C. (1948), *Caste, Class and Race: A Study in Social Dynamics*, New York: Monthly Review Press (repr. 1970, New York and London: Modern Reader Paperbacks).

Crook, Richard and James Manor (2000), "Democratic Decentralization", OED Working Paper Series No. 11, Summer, World Bank, Washington, DC.

Dangdai Zhongguo Shehui Ge Jieceng Fenxi (2007 Nian Ban) 当代中国社会各阶层分析 (2007年版) [Social strata analysis of contemporary China, 2007 edition] (by Zhu Guanglei 朱光磊 *et al.*), Tianjin: Tianjin Renmin Chubanshe 天津人民出版社, 2007.

Deng Xiaoping (1986), "Take a Clear-Cut Stand against Bourgeois Liberalization", 30th December. <*http://web.peopledaily.com.cn/english/dengxp/vol3/text/c1630.html*>

DeVos, George A. (1972), "Japan's Outcastes: The Problem of the Burakumin", in Ben Whitaker (ed.), *The Fourth World: Victims of Group Oppression*, London: Sidgwick & Jackson, pp. 308-327.

Diamond, Larry (2002), "Elections without Democracy: Thinking about Hybrid Regimes", *Journal of Democracy*, Vol. 13, No. 2, April, pp. 21-35.

Dickens, Charles (1859), *A Tale of Two Cities*, with illustrations by Hablot K. Browne ('Phiz'), London: Chapman and Hall (edited with introduction by George Woodcock, London: Penguin Books, 1970, 1985).

Dorff, Robert H. (1994), "Federalism in Eastern Europe: Part of the Solution or Part of the Problem?", *Publius: The Journal of Federalism*, Vol. 24, No. 2, Spring, pp. 99-114.

Duchacek, Ivo D. (1988), "Dyadic Federations and Confederations", *Publius: The Journal of Federalism*, Vol. 18, No. 2, Spring, pp. 5-31.

Enloe, Cynthia H. (1980), *Police, Military and Ethnicity: Foundations of State Power*, New Brunswick: Transaction Books.

Escobar-Lemmon, Maria (2001), "Fiscal Decentralization and Federalism in Latin America", *Publius: The Journal of Federalism*, Vol. 31, No. 4, Fall, pp. 23-41.

Evans, Peter B., Dietrich Rueschemeyer and Theda Skocpol (1985), "On the Road toward a More Adequate Understanding of the State", in Peter B. Evans, Dietrich Rueschemeyer and Theda Skocpol (eds), *Bringing the State Back In*, Cambridge and New York: Cambridge University Press, pp. 347-366.

Fan Xiaojian 范小建 (2008), "Zhongguo Fupin Kaifa: Huigu yu Zhanwang 中国扶贫开发: 回顾与展望 [China's poverty assistance development: review and prospects]", in Fan Xiaojian 范小建 (ed.), *Fupin Kaifa Xingshi he Zhengce* 扶贫开发形势和政策 [The situation and policy of poverty assistance development], Beijing: Zhongguo Caizheng Jingji Chubanshe 中国财政经济出版社, pp. 14-20.

Fang, Lizhi 方励之 (1991), *Bringing down the Great Wall: Writings on Science, Culture, and Democracy in China*, editor and principal translator: James H. Williams, New York: Alfred A. Knopf.

Freedom House (2009), *Freedom in the World 2009. <http://www.freedomhouse. org/uploads/fiw09/FIW09_Tables&GraphsForWeb.pdf>*

Frye, Timothy and Andrei Shleifer (1997), "The Invisible Hand and the Grabbing Hand", *American Economic Review*, Vol. 87, No. 2, May, pp. 354-358.

Garcia-Milà, Teresa (2003), "Fiscal Federalism and Regional Integration: Lessons from Spain", July. *<http://www.crei.cat/people/gmila/papers/book1-july03.pdf>*

Garcia-Milà, Teresa and Therese J. McGuire (2002), "Fiscal Decentralization in Spain: An Asymmetric Transition to Democracy", revised 22nd March. *<http://www.crei. cat/people/gmila/selected%20publications/march02.pdf>*

Geertz, Clifford (1963), "The Integrative Revolution: Primordial Sentiments and Civil Politics in the New States", in Clifford Geertz, (ed.), *Old Societies and New States: The Quest for Modernity in Asia and Africa*, New York: The Free Press of Glencoe, pp. 105-157.

Gellner, Ernest (1983), *Nations and Nationalism*, Ithaca: Cornell University Press.

Gheorghe, Nicolae (1991), "Roma-Gypsy Ethnicity in Eastern Europe", *Social Research*, Vol. 58, No. 4, Winter, pp. 829-844.

Gladney, Dru C. (1991), *Muslim Chinese: Ethnic Nationalism in the People's Republic*, Council on East Asian Studies, Harvard University.

Gladney, Dru C. (2003), "China's Minorities: The Case of Xinjiang and the Uyghur People", paper for the Ninth session of the Working Group on Minorities, Sub-Commission on Promotion and Protection of Human Rights, United Nations Commission on Human Rights (UNCHR), 12th-16th May 2003. *<http://www.unhchr.ch/huridocda/huridoca.nsf/AllSymbols/ 79E5FCFFB0A0E39CC1256D26004661FC/$File/G0314169.pdf?OpenElement>*

Gorbachev, Mikhail Sergeyevich (1991), *The August Coup: The Truth and the Lessons*, New York: HarperCollins.

Gordon, Milton (1978), *Human Nature, Class and Ethnicity*, New York: Oxford University Press.

Greenwood, Davydd James (1985), "Castilians, Basques, and Andalusians: An Historical Comparison of Nationalism, 'True' Ethnicity, and 'False' Ethnicity", in Paul R. Brass (ed.), *Ethnic Groups and the State*, London: Croom Helm, pp. 202-227.

Gu, Qingyang and Kang Chen (2002), "Impact of Fiscal Re-Centralization on China's Regional Economies: Evidence from a Multi-Regional Model", paper presented at the International Conference on Policy Modeling, Brussels, 4th-6th July 2002.

Gunther, Richard (1980), *Public Policy in a No-Party State: Spanish Planning and Budgeting in the Twilight of the Franquist Era*, Berkeley and Los Angeles: University of California Press.

Gurgur, Tugrul and Anwar Shah (2000), "Localization and Corruption: Panacea or Pandora's Box?", November. <*http://web.nps.navy.mil/~relooney/EconIntel_23.pdf*>

Hage, Jerald, Robert Hanneman and Edward T. Gargan (1989), *State Responsiveness and State Activism: An Examination of the Social Forces and State Strategies That Explain the Rise in Social Expenditures in Britain, France, Germany and Italy, 1870-1968*, London: Unwin Hyman.

Hebbert, Michael (1989), "Spain – A Centre-Periphery Transformation", in Jens Christian Hansen and Michael Hebbert (eds), *Unfamiliar Territory*, Aldershot: Avebury.

Heiberg, Marianne (1979), "External and Internal Nationalism: The Case of the Spanish Basques", in Raymond L. Hall (ed.), *Ethnic Autonomy – Comparative Dynamics: The Americas, Europe and the Developing World*, New York: Pergamon Press, pp. 180-200.

Heywood, Paul (1995), *The Government and Politics of Spain*, Basingstoke & London: Macmillan Press Ltd.

Hobbes, Thomas (1651), *Leviathan, The Matter, Forme and Power of a Common Wealth Ecclesiasticall and Civil*, published by Andrew Crooke / *Leviathan* (Oxford World's Classics), New York: Oxford University Press, 2009.

Hobsbawm, Eric J. (1990), *Nations and Nationalism since 1780: Programme, Myth, Reality*, Cambridge: Cambridge University Press.

Hoetink, Harmannus (1967), *The Two Variants in Caribbean Race Relations: A Contribution to the Sociology of Segmented Societies*, tr. by Eva M. Hooykaas, London: Oxford University Press.

Hoetink, Harmannus (1973), *Slavery and Race Relations in the Americas: Comparative Notes on Their Nature and Nexus*, New York: Harper & Row.

Hoetink, Harmannus (1975), "Resource Competition, Monopoly, and Socioracial Diversity", in Leo A. Despres (ed.), *Ethnicity and Resource Competition in Plural Societies*, The Hague: Mouton Publishers, pp. 9-25.

Hu, Angang (ed.) (2006), *Economic and Social Transformation in China: Challenges and Opportunities*, Abingdon, Oxon, London and New York: Routledge.

Hu Lianhe 胡联合, Hu Angang 胡鞍钢 and Wang Lei 王磊 (2006), "Yingxiang Shehui Wending de Shehui Maodun Bianhua Taishi de Shizheng Fenxi 影响社会稳定的社会矛盾变化态势的实证分析 [Empirical analysis of the change and trend of social contradictions that affect social stability]", *Shehuikexue Zhanxian* 社会科学战线 [Frontline of social science], Vol. 4, pp. 175-185.

Huang Taiyan 黄泰岩 and Niu Feiliang 牛飞亮 (2007), *Zhongguo Chengzhen Jumin Shouru Chaju* 中国城镇居民收入差距 [Income differentials amongst China's urban population], Beijing: Jingjikexue Chubanshe 经济科学出版社.

Huther, Jeff and Anwar Shah (1998), "A Simple Measure of Good Governance and Its Application to the Debate on Fiscal Decentralization", World Bank Policy Research Working Paper Series No. 1498, World Bank, Washington, DC.

Hutton, Will (2006), *The Writing on the Wall: China and the West in the 21st Century*, London: Little, Brown.

IDE Spot Survey – China's Western Development Strategy: Issues and Prospects (edited by Yasuo Onishi), Chiba, Japan: Institute of Developing Economies/IDE-JETRO, December 2001.

International Monetary Fund (IMF), *Government Finance Statistics Yearbook*, various years.

Katznelson, Ira (1971), "Power in the Reformulation of Race Research", in Peter Orleans and William Russell Ellis, Jr (eds), *Race, Change, and Urban Society* (*Urban Affairs Annual Reviews*, Vol. 5), Beverly Hills, California: Sage.

Kaup, Katherine Palmer (2000), *Creating the Zhuang: Ethnic Politics in China*, Boulder, Colorado: Lynne Rienner Publishers.

Keating, Michael (1993), "Spain: Peripheral Nationalism and State Response", in John McGarry and Brendan O'Leary (eds), *The Politics of Ethnic Conflict Regulation: Case Studies of Protracted Ethnic Conflicts*, London: Routledge, pp. 204-225.

Keidel, Albert (2005), "The Economic Basis for Social Unrest in China", paper for The Third European-American Dialogue on China, George Washington University, 26th-27th May. *<http://www.carnegieendowment.org/files/Keidel_Social_Unrest.pdf>*

Kristof, Nicholas D. and Sheryl WuDunn (1994), *China Wakes: The Struggle for the Soul of a Rising Power*, New York: Time Books.

Krug, Barbara and Ze Zhu (2004), "Is China a Leviathan?", ERIM Report Series "Research in Management", Erasmus Research Institute of Management, Rotterdam School of Management/Rotterdam School of Economics, ERS-2004-103-ORG. *<http://hdl.handle.net/1765/1821>*

Krug, Barbara, Ze Zhu and Hans Hendrischke (2004), "China's Emerging Tax Regime: Devolution, Fiscal Federalism, or Tax Farming?", ERIM Report Series "Research in Management", Erasmus Research Institute of Management, Rotterdam School of Management/Rotterdam School of Economics, ERS-2004-113-ORG. *<http://hdl.handle.net/1765/1841>*

Kuper, Leo (1974), *Race, Class and Power: Ideology and Revolutionary Change in Plural Societies*, London: Duckworth.

Levi-Strauss, C. (1967), *Structural Anthropology*, New York: Anchor Doubleday.

Li, Linda Chelan (2003), "The Nature of Central-Provincial Relations in China: A Comparative Note", January. *<http://personal.cityu.edu.hk/~salcli/paperforweb/webarticle/Natureoncprelations.pdf>*

Lijphart, Arend (1977), *Democracy in Plural Societies: A Comparative Exploration*, New Haven: Yale University Press.

Lin Buowen 林博文, "Mi Yven Haiwai de Hueiyilu: Cong Zhao Zeuyang Zhueisu Hclusvefu 祕運海外的回憶錄 —— 從趙紫陽追溯赫魯雪夫 [Memoirs secretly transported overseas: From Zhao Ziyang recalls Nikita S. Khrushchev]", special article in Zhao Ziyang 趙紫陽 (2009, posthumously), *Quozia de Cioutu: Zhao Zeuyang de Mimi Luyin* 國家的囚徒 —— 趙紫陽的祕密錄音 [Prisoner of the State: The secret voice recordings of Zhao Ziyang] (*Prisoner of the State*), edited by Bao Pu 鮑樸, Taipei: Sheubao Wenhua Chuban Ciye 時報文化出版企業, pp. 350-358.

Lin Hueisiang 林惠祥 (1936), *Zhongquo Minzu Sheu* 中國民族史 [History of China's nationalities], Volume 2, Shangwu Yinshuquan 商務印書館, photo-reprint first printing 1993 published by Shangwu Yinshuguan 商务印书馆, third printing 1998.

Lum, Thomas (2006), "Social Unrest in China", CRS Report for Congress, 8th May. *<http://www.fas.org/sgp/crs/row/RL33416.pdf>*

Lü Yuanli 呂元礼 (2007), *Xinjiapo Weishenme Neng – Shang Juan: Yi Dang Changqi Zhizheng Heyi Baochi Huoli, Lianjie?* 新加坡为什么能 —— 上卷: 一党长期执政何以保持活力、廉洁? [Why can Singapore do it – Volume 1: How are vitality and cleanliness preserved in long-term one-party rule?], 2nd ed. (Volumes 1 & 2), Nanchang: Jiangxi Renmin Chubanshe 江西人民出版社 (2008, 6th printing).

Lye Liang Fook (2009), "China's Media Reforms and Prospects for Media Liberalization", in Emile Kok-Kheng Yeoh (ed.), *Regional Political Economy of China Ascendant: Pivotal Issues and Critical Perspectives*, Kuala Lumpur: Institute of China Studies, University of Malaya, pp. 215-240.

MacFarquhar, Roderick (2009), "Foreword", in Zhao Ziyang 赵紫阳 (2009, posthumously), *Prisoner of the State: The Secret Journal of Zhao Ziyang*, translated and edited by Bao Pu, Renee Chiang and Adi Ignatius, New York: Simon & Schuster.

Mansvelt Beck, Jan (1991), "Basque and Catalan Nationalisms in Comparative Perspective", in J.M.M. (Hans) van Amersfoort and Hans Knippenberg (eds), *States and Nations: The Rebirth of the 'Nationalities Question' in Europe*, Utrecht: Koninklijk Nederlands Aardrijkskundig Genootschap; Amsterdam: Instituut voor Sociale Geografie, Universiteit van Amsterdam (*Netherlands Geographical Studies*, 137), pp. 153-170.

Marden, Charles F. and Gladys Meyer (1962), *Minorities in American Society*, 2nd edition, New York: American Book Company.

Marx, Karl (1852), *The Eighteenth Brumaire of Louis Bonaparte*, original version published in the first number of the monthly *Die Revolution* in 1852 (excerpts included in *Karl Marx and Friedrich Engels: Basic Writings on Politics and*

Philosophy, edited with introduction by Lewis S. Feuer, New York: Doubleday/ Anchor Books, 1989).

Mason, Philip (1970), *Race Relation*, London: Oxford University Press.

Minzner, Carl (2006), "Social Instability in China: Causes, Consequences, and Implications", Center for Strategic and International Studies, November. <*http:// csis.org/files/media/csis/events/061205_mizner_abstract.pdf*>

Molero, Juan-Carlos (2001), "Analysis of the Decentralization of Public Spending in Spain", *Public Finance and Management*, Vol. 1, No. 4, pp. 500-556. <*http://www. unav.es/economia/economiasectorpublico1/archivos/Analysis of the decentr.in SPAIN.JCMolero.pdf*>

Mommen, André (1994), *The Belgian Economy in the Twentieth Century*, London & New York: Routledge.

Montero, Alfred P. (2001), "After Decentralization: Patterns of Intergovernmental Conflict in Argentina, Brazil, Spain, and Mexico", *Publius: The Journal of Federalism*, Vol. 31, No. 4, Fall, pp. 43-64.

Moscovici, Serge (1985), "Innovation and Minority Influence", in Serge Moscovici, Gabriel Mugny and Eddy van Avermaet (eds), *Perspectives on Minority Influence*, Paris: Maison des Sciences de l'homme and Cambridge: Cambridge University Press, pp. 9-51.

Moseley, George (1966), *The Party and the National Question in China*, Cambridge, Massachusetts: Massachusetts Institute of Technology.

Murphy, Alexander B. (1995), "Belgium's Regional Divergence: Along the Road to Federation", in Graham Smith (ed.), *Federalism: The Multiethnic Challenge*, London & New York: Longman, pp. 73-100.

Nee, Victor (2000), "The Role of the State in Making a Market Economy", *Journal of Institutional and Theoretical Economics*, Vol. 156, pp. 64-88.

O'Donnell, Guillermo and Philippe C. Schmitter (1986), *Transitions from Authoritarian Rule: Tentative Conclusions about Uncertain Democracies*, Baltimore: Johns Hopkins University Press.

Oi, J.C. (1992), "Fiscal Reform and the Economic Foundations of Local State Corporatism in China", *World Politics*, Vol. 45, No. 1, pp. 99-126.

Oi, J.C. (1995), "The Role of the Local State in China's Transitional Economy", *China Quarterly*, Vol. 144, pp. 1132-1150.

Olson, Mancur (2000), *Power and Prosperity: Outgrowing Communist and Capitalist Dictatorships*, New York: Basic Books.

Ortiz Junquera, Pilar y José Antonio Roldán Mesanat (1988), «La evolución del sector público territorial desde la aparición de las Comunidades Autónomas», *Papeles de Economía Española*, N° 35, pags. 434-456.

Paine, Thomas (1776), *Common Sense*, issued at Philadelphia (edited with introduction by Isaac Kramnick, published by Penguin Books Ltd., Harmondsworth, Middlesex, England, 1976, reprinted 1986; included in *The Life and Major Writings of Thomas Paine*, collected, edited and annotated by Philip S. Foner, New York: Carol Publishing Group/Citadel Press, 1993).

Paine, Thomas (1794), *The Age of Reason, Part First*, Paris: Barras (included in *The Life and Major Writings of Thomas Paine*, collected, edited and annotated by Philip S. Foner, New York: Carol Publishing Group/Citadel Press, 1993).

Pei, Minxin (2006), *China's Trapped Transition: The Limits of Developmental Autocracy*, Cambridge, MA: Harvard University Press.

Poole, Steven (2006), *Unspeak*, London: Little, Brown.

Puddington, Arch (2009), "Freedom in the World 2009: Setbacks and Resilience", Freedom House. <*http://www.freedomhouse.org/uploads/fiw09/FIW09_OverviewEssay_Final.pdf*>

Rabushka, Alvin (1974), *A Theory of Racial Harmony*, Columbia: University of South Carolina Press.

Rex, John (1986), "Preface", in John Rex and David Mason (eds), *Theories of Race and Ethnic Relations*, Cambridge: Cambridge University Press (ppb. ed. 1988, repr. 1990).

Roig Alonso, Miguel (1987), «El endeudamiento de los distintos niveles de administraciones públicas españolas», *Papeles de Economía Española*, N° 33, pags. 155-171.

Schattschneider, E.E. (1961), *The Semisovereign People*, New York: Holt, Rinehart and Winston.

Schermerhorn, R.A. (1970), *Comparative Ethnic Relations: A Framework for Theory and Research*, New York: Random House.

Schneider, Aaron (2003), "Decentralization: Conceptualization and Measurement", *Studies in Comparative International Development*, Vol. 38, No. 3, Fall, pp. 32-56.

Schumacher, E. F. (1973), *Small Is Beautiful: Economics as if People Mattered*, New York: Harper and Row.

Semyonov, Moshe and Andrea Tyree (1981), "Community Segregation and the Costs of Ethnic Subordination", *Social Forces*, Vol. 59, No. 3, March, pp. 649-666.

Shah, Anwar and Zia Qureshi, with Amaresh Bagchi, Brian Binder and Heng-fu Zou (1994), "Intergovernmental Fiscal Relations in Indonesia: Issues and Reform Options", World Bank Discussion Papers, No. 239, October. <*http://info.worldbank.org/etools/docs/library/206941/IntergovernmentalFiscalRelationsinIndonesia.pdf*>

Shleifer, A. and R. Vishny (1994), "Politicians and Firms", *Quarterly Journal of Economics*, Vol. 109, pp. 995-1025.

Shleifer, A and R. Vishny (1998), *The Grabbing Hand*, Cambridge, MA: Harvard University Press.

Smith, M.G. (1986), "Pluralism, Race and Ethnicity in Selected African Countries", in John Rex and David Mason (eds), *Theories of Race and Ethnic Relations*, Cambridge: Cambridge University Press, pp. 187-225.

Smith, M.G. (1987), "Some Problems with Minority Concepts and a Solution", *Ethnic and Racial Studies*, Vol. 10, No. 4, October, pp. 341-362.

Solé-Vilanova, Joaquim (1989), "Spain: Developments in Regional and Local Government", in Robert J. Bennett (ed.), *Territory and Administration in Europe*, London: Pinter and New York: St. Martin Press, pp. 205, 209-213.

Steiner, Jürg (1974), *Amicable Agreement versus Majority Rule: Conflict Resolution in Switzerland*, rev. ed., Chapel Hill: University of North Carolina Press.

Stepan, Alfred (1985), "State Power and the Strength of Civil Society in the Southern Cone of Latin America", in Peter B. Evans, Dietrich Rueschemeyer and Theda Skocpol (eds), *Bringing the State Back In*, Cambridge and New York: Cambridge University Press, pp. 317-343.

Stone, John (1985), *Racial Conflict in Contemporary Society*, London: Fontana/ Collins.

Sun Yan (2005), "Corruption, Growth, and Reform: The Chinese Enigma", *Current History*, Vol. 104, no. 683, pp. 257-263.

Tan Chee-Beng (2004), "Southeast Asia and China Studies", roundtable presentation at the conference "Emerging China: Implications and Challenges for Southeast Asia", University of Malaya, Kuala Lumpur, 22nd-23rd July.

Tanner, Murray Scot (2004), "China Rethinks Unrest", *The Washington Quarterly*, Summer, pp. 137-156.

Tanner, Murray Scot (2005), "Chinese Government Responses to Rising Social Unrest", prepared testimony before the US-China Economic and Security Review Commission Public Hearing on "China's State Control Mechanisms and Methods", 14th April. <*http://www.uscc.gov/hearings/2005hearings/written_testimonies/05_04_14wrts/tanner_murray_wrts.htm*>

Tiebout, Charles M. (1956), "A Pure Theory of Local Expenditures", *Journal of Political Economy*, Vol. 64, No. 5, October, pp. 416-424.

Tilly, Charles (1985), "War Making and State Making as Organized Crime", in Peter B. Evans, Dietrich Rueschemeyer and Theda Skocpol (eds), *Bringing the State Back In*, Cambridge and New York: Cambridge University Press, pp. 169-191.

Turnley, David, Peter Turnley, Melinda Liu and Li Ming (1989), *Beijing Spring*, New York: Stewart, Tabori & Chang.

Unger, Jonathan and Anita Chan (1995), "China, Corporatism, and the East Asian Model", *The Australian Journal of Chinese Affairs*, No. 33, January, pp. 29-53.

Unger, Jonathan 安戈 and Anita Chan 陈佩华 (2001), "Zhongguo, Zuhezhuyi ji Dongya Moshi 中国、组合主义及东亚模式" [China, corporatism, and the East Asian model], *Zhanlüe yu Guanli* 战略与管理 [Strategy and management] (Beijing), No. 44, January, 2001年第01期 (updated version of the 1995 AJCA article).

van Amersfoort, J.M.M. (Hans) (1978), "'Minority' as a Sociological Concept", *Ethnic and Racial Studies*, Vol. 1, No. 2, April, pp. 218-234.

van Dijk, Teun A. (2005), expanded edition of *Dominación Étnica y Racismo Discursivo en España y América Latina* (Barcelona: Gedisa, 2003), Amsterdam: Benjamins (pre-publication accessed at *http://www.discourse-in-society.org/Racism.htm*).

Vinuela, Julio (2000), "Fiscal Decentralization in Spain". *<http://www.imf.org/external/pubs/ft/seminar/2000/fiscal/vinuela.pdf>*

Wagley, Charles (1959), "On the Concept of Social Race in the Americas", in *Actas del XXXIII Congresso Internacional de Americanistas*, San José, Costa Rica, reprinted as "The Concept of Social Race in the Americas" in Charles Wagley (1968), *The Latin American Tradition*, New York: Columbia University Press, pp. 155-174.

Wagley, C. and M. Harris (1967), *Minorities in the New World*, New York: Columbia University Press.

Warner, W. Lloyd (1936), "American Caste and Class", *American Journal of Sociology*, Vol. 42, No. 2, September, pp. 234-237.

Weber, Max (1914), "Ethnic Groups", Chapter V (pp. 385-398) in Vol. 1 of Max Weber (1968), *Economy and Society: An Outline of Interpretive Sociology* (2 vols), ed. by Guenther Roth and Claus Wittich, tr by Ferdinand Kolegar *et al.*, New York: Bedminster Press and Berkeley: University of California Press (revised from "Ethnic Groups", written by Max Weber in 1910-1914, tr. by Ferdinand Kolegar in Talcott Parsons *et al.* (eds) (1961), *Theories of Society*, Vol. 1, New York: The Free Press of Glencoe).

Wirth, Louis (1945), "The Problem of Minority Groups", in Ralph Linton (ed.), *The Science of Man in the World Crisis*, New York: Columbia University Press, pp. 347-372.

Wolpe, Harold (1988), *Race, Class & the Apartheid State*, Paris: UNESCO and London: James Currey.

Xinjiang Tongji Nianjian - 2007 新疆统计年鉴 - 2007/*Xinjiang Statistical Yearbook - 2007* (compiled by the Xinjiang Weiwuer Zizhiqu Tongji Ju 新疆维吾尔自治区统计局/Statistics Bureau of Xinjiang Uygur Autonomous Region), Beijing: Zhongguo Tongji Chubanshe 中国统计出版社/China Statistics Press, 2007.

Xizang Tongji Nianjian - 2007 西藏统计年鉴 - 2007/*Tibet Statistical Yearbook - 2007* (compiled by the Xizang Zizhiqu Tongji Ju 西藏自治区统计局/Tibet Autonomous Region Bureau of Statistics and Guojia Tongji Ju Xizang Diaocha Zongdui 国家统计局西藏调查总队/Tibet General Team of Investigation under the NBS), Beijing: Zhongguo Tongji Chubanshe 中国统计出版社/China Statistics Press, 2007.

Xu Chenggang 许成钢 (2008), "Zhengzhi Jiquan xia de Difang Jingji Fenquan yu Zhongguo Gaige 政治集权下的地方经济分权与中国改革" [Local economic decentralization under political centralization and China's reform], in Masahiko Aoki 青木昌彦 and Wu Jinglian 吴敬琏 (eds), *Cong Weiquan dao Minzhu: Kechixu Fazhan de Zhengzhijingjixue* 从威权到民主: 可持续发展的政治经济学 [From authoritarian developmentalism to democratic developmentalism: the political economy of sustainable development], Beijing: Zhongxin Chubanshe 中信出版社 (China Citic Press), pp. 185-200.

Yan Jiaqi (Yan Ziaci) 嚴家其 (1992), *Lianbang Zhongguo Qousiang* 聯邦中國構想 [Conception of a federal China], Hong Kong: Ming Bao Chubanshe 明報出版社 (Ming Pao Press).

Yazhou Zhoukan 亞洲週刊 (1989), *Zingtiandongdi de Yibai Jeu* 驚天動地的一百日, Hong Kong.

Yeoh, Emile Kok-Kheng (2003), "Phenotypical, Linguistic or Religious? On the Concept and Measurement of Ethnic Fragmentation", *Malaysian Journal of Economic Studies*, Vol. XXXX, Numbers 1 and 2, June/December, pp. 23-47.

Yeoh, Emile Kok-Kheng (2006a), "Ethnic Coexistence in a Pluralistic Environment", *GeoJournal: An International Journal on Human Geography and Environmental Sciences*, Springer, Vol. 66/3, pp. 223-241.

Yeoh, Emile Kok-Kheng (2006b), "Demographic Diversity and Economic Reform in a Globalizing World: Regional Development and the State in China", in Emile Kok-Kheng Yeoh and Hou Kok Chung (eds), *China and Malaysia in a Globalizing World: Bilateral Relations, Regional Imperatives and Domestic Challenges*, Kuala Lumpur: Institute of China Studies, University of Malaya, pp. 208-273.

Yeoh, Emile Kok-Kheng (2007), "China at a Crossroads: Fiscal Decentralization, Recentralization and Politico-economic Transition", in Emile Kok-Kheng Yeoh and Evelyn Devadason (eds), *Emerging Trading Nation in an Integrating World: Global Impacts and Domestic Challenges of China's Economic Reform*, Kuala Lumpur: Institute of China Studies, University of Malaya, pp. 233-305.

Yeoh, Emile Kok-Kheng (2008a), "China's Regional Policy, Poverty and the Ethnic Question", in Emile Kok-Kheng Yeoh and Kate Hannan (guest editors), *The Copenhagen Journal of Asian Studies*, Vol. 26, No. 2 (*Special Issue: Transforming China*), pp. 26-59.

Yeoh, Emile Kok-Kheng (2008b), "Beyond Reductionism: State, Ethnicity and Public Policy in Plural Societies", in Nicholas Tarling and Edmund Terence Gomez (eds), *The State, Development and Identity in Multi-Ethnic Societies: Ethnicity, Equity and the Nation*, Oxford, London and New York: Routledge, pp. 57-96.

Yeoh, Emile Kok-Kheng (2008c), "China's Transformation: A Multi-faceted Enigma", in Emile Kok-Kheng Yeoh (ed.), *Facets of a Transforming China: Resource, Trade and Equity*, Kuala Lumpur: Institute of China Studies, University of Malaya, pp. 3-35.

Yeoh, Emile Kok-Kheng (2008d), "Disparity in China: Poverty, Inequality and Inter-regional Imbalance", in Emile Kok-Kheng Yeoh (ed.), *Facets of a Transforming China: Resource, Trade and Equity*, Kuala Lumpur: Institute of China Studies, University of Malaya, pp. 149-205.

Yeoh, Emile Kok-Kheng (2008e), "Poverty Reduction: The China Experience", in Emile Kok-Kheng Yeoh and Joanne Hoi-Lee Loh (eds), *China in the World: Contemporary Issues and Perspectives*, Kuala Lumpur: Institute of China Studies, University of Malaya, pp. 87-123.

Yeoh, Emile Kok-Kheng (2009a), "China in the Regional Political Economy", in Emile Kok-Kheng Yeoh (ed.), *Regional Political Economy of China Ascendant: Pivotal Issues and Critical Perspectives*, Kuala Lumpur: Institute of China Studies, University of Malaya, pp. 3-15.

Yeoh, Emile Kok-Kheng (2009b), "Leviathan at a Crossroads: China's Reforms and the Pitfalls and Prospects of Decentralization", in Emile Kok-Kheng Yeoh (ed.), *Regional Political Economy of China Ascendant: Pivotal Issues and Critical Perspectives*, Kuala Lumpur: Institute of China Studies, University of Malaya, pp. 241-303.

Yeoh, Emile Kok-Kheng, Lionel Wei-Li Liong and Susie Yieng-Ping Ling (2009), "Fiscal Reform and Dimensions of Decentralization: Some Observations on China", in Emile Kok-Kheng Yeoh, Chan Sok Gee, Wendy Chen-Chen Yong and Joanne Hoi-Lee Loh (eds), *China-ASEAN Relations: Economic Engagement and Policy Reform*, Kuala Lumpur: Institute of China Studies, University of Malaya, pp. 168-185.

Yinger, J. Milton (1986), "Intersecting Strands in the Theorisation of Race and Ethnic Relations", in John Rex and David Mason (eds), *Theories of Race and Ethnic Relations*, Cambridge and New York: Cambridge University Press, pp. 20-41.

Yu, George T. (2004), "Political Change and Reform in China", paper presented at the conference "Emerging China: Implications and Challenges for Southeast Asia", University of Malaya, Kuala Lumpur, 22nd-23rd July

Zhang Liang (pseudonym, compiler), Andrew J. Nathan and E. Perry Link (editors and translators) (2001), *The Tiananmen Papers: The Chinese Leadership's Decision to Use Force against Their Own People – In Their Own Words*, New York: Public Affairs.

Zhao Ziyang 赵紫阳 (2009a, posthumously), *Prisoner of the State: The Secret Journal of Zhao Ziyang*, translated and edited by Bao Pu, Renee Chiang and Adi Ignatius, New York: Simon & Schuster.

Zhao Ziyang 趙紫陽 (2009b, posthumously), *Qaige Licheng* 改革歷程 [Journey of reform] (*The Secret Journal of Zhao Ziyang*), edited by Bao Pu 鮑樸, Hong Kong: Sin Sheuzi Chubanshe 新世紀出版社 (New Century Press).

Zhao Ziyang 趙紫陽 (2009c, posthumously), *Guozia de Cioutu: Zhao Zeuyang de Mimi Luyin* 國家的囚徒 —— 趙紫陽的祕密錄音 [Prisoner of the State: The secret voice recordings of Zhao Ziyang] (*Prisoner of the State*), edited by Bao Pu 鮑樸, Taipei: Sheubao Wenhua Chuban Ciye 時報文化出版企業.

Zheng, Yongnian 郑永年 (1999), *Zhu Rongji Xinzheng: Zhongguo Gaige de Xin Moshi* 朱榕基新政: 中国改单的新模式 (Zhu Rongji's New Deal: A New Model for Reforming China), Singapore: World Scientific.

Zheng Yongnian and Lye Liang Fook (2004), "Reform, Leadership Change and Institutional Building in Contemporary China", paper presented at the conference "Emerging China: Implications and Challenges for Southeast Asia", University of Malaya, Kuala Lumpur, 22nd-23rd July.

Zhongguo Caizheng Nianjian 中国财政年鉴/*China State Finance Yearbook*, Beijing: Zhongguo Caizheng Jingji Chubanshe 中国财政经济出版社 / Zhongguo Caizheng Zazhi She 中國財政雜志社, various years.

Zhongguo Fazhan Baogao 2007 – Zai Fazhan zhong Xiaochu Pinkun 中国发展报告 2007 —— 在发展中消除贫困 [China development report 2007 – Eliminating poverty through development in China] (by Zhongguo Fazhan Yanjiu Jijinhui 中国发展研究基金会 [China Development Research Foundation]), Beijing: Zhongguo Fazhan Chubanshe 中国发展出版社, 2007.

Zhongguo Fazhan Shuzi Ditu 中国发展数字地图 [Atlas of China's development in figures] (chief editors: Lian Yuming 连玉明 and Wu Jianzhong 武建忠), Beijing: Zhongguo Shidai Jingji Chubanshe 中国时代经济出版社 (China Modern Economic Publishing House), 2006.

Zhongguo Minzu Fazhan Baogao (2001-2006) 中国民族发展报告 (2001-2006) [China's ethnic minorities development report, 2001-2006] (*Minzu Fazhan Lan Pi Shu* 民族发展蓝皮书/*Blue Book of Ethnic-Affairs*) (edited by Hao Shiyuan 郝时远 and Wang Xi'en 王希恩), Beijing: Shehuikexue Wenxian Chubanshe 社会科学文献出版社 (Social Sciences Academic Press), 2006.

Zhongguo Renkou Pucha 2000 中国人口普查 2000/*2000 Population Census of China*, Beijing: Zhonghua Renmin Gongheguo Guojia Tongji Ju 中华人民共和国国家统计局/National Bureau of Statistics of China, 2002.

Zhongguo Renkou Wenhua Suzhi Baogao 中国人口文化素质报告 [China population qualities report] (edited by Gao Shuguo 高书国 and Yang Xiaoming 杨晓明), Beijing: Shehuikexue Wenxian Chubanshe 社会科学文献出版社 (Social Sciences Academic Press), 2004.

Zhongguo Shehui Tongji Nianjian - 2008 中国社会统计年鉴 - 2008/*China Social Statistical Yearbook 2008* (compiled by the Guojia Tongji Ju Shehui he Keji Tongji Si 国家统计局社会和科技统计司/Department of Social, Science and Technology Statistics of the National Bureau of Statistics of China), Beijing: Zhongguo Tongji Chubanshe 中国统计出版社/China Statistics Press, 2008.

Zhongguo Tongji Nianjian 中国统计年鉴/*China Statistical Yearbook* (compiled by the Zhonghua Renmin Gongheguo Guojia Tongji Ju 中华人民共和国国家统计局/National Bureau of Statistics of China), Beijing: Zhongguo Tongji Chubanshe 中国统计出版社/China Statistics Press (various years).

Zhongguo Xibu Jingji Fazhan Baogao (2007) 中国西部经济发展报告 (2007) [Report on economic development in western region of China (2007)] (*Xibu Lan Pi Shu* 西部蓝皮书/*Blue Book of Western Region of China*) (chief editors: Yao Huiqin 姚慧琴 and Ren Zongzhe 任宗哲), Beijing: Shehuikexue Wenxian Chubanshe 社会科学文献出版社 (Social Sciences Academic Press), 2007.

Zhou Tianyong 周天勇, Wang Changjiang 王长江 and Wang Anling 王安岭 (eds) (2007), *Gongjian: Shiqi Da hou Zhongguo Zhengzhi Tizhi Gaige Yanjiu Baogao* 攻坚: 十七大后中国政治体制改革研究报告 [Attack the fortress: Research report on China's political reform after the 17th Party Congress], Wujiaqu 五家渠, Xinjiang: Xinjiang Shengchan Jianshe Bingtuan Chubanshe 新疆生产建设兵团出版社.

Index